Tasting Tourism: Travelling For Food and Drink

Tasting Tourism: Travelling For Food and Drink

Satendra Tripathi

RANDOM PUBLICATIONS
NEW DELHI (INDIA)

Tasting Tourism: Travelling for Food and Drink

ISBN 978-93-5111-550-2

Published in 2015 in India by

RANDOM PUBLICATIONS

4376-A/4B, Gali Murari Lal, Ansari Road
New Delhi-110 002
Phone : +9111-43580356, 011-23289044, 011-43142548
e-mail: sales@randompublications.com,
info@randompublications.com, randomexports@gmail.com

Reprinted 2018

Type Setting by : Friends Media, Delhi-110089
Digitally Printed at: Replika Press Pvt. Ltd.

Preface

Travelers who participated in wine, beer and food tasting are among the most frequent consumers of travel-related media including the travel sections of newspapers, travel magazines, travel websites and travel television shows. Over the last two years, 17.7% of adult Canadians (4,389,525) participated in a wine, beer or food tasting while on an out-of-town, overnight trip of one or more nights. A day visit and tasting at a winery (12.4%) was the most common tasting experience on a trip. A visit to a food processing plant such as a cheese factory (4.8%) was the next most common activity followed by a day visit and tasting at a brewery (4.5%) and a cooking or wine tasting course (2.7%). Participating in wine, beer or food tasting while on trips was the 7 most frequent culture and entertainment activity type undertaken by Canadian Pleasure Travelers in the past two years. Participating in a wine, beer or food tasting was typically not the main reason for travel. In fact, only 17.7% (776,895) reported that this activity was the main reason for taking at least one trip in the past two years (the 20 most frequent reason for travel of the 21 culture and entertainment activity types). Ta king a cooking or wine tasting course was more likely than other tasting activities to be cited as the main reason for taking at least one trip in the last two years.

I would like to thank my team for standing beside me throughout my career and writing this book. My special thanks go to "Random Publications" who have published the book.

– *Satendra Tripathi*

Contents

1

Tasting Tourism and Restaurant Sector

INTRODUCTION

The enormous variety of food and beverage outlets makes it a challenge when one is trying to differentiate between them. Some are distinctly different. Others are harder to categorize. The list of sectors in food and beverage management in this book is not exhaustive and as trends change so will new sectors emerge. The restaurant sub sectors are covered with relevant descriptions drawing from the experience of food and beverage managers, educators and research in current sector definitions. For each subsection the basic policies, financial, and catering issues specific to that type of outlet is discussed. Where possible average spent, typical capacity, production capabilities and available technology issues are discussed.

FULL SERVICE RESTAURANTS AND LICENSED RETAIL

In this part of the stage full service restaurants are categorized by revenue stream. Operations with food as their main revenue source and operations that their main revenue is generated from sales of beverages are explored. Examples of mainstream restaurant guides are also explored in this part. As licensing laws differ from country to country the restaurant guides provide a good point of reference when trying to distinguish restaurant types and styles.

RESTAURANT GUIDES

Consumers will often refer to restaurant guides when they wish to choose which establishment they might wish to visit. Restaurant guides can provide an easy way of classifying food and beverage establishments and for the food and beverage manager listing in a restaurant guide may mean the difference between a successful operation or failure to attract business. An understanding of the most predominant restaurant guides is therefore a necessary asset for any food and beverage manager. The Michelin guide is a famous guide awarding restaurants from 1 to 3 stars depending on quality of their cuisine. The guide also features the face of the Michelin Man for restaurants that offer good food at reasonable prices and has a rating for the atmosphere décor and general feeling of the establishment with a scale of five levels ranging from quite comfortable to Luxurious establishment. In 2006, Michelin released a New York city guide. Unfortunately in some cases a Michelin star can be taken by the proprietor as license to charge extravagant prices.

The Mobil travel guide is the USA guide for restaurants and ratings range from 1 star to 5 stars. Ranging from a restaurant that provides a distinctive experience through culinary speciality. The AAA is another travel guide that rates restaurants on a 1 to 5 Diamond scale. Three, four and five star/diamond ratings are somewhat equivalent to the Michelin one, two, and three star ratings. Specific to the India the 'Good Food Guide' is an annual publication using anonymous inspectors to grade restaurants from 1 to 10 were by 1 is a recommended restaurant that makes the top 1% of the countries restaurants whilst a 10/10 would be the equivalent of a 3 star Michelin restaurant. Another guide worth mentioning is the 'AA restaurants and Pub Guide'. An alternative guide is the Zagat survey. The Zagat survey compiles individuals' comments about restaurants but does not pass an official judgement of the establishment. The web site features over 16,000 restaurant menus in various US cities. It is a great resource for any food and beverage manager to get ideas on what to do or what not to do when designing their own menus.

FINE DINING

Fine dining restaurants are those establishments that offer very high standards in all aspects of their operation–an extensive à la carte menu, silver service, good quality facilities and décor, service accompaniments, etc. They can be found in four and five star hotels or as free standing restaurants. The percentage of restaurants today that may be described as fine dining restaurants is small; indeed it may be as little as 3–5% of the total number of restaurants in all sectors of the catering industry. However, the narrow market for which quality restaurants cater will continue to be present in the future, because there will always be that percentage of the eating-out market that demands the highest standards in all aspects of a restaurant operation, and can afford to pay the high prices charged.

Financial Implications

Fine dining restaurants are profit orientated and this is reflected in their financial policies. The higher GP levels of the à la carte and high quality restaurants are mainly due to the lower percentage of variable costs of these operations and the need to cover the higher staff costs. The high percentage of fixed costs associated with the fine dining restaurants affects the margin of safety of these operations; this is the difference between the operation' s break-even point and its maximum potential output. High fixed cost operations have a smaller margin of safety than those with lower fixed costs, so that a drop in the volume of sales would seriously affect the profitability of high fixed cost establishments. In addition, the wide range of price discretion that is available to hotels and quality restaurants further complicates their pricing structure. The balance between the price level of these establishments and their volume of sales must therefore be carefully calculated, and this again would be contained in their financial policies.

The average spend per customer in the fine dining may range from ₹50 to ₹120 or even more per customer. In the higher average spending power operations, the cost of the meal to the customer is not such an important variable in determining the sales of the operation; broadly speaking, the higher the price level of an operation, the less elastic its demand. The demand for those catering facilities offered by quality restaurants and hotels, therefore tends to be relatively inelastic, that is, a large change in price will not have a very substantial effect on the sales of the establishment.

Marketing

Because of the narrowness of the market for which quality restaurants cater, the marketing policies of these operations are able to quite clearly identify their market and target their advertising and merchandising campaigns at this market level. The high ASP of such establishments must be reflected in their marketing policies; if th2ey cannot compete with other catering operations on the basis of price, they must look to the other aspects of their operation, such as food quality and standard of service as a basis for competition. Often such restaurants will feature a Celebrity chef as their executive chef. Other times the acquisition of a Michelin star due to the quality of the food will send demand levels to such a high that soon the menu prices follow. Fine dining restaurants are characterized by the need for a high capital outlay and have a correspondingly high percentage of fixed costs; the perish ability of their product; and a demand for that product that is unstable. All these factors lead to a high dependence of these operations on the demands of the market, so that hotels and quality restaurants may be said to be highly market orientated. In comparison to the welfare sector cost- orientated operations, fine dining restaurants are more dependent on their market for the survival of their operation, and this has important implications for their basic policymaking decisions.

In fining dining restaurants marketing has to be subtle for example, advertising in quality magazines–obtaining free writeups of the restaurant in quality newspapers and magazines–joint promotion with credit card companies. These can enhance the type of image the restaurant is trying to create. Often the restaurant will hire a public relations company that has the expertise, resources and networking to do just that.

Product and Service Styles

The most widely used method of food production in the kitchens of fine dining restaurants is still the conventional method of production, based on the party system. The party system is a method of kitchen organization in which production is divided into separate areas just as to the type of food being produced. In a large hotel kitchen, for example, there may be as many as seven main production parties: roast; vegetables; larder/salads; entree; fish; soup; and pastry, and each of these parts may be further subdivided depending on the quantity of food to be produced by the party.

In fine dining restaurants fresh ingredients define the product and the use of any convenience food stuff is eliminated or reduced to a bare minimum. Food service styles are not only dependent on the type of catering operation, but also on its price level. Generally speaking, the higher the price level of an operation, the more elaborate and sophisticated the service style becomes. However in fine dining restaurants we have seen a move away from silver service and towards plated service styles. This is mainly because the chef can far better control the appearance of a plate in the kitchen. When a customer is paying ₹40 for a main course, they would expect excellent quality of food but excellent dish appearance as well. Furthermore the luck of skilled staff in the industry has made styles such as Flambé and silver service redundant. It is worth noting however that a renaissance of the Flambé service in front of the customer might be back on the menu.

Although flambé dishes still exist on the menu they are mainly prepared in the kitchen but recent trend would suggest that in fine dining at least Flambé service style might be resurrected. As the sophistication of food service styles increases with the price level of an operation, so too do beverage service styles. The service of wines, for example, is considerably more elaborate in an à la carte quality restaurant than in an operation featuring a table d' hôte menu. In a quality restaurant an extensive wine list would be available and a wine waiter would serve the wine throughout the duration of the meal. In a lower ASP catering outlet a more limited wine list would be offered and the service of the wine would usually be by the member of staff serving at the customer' s table, rather than a separate wine waiter. Adjacent to quality restaurants may be a cocktail bar or some other form of bar where beverages are served to customers at individual tables. In the lower ASP operations, this bar arrangement is not often found; patrons for the table d' hôte restaurant would usually use the main hotel bar.

Staffing

The organization of fine dining restaurants has changed mainly at the top over the past years. An executive chef might often be the owner or the manager of such an establishment as the product is what differentiates the restaurant from its competitors. However the traditional hierarchy will still exist with a sous chef responsible for the operations and the chefs de party responsible for parts of the kitchen whilst a number of commis chefs will assist the chefs de party with the more menial tasks. In the front of house a Restaurant Manager is now often the title used for what in more traditional settings be the Maitre' D a head waiter, a chef de rang responsible for a station with a commis waiter. Also a wine waiter with a commis might be present especially in operations that feature an extended wine list.

BARS, NIGHTCLUBS AND PUBS

Although bars strictly speaking are focusing in the sale of beverages only and the provision of entertainment, Nightclubs often feature restaurants within their premises and pubs have taken the food agenda in their premises even further with the relatively new phenomenon known as Gastro pubs. Mintel, the India market shows a positive growth in the future.

Table. Restaurant Sector Forecasts

All current Prices	2007	2008	2009	2010	2011	2012	% change 2007-12
			Fast food				
Burgers	2.4	2.47	2.5	2.49	2.48	2.48	3
Ethnic takeaway	1.8	1.87	1.94	1.98	2.04	2.09	16
Pizza and Pasta	1.35	1.42	1.51	1.57	1.64	1.7	26
Fish and chips	1	1.04	1.07	1.09	1.12	1.14	14
Fried chicken	1	1.1	1.19	1.24	1.31	1.37	37
Other fast food	0.17	0.17	0.18	0.19	0.19	0.2	18
Total fast food	**7.72**	**8.07**	**8.39**	**8.55**	**8.77**	**8.96**	**16**
			Restaurants				
Pub catering	7.25	7.67	8.21	8.5	8.9	9.26	28
Hotel catering	4.31	4.43	4.48	4.54	4.66	4.69	9
Restaurant meals	4.5	4.79	5.15	5.34	5.6	5.85	30
Ethnic restaurants	2	2.02	2.07	2.12	2.2	2.23	11
In-store	1.4	1.5	1.59	1.66	1.75	1.82	30
Roadside	0.53	0.54	0.54	0.54	0.54	0.54	2
Total restaurant	**19.98**	**20.93**	**22.05**	**22.7**	**23.65**	**24.39**	**22**
Other	2.75	2.99	3.02	3.07	3.21	3.24	18
Total	**30.45**	**31.99**	**33.46**	**34.32**	**35.64**	**36.6**	**20**

The Gastro pub is a traditional pub that has been updated with a full service restaurant that can often be compared in product to a fine dining establishment.

Technology

In fine dining restaurants communication between service and production staff is of paramount importance. If the Chef has prepared an exquisite dish only to find it melting away in the hot plate because service staff could not be alerted on time, the restaurant will not uphold its reputations. Electronic point of sale and mobile point of sale systems technology have made huge advancements. The waiter can be alerted through the MPOS, the waiter can input specific instructions about a dish without having to physically go to the kitchen. The Chef can instantly alert all waiters with how many portions of a specific dish is left or if he wants to push a particular dish. Staff performance has become much easier to quantify as a result of technology. POS systems can provide information about an employee, how many customers he/she serves per hour, how much revenue he/she generates, how long it took to service a table, how much tips tables leave and the lists goes on. Such information can be used to establish whether a member of staff needs more training, needs to be appraised for brilliant work or needs to be evaluated, as they do not seem to match the required standards. The ease of obtaining such information allows for the information to be shared around with the team and that in its self can help motivate staff as they can share what is going on in the workplace.

Financial Implications

The sale of beverages has always been a favourite with every food and beverage manager. With a gross profit of 65–70% beverages often help to sustain a business through rough times. With nightclubs there may be further income as many charge an entrance fee but this is mainly in order to cover the entertainment expenses such as the fee of a DJ or a band. With new antismoking regulations in place there has been a fear that such establishments would see a significant reduction in their revenues, however in May 2007 it was reported that the antismoking laws have not deterred punters and companies such as Wetherspoons in the India have announced a 3% higher profits than predicted.

Marketing

Whilst bars and nightclubs tend to attract younger audiences the traditional pub is an establishment seen in the India that bases its operation mainly in the local community with often a catchment area of no more than 5 mile radius. To counter that pub man agers will often have a live music night or put together and advertise event nights such as Bingo nights or Karaoke nights. Bars and nightclubs will often advertise in local newspapers and magazines as well as local radio and TV stations. Often a nightclub will have young people distributing leaflets when they attempt to advertise a big event. Similarly to a pub they will often have themed nights or a special attraction in an attempt to attract further audiences.

Product and Service Styles

Bars and nightclubs will often feature an extended beverage and cocktail menu. The service in bars and pubs is always counter style service and in some nightclubs one may find table service or in the case of an event a butler style service. This style of service is common when a drink might be included in the entrance price and the customer might give a ticket whilst collecting a drink from staff passing around with a tray full of the specified drink. Pubs will often offer at least ten types of beer and or ale, often products from local breweries might feature in the menu, but today most pubs are owned by large companies that they rent the pubs out to owners who are then obliged to buy the products from the company' s brewery.

Staffing

Bars and nightclubs will need to have well-trained bar staff behind the counter as often the volume of business is extremely high and one barperson might have to serve one order per 1–3 minutes. The volume of business in pubs is not as high as in bars and nightclubs and as most punters will require beer the skills needed are not as demanding. Another staff consideration for bars and nightclubs is that of security. As insurance costs can be quite high often an operator will decide to outsource their security to a security company.

Technology

We have already talked about the advantages of EPOS technology but together with advancements in beverage dispensing technology these types of operation that traditionally suffered loses from beverage spillage or theft can now pinpoint exactly what was sold when and by whom. Making it far easier to keep track of stock and reducing opportunities for theft. Wine cooling and dispensing technology has also advanced allowing the establishments to offer more wines by the glass without having to throw the unfinished bottle of wine within a few days. Recent technology in beer dispensing has allowed for extra cool beer to be dispensed and self-cleaning pipes for the beer dispensing system can reduce staff costs.

HOTEL RESTAURANTS AND PRIVATE CLUBS

Hotel food and beverage management may be described as one of the most complex areas of the catering industry because of the variety of catering outlets that may be found in any one hotel. The different types of catering services associated with hotels include the following: luxury haute cuisine restaurants, coffee shops and speciality restaurants, room and lounge service, cocktail bars, banqueting facilities and staff restaurants.

Additionally, some hotels will provide a catering and bar service to areas of the hotel such as swimming pools, and health complexes, discos and other leisure areas as well as often providing some vending facilities.

The type and variety of catering outlets in hotels will depend to a large extent on the size of the hotel. Small hotels of up to 30–40 bedrooms may have a licensed bar, and a restaurant which may offer a limited table d' hôte or à la carte lunch and dinner menu.

A medium-sized hotel of up to 100 bedrooms would usually have a licensed bar and two restaurants; these may include a grill room/coffee shop offering a table d' hôte menu and a separate à la carte restaurant. The bar in this size of hotel may also offer a limited selection of snacks. Today, room service in these small- and medium-sized operations is limited; facilities for tea and coffee making within the room are more usually provided as an alternative. In the large hotels with several hundred bedrooms, the largest variety of catering outlets is found–the traditional haute cuisine restaurant alongside the more unusual speciality restaurant; lounge and cocktail bars; several coffee shops, some offering a very limited selection of snacks, others offering more substantial menu items; and varying degrees of room service.

The different types of catering outlets in hotels depend not only on the size of the operation, but also on its nature and the market for which it is catering. A medium-sized resort hotel, for example, where a guest' s average length of stay may be 2–3 weeks, may need to offer a variety of food and beverage facilities to cater for the guests' different and changing needs during their stay.

A transient hotel, however, such as one situated near an airport where the guest' s average length of stay may be one or two nights, may only need to provide comparatively limited catering facilities. As for the future demands for catering services in hotels, this is closely allied to the demand for hotel accommodation itself. The continually growing tourism industry both in the India and abroad guarantees a future demand for some form of hotel accommodation to be provided for tourists, and with this a demand for food and beverage services. Private gentlemen' s Clubs feature the dining room a type of restaurant that pre-dates the member' s only exclusive restaurant concept such as Mosimann' s in London. It is worth mentioning as it educates us as to how the member only restaurants have evolved.

HOTEL FOOD AND BEVERAGE OUTLETS

In many hotels, the importance of the food and beverage department in operating an à la carte restaurant and a 24-hour room service, neither of which may be significant net profit contributors, is essential for the hotel to obtain a four or five star grading, with their input of service and facilities enabling the hotel to signifi cantly increase its prices for accommodation.

Table. Food and Beverage as a Percentage of Hotel Revenue

Hotel revenue source %	2006	2005
Rooms revenue	57.3	56.6
Miscellaneous revenue	7.2	6.8
Food revenue	21.2	21.7
Beverage revenue	9.4	9.7
Other F&B revenue	4.9	5.2
Total F&B revenue	35.5	36.6
	100.0	**100.0**

In so doing the hotel is more likely to be able to increase its total revenue and net profit figures. It should be noted that hotels have realised the lost potential of their restaurants the latest figures suggest that the food and beverage area is a substantial source of income for most hotels and two main options were followed by many hotel operators.

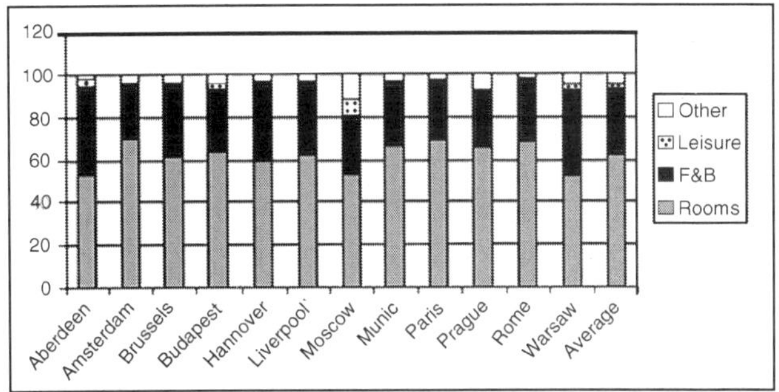

Fig. Departmental Revenue Mix by City

The easiest one is that of outsourcing. With outsourcing the hotel simply rents the space of the restaurant to a management company who in turn create a product that is marketable not only to residents of the hotel but also the public. Catering companies have dedicated branches that specialize in restaurant outsourcing. For example, the Compass Group branch that specializes in outsourcing is Restaurant Associates. The second option for the hotel management is to re-vamp the restaurant themselves.

This can be costly at first but the benefits can outweigh the 'rent' received by outsourcing the space. For example, one of the greatest problems hotel restaurants faced is that their restaurants would be located in a middle floor and the customer would have to go through a reception and up an elevator to eventually find a restaurant with often overpriced and outdated menus.

Many potential customers would walk by such hotels and not even consider attempting to try out the restaurant. The solution would be to have the restaurant at ground level with an entrance to the high street separate from the entrance the hotel residents might use. Updated menus that can compete with other high street restaurants are crucial as well as highly trained and motivated staff.

Fig. Radisson Edwardian Ascots Restaurant

Financial Implications

Generally speaking the average spend of customers in hotel catering outlets, is higher than in similar catering operations found outside a hotel. This is particularly evident with reference to the hotel' s high ASP quality restaurants, but also in the less expensive outlets such as coffee shops; here the ASP of the hotel customer may again be higher than in comparable operations found, for example in a town' s high street. The higher prices charged by these types of catering facilities result in higher sales per employee, and a higher revenue per trading hour.

In fast-food operations with their lower ASP per customer, the long trading hours of these establishments are often necessary in order to achieve high volume sales. In the catering outlets of hotels similar long trading hours are not characteristic of all the facilities; the lower ASP coffee shops may stay open for most of the day, but the higher ASP restaurants in the hotel, like the quality restaurants found outside, will only open for the lunch and dinner periods, approximately 3 hours and 4–5 hours, respectively.

In the larger hotels some form of food and beverage service is generally available 24 hours a day and most of the catering facilities are usually open 7 days a week; quality restaurants situated outside the hotel, however, may only open 6 days a week. The catering policy of the hotel or quality restaurant in conjunction with the financial policy of the establishment will, however, determine the opening hours of the operation based on such information as revenue per trading hour, sales per employee per hour, etc. Payment for food and beverages in hotels may be made in several ways. If customers are residents, the charges may be debited to their hotel account.

Alternatively, payment may be made on a cash or credit basis. Generally speaking, the higher the price level of a restaurant, the more likely that credit facilities will be available. Some hotels and quality restaurants include a service charge in the price of their meal, while others leave it to the discretion of the customer. This is the sector of the industry where the practice of tipping is most commonly found and the 'trunc' system of sharing pooled by the employees.

Marketing

The marketing policy of a hotel is very complicated because of its variety of catering outlets and the corresponding variety in the types of customers these facilities will attract; the customer frequenting the hotel' s coffee shop, for example, may not be the same customer to use the hotel' s à la carte restaurant. The danger of catering for mixed markets within the same establishment must therefore be recognized and planned for accordingly.

The marketing policy of a hotel may vary with different times of the year because it can see opportunities for marketing its catering facilities to different markets. A hotel in a coastal resort, for example, may cater largely for families and groups of tourists during the summer months, during which time its catering facilities may be well patronized. In the winter months, however, this market may no longer be available and the hotel may therefore alter its marketing policy and promote its catering facilities as part of banqueting and conference 'packages'.

In this way the hotel' s catering facilities may be utilized throughout the year without the danger of mixing its markets, and adversely affecting the hotel' s total image, whilst also ensuring a consistent revenue and maximum utilization of the hotel' s capital equipment. A hotel' s marketing policy will also contain its intentions with regard to its resident and non-resident markets. For example, is the hotel going to concentrate mainly on trade generated from within, that is, residents, or to what extent is it going to attempt to attract outside custom? Some hotels aim almost exclusively at the resident guest and may offer comparatively limited catering facilities, compared with those hotels seeking to also attract the non-resident customer by offering a wider range of catering outlets–restaurants, bars, banqueting facilities, etc. 'Crisscross' advertising is a technique available to hotels where there is more than one type of catering facility in the hotel; for example, the cocktail bar may use tent cards to advertise a special promotion week in the à la carte restaurant.

Where the hotel is part of a large organization, inter-hotel advertising may be used which usually features the catering outlets of the group' s hotels in the company sales literature which is distributed to all hotel units throughout the country, and sometimes abroad. It is also possible to advertise the food and beverage facilities of the hotel in conjunction with its other services; for example, a number of large hotel chains now offer 'bargain week ends', where for an inclusive price a guest may stay at the hotel for 2 or 3 days on demi pension or en pension terms. Gourmet and wine weekends may be offered during off-peak winter months. Discounts are given to hotel residents dining in the à la carte restaurant, a free bottle of wine is offered with the meal, or two meals for the price of one during the quieter weekdays. It is important therefore for all possible advertising techniques to be reviewed for the marketing of catering outlets, as they may often not only be marketed in isolation, but also may be advertised in conjunction with the establishment' s other facilities such as accommodation.

Product and Service Styles

Hotel restaurants like fine dining restaurants still use mainly the party system. Other production styles such as cook-chill and sous-vide are making inroads into this previous bastion of hotel tradition, these inroads are mainly in specific areas, for example, function catering, where they may be used to complement the traditional methods rather than replace them. The variety of food service styles used in hotels is dependent upon the different types of catering outlets in the establishment. In a small hotel, for example, where one restaurant is used for the service of all meals, and features table d' hôte menus for lunch and dinner, plated meals may be served to the guests by service staff.

In a large hotel, however, with four or five different types of outlets, there can be a corresponding variety in the ser vice styles. Breakfast service in the hotel, for example, can be on a self-service basis in the coffee shop, or waiter service in the main restaurant. For lunch and dinner the coffee shop can serve a limited selection of plated snacks and meals directly to customers at their table, and the outlet may also incorporate a self- service buffet or carvery. The hotel grill room or themed restaurant could feature a table d' hôte menu with plated meals, and the à la carte restaurant would offer silver service, both with waiter service.

In addition to the main dining areas the hotel bar can offer a limited snack service and the hotel could also offer room service facil ities; because room service is, however, a highly labour intensive and time-consuming method of food service, the majority of hotels offering room service today usually provide only a very limited menu selection, except for the large luxury establishments; the room service menus often containing some items from the main restaurant menu. This same variety of service styles is not, however, found in quality restaurants. This level of operation usually only offers a similar service style to that found in the à la carte restaurants of hotels, that is, silver service to the table.

Staffing

Staffing organization in hotels restaurants depends to a large extent on the size of the establishment and the level of service being offered; the larger the operation and the more staff employed, the greater the departmentalization and specialization of the catering personnel. In a small hotel with one restaurant offering a limited menu, there may be as few as five or six production staff and a similar number of service staff; this would constitute the catering department. In a large hotel, however, with a number of catering outlets, the catering department may consist of several hundred personnel. In the smaller hotel little staff hierarchy would be present; in the larger hotel a very clearly defined hierarchy would be identifiable for each catering outlet. As the staff hierarchy in a catering operation increases, so does the specialization of the staff functions.

The head chef of a large hotel may therefore have several sous chefs who would deputize in his absence, and under the sous chefs would be the chefs de partys; these are each responsible for the main parts in the kitchen–roast, vegetables, fish, larder, pastry, soup and sauces, etc. The chefs de partys may have several commis, or assistant chefs, reporting to them, depending on the size of the part, and finally there can be a number of general apprentices working in the kitchen in any one of these parts. In the large kitchens organized on this traditional party system, each part is quite autonomous; in smaller kitchens where less specialization is found, the kitchen staff may be required to perform a variety of tasks that would normally be associated with specific parts in a large production area.

The head chef of a large kitchen is usually involved to a far greater extent with the administrative side of the operation, rather than in the physical preparation of meals. In a small establishment, however, the head chef is more involved in the production of restaurant meals, leaving the majority of the administration to the hotel owner or proprietor. On the food service side of catering operations a similar staff hierarchy is found just as to the size of the establishment. In a large operation, for example, the staffing organization for a lunch or dinner service in a quality restaurant serving 80 or more covers, from an à la carte menu, may be as follows: the restaurant manager or his assistant, one head waiter, two chef de rang, one wine waiter, one commis wine waiter, and three commis waiters. In a smaller operation, however, there may only be the restaurant manager or head waiter, and several assistants, with no separate staff hierarchy for beverage service.

Technology

Hotel restaurant service has been changing dramatically as a result of new technology. A challenge that the industry faces is to provide a meal when and where the customer wants it, with guaranteed food safety and nutritional value, offering authentic recipes and customer specific engineered menus. Guests give their order to a waiter holding a wireless POS the order is transmitted to the Kitchen, speeding service reducing errors, and increasing time spent by server staff with guests. The data from the handheld device, now in the restaurant' s computer system, pass through an interface to the inventory and supply ordering software.

Wireless point-of-sale systems are ideal for difficult-to-wire environments such as pool areas, casino floors, leisure centres or common areas, as well as historic buildings and properties with large open spaces, providing point-of-activity revenue opportunities and new service offerings. Wireless pen-based terminals integrated with leading-edge restaurant systems can provide food and beverage facilities with breakthrough solutions that optimize efficiency, diminish lines and eliminate waits in a wide variety of hospitality applications. Wireless customer pads enable customers to give feedback if they are dissatisfied before they leave the restaurant.

Guest pagers that light up or vibrate mean that the hostess does not have to hail customers on a loudspeaker system. Pagers can alert waiting staff when orders are ready in the kitchen. Guest initiated pagers alert servers when a table is ready to have their order taken, saving time and preventing unnecessary trips to the table.

Restaurant processes such as order taking, payment processing, inventory control, wait-list management, valet parking, frequent diner programme interface and other applications can dramatically increase productivity, reduce costs and improve customer service. In addition, the introduction of new technologies in Room Service has also allowed greater flexibility. Room service staff can be supplied with internal phones that allow them to be in constant contact with food, beverage and banquet personnel, while roaming throughout the property. The productivity enhancements and responsiveness by re-directing staff to deliver and/or pick up food service orders while being mobile are phenomenal. By installing a wireless transmitter, hotels can provide Internet connectivity to sales people who happen to entertain customers in the hotel restaurant or even to guests who may wish to use their laptops.

New accounting software interface direct with POS systems, enabling credit card authorization and payment, storing customer information for future use and providing up to date reports for managers. Specialized software can analyse profitability, productivity, costing, and realization at multiple levels from companywide to the individual client or staff member. Tax, Social Security and statistical updates can also be automated and payroll software can maximize payroll processing productivity and enhance profits.

POS and Sales and Catering systems have provided new management and accounting tools. Accounting software can print reports that enable the accounting office to spot costs and trends. Managers can visualize better and faster where money is coming from and tactical decisions can be made faster and safer. Computerized systems identify true food and beverage expenses much faster than with systems that do not utilize information technology, and save time in accounting and food and beverage management. Time and money saved in accounting processes can be invested in training staff or bettering products and services

DINING ROOMS

Private Gentlemen' s Clubs are organizations that resemble hotels but in order for a customer to use their facilities they have to become a member. Often the organization is so exclusive that a 2 year waiting list is a common phenomenon amongst the more exclusive clubs. In such organizations the restaurant often takes the form of a dining room which keeps the traditions of the old fine dining restaurants whilst offering a high quality product at lower prices than their high street counterparts.

Financial Implications

These restaurants often offer lower prices on their menu as they are subsidized by the membership fee. Often they are there simply to offer the service to their members and may not function as a profit making outlet. Considering that these types of restaurants still have labour costs to cover and the fact that they may not offer services to the public they more often make a loss than break even.

Marketing

Private clubs often have their own newsletters or magazines and they will advertise their new menu in those or have notices of a special menu around the premises of the club and in the bedrooms if they offer accommodation. Apart from in house marketing there is not much more they can do to attract the business due to the restrictions imposed in them by the clubs regulations. However, sometimes clubs will allow members of other clubs to use the facilities. Those clubs are known as reciprocal clubs and often are allowed to advertise their services in the reciprocal clubs magazine.

Product and Service Styles

The product is often of a fine restaurant standard and these are establishments were one would expect to find full silver service and flambé, a Carving Trolley and Cheese or Dessert Trolleys. The menu tends to be restricted however and more often is a Table d' hôte as the low volume of business may not allow for an extended à la carte menu. A well-stocked cellar is often the pride of such establishments and an extended wine list is not uncommon.

Staffing

Customers would expect to find the same hierarchy that is found in a fine dining restaurant. Members Clubs tend to have a smaller team and the environment and pace of business tends to be more relaxed than in a hotel. Unlike a corporate hotel clubs enjoy almost 100% repeat business. As members join they will tend to use the facilities a number of times over a year, staff will often know customers by name. A more relaxed atmosphere and a closer, smaller team reinforces club loyalty which can result in lower staff turnover.

Technology

Often there is limited investment in technology in such dining rooms and although in the kitchen one might find some of the latest equipment in the front of house a basic EPOS will be considered a luxury.

FAST FOOD

Fast food may be defined as that sector of the catering industry primarily concerned with the preparation and service of food and beverages quickly, for immediate sale to the customer. McDonalds, Burger King, KFC and Wendy' s are some of the better known fast-food operators. Although differing from one another in certain aspects, these catering outlets have a number of characteristics which are common to all these types of operations–they offer a limited menu range; the operation tends to focus around one product, namely burger, pizza or chicken.

These operations cater mainly for the relatively lower average spend markets with lower prices being charged than those found in other food and beverage establishments; there is a low ratio of service staff to customers with many of these operations being a form of self-service; consumption of the food may be on or off the premises; less rigid meal times are observed by these establishments, with some form of menu usually available throughout the day; and finally, all aspects of the operation are highly standardized, leading to a high volume throughput with resulting economies in food, labour and other operating costs.

SANDWICH BARS

Sandwich bars are fast-food outlets that their main product is sandwiches. They often provide fruit juices and other refreshments and they may venture into the sales of hot beverages. Mintel Report the sandwich showed a 23% increase from 2002 and is now worth over ₹4 billion. This strong growth has been driven by the introduction of specialist sandwich bars, as well as a focused innovation and new product development.

A possible threat to future growth is the growing competition from other snack style foods and lunch options such as soups, sushi and other convenience foods.

On the plus side, the sandwich supply structure continues to expand, thus widening the locations where sandwiches can be purchased. With India consumers continuing to work long hours and take shorter lunch breaks than their European counterparts the sandwich fits in well with such a lifestyle. When McDonald' s first bought a high share in Prêt A Manger, a India-based chain of Sandwich Bars, food and beverage managers around the world realised that sandwich bars have stopped been a mere 'pawn' in the 'Chess board' of food and beverage management.

Consumers were looking out for a healthier option and they found it in the marketing promises of sandwich bars. Retail operations such as supermarkets have ventured into sandwich bars.

Financial Implications

Sandwich bars, rely on high turnovers and the fact that they have very low fixed costs. In some cases extra income may arrive from the sale of hot and cold beverages but the main focus remains the sandwich or baguette.

Depending on the type of operation, goods can be perishable often expiring within a few days of packaging therefore it is important to ensure high sales of the items. The average spend can range from ₹3 to ₹5 with food cost at around 20–30% and minimum labour, a sandwich bar can be a very profitable operation that involves relatively low start-up costs.

Marketing

Some operations will have a Unique Selling point which might be the freshness of the product or the speed of service or the spirit of hospitality and ethics in the organization. Often organiza tions will attempt to communicate the essence of their business to stake holders through the use of a mission statement, sometimes the unique selling point of the organization may appear in the mission statement as well. For example, in the Pret A Manger mission statement one can see their unique selling point as the freshness of the ingredients and their passion for food. Sandwich bars will market their product to a huge range of market segments and they are generally placed on a high street or strategic points were there are a high number of people passing by.

Product and Service Styles

Some operations will place the importance on the quality of ingredients or range of ingredients available. Outlets may have prepackaged products on sale or prepare products on order. Generally speaking the smaller operations which cannot guarantee a high volume of sales every day will opt for the customised option, whilst larger operations will tend to have a high number of prepackaged products, although product customization will still be a choice available to their customers. Although traditionally convenience foods have been used in those type of operations, consumer awareness has generally steered such type of operations to more healthy options.

How much convenience food is to be used and when can be the key to a successful operation as often the kitchen space available may only be a counter and the 'Kitchen' is really nothing more than a finishing kitchen. Often big sandwich chains will have centralized Kitchens were they prepare and even assemble the finished product for distribution to the various outlets. Portion control and costing is of paramount importance as the net profit per sandwich sold is minimal so production can be highly standardized. Equipments used are minimal and might involve a toaster or sandwich grill whilst refrigeration space is a must for every sandwich bar. Service styles tend to be either counter service or self-service. Speed of service is extremely important especially at the peak times which is very likely to be around lunchtime. Some operations will offer seating space with different pricing for eating in or taking away.

Staffing

Staff levels are kept to a minimum. Depending on the size of operation there can be one or two members of staff behind a counter. It is not uncommon for small establishments to only have one member of staff per shift, who may be both produ cing the end product and serving the customer. It is often the case that one staff member may serve a few hundreds of customers per day. Staff to customer contact time is extremely limited.

Technology

Bar code and scanner technology is not uncommon in established sandwich chains. The technology speeds up service dramatically enabling servers to deal with even more customers per hour. EPOS systems are also used as sandwich bars now analyse their peak times, service levels and even waiting times of customers to ensure faster and better service to their customers.

Product popularity can also be tracked and analysed a helpful tool especially when new products are introduced. Stock control software is also extensively used as it can help reduce costs. Really high-tech sandwich bars with seating capacity may offer WIFI connection.

POPULAR CATERING

These types of outlets have many similarities to fast-food outlets and although they could be categorized as such they often offer full table service and that alone can be considered a reason enough to slightly distinguish them from fast-food type outlets. Although differing from one another in certain aspects, these catering outlets have a number of characteristics which are common to all these types of operations–their menu is focused around a certain product, for example, pizza or chicken or offer a limited range of products.

The food and beverages sold are of a consistent standard and quality with a high percentage of convenience and pre-cooked foods being used. These operations cater mainly for the relatively lower average spend markets with lower prices being charged than those found in other food and beverage establishments; there is a low ratio of service staff to customers with many of these operations being a form of self-service; consumption of the food may be on or off the premises; less rigid meal times are observed by these establishments, with some form of menu usually available throughout the day; and finally, all aspects of the operation are highly standardized, leading to a high volume throughput with resulting economies in food, labour and other operating costs.

Financial Implications

Popular catering establishments have a number of characteristics which enable their particular business orientation to be identified. Relatively speaking, they do not require such a high initial capital outlay nor a high percentage of fixed costs, although they do normally have a higher percentage of variable costs. Although the products offered for sale by these establishments are perishable, they are not as perishable as similar food and beverage products offered by other types of catering establishments; this is mainly due to the high level of convenience foods used by popular catering outlets, and the fact that often most of the foods are 'cooked to order' and do not have to be prepared sometime in advance; also because the products are not so highly perishable, these operations do not suffer from such sales instability as do hotels, for example, and they therefore have a lesser degree of dependence on market demand.

All these factors contribute to making the fast food and popular catering operations both costorientated and market-orientated. In these lower average spend operations, the cost of the meal to the customer is an important variable in determining the sales of the operation; because fast food and popular operations demonstrate a very elastic demand, an increase in an establishment' s prices of, for example, 10%, is likely to have a substantial effect on its sales.

Variable costs in fast-food operations account for a large part of the product' s selling price and the range of price discretion is consequently low. The prices charged by these establishments must therefore be carefully calculated, particularly in relation to competitors' pricing levels. The average spend per customer can be relatively low, ranging from ₹10 to ₹20 although these relatively low average spends are compensated by the volume sales achieved.

The financial policies of such operations would include the envisaged profitability of the establishment and the way in which it may be achieved, by controlling costs, balancing selling prices against volume sales, determining the profit margins on the food and beverage items, etc.

Marketing

The marketing policy for the modern popular and fast-food organization is the key to success in this sector of the industry. A study of many of these organizations provides an outline to the marketing policy which may be discussed under the variables of product, promotion, place, price, process, physical evidence and participants.

Product and Service Styles

The products sold by popular catering operations are highly standardized and portion controlled, particularly in take-away operations. The larger organizations, such as Pizza Hut, have vertically integrated their supply chains, controlling food production through to product sales, ensuring total product control and specification. Other companies may buy in pre-prepared and packaged products from the food manufacturers and sell them directly to the customer, for example, pre-wrapped pies, biscuits, butter, etc.

In this situation the fast-food operation closely resembles a retail trading outlet in which it has bought from the wholesaler and is selling to the customer without altering the product in any way. This is a particularly useful way for an operation to increase its menu range without increasing the work load on the kitchen staff or requiring additional space or equipment to prepare a menu item with fresh produce. The menu as a sales tool is important in any food and beverage operation, but is particularly so in these types of operations where staffing levels are reduced to a minimum and the oper ation's only vehicle for selling its products is via its menu and visual displays. In situations such as takeaways where contact time with the service staff is minimal, the menus are featured very prominently, usually with pictorial representation of the dishes. In these operations it is not so much a question of whether or not to use convenience foods, but of those available which ones to use and to what extent.

The amount of convenience foods used by an establishment will depend on a number of factors: the cost of buying in manufactured foods compared with the cost of producing the same products on the premises; the standard of food that the establishment wishes to offer; the variety of menu items to be offered; whether the additional costs of buying manufactured foods is offset by savings in production and labour costs, etc.

Staffing

Staffing levels are, where possible, kept to a minimum. The ratio of service staff to customers is dependent upon a number of factors which include the type of establishment, the range of menu items, and the prices charged. The labour intensity of an operation is particularly related to its price level; broadly speaking, the higher the price of the meal to customers, the more service they expect to receive.

The staff to customer ratio increases as the operation becomes more sophisticated so that in waiter service establishments, for example, one waiter may only serve 12 to 16 customers.

Technology

Apart from the advancements in EPOS and production technologies and its worth mentioning the use of the Internet that has enabled smaller businesses to use this new and exciting medium for marketing efforts. Restaurants of various sizes around the world have seized the opportunity by creating web sites.

These can range from simple information 'electronic billboards' sites to more interactive web sites where customers can book seats in the restaurant online. Web sites are just one piece of the overall marketing strategy that can help operators realise some of their business goals. Innovative and cohesive web sites combined with other online tools such as, mail list, newsletters, and auto-responders, can generate a high degree of visibility for a company that is necessary to increase sales or business to business contacts.

TAKEAWAY AND HOME DELIVERIES

The take-away, or take-out service as it is more commonly known in the US, is a method of food service that exploits to the full the concept of 'fast foods'. The products offered by these establishments are highly standardized, as are most of the features of the operations–service, sales control, product packaging, etc.

The take-away operation offers a limited basic menu to the customer, but within this menu there may be a number of variations on the basic items. These operations aim to achieve volume sales by offering low- to medium-priced foods, and they have become a popular segment of the food and beverage market because they fill a need for a quick snack or meal.

The time between customers placing orders and receiving their meals, aims to be faster than any other method yet discussed; some operations aim for a 30 second service time.

The customer may either take the food out of the takeaway to eat, or it may be consumed on the premises; a large number of so-called 'take-away' outlets now provide very extensive seating areas, often for more than several hundred.

A number of take-away restaurants would also offer a Home delivery service. The practice, traditionally linked to Pizzas expanded to Indian and Chinese and even sit in restaurants. Home delivery is one of the upcoming markets as it is predicted to have a high growth in the India in the next few years.

Financial Implications

Traditional restaurants tend to be limited by the number of seats in their facility, a takeaway or home delivery restaurant however, can capitalize on the fact that the faster they produce and deliver food the higher the earnings. Average spend can range from ₹2 to ₹8 depending on the type of takeaway and for home deliveries average spend tends to be in the range of ₹8 to ₹12.

Marketing

Because take-away outlets aim for a high rate of customer turnover, their situation in relation to their markets is crucial; they are usually found in high streets and main shopping centres where they have a high percentage of passing trade.

Although the ASP of customers in takeaways may be considerably lower than for some of the other food service methods discussed, this is compensated by their high rate of customer throughput.

Home delivery operators tends to spend most of their marketing budget in leaflets that they distribute in houses in their catchments area.

Apart from the menu itself, other typical information will include operating hours and contact telephone numbers although increasingly operators will accept orders via e-mail or their web site.

As the majority of consumers will consider such menus junk mail, increasingly the use of the web site will be paramount and the operators will revert to using business card style leaflets to draw potential customers to their web site portal.

Product and Service Styles

Today there is a wide selection of products that takeaway can offer for sale; the growth of the traditional fish-and-chip shops has now taken second place to the other types of foods now offered–hamburgers, pizzas, Chinese, Indian and Mexican food, to name a few. Menu is normally limited to allow for either pre-cooked goods that can be easily reheated and served to customers or batch cooking which can be an efficient production for a busy high street takeaway.

Even fish and chip shops will often batch cook a number of portions and keep in a hot plate especially in busy times of the business. Self-service is therefore a method of food service in which customers collect their own food from some form of service counter, in return for which they pay a lower price for the meal than they would, for example, in operations offering a waiter service. In self-service operations payment for the meal is made either before the meal, for example, in vending operations or after the meal as in some cafeterias.

In the industrial sector of the catering market this method of food service has become firmly established; in the majority of cases people' s main meal is in the evening, so that they only require a snack-type short lunch which a self-service operation can adequately provide. In the welfare sector this utilitarian method of food service is also used extensively, leaving the more leisurely dining to that part of the day which is not associated with work.

Staffing

A take-away restaurant focuses its labour expenditure mainly in production staff with just one person serving the customers; often the same person may prepare some easy menu items such as salads. In the case of Home delivery the person in the counter will also take any calls and allocate orders to the delivery staff. The number of delivery staff will vary with the volume of business but a good home delivery restaurant would need at least three delivery staff to be able to deliver orders on time.

Technology

Increasingly home delivery restaurants are utilizing database software, so once a customer has made a call their address and phone number is stored so that the next time they call the call receiver knows correct address customer menu preferences and past purchases. Innovation in credit card and Internet technology has allowed for orders to be made via the Internet enabling the operation to be more efficient.

COFFEE HOUSES AND TEA ROOMS

Coffee houses often feature large comfortable sitting areas were customers may purchase hot beverages and cold snacks for consumption primarily in house.

Often to take away. In the US from late 1950s onward, coffee houses also served as a venue for entertainment, most commonly folk performers, especially since young audiences are not allowed entry to bars until the age of 21. For example, Bob Dylan began his career performing in coffee houses. A Coffee house is not to be confused with the term Café. In the US the term is used to describe a small restaurant whilst in France a café may sell alcoholic beverages. In the India the coffee shop market has evolved rapidly since the 1990s and is now a major market with Starbucks leading the way but brands such as Costa and Nero following the example.

Tea rooms are found mostly in Britain and tend to be small businesses that offer a variety of teas as well as scones, pancakes and other cakes. Tea rooms can also be found in countries such as Australia, India and New Zealand and generally countries that have been in some way influenced by the India. Although the traditional tea room is beyond its maturity stage, tea consumption is on the increase particularly with herbal and aromatic tea varieties, and the concept might find a revival in future years.

Financial Implications

Coffee houses in the US just as to Mintel the market experienced 157% growth between 2000 and 2005 to reach some ₹8,372 million. Over the next 5 years sales are expected to grow by a further 125% to reach an impressive ₹18,839 million by 2010. This is over twice the growth rate seen in the British coffee shops market which is not as established as in the US.

Table. Market Size and Forecast of Branded Coffee Shops

Year	2005 prices	Index	At 2006 prices	Index2
2001	305	45	355	53
2002	375	56	420	62
2003	450	67	489	72
2004	530	79	561	83
2005	610	90	627	93
2006	675	100	675	100
2007	736	109	716	106
2008	801	119	760	113
2009	874	129	806	119
2010	948	140	848	126
2011	1,023	152	890	132

The total number of coffee shops in the US increased by 70% between 2000 and 2005, bringing the total to a staggering 21,400 or one coffee house for every 14,000 Americans. Mintel the number of shops could well continue to rise until there is a coffee shop for every 10,000 Americans. In the India, the market is worth over ₹700 million and forecasts suggest a growth well into 2011 although the market would soon reach maturity stage.

Tea rooms today, are not a significant market in terms of financial implications but they worth a mention from a cultural point of view.

Marketing

The market for coffee shops today is highly segmented. From business people conducting meetings to mothers with toddlers during the day and young people during the weekends it is a product that has attracted such a wide market that it can be hard to distinguish one significant market segment. As coffee shops tend to be opened by a chain, the brand increasingly becomes a prime criteria for consumers when choosing which coffee shop to select. The tea room market tends to be elderly customers although tea rooms are often seen as a tourist attraction by tourists of all ages.

Product and Service Styles

The main product is the large variety of types of coffee that the consumer can find in a coffee shop. Apart from the large variety of coffee beans that each shop may feature there can be a var iety of products that all are made using the same coffee bean.

For example a latte a cappuccino and an espresso can all have the same coffee as the base ingredient. A typical coffee shop menu will feature 10–15 types of coffee and other hot beverages such as tea or hot chocolate. Often the shops may sell their own brand of coffee beans for consumption at home. Interestingly Starbucks, the global leader of the coffee shop, is diversifying by selling hot food rather than cold snacks.

If other brands follow suit the coffee shop concept will be reinventing itself and we may well see a number of coffee shop chains mutating into the café concept often found in France. Counter service is now a norm in most coffee shops although some privately owned may still offer table service. On the other hand with tea rooms table service is the norm or a combination of counter and table service, where by the customer gives the order over the counter and the product is served at the table.

Staffing

Coffee shops depending on their size will have two or more baristas. A barista is a counter clerk and the word derives from the Italian word for bartender. As the quality of the hot beverage is affected by the skills of the barista it is very important for all staff to be properly trained in the use of the equipment.

High street coffee shops tend to have their busiest times during morning hours and the lunch period so the coffee shop manager would have to take that in consideration when creating the rotas. As most tea houses tend to be family owned businesses the staff tend to be members of the family, in the India tea houses tend to get busier during the summer months and weekends when tourists would visit the destination but often seating space is so limited that the necessity for extra staff would not normally arise.

Technology

EPOS systems have enabled coffee houses to deal with higher volumes of costumers and better stock control. Even more importantly the advancement of coffee dispensing technology has enabled coffee shop chains to be able to deliver consistent quality of their beverages throughout their branches. The technology however is not yet that far advanced that can deliver a complete finished product and well-trained baristas are still a must.

2

Contract, Travel and Public Sector Catering

INTRODUCTION

We examine the contract, travel and public sector catering. In many occasions the public sector and travel catering operations, are often serviced by contract caterers. However, there are still occasions where organizations provide their own in-house catering and by dividing the sector into three subdivisions, it allows us to discuss the distinct differences between the various operations. The three subsectors have shown a dramatic increase in the past few years with some sectors such as the cruise ships showing a growth in business looking to continue in the next ten years or more. The stage aims to give an overview of the sectors to enable the reader to get an understanding of the type of technology often used as well as the marketing and financial implications for each sector.

CONTRACT CATERING

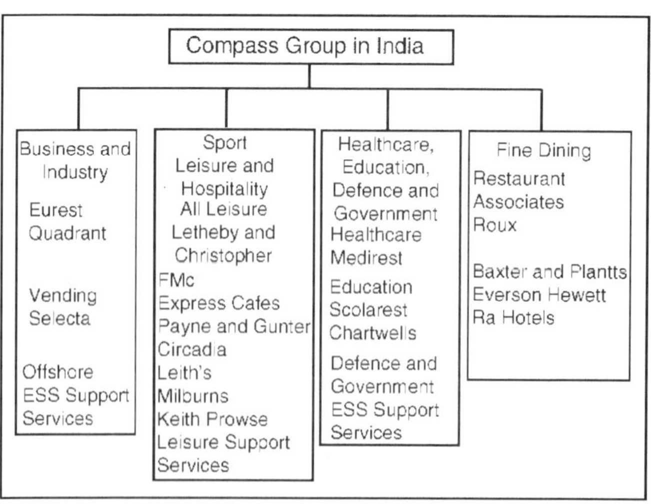

Fig. Structure of Compass Group the Largest Catering Company in the India.

Contract catering has evolved greatly in the past ten years and it is not uncommon to find contract catering companies investing in any of the sectors that are covered in this stage. Traditionally, contract catering has been associated with non-profit or institutional catering, including workplace canteens, hospitals and schools however, today contract catering firms such as Compass or Sodexho have branched outside the remits of traditional contract catering and today it is not uncommon for contract catering firms to develop brands under which they operate restaurants.

Compass Group employs 90,000 employees and has 8,500 sites in the India alone. Worldwide the compass group employees 400,000 employees and annual revenue of approximately ₹11 billion. The BHA in 2006 in the India alone contract catering reached revenues of just under ₹4 billion, showing a 0.8% drop in turnover from the previous year. Worth noting is the decline of contract catering in Health care, MOD, Local authority and private education.

Table. Contract Catering Market Segments by Number or Means served

	2001		2003		2005		% change 2001-2005
	m	%	m	%	m	%	
Business and industry	588	38	613	36.9	645	41.2	9.7
State education	227	14.7	281	16.9	265	16.9	16.7
Public catering	177	11.4	185	11.1	210	13.4	18.6
Healthcare	238	15.4	232	14	204	13	−14.3
MOD	135	8.7	161	9.7	105	6.7	−22.2
Private education	125	8.1	135	8.1	100	6.4	−20
Local authority	42	2.7	37	2.2	22	1.4	−47.6
Oil rigs, training centers, construction sites	15	1	14	1	16	1	6.7
Total	**1,547**	**100**	**1,661**	**100**	**1,567**	**100**	**1.3**

For the purposes of this text we shall define contract caterers as: individuals or firms who undertake the responsibility of operating and controlling a company' s catering facilities within that company' s guidelines for a specified contract arrangement. Contract caterers are usually engaged for a specific period of time, after which the contract may be renewed or dissolved as both parties wish. Catering contracts can be classified mainly in five types:

- *Cost plus/management fee*: These are contracts where the client is billed for the cost of the operation plus a management fee.
- *Fixed price/performance guarantee*: Contracts where the clients agree a total subsidy and the costs may not rise above the agreed figure.
- *Profit and loss concession*: The client and the caterer agree to share the profits or loss of the operation.
- *Total risk*: Total investment covered by the caterer who earns all profits.
- *Purchasing*: A contract for purchasing only.

Contract caterers are involved in all types of industrial catering situations, ranging from the small independent concerns to the large multinational organizations and may become involved for different reasons: for example, the organization' s dissatisfaction with the existing services; complaints about the standard of catering have been made at staff meetings and repeated attempts to improve the facilities have failed, or the company does not wish to become involved in operating the catering facilities itself as it may not be its core business or recognizes that it does not have the expertise and so engages the services of contract caterers.

INDUSTRIAL CATERING

Industrial catering can be defined as catering taking place in businesses. For example, major retail operators will offer catering to their employees and whilst sometimes they may have an in-house catering division, most often they will hire a contract caterer.

Another example of industrial catering is the catering supplied to employees of organizations that provide financial services. Other businesses that may be included would be catering in oil rigs, construction sites, and training or conference centres. Indeed the subsector is so large that it exceeds an annual turnover of ₹660 million. Typical contracts agreed between organizations and caterers tend to be fixed price and profit/loss concession and total risk.

Financial Implications

Product pricing is a major issue for industrial catering. The market can be characterized as semi-captive as it would be convenient for employees to use the caterer but they also have the choice to use other food and beverage providers or bring in their own lunch. Of course there are exceptions to this such as catering provided in oil rigs where employees have no alternative but to consume what is provided by the caterer.

Supermarkets tend to offer good quality luncheons not only in the form of sandwiches but also in hot and freshly prepared food at very competitive prices. Caterers have to ensure good quality of food is provided with food items that are around the range of ₹3–₹5.

Marketing

Ensuring that the caterer is the prime choice for the employees of the business can be affected by the marketing efforts of the caterer. Day specials and promotional packages will often be advertised on a company' s intranet or message board.

Traditional methods such as flyers may also be used but the speed and cost effectiveness of an e-mail makes it a prime method of communicating with potential clients.

Product and Service Styles

Counter service and take-away service styles tend to be the preferred service style for such operations, however buffet style and self-service may be used. The main products are snacks and take-away food, so product packaging can be important as some caterers may have limited seating space and employees may also chose to buy the product and consume it later.

Staffing

These operations tend to be staffed by regular members of staff. Caterers will often have other operations in nearby sites so staff mobility between operations can be an option. This flexibility can become important especially when there is need to cover staff leave or sickness periods from one outlet to another.

Technology

Food holding technology is very important. An off-site central kitchen may be used that supplies a number of operations. Ensuring that the quality of food is maintained through the transportation and delivery is paramount. Electronic point of sale technology can help with forecasting of sales thus reducing wastage. Communication technologies such as access to host company electronic boards or intranets and group mailing lists can be a great advantage to the caterer for marketing purposes.

EVENT MANAGEMENT

An increasingly important area in Hospitality Management is that of Event Management. Although event management involves all those aspects that are required to organize a successful event, the provision of food and beverage is often of paramount importance to guarantee the success of the event. Policy decisions relating to function catering are largely determined by a number of characteristics inherent in this type of catering.

The first is the season. The second is the concentration of events during these months, which are mainly at weekends, particularly Friday and Saturday events, during which time an operation must seek to maximize its sales potential. Third, a considerable amount of information is available to the caterer in advance of the organized functions; this includes the number of guests to be catered for and for which meal periods, for example lunch or dinner; their time of arrival and departure; the menu they are to be given and the price being paid per guest. The basic policies relating to function catering are usually quite specific to this form of catering.

If function trade is an establishment' s only source of business then the policies laid down will only relate to this type of trade. In other establishments, however, such as hotels, the function facilities may be one of a number of catering outlets, although even in these organizations the banqueting department will often have policy decisions relating specifically to this department.

Banqueting and Functions and Large-scale Events

Function and event catering may be described as the service of food and beverages at a specific time and place, for a given number of people, to an agreed menu and price. Examples of function catering include social functions, such as weddings and dinner dances; business functions such as conferences, meetings and working lunches; and those functions that are organized for both social and business reasons such as outdoor catering at a sports event, show or exhibition. Function catering is found in both the commercial and non-commercial sectors of the catering industry.

The term 'banqueting' can often be used within hotels to describe the department that deals with function catering. The typical hotel function or banqueting 'season' runs between the months of October and May with the busiest months being December and January. For the rest of the year some of the facilities may be used for providing separate restaurant facilities for tour groups who normally have limited time available for meals and whom the hotel may wish to keep apart from the normal day-to-day restaurant business. The function facilities may also frequently be let on a day or half-day basis for such occasions as antique shows, trade exhibitions, fashion shows, etc. where the requirement of food and beverages may be very limited.

This function season is more noticeable in certain types of establishments, particularly those organizations whose sole purpose is function catering, and those that offer purpose-built facilities such as hotels. In other establishments such as public houses, department store restaurants, industrial cafeterias, etc. the function season is not so evident, as existing dining facilities are usually adapted for function events rather than specific facilities being available; however, even these types of operations are still likely to experience peak periods during the year when the function facilities are in greater demand than at other times. This characteristic fluctuating of demand associated with function catering has implications for such establishments' basic policy decisions.

Financial Implications

The logistics required for such events can be extremely complicated. Often the event might take place in a location that there is no production capabilities and the food and beverage will have to be produced at another site and then transported and served on-site.

For the company taking on such a project there are the additional costs of transportation to take into account. When negotiating the contract the caterer will have a number of ready-made and coasted menus but often in events such as weddings the customer might require a very specific product that the caterer will have to customise. Using the wedding as event example, beverages will often be included in the cost per head or cover. Meaning, cost per customer. Because the margins per head are normally very small the caterer makes the money on the volume of the event.

The pricing structure for an establishment' s function catering facilities will be largely determined by its cost structure, with particular reference to its fixed and variable costs. This is most in evidence in the non-commercial sector where functions may not be fully costed, that is not taking into account the fixed costs of the operation.

Where the costing of function menus is based mainly on covering food and labour costs, it is important to remember that both of these increase with the size and quality of function offered.

However, due to the volume of sales the food and labour costs as a percentage of actual sales will slightly decrease; it is necessary therefore to not only consider the food costs per function but also the potential benefits to be gained from a reduction in labour costs. There are a variety of pricing structures that may be used for costing functions, the adoption of any one being determined by such factors as the type of organization, the standards of food and beverage service to be offered, and the cost structure of the establishment.

Marketing

There is such a varied type of events that a catering company or a hotel banqueting department may use any of the traditional marketing such as Leaflets, radio, TV, magazine and newspaper adverts. Brewin Dolphin, a financial research company, the market for weddings is worth ₹4.2 billion each year with the average wedding to about ₹16,000 no wonder hotel banqueting departments and contract catering operators are competing for this lucrative segment. Sample function menus produced by an establishment need to be of a good quality and appearance as the customer will often wish to take them away to study before deciding on the function menu.

These sales tools should also be of a standard consistent with the level of operation and the type of image it is trying to project. Function 'folders' containing details of all the different facilities offered by an establishment are often produced by organizations which may be distributed to prospective clients advertising the establishment' s function facilities.

A function 'folder' often colour-coded for easy reference by the client, would most likely be composed of the following:

- An envelope type folder with the company' s logo, title and address clearly displayed.
- A personal letter from the function/banqueting manager to the client.
- A list of function rooms together with details of the numbers that could be accommodated for different types of functions, for example

a formal lunch or dinner, a dinner dance, a buffet type reception, a theatre-style conference/meeting, etc.

- Plans of the room with basic dimensions, position of power points, telephone points, ceiling heights, etc.
- Sample menus for lunch, dinner, buffets, meetings, etc.
- Details of audio-visual equipment available for meetings, for example lecterns, microphones, overhead projectors, screens, etc.
- Details of accommodation facilities available, often at special rates for guests attending a function/meeting.
- Coloured postcards of the hotel/function rooms.
- Relevant simple maps and parking arrangements where necessary.

Product and Service Styles

The product may vary depending on the type of the event and it may be anything from buffet style service to full table ser vice depending on the customer request. Silver service and family service styles are quite common when table service has been requested. Functions may include a reception stage where canapés and appetisers are served by "satellite waiters". This is often known as the Butler style of service.

Staffing

Caterers as well as banqueting departments will normally have a core of staff and will then use agency staff to cope with larger events. Because of this the quality of service may suffer as the operator cannot guarantee the skill level of the agency staff. Some contract catering companies train their own casual staff and they then have a 'Bank' of casual staff that they may call upon when needed.

Technology

Food holding technology is very important to contract caterers. Because the business is more predictable as the numbers of customers are known hotel kitchens may use their staff to prepare the food for a large function before hand and load it to already plated to specially designed racks that can fit into combination ovens. Food can then be either completely cooked at the time needed and served straight from the racks or pre-cooked/chilled and then re-constituted.

SPORT VENUE CATERING

Sport venue catering includes catering offered in stadia, football, cricket, rugby, horse racing venues, private health and fitness clubs, golf and other sports. The sector is hard to quantify as each country has a large number of venues and catering operations are largely fragmented. In 2004, Mintel was estimating the sector in the India to worth ₹354 million. With the introduction of new venues since 2004 including the Wembley and Arsenal Stadia in London in 2007 and 2006, respectively, the India sector is estimated to exceed the ₹400 million mark in revenue today.

In the India there are 365 stadia whilst the USA currently has 1,726. With 9,379 stadia around the world the revenues generated through the sale of food and drinks alone must be well over the ₹10 billion mark today.

Table. Number of Satdia Around the World

	Number of Menu
Africa	525
Asia	884
Central America	260
Europe	3,780
Middle East	424
North America	2,125
Oceanla	260
South America	1,121
Total	**9,379**

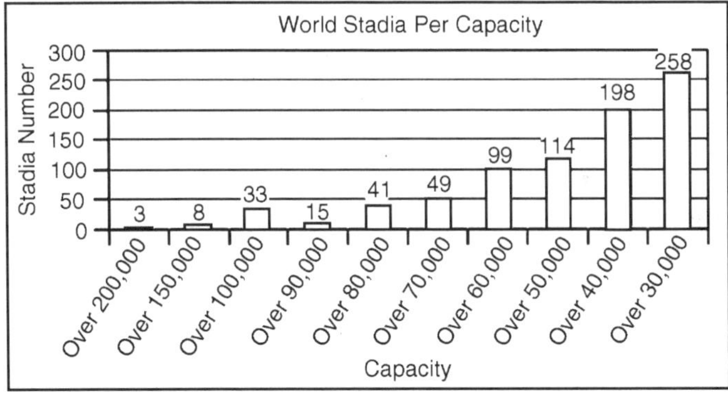

Fig. Number of World Stadia Per Capacity

There are three common types of contracts often found between caterers and venue operators. The first is where the venue takes a percentage of the revenue generated by the contract caterer. The second is where the venue simply leases their facilities therefore enjoying a fixed stream of income. The third is a relatively newer type of arrangement where both caterer and venue work in partnership setting a joint venture and splitting the profits generated equally.

Financial Implications

With approximately 9% of the world' s stadia having a capacity of over 30,000 the logistics required for the catering of such large operations can be extremely complex. If we consider the newly finished Wembley stadium in London, India, the catering logistics required are phenomenal. The stadium has a capacity of 90,000. With 60 bars and 41 food and beverage outlets the stadium hospitality facilities include conference rooms of up to 1,000 cap acity and reception rooms for up to 3,000 capacity. With 803 points of sale and a total of 3,000 hospitality employees, Wembley is one of the biggest catering sites in Europe. It includes a 950 cover Atrium restaurant, serving buffet food, the great hall and banquet space for up to 1,500 people, as well as four signature restaurants of 650 covers each, including two à la carte eateries and two brasseries. It also features two Champagne and seafood bars as well as two large free-flow public catering areas, 162 private boxes, two super boxes and a royal suite for up to 400 people Kühn.

Marketing

Many of the venues will try to entice the consumer earlier than the starting time of the event to maximize sales. Often leaflets might be handed at to the public featuring 'early bird' offers as well as the type of food and drinks on offer at the venue.

Meal deals often seen in fast-food operations are also a popular promotional tool to increase multiple item purchasing. For example, a consumer may be offered to buy a pint of specific lager and a pie and gets a bag of crisps for free. The major contract caterers such as Delaware North, Compass and Sodexho use the Internet extensively as a marketing and promotional tool.

Product and Service Styles

Soft and hot drinks and sandwich markets appear to be the most popular items just as to Mintel. However, it is not uncommon for exclusive restaurants to be featured in many of the worlds stadia. However, it is worth mentioning something specific to stadia in terms of service styles; often catering staff may be seen moving around the stadium selling food and beverages whilst a game is taking place. They can be on foot carrying trays or in some cases in specially converted bicycles that allow the sale of cold bottled beverages or even warm food.

Staffing

Staffing can be a major 'headache' for the human resources management of such an operation. Because of the fluctuation of the events that could range from the corporate entertainment of a handful of people to that of a few thousands the organizations involved tend to have a core of permanent staff whilst they manage an often enormous database of casual staff that can be called upon to cover a certain event. Two major problems emanate from such a setup. The first is that of consistency, so organizations will have to ensure that all staff are trained to ensure standards of production and service are maintained at all times. The second is ensuring that the casual staff in the database get enough work every week to keep them interested in coming back for more work in the future.

Technology

Two key considerations in such environments are paramount: health and safety, and speed of service. Advancements in technology enable operators to have better control of their food production ensuring health and safety standards are maintained throughout the production and service delivery. With large stadia that often have an excess of 500 selling points, EPOS systems and networking technology has to be extremely robust. Technology can also ensure that food production and food holding can be achieved with larger numbers than ever before. The new Wembley stadium in the India features a beer dispensing system that has the pumping capability of four pints per sixteen seconds with the stadium number of sales points that means at optimum production their 803 points of sale can produce 45,169 pints in fifteen minutes. That is half the total possible capacity of the stadium and in theory it would mean the end of customer queuing for a pint.

LEISURE VENUE CATERING

Leisure venue catering is catering offered in venues such as museums, theatres, cinemas, historic buildings, zoos, wildlife parks, art galleries. Perhaps, because of the captive nature of the market the key management issues that appear to be prevalent are that of pricing and quality. In the India, the market has exceeded the ₹2 billion mark since 2006. However, the growth of the sector compared to that of free-standing restaurants is quite slow suggesting that improvements could be made.

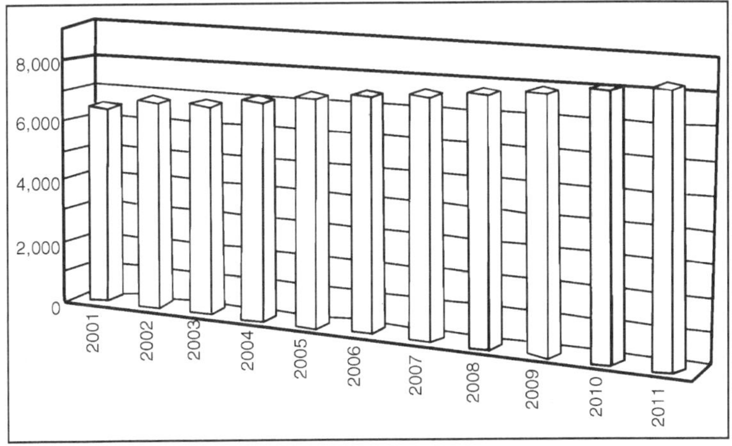

Fig. Trends in the Leisure Venue Catering Market, 2001-2002 (in million Pounds)

Although the majority or leisure venues outsource their catering a significant number chooses to keep their catering in house. This is more prevalent in cinema and theatre catering.

Financial Implications

Although catering in museums has shown the largest growth in the leisure venue catering in recent years Museums and art galleries in the India have lost a major competitive advantage. With the introduction of free admission consumers have the option to go to a high street restaurant and re-enter the museum or gallery later. What was once a captive market has now become at best a semi-captive one. This meant that catering in such establishments has to offer a better value for money than it has done in the past, ensuring that costs remain low whilst quality of product and price remains competitive enough to entice visit ors to buy from their outlets. In order to ensure higher profit margins whilst remaining competitive leisure caterers will have to ensure that they maximize their sales per available customer within the venue. That means that vendors must ensure that the long queues that often put off consumers must be minimized.

Marketing

Apart from the common promotional techniques used such as meal deals and discounted offers, catering in leisure venues over the past years had a reputation of bad value for money. Caterers today must not only ensure that customers are enticed to buy their in-house products but also that they develop a brand that communicates quality and efficiency to the consumer. This one of the main reasons leisure venue operators will often chose to outsource their food and beverage provision to well-established contract catering companies. The main operators in the India are Compass, Sodexho and Elior although there are other operators such as DO&CO, Searcy and Caterleisure.

Product and Service Styles

Table. Types of Food Bought at Leisure Venues, 2007

	Percentage of a sample of 809 visitors
Cold snacks (e.g. crisps, chocolate, nut)	47
Hot take-away food (e.g. hotdog, burger, hot pie/pastry	45
Cold take-away food (e.g. sandwiches, ice cream)	45
Hot snacks (e.g. chips, nachos)	30
Hot sit-down meal (e.g. pizza) pasta , shepherds pie,curry)	27
Cold sit-down meal (e.g. salad, sandwiches)	19
Healthy snacks (e.g. fruit, energy/ cereal bars)	19
Others	1
Did not buy food	15

The majority of visitors purchase snacks or take-away food such as burgers, hot dogs, crisps and chocolate. Therefore the majority of the food provision can take often the form of retail. Counter, buffet and take-away service styles tend to be amongst the more popular for leisure catering.

Staffing

In recent years, the minimum wage in the India has been increased much faster than inflation rates. This has caused an added challenge to operators and for a sector that was traditionally perceived as an expensive one compared to high street vendors transferring the added cost to the consumer farther expanded the gap between consumer expectations and value for money delivered. When catering is kept in house, operators have a separate staff division that focuses on hospitality. Casual staff are also used as there is a fluctuation of visitors depending on day of the week, weather and time of the year. During weekends and school breaks, for example, leisure parks tend to be at their busiest. This in turn does affect the quality of service especially with the larger operators.

Technology

One of the key allies in recovering product and service quality lies in the investment of information technology. The latest EPOS technology can help managers keep track of customer preferences as well as employee productivity, this can be a great tool in allowing the manager to identify a member of staff that may be in need of further training or even award that excellent member of staff that could otherwise go unnoticed.

TRAVEL CATERING

Travel catering has a number of characteristics not commonly associated with other food and beverage outlets. It frequently involves the feeding of a large number of customers arriving together at a catering facility, and who need to be catered for in a specific time, for example, on board a plane. The plane only carries sufficient food and beverage supplies for a specific number of meal periods.

If for any reason this food cannot be served to customers, alternative supplies may not be readily available.

The service of the food and beverages may be particularly difficult due to the physical conditions within the service area, for example, turbulence on board a plane. The types of restaurants described previously are usually catering for a specific and identifiable socio-economic market. Travel catering often has to cater for 'mixed markets'.

Finally, there are the problems of staffing these food and beverage facilities: the extra costs involved in the transportation and service of the food and beverages; space restrictions and the problem of security while the operation is in transit. Four main types of travel catering may be identified: Airline catering, Cruise ship and Ferry boat catering, Train catering and Motorway catering.

AIRLINES

The major new trend of the past ten years in the Airline industry in Europe has been the introduction and substantial growth of the budget or 'no frills' airline phenomenon. Companies such as Easyjet and Rynair have shown amazing growth. The total airline growth from the year 2000 to 2006 has been an amazing 30% but mainly due to the increase in budget airlines the in-flight catering expenditure had a downward trend in recent years.

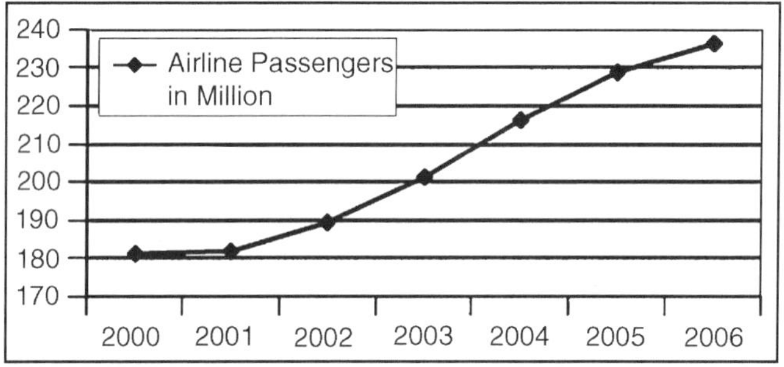

Fig. Airline Passengers, 2000-2008

Table. Onboard Catering Market, by Sector

	2002		**2005**		**2007**		**% change 2002-2007**
	₹m	%	₹m	%	₹m	%	
In-flight	613	72	590	72	577	72	–6.0
Ferry	170	20	155	19	152	19	–10.6
Rail	69	8	75	9	73	9	+4.2
Total	**852**	**100**	**820**	**100**	**802**	**100**	**–5.9**

Airline catering has increased and developed considerably over the past twenty-five years. Originally consisting of sandwiches and flasks of tea, coffee and alcoholic beverages, the progress to today' s full and varied service has paralleled that of aircraft development itself. In budget airlines, however, the product has gone back to the basic trolley with sandwiches, snacks chocolate and limited selection of beverages on offer. Airline catering falls into two main areas: terminal catering, and 'in-transit' or 'in-flight' catering.

Financial Implications

The cost of a hot meal and beverage to the airline is about ₹6.50 but the biggest cost to the airline is the waiting to restock the aircraft and time at an airport can mean a big loss of income to the carrier. If, for example, a carrier flies from London, India to Athens, Greece, it may cost the airline less to stock up for the return trip as well, limiting the waiting time at the Greek airport. This is especially true for budget airlines as they are well known for their strategy of limiting their turnaround time.

Marketing

Airlines have tried to different experiments to alleviate the widely held customer perception that airline food is bland. Some airlines have tried introducing high street brands in their food packaging. Quite often the quality of the food is used in their marketing campaigns as a unique selling point, and airlines will employ a well-known chef to design their menu as part of their marketing efforts

Product and Service Styles

The in-flight catering service varies considerably with the class of travel, type and duration of flight. For the economy travellers, the food and beverage portions are highly standardized with the meals portioned into plastic trays that are presented to the passengers and from which they eat their meals. Disposable cutlery, napkins, etc. may be used to increase the standard of hygiene and reduce the weight carried and storage space required.

Gourmet food in the airlines is another recent trend. Stephan Pyles, of the Dallas restaurant, working with American Airlines whilst Charlie Trotter, the Chicago chef, introduces dishes created for premier United Airlines passengers. The lower than normal air pressure can affect customer perception of taste as well as digestion and executive chefs designing a menu will often taste it mid-air to ensure they have compensated for this.

Added to that is the fact food is not cooked on board, it is just warmed. Meals are prepared twelve to sixteen hours in advance chilled and then held at low temperatures. Service is from a gueridon trolley, where food is portioned in front of the customers and any garnishes, sauces, etc. are added just as to their immediate requirements. The crockery used may be bone china and this combines with fine glassware and cutlery to create an atmosphere of high-class dining. Some airlines offer full silver service menu for their first class and business travellers.

A characteristic of airline catering is that this service is often contracted out to a specialist catering firm, which will supply a similar service to many airlines. The meal is usually included in the price of the fare with the exception of budget airlines.

The growth in air travel has made competition fierce, and the area of food service is now a particularly competitive aspect of the total service offered by an airline. An interesting concept currently in the USA is that of gourmet meals delivered to the airport by the SkyMeals company.

Staffing

Food and beverage outlets at air terminals usually consist of selfservice and waiter service restaurants, supplemented by vending machines and licensed bars. The major restaurant brands often seen in high streets can also be seen in airport terminals. In flight catering service is delivered by the flight attendants, who often see the service of food and drinks as secondary to their responsibility of ensuring the health and safety of passengers, this can be especially true if customers are flying in the economy class. Although health and safety should always remain flight attendants primary responsibility airlines that wish to claim a competitive advantage ought to train and offer incentives to individuals that offer exceptional service.

Technology

The main issues with aircraft are that of space and weight. Ensuring that on-board ovens are lighter, take less space and consume less energy are of primary importance. Advancements in technology may mean that airlines may be able to offer a menu fully cooked on board one day.

CRUISE SHIPS/FERRY BOATS

The cruise ship sector is one of the fastest moving sectors in the hospitality industry. The number of passengers has grown to more than 12 million in 2006 from approximately 500,000 in 1970.

Forecasts suggest that by 2012 the global industry will reach 20 million passengers with the USA and India leading in terms of cruise ship passengers.

Budget or 'no frills' cruise liners are making an appearance with new companies such as Caspi Cruises, Easy Cruise, whilst older budget companies such as Thomson or Louis Cruise Line increase their fleet capacity.

On the other hand, Ferry boat catering has slumped as the numbers of Ferry travellers has dramatically decreased due to the increase of low-cost airlines. In India, the onboard catering market was valued at ₹155 million for 2005, a 19% decrease since 2000, and the trend is still going today.

Financial Implications

Whilst cruise ship catering promises growth Ferry boat catering is extremely competitive. Mintel is forecasting a downward trend continuing well into 2010. Traditional cruise liners are looking to be more innovative continuing with all inclusive packages but offering optional extras. Wedding and honeymoon packages are another two products often offered by cruise liners.

Marketing

Cruise liners are expanding their marketing strategies to target non-traditional market segments. Increasing competition in the budget sector forces them to think innovatively in finding ways to sell their product without conflicting the more traditional brands.

Special promotions, discounts during low season, special occasions, anniversary gifts to customers are some of the promotional tools used by most liners.

Product and Service Styles

Sea or marine catering varies from the provision of food and beverages on the short sea route ferries to the large cruise or passenger liners where the catering facilities are an important part of the service offered by the shipping line and are usually included in the price of the fare. On the cruise liners the standard of catering facilities is high because they are an important sales feature in a competitive activity.

On the short sea routes, however, price is usually a more important factor and because of the necessity to feed large numbers of people in a short time the catering service provided is usually of the popular and fast-food type.

In the cruise liners companies appear to be more innovative than ever with companies such as Princess Cruises serving dinner in customer cabins or suite balconies ensuring extra food and beverage income.

The Gourmet 'bug' is also appearing in the cruise sector with celebrity chefs such as Todd English on Queen Mary 2; Nobu Matsuhisa and Wolfgang Puck on Crystal; Marco Pierre White on the new P&O Ventura and Gary Rhodes on two P&O' s ships, Oriana and Arcadia. Service styles can range depending on cruise liner from full silver service to self-service and buffet. With Ferry boats the service style often is cafeteria or take away due to the short journeys involved.

Staffing

After casino sales one of the largest revenue generators in cruise liners is beverage sales. Staff are trained extensively in up- selling techniques and with traditional cruise liners the recruitment process ensures that some of the best staff are hired. With the added incentive of tax-free incomes many hospitality professionals consider a few months on a cruise liner.

The organization on cruise ships can be extremely hierarchical. Most front line employees tend to stay for only a few trips as the nature of the ship means that there is not much to do but work whilst on a cruise ship.

Technology

Advanced EPOS technology and bar dispensing equipment mean better control of sales, stock control and wastage ensuring better profit margins as well as the facilitation of special discounts.

Advancement in waste disposal technology ensures waste is better compacted shredded and incinerated.

TRAINS

Mintel Reports, unlike Ferry and in flight catering, rail catering is showing an upward trend in revenues generated. Rail catering may be conveniently divided into two areas: terminal catering and in-transit catering.

There are 2,500 rail stations across the India. The main rival to rail is the low-cost airlines but the introduction of Eurostar in 2003 raised the rail market share in the India. The improvements of the West Coast Mainline and the introduction of the Pendolinos train by Virgin Trains passenger numbers increased by a 20%. In the US sales reached $79 million in 2005.

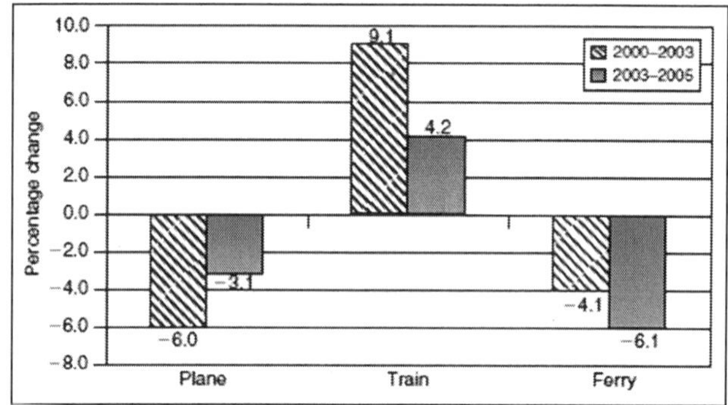

Fig. Percentage Change in Value of the UK Onboard Catering

Table. Rail F&B Gross Profit, 2005

F&B sales	₹78,929,599
Food	₹30,237,417
On train food condemnage	₹222,920
Liquor and tobacco	₹3,395,625
Total cost of goods sold	₹33,855,963
Gross profit	₹45,073,636
%Gross profit	57%

Financial Implications

With a 4.2% increase in rail catering revenue the sector appears a positive one. The main products purchased are hot beverages and snacks so the focus is in the reduction of costs to ensure higher profit margins. Spend per passenger increases as the length of journey increases, however some companies offer all inclusive ticket prices which help raise the food and beverage revenue generated.

Marketing

The provision of food and beverage in rails is often used as promotional tool. Ticket inclusive packages are often advertised in an effort to entice customers away from low-cost airlines. The sector is not as aggressive as it could be with its promotional efforts on food and beverage sales. The majority of train companies advertise their services in their in-house magazine whilst some have an e-marketing campaign and also use local and international media advertising.

Product and Service Styles

Catering at railway terminals usually comprises licensed bars, self-service and waiter service restaurants, fast food and takeaway units, supplemented by vending machines dispensing hot and cold foods and beverages. In-transit catering can feature three kinds of service. The first is the traditional restaurant car service where breakfast, lunch and dinner are organized in sittings and passengers go to the restaurant car for service where appropriate seating accommodation is provided, and then return to their seats on the train after their meal. In a Pullman service, these meals are delivered direct to the seat of first-class passengers only.

The second type of service is the buffet car, which is a self-service operation in which passengers go to the car and buy light refreshments over the counter. The third is a trolley service where snacks and drinks are delivered to customers at their seats. Innovative approaches to catering on trains are also in evidence such as the operation of 'Cuisine 2000' using cook-chilled foods prepared centrally, buffet cars turned into bistros on the London to Birmingham route, and on the east coast Anglo- Scottish route 'A taste of Scotland' restaurant service.

Staffing

In the India, the Network rail is undertaking a project that looks to rejuvenate the provision of skills in the rail catering and other rail staff. In partnership with local colleges the programme aims to bring all staff to a National Vocational Qualification standard. For example, in 2004 the country' s first Rail Academy–run by York College in partnership with the National Railway Museum the academy was funded with ₹1.25 million. Other similar initiatives have been introduced all over the India ensuring that rail employees are well trained.

Technology

There have been a number of advancements in railway kitchen design and technology enabling operators to serve more complicated menus than ever before. Also the same benefits enjoyed by the other sectors with the advancement of EPOS and beverage dispensing technologies are also enjoyed by the rail sector.

ROADS/MOTOR SIDE

Road catering has progressed from the inns and taverns of earlier days used by those travelling on foot and horseback to the present-day motorway service areas and other roadside catering outlets. High street fast-food operations are also now appearing both on MSAs and as free-standing drive-through. As an example, in the India, there are 86 MSAs. Moto is the biggest MSA operator with 42 sites followed by Welcome Break and Roadchef. These three operators control 89% of the market whilst McDonalds are slowly emerging as a significant MSA operator.

Financial Implications

The numbers of cars on the road are on the increase. In India from 1999 to 2004 there was an increase of almost 3 million cars.

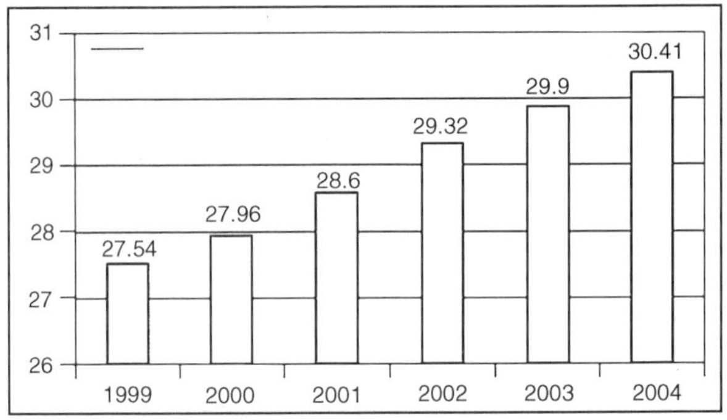

Fig. Cars, 1999-2004

There is a constant decrease of households without cars whilst the percentage of females holding driving licences has risen from 49% in 1989/1991 to 61% in 2002/2003. This does have implications as demographics change so do trends in consumer expenditure. Public transport in the India only accounts for 12% of traffic, this would suggest a steady growth of motorway catering revenue well into 2010.

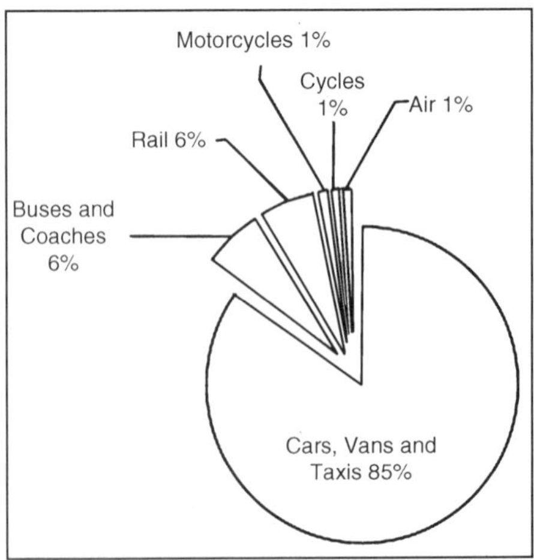

Fig. Transpor by Mode 1999-2003

Marketing

MSAs main marketing tool are the road signs. The main motive for consumers stopping at such a facility is that of convenience. Advertising is heavily regulated and often operators may not be allowed to use their own brand in motorway signage.

Product and Service Styles

MSAs provide a valuable catering service to the travelling public and their food and beverage facilities usually include self-service and waiter service restaurants, vending machines, and take-away foods and beverages.

Staffing

These service areas are often open twenty-four hours a day and have a particular problem of staffing as some employees have to be brought to and from work over a distance of 20–30 miles. Also, because of their isolated locations, the hours they are open and the sheer volume of numbers involved at peak periods, these service areas are also particularly prone to vandalism and littering.

Technology

In the USA, public wireless Local Area Network is widely available. In the India, talks for public wireless LAN in MSA' s first started in 2003 with the first hotspots installations around 2004. This added service may have an effect on the average food and beverage expenditure of customers in MSAs. The longer a business person spends online whilst at an MSA the more likely they will need to purchase food or drinks.

VENDING MACHINES

Vending today has become synonymous with selling from a machine. It is also known as 'automatic retailing' or selling from an 'electronic cafeteria' and involves a machine providing the customer with a product in exchange for some form of payment, coins, credit cards, etc.

Table. Forecast of Expenditure on Vended Products by Sector

Drinks	Confectionery/snacks/meals				Total	
	₹m	Index	₹m	Index	₹m	Index
2004	815	100	640	100	1,455	100
2005	877	108	682	107	1,559	107
2006	917	113	726	113	1,643	113
2007	974	120	767	120	1,741	120
2008	1,007	124	798	125	1,805	124
2009	1,045	128	826	129	1,871	129

Although vending was in evidence in the India prior to the Second World War, mainly in the form of chocolate and cigarette machines, it was not until the 1950s that the vending of drinks and snack items really became established in this country. The markets for vended products have grown steadily over the last forty years. In beverage vending, canned drinks, cartons and bottles have shown the greatest increase in growth whilst snack foods have increased the greatest.

Mintel, the value of the vending market grew by 15% between 1999 and 2004 to reach ₹2.2 billion. However, the market has actually declined by 3% in real terms, although their forecasts show a steady growth both in revenue and numbers of vending machines showing a 5% steady increase.

The number of machines increased by 13% over the same period, indicating that the growth in the market can be attributed mainly to the expansion in the number of machines, rather than a rise in the unit value of products.

Factors to consider when outsourcing vending operations to a contractor:

- No capital outlay for machine–it is supplied by contractor.
- Some installation costs paid by client, for example water and electricity.
- Operating costs such as ingredients, commodities, cups, maintenance, cleaning and servicing done by contractor.
- Selling prices set between client and contractor. Reimbursement costs, direct and indirect to contractor.

The range of vending machine equipment or hardware is divisible into two major groups:

- *Beverage venders*: Beverage vending machines have accounted for the largest share of vending sales over the last thirty years and consequently their design has been developed further than the food vending machines.
- *Food vending machines or merchandisers*: Food vending machines may vend a variety of food products - confectionery, snacks, plated meals, etc. and are usually vended in one of three types of machine:
  - *Snack machines*: Confectionery, crisps, biscuits, etc. are usually vended from an ambient temperature machine as these items have a relatively long shelf life and do not have any special temperature requirements. Because of these factors, servicing of the machines except for re-stocking purposes, can be kept to a minimum thereby also reducing operating costs.
  - *Refrigerated machines*: Snack items such as sandwiches and rolls have a limited shelf life and need to be date-stamped and vended through a refrigerated machine. Plated foods such as salads, cold meats, etc. must be vended from refrigerated machines where the holding temperature is between 2°C and 5°C. At this temperature the food may be kept for 2-4 days, although some operations work on a twenty-four hour cycle only.

- *Hot meal machines*: Food for a hot vending service may be vended in a number of ways. The first is the heated food vendor which will hold the temperature of the plated food at about 69°C for up to six hours. The second is the hot can vendor which usually offers a choice of items. The selection of hot canned meals, for example soups, baked beans, pasta dishes, casseroles, etc. are held at a temperature of 68°C in the machine without deterioration in the quality of the food. Money is placed into the appropriate slot and the hot can is vended together with a disposable bowl and suitable cutlery to eat the food with; the can is easily opened by the use of a ring pull top. The third involves the use of a microwave oven adjacent to a refrigerated merchandiser. Cooked food is plated by kitchen staff, rapidly cooled and placed into a refrigerated merchandiser; if limited kitchen facilities are available, ready plated or semi-prepared foods may be bought in from a supplier, plated and put in the vending machine. The food is heated when placed in the microwave, which has an automatic timing device for the different foods which begins when a token or code is put into the microwave. The time taken for a meal to be heated thoroughly depends on whether it is a snack item or a full meal. Snack items being heated from a refrigerated state takes between ten and thirty seconds, and a main meal between forty and sixty seconds, depending on the quantity and depth of the food, and the power supply feeding the microwave. The range of products available for hot meal vending is now quite considerable although snacks and sandwiches still account for the largest percentage.

Within each of these groups the type of vending machine used will depend largely on the type of product being vended. For confectionery and pre-packed goods a simple mechanical unit with a drawer at the base of the column is all that is required; it can be free-standing, wall-mounted or be positioned on a fixed surface and does not require any electricity or water supply.

Snack and sandwich vending machines require a power supply only and because their products are easily consumed, the machines can be situated outside wards, in the corridors of hotels, etc. close to the customer market.

Machines vending plated meals need to be situated close to the kitchen facilities and adjacent to the dining area; some banks of vending machines are sited such that the kitchen is behind the machines for ease of stocking and the dining area is in front of them.

These types of machines may be a rotating drum or revolving shelf design whereby a button is pushed rotating or revolving shelves until the required item is reached and then removed through a flap door.

The basic question of whether to use vending machines or not should be taken after careful consideration of the organization' s catering and financial policies and an assessment of what vending has to offer.

The main advantages associated with vending include the following:

- *Flexibility*: Vending can provide a twenty-four hour food and beverage service, either alone or in conjunction with other catering services. Customers can use a vending machine when they want to, rather than only when a cafeteria is open.
- *Situation*: Vending machines can be sited close to the customer market, for example in office corridors, thus reducing workers ' time away from the workplace queuing for a snack or drink; customers are also more likely to take a vended drink back to their workplace and consume it there, rather than spend time away from their work, for example in a cafeteria. Satellite vending machines can also be used to serve areas that would not normally benefit from a catering facility; for example, in a large industrial complex, machines can be sited some distance from the main kitchen and dining area.
- *Quality control*: In terms of quality, vending machines can sell a consistent product, particularly beverages, pre-packed snacks and bought in meals from a supplier. Meals prepared in the kitchen can also be plated under tighter quality and portion control.
- *Hygiene control*: Reduced handling of vended foods also reduces the possibilities of food contamination. Many beverage machines now also have built-in, self-clean mechanisms.
- *Operating control*: Labour savings can be made as once cleaned and stocked vending machines should require the minimum of maintenance, thus reducing labour costs. Wastage, pilferage and cash losses should also be negligible.
- *Speed*: Vending machines can 'sell' products quickly and efficiently, for example a hot chips machine which can vend portions of freshly prepared chips, always giving a standard product, at a standard price.
- *Sales promotion*: Products for sale in a vending machine can look attractive and stimulate 'impulse purchases', particularly glass-fronted merchandisers displaying fresh fruits, sweets, etc.

The disadvantages associated with using vending include the following:

- *Impersonality:* Vending machines lack the 'personal touch' and some customers will always prefer to be served food and beverages in the traditional manner rather than from a machine.
- *Inflexibility of the product*: Initially the range of products available for vending was quite limited; today, however, vending machines offer a much wider selection, and beverages in particular can be highly customised.

- *Reliability:* One of the major causes of dissatisfaction with vending machines in the past has been that the coin mechanism could become jammed and the machine would give no service. This in turn left the machines open to abuse and vandalism. Since their introduction the vending machines' coin mechanism has been a mechanical device which could be regularly jammed with foreign coins, washers, etc. Today, however, the electronic coin mechanism can detect even the most accurately produced fake coins, which even when fed into the machine, do not jam it. Electronic mechanisms are constantly being improved and are incorporated into the majority of new machines. These electronic mechanisms are also capable of accepting different valued coins, displaying a running total as they are added and of giving change.
- *Limiting:* For large-scale food and beverage service, vending machines have limitations. In some situations they are best suited as a backup to the main catering services although a bank of vending alleviates queuing and waiting time. They are also of less use in up-market situations, except in the form of mini-bars, for example in hotels.

Financial Implications

The vending market is a retail-based operation and profits rely on high volume turnover, however the sector is highly competitive and pricing wars by different vendors may eat into profits.

The vending market grew by 15% between 1999 and 2004, the market has actually declined by 3% in real terms, as the slump in the cigarette segment and inflationary pressures slowed year-on-year growth.

The number of machines increased by 13% over the same period, indicating that the growth in the market can be attributed mainly to the expansion in the number of machines, rather than a rise in the unit value of products.

Table. Forecast of the Number of Vending Machines, 2004-2009

Machines (in Thousand Units)*	Index		Machines (in Thousand Units)*	Index	
2004	770	100	2005	785	102
2006	805	104	2007	820	106
2008	842	109	2009	866	112

* Number of machines in circulation

However, it is expected that sales of the vending industry will fall from ₹14 billion to ₹12.5 billion by 2010.

Marketing

The markets available for vended products are varied and numerous and may be grouped into three main areas:

- The general market vending machines and their products may be situated in areas to which the general public largely has access; for example, shopping courts, MSAs, garage forecourts, airports, seaports, ferries, rail and bus terminals, libraries, swimming and leisure centres, stadiums, exhibition centres, cinemas and theatres.
- The industrial market includes those establishments where vending machines are provided for employers and employees in office blocks and shops, factories and sites, etc. Eighty per cent of companies in the India having installed vending machines at some or all of their premises.
- The institutional market includes establishments such as hospitals and schools, prisons, sports complexes, universities and colleges and more recently hotels, replacing to some extent floor service.

Product and Service Styles

Vending operates in a very competitive market and a number of developments and market trends may be identified in the vending sector:

- *Cashless systems:* The development of card operated vending has probably been the most important technological development in vending. The leading supplier of this type of system is Girovend, the main component being a credit card type of pass or card which can record the user' s own data; it can be used for personnel control such as security, identity passes, attendance recording, leisure facilities, etc. For catering purposes, customers can buy any food and beverage items from a vending machine by placing their card into the machine instead of cash; their card is then debited with the amount for the items purchased.
  - The card first has to be loaded with credit and this can be done in a number of ways. First, supervised loading whereby a supervisor collects customers' cash amounts and loads the cards via a vending machine; the disadvantage to this method is that the handling of cash is still involved and at least one person has to be employed to do this job. Second, customers self-load their own cards with a cash value before making their purchases. By inserting the card into the loader a customer can check its balance and increase the amount by feeding the appropriate money into the machine; this method' s disadvantage is that special loaders are required and cash is still handled. Third, is the direct-debit loader linked to the wages department so that a card holder may

direct debit different values from his/her salary; in this way cash hand ling is eliminated completely.

- The advantages to the customer of card vending are that it is a convenient method of payment; loose change does not have to be carried, it is not 'lost' in the machine and, overall, a faster service can be given.
- The card holders can be divided into user type groups and these categories may then be separated into different price bands. Vending machines payments can be broken into cashless, free-vend and coin operated systems. This enables different charges to be made for the same product, for example for regular employees, temporary staff, free vend for visitors, etc. Cash refunds can be given to users giving up their cards, or money can be paid back into an employee account; machines can also be programmed to stop accepting stolen cards. Finally, the sales information stored in these machines can be printed out by item, price list or type of user, and a comparison between actual and cash loaded on to the cards can be given; such upto- date information greatly aids financial control and cost accounting.

- *Mixed product vending*: Where the design of the machine allows, different products may be vended together and complement each other, for example, pre-packed snacks with carton juices together form a substitute for a main meal at certain times of the day. Smaller units, for example vending confectionery, can also be attached to the side of the larger machines and utilize their coin or card mechanism.
- *Fresh brew vending*: Machines using fresh brew systems for tea and coffee ensure that a better quality end product is dispensed to the customer. In-cup drink machines where the ingredients are already in the cup also offer better hygiene, operation and servicing, control and range of products. Some beverage machines are now capable of offering 100 different selections for both hot and cold drinks and have capacities of up to 1,000 cups.
- *Space economization*: The efficient utilization of business space in offices, factories, hospitals, industrial units, etc. is of great importance today. This has led many operations to critically review their catering facilities and the space allocated to them, particularly where a twenty-four hour service is needed. In many situations vending is being used as a space and cost saving alternative to installing traditional catering services. Furthermore, the vending manufacturers themselves are aware of the amount of space vending machines need, and are researching ways of reducing their overall size yet at the same time trying to increase the range and quality of products they can offer.

- *Compatibility with cook-chill*: The cook-chill method of food preparation serves the vending industry well by allowing plated meals to be prepared in advance and vended for later consumption either in a chilled state, for example salads, cold meats, pâtés, etc. or for use in conjunction with some type of heating system, for example microwaves.

Vending has now established itself as a method of food service that may be considered for many types of operations and situations. In some sectors of the catering industry it is employed as a total feeding system, for example staff cafeterias and restrooms, hospital canteens, etc. in others it is an economic alternative to other types of catering service at different times of the day, for example, night shifts in hospitals, twenty-four hour factories, offices, etc.

Staffing

The reduced labour costs is one of the biggest advantages of the vending machines along with the availability of the product. Operators can stock a large number of machines with a very small number of staff and with very little training. However, often, there are hidden costs such as maintenance costs.

Technology

Without advancements in technology vending machines would not exists and similarly if technology did not evolve the consumer would prefer alternative means of purchasing the goods. Today technological advancements in stock control and maintenance have enabled vending machines to become more reliable. Telemetry and on-site hand-held systems have helped to reduce the number of out-of-stock situations, or quickly identify malfunctioning machines. With advancements in Internet technology vending machines can be easily monitored for conditions and levels of stock. Vending machine technology has improved the storage conditions for perishable goods, and has enabled hot food vending.

SCHOOLS

The school meals catering service was formerly structured on a dietary basis with a daily or weekly per capita allowance to ensure that the children obtained adequate nutritional levels from their meals. Most of the schools used to operate their dining rooms on a family type service or a self-service basis with the traditional 'meat and two veg' lunch being very much the norm.

There has been a shift away from this conventional arrangement to the provision of a snack type lunch as an alternative to or replacement for the main meal. Many schools now provide 'snack meals' such as baked potatoes, pizzas, sandwiches, rolls, pies, soups, yoghurts, etc. and the children may choose from this selection in a normal cafeteria fashion. Some areas have drastically cut their school meal service and are simply providing dining-room space for the children to bring in their own lunches from home. Whether this trend will continue in the future is debatable. It does seem likely, however, that now introduced, the snack type meal will remain as an alternative to the traditional school meal. Many local education authorities contract out this service to specialist contract caterers. Celebrity Chef Jamie Oliver started his campaign for school dinners in 2005 and his TV programme was quite influential in government circles that promised increases in the school budget to ensure a better quality of food in schools.

UNIVERSITIES AND COLLEGES

All institutions of further and higher education provide some form of catering facilities for the academic, administrative, technical and secretarial staff as well as for full- and part-time students and visitors. The catering service in this sector of the industry suffers from an under-utilization of its facilities during the three vacation periods and in many instances at the weekends.

Universities are autonomous bodies and are responsible for their own catering services. They are, however, publicly accountable for their expenditure to the Higher Education Funding Council for England which allocates them funds on behalf of the exchequer. The HEFCE' s policy on catering allows for a subsidy on capital costs, that is, buildings and equipment, 'landlord' s' expenses and rent and rates where applicable. Apart from a few special exemptions to named universities, they are expected to break-even. University catering units have traditionally been of two basic kinds: residential facilities attached to halls that may serve breakfast and evening meals within an inclusive price per term, and central facilities that are open to all students and staff and usually serve lunches and snacks throughout the day with beverages.

These catering facilities have to compete openly with the students' union services and independently staffed senior common rooms. Residential students pay in advance for their board and lodgings. This method has been abandoned by many universities in recent years who have provided reasonable kitchen facilities in the residences to enable students to prepare and cook their own meals if they wish to. Others have introduced a pay-as-you-eat system for residential students. Unfortunately, this has led to reduced catering revenue from students.

Non-residential students are provided with an on-site catering provision that has to compete against all other forms of locally provided catering, with ease of accessibility and some level of subsidy being the main attractions. Increasingly, caterers are turning to ideas from the high street operations to attract and keep their predominantly young adult clientele. To offset the losses incurred and to achieve a position of break-even in catering, universities have seen the advantages of making their residential and catering facilities available at commercial rates to outside bodies for meetings, conferences and for holidays during the vacation periods.

HOSPITALS

Hospital catering facilities have improved considerably over the past ten to twenty years with the result that new hospitals in particular are benefiting from well planned and managed catering services. Hospital catering is a specialized form of catering as the patient is normally unable to move elsewhere and choose alternative facilities and therefore special attention must be given to the food and beverages so that encouragement is given to eat the meal provided. The hospital catering service is normally structured on a per capita allowance for patients but with staff paying for all of their meals.

A decentralized approach was used in many hospitals where the patients' food and beverages were portioned at the point of delivery in the wards. This often resulted however, in patients receiving cold, unappetizing meals because of the time between the food being prepared and the patients actually receiving it. This method of food service is commonly replaced by a centralized approach that involves the preparation of the patients' trays in or close to the main production area.

From here they are transported by trucks or mechanical conveyors to the various floors, and from there directly to the patients so that there should be little delay between the food being plated and served to the patient.

Another trend has seen hospital catering open for tender by contract caterers where in many instances a centralized production system for several nearby hospitals may have to be operated to be viable. In May 2001, the Better Hospital Food initiative was launched.

The programme' s aims were to:

- Produce a comprehensive range of tasty, nutritious and interesting recipes that every NHS hospital could use;
- Re-design hospital printed menus to make them more accessible and easier to understand;
- Introduce twenty-four hour catering services to ensure food is available night and day;
- Ensure hot food is available in hospitals at both mid-day and early evening mealtimes.

Perhaps evidence that caterers are committed on improving the catering of the health care sector can be seen at the Hospital Caterers Association, at a recent conference programme. The catering experience and food nutrition are prominent subjects as well as cultural and environmental issues in hospital catering.

THE SERVICES

The services include the armed forces: the Royal Navy, Army and Royal Air Force; the police and fire service; and some government departments. The armed forces often have their own specialist catering branches, for example the army catering is provided by the Royal Logistics Corp. Civil service organizations such as the Metropolitan Police force also have their own catering departments.

The levels of food and beverage facilities within the services vary from the large self-service cafeterias for the majority of personnel, to high-class traditional restaurants for more senior members of staff. A considerable number of functions are also held by the services leading to both small- and large-scale banqueting arrangements.

PRISONS

There are over 9 million people detained in penal institutions around the world and over 2 million of them are held in US institutions whilst over 1.5 million in China. The population of detainees in all penal institutions in England and Wales is more than 75,000 and continues to grow. Working on a very limited budget, the diet for the inmates is based upon fixed weekly quantities of specific named food commodities with a small weekly cash allowance per head for fresh meat and a further separate weekly cash allowance per head for the local purchase of dietary extras of which a proportion must be spent on fresh fruit. The catering within the prisons is the responsibility of the prison governor with delegated responsibility being given to a catering officer, with much of the actual cooking and service being done by the inmates themselves.

3

Safe Handling of Foods in Tasting Tourism

FOOD SELECTION AND STORAGE

FOOD QUALITY AND SAFETY

Storage does not improve the quality of any food. The quality of a food will also not decrease significantly during storage as long as the food is stored properly and used within the recommended time frame. Quality is not the same as safety.

A poor-quality food may be safe such as stale cereal, overripe fruit or soured pasteurized milk. An unsafe food may have good quality in terms of appearance and taste, but have a high bacterial count.

For example, improperly canned food may contain Clostridium botulinum thus making food unsafe. Or cooked chicken may be placed on a plate that held the raw chicken and become contaminated. The goal of home food storage is to provide both safe and high-quality foods. Maintaining a food's quality depends on several factors: the quality of the raw product, the procedures used during processing, the way the food is stored and the length of storage.

For example, fresh-picked corn will store better than corn that has been in the market for a few days; a tightly folded inside cereal box liner will prevent a ready-to-eat cereal from becoming limp. The recommended storage time takes these factors into consideration. Since bacteria frequently get into food through careless food handling, keep everything—hands, pantry, shelves and storage containers—clean.

SELECTION GUIDELINES

To help assure quality, some products have "open dates" on the package. Product dating is optional on most products. Dates may also be "coded" by the manufacturer and only understood by them.

The most commonly used open dates are:

- *Sell-by Date*: This is the last recommended day of sale. The date allows for home storage and use. You will find the date after the statement "sell by." Breads and baked goods may have "sell-by" dates.

- *Use-by Date*: Tells how long the product will retain top quality after you buy it. You will find this date after statement "Use by." Some packaged goods have "use-by" dates.
- *Expiration Date*: This is the last day the product should be used or eaten. You may find this date after the statement, "Do not use after." Yeast and baking powder have expiration dates.
- *Pack Date*: Canned or packaged foods may have pack dates, which tell you when the product was processed. This does not tell you how long the food will be good.

These are guidelines; if a food is not properly handled, its storage life will be shortened. Follow these tips for purchasing top-quality foods that have been handled safely.

- Look for packages of food that are not torn or broken.
- Canned goods should be free of dents, cracks and bulging lids.
- Refrigerated food should feel cold and frozen food should be frozen solid. Purchase these foods last.
- When shopping, place packaged raw meat, poultry and fish in plastic bags and keep from contact with other foods.
- Take perishable foods home quickly to refrigerate. If travel time will exceed one hour, pack fresh meats in a cooler with ice and keep in the passenger area of the car in warm weather.
- At home, refrigerate perishable food immediately. The "Danger Zone" for most food is 40 to 140 °F. Bacteria grow most rapidly in this range of temperatures, doubling in number in as little as 20 minutes.

STORAGE GUIDELINES

For best results in maintaining product quality practice the rule, First In, First Out. This means you use the oldest products first and the newest products later.

A good practice in the home is to place the newly purchased products in back of the same products already on the shelf. It may help to write purchase dates on products without "open dates" on the package. Follow recommended storage times for the refrigerator, freezer and pantry.

Freezer

- Keep freezer temperature at or below 0 °F. A good indication of proper temperature is that ice cream will be frozen solid.
- Use moisture-proof, freezer-weight wrap. Examples are foil, freezer bags and freezer paper. Label and date all packages.
- Food stored beyond the recommended time will be safe to eat, but eating quality and nutritive value will be reduced.
- Keep an inventory of freezer contents.

Refrigerator

- Use a thermometer to check temperature; it must be between 34 °F and 40 °F at all times. Avoid frequently opening the refrigerator door, especially in hot weather.
- Wrapping perishable food prevents the loss of flavour and the mixing of flavour and odours resulting in, for example, onion-flavoured milk.
- Raw meat and poultry should be wrapped securely so they do not leak and contaminate other foods. Place the store packages in a plastic bag or place the package on a plate to contain any juices. Clean up leaks with warm soapy water and sanitize with a solution of 1 teaspoon chlorine bleach to 1 quart water.
- Cooked meats and leftovers should be tightly wrapped to prevent leakage and drying out.

Pantry

- Storage cabinets should be cool and dry. Storage areas near oven ranges, hot water pipes or heating ducts should not be used because heat and moisture can cause a food to lose its quality more rapidly.
- High temperature or humidity may reduce storage time considerably.
- Insect infestation can occur in any home. Susceptible foods include cereals, flour, seeds, baking mixes, spices, candy, dried fruits and dry pet foods. Avoid purchasing damaged packages of foods and keep cupboard shelves clean. Storing food in tightly sealed glass, metal or rigid plastic containers may help.
- Pantry foods will probably be safe beyond recomm-ended storage time, but eating quality and nutritive value will be reduced.

SAFE HANDLING OF SEAFOOD

SELECTING THE BEST

Federal regulations require that all parts of the seafood industry implement safe handling practices to keep seafood safe. The regulations require that those handling seafood have a Hazard Analysis and Critical Control Points, or HACCP plan in place in their operation. HACCP is a science-based system that examines each step in processing food, isolates possible hazards and sets limits, or critical control points, within which the food is safe.

These regulations help consumers to select safe, quality seafood. In addition, state law mandates the inspection of oyster and clam beds and other waters where seafood is harvested.

The bacterial levels of these waters are inspected and are closed to the harvesting of shellfish if the levels are considered too high. Seafood poisoning can occur from eating seafood that has not been handled properly, raw or improperly cooked seafood or fish from tropical water that harbours a toxin.

Consumers can protect themselves by purchasing seafood only from certified processors and dealers and by following the suggestions given here for safe handling.

Spotting a Safe Seafood Seller

Always purchase fish from a certified dealer that maintains high quality. *Based on FDA's Food Code, here are some ways of spotting a safe fish dealer:*

- Employees should be in clean clothing and wearing hair coverings.
- Employees should be in clean clothing and wearing hair coverings.
- They should not be smoking, eating or playing with their hair.
- They should not be sick or have any open wounds.
- Employees should be wearing disposable gloves when handling food and change gloves after doing nonfood tasks and after handling raw fish.
- Fish should be displayed on a thick bed of fresh—not melting—ice, preferably in a case or under some type of cover. Fish should be arranged with the bellies down so that the melting ice drains away from the fish, thus reducing the chances of spoilage.

Shrimp

Fresh shrimp have a mild odour and firm-textured meat. The shell or meat is not slippery, and there are no black spots, or patches on the shell or meat. The shell of raw shrimp may be grayish-green, pinkish-tan, or light pink. When cooked, the shell turns red and the meat takes on a reddish tint. Cooked shrimp have firm meat and a mild smell.

Crabs, Lobsters and Crayfish

Live crabs, lobsters, spiny lobsters and crayfish move their legs. The "tail" of a live lobster curls under the body and does not hang down when you pick it up. Frozen spiny or rock lobster tails have clear white meat, no odour and are hard-frozen. Cooked crabs, lobsters and crayfish have bright orange to red shells and are free of any disagreeable odour.

Clams, Oysters and Mussels

Purchase raw shellfish carefully. Buy raw clams, oysters and mussels only from reputable markets. If in doubt, ask the seafood market personnel to show you the certified shipper's tag that accompanies "shell on" products or check the shipper number on shucked oyster containers.

Clams, oysters and mussels in the shell are alive, and the shells close tightly when tapped. Gaping shells indicate that the shellfish are dead and not edible. Shucked oysters are plump, and have a mild odour, a natural creamy colour, and clear liquid or nectar.

Scallops

Fresh scallops have a sweetish odour and are free of excess liquid when packaged. The meat of the large sea scallop is white, orange or pink. Smaller bay and calico scallops are white, light tan or pinkish.

Frozen Seafood

Flesh is solid, and there is no discolouration or drying on the surface. Odour is not evident or is fresh and mild. Wrapping material is moisture- and vapour-proof, fits closely around the product and is undamaged. Packaging materials do not contain ice crystals or have water stains or other indications that the product had thawed at any point.

Packaged breaded and unbreaded products have a clean and uniform appearance. Individual pieces separate easily. Breading is intact. Packaged frozen seafood may have an expiration date stamped on the label. Use the seafood before the expiration date.

STORAGE

Safe Handling after Purchase

Whether you've purchased seafood that is fresh or frozen, always keep it cold. Never leave perishable items in a hot car unless packed in ice or in a cooler; seafood products must be kept cold to ensure peak quality.

It's always a good idea to keep your refrigerator temperature between 32 and 38 °F, and your freezer at 0 °F or colder. Plan to use your seafood purchases within one to two days, or freeze them.

Refrigeration

Place seafood immediately in the refrigerator when you get home from the seafood market. Wrap fresh seafood in cling wrap or store in airtight containers. Store fresh, pasteurized or smoked seafood products at 32 to 38 °F. Refrigerate live clams, oysters, mussels, crabs, lobsters and crayfish in well-ventilated containers. Cover the container with a damp cloth or paper towel.

Do not store live shellfish in airtight bags or containers. Storing live shellfish in salt water shortens their shelf life. Storing them in fresh water kills them. Keep live shellfish alive. Do not cook or eat shellfish that have died during storage.

Live clams, oysters and mussels have tightly closed shells, or the shells will close when tapped. Live crabs, lobsters and crayfish move their legs. Dead shellfish spoil rapidly and develop off-flavour and off-odours.

Freezing

Store frozen seafood products immediately in the freezer when you get home from the seafood market. Store them in their original moisture-and vapour-proof packages. Frozen seafood packaged in over wrapped trays should be repackaged in moisture-and vapour-proof plastic freezer wrap, freezer paper or foil before you store them in the freezer. Keep frozen seafood products at 0 °F or below until ready to use.

PREPARATION

Cleanliness

Always wash hands thoroughly with hot, soapy water before preparing foods and after handling raw seafood. Don't let raw meat or juices touch ready-to-eat foods either in the refrigerator or during preparation. Don't put cooked foods on the same plate that held raw seafood.

Always wash utensils that have touched raw seafood with hot, soapy water before using them for cooked seafood. Wash counters, cutting boards and all surfaces raw seafood has touched.

Thawing

While freezing seafood quickly keeps more cell walls intact, the opposite is true for thawing. Defrost gradually so cells are disturbed less and fewer juices leak out. The best way to thaw is overnight in the refrigerator. Avoid thawing at room temperature. If you must thaw seafood quickly, here are safe options: seal seafood in a plastic bag and immerse in cold water for about an hour OR microwave on the "defrost" setting, stopping when seafood is still icy but pliable.

Marinating

Marinate seafood in the refrigerator, not on the counter. Discard the marinade after use because it contains raw juices, which may harbour bacteria. If you want to use the marinade as a dip or sauce, reserve a portion before adding raw food.

COOKING

Basic Cooking Tips for Shellfish

Shrimp, crabs, scallops, clams, mussels, oysters or lobster become tough and dry when overcooked.

To cook raw shellfish, shucked or in the shell, follow these basic guidelines:

- Raw shrimp turn pink and firm when cooked. Depending on the size, it takes from 3 to 5 minutes to boil or steam 1 pound of medium-sized shrimp in the shell.
- Shucked shellfish become plump and opaque when cooked thoroughly and the edges of the oysters start to curl. The Food and Drug Administration suggests boiling shucked oysters for 3 minutes, frying them in oil at 375 °F for 10 minutes or baking them for 10 minutes at 450 °F.

- Clams, mussels and oysters in the shell will open when cooked. The FDA suggests steaming oysters for 4 to 9 minutes or boiling them for 3 to 5 minutes after they open.
- Scallops turn milky white or opaque and firm. Depending on size, scallops take 3 to 4 minutes to cook thoroughly.
- Place lobster in a pan of boiling water to cover, and return water to boil. Boil a 1-pound lobster for 10 minutes, and allow an extra 3 minutes for each additional pound. If steaming, allow 15 to 18 minutes for a 1½-to 2-pound lobster.

Guidelines for Cooking Fish

Cooked to perfection, fish is at its flavourful best and will be moist, tender and have a delicate flavour. In general, fish is cooked when its meat just begins to flake easily when tested with a fork and it loses its translucent or raw appearance. Like most foods, fish should be thoroughly cooked.

The suggests cooking fish until it reaches an internal temperature of 145 °F. One helpful guideline is the 10-minute rule for cooking fish. Apply it when baking, broiling, grilling, steaming, and poaching fillets, steaks or whole fish. Practice makes perfect and cooking fish properly is all in the timing.

Here's how to use the 10-minute rule:

- Measure the seafood product at its thickest point. If the fish is stuffed or rolled, measure it after stuffing or rolling.
- At 450 °F, cook it 10 minutes per inch thickness of the fish, turning the fish halfway through the cooking time. For example, a 1-inch fish steak should be cooked 5 minutes on each side for a total of 10 minutes. Pieces of fish less than half an inch thick do not have to be turned over.
- Add 5 minutes to the total cooking time if you are cooking the fish in foil or if the fish is cooked in a sauce.
- Double the cooking time for frozen fish that has not been defrosted.

Fish is the original "fast food." It cooks quickly, within minutes, because it lacks the connective tissue of red meats and poultry. Some of the best cooking methods for fish include poaching, broiling, grilling, baking and microwaving because they bring out flavour without adding fat.

SERVING

Basic Tips

Wash hands with soap and water before serving or eating food. Serve cooked products on clean plates with clean utensils and clean hands. Never put cooked foods on a dish that has held raw products unless the dish is washed with soap and hot water. Hold hot foods above 140 °F and cold foods below 40 °F. Never leave foods, raw or cooked, at room temperature longer than two hours. On a hot day with temperatures at 90 °F or warmer, this decreases to one hour.

LEFTOVERS

Basic Tips

Always use clean utensils and storage containers for safe storage. Divide large amounts of leftovers into small, shallow containers for quick cooling in the refrigerator. For frozen storage, wrap seafood in heavy foil, freezer wrap or place in freezer container. For optimum taste, use seafood within a month. When reheating leftovers, make sure that they have been cooked to 165 °F. If you may have kept the food refrigerated for too long, throw it out. Never taste food that looks or smells strange to see if you can still use it.

Recommended Times for Refrigerator and Freezer Food Storage Food	Refrigerator	Freezer
Fresh Seafood		
Fresh lean fish: cod, flounder, trout, haddock, pollack, perch	1-2 days	4-6 months
Fresh fatty fish: mullet, smelt, salmon, mackerel, bluefish, tuna, and swordfish	1-2 days	2-3 months
Live crabs and lobster	Same day purchased	*
Live mussels and clams	2-3 days	*
Live oysters	7-10 days	*
Shucked mussels and clams	1-2 days	3-4 months
Shucked oysters	5-7 days	3-4 months
Shrimp, crabmeat	2-3 days	4 months
Scallops	2-3 days	3 months
Cooked Seafood		
Crab	1-2 days	3 months
Shrimp	3-4 days	2 months
Fish sticks, commercial	*	18 months
Breaded shrimp, commercial	*	1 year
Cooked fish pieces	3-4 days	3 months

Notes:

* Storage by this method is not recommended due to safety or quality issues.

SELECTING AND STORING FRUITS AND VEGETABLES

SELECTING THE BEST

With satiny yellow skin and a rosy blush, it looks like the perfect peach. But how will it taste once you get it home? Choosing fresh and flavourful produce can sometimes be your greatest challenge in the supermarket. Here are some tips to find great-tasting fruits and vegetables and increase your enjoyment of these healthful foods.

FIND IT FRESH

With modern farming, processing and delivery, many stores are able to put produce out for sale within a day or two after it is picked. Ask your store's produce manager for delivery days so you can get to your favourite fruits and veggies before quality declines.

SELECT WISELY

Vegetables that are characteristic colour, shape and size generally have the best taste and texture. However, good produce doesn't have to be picture perfect. Some of the best products don't look very good. Most bananas, for example, have a fuller flavour if they are speckled.

USE YOUR SENSES

Contrary to some consumer practices, thumping or shaking a melon does not indicate ripeness. Instead, authorities recommend feeling a product. In general, produce that's too soft is too ripe; if it's too hard, it's not ripe enough. Try the sniff test, too. With certain fruits, like peaches and melons, a strong scent means they're ripening nicely.

GET THE GRADE

The United States Department of Agriculture (USDA) has established grade standards for most fresh fruits and vegetables. The grades are most often seen on pre-packaged apples, potatoes and onions. "U.S. Fancy" is the top grade, while "U.S. No. 1" is the most common designation. "U.S. No. 2" and "U.S. No. 3" mean lower quality.

LOOK FOR LOCAL PRODUCE

Fruits and vegetables grown by local farmers may be fresher and tastier than those shipped long distances from larger farms. Once again, ask your grocery store's produce manager if any is in stock.

GO TO MARKET

Many communities sponsor weekly farmers' markets to provide a central, in-town site for small farms to sell their produce directly to consumers.

TAKE A STAND

Take a weekend drive into the country to look for roadside stands where farm families sell their produce, usually picked just hours before you buy it. Or visit a farm that allows you to pick your own strawberries, blueberries, peaches and apples. Your local county Extension agent can direct you to such places.

SHOP SEASONALLY

Probably one of the most important tips for finding great-tasting produce is to buy in season, when possible.

Here's a guide to when certain fruits and vegetables are at their peak:

- *Summer*: Apricots, blueberries, cherries, eggplant, fresh herbs, green beans, hot peppers, melon, okra, peaches, plums, sweet corn, sweet peppers, tomatoes, zucchini.
- *Fall:* Apples, broccoli, brussels sprouts, cauliflower, collards, grapes, kale, pears, persimmons, pumpkins, winter squash, yams.
- *Winter:* Beets, cabbage, carrots, citrus fruits, daikon radishes, onions, rutabagas, turnips, winter squash.
- *Spring:* Asparagus, blackberries, green onions, leeks, lettuces, new potatoes, peas, red radishes, rhubarb, spinach, strawberries, watercress.

WAX COATING

Why are wax coatings used on some fruits and vegetables? Are they safe? Many fruits and vegetables make their own natural waxy coating to help retain moisture because most produce is 80 to 95 per cent water. After harvest, but before the produce is packed and sent to the supermarket, it is repeatedly washed to clean off dirt and soil. Such extensive washing also removes the natural wax. Therefore, waxes are applied to some produce items at the packing shed to replace the natural ones that are lost.

Waxes are applied in order to:

- Help retain moisture in fruits and vegetables during shipping and marketing;
- Help inhibit mold growth;
- Protect fruits and vegetables from bruising;
- Prevent other physical damage and disease;
- Enhance appearance.

By protecting against moisture loss and contamination, wax coatings help fresh fruits and vegetables maintain wholesomeness and freshness. Waxing does not improve the quality of any inferior fruit or vegetables; rather, waxing-along with proper handling-contributes to maintaining a healthful product. Waxes by themselves do not control decay; rather, they may be combined with some chemicals to prevent the growth of mold. The Food and Drug Administration and the Environmental Protection Agency strictly regulate the safety and use of these substances. Waxes are also used on candies, pastries and gum and come from natural sources. Wax sources generally are plants, food-grade petroleum products or insects. Some waxes can be made from dairy or animal sources, but we are not aware of any such coatings being used on fruits and vegetables in this country. This is particularly important for people following Kosher or vegetarian diets and who don't want any animal-based wax on their produce. Any commodities that do have this type of coating must be labeled "Coated with animal-based wax." Waxes are used only in tiny amounts. In fact, each piece of waxed fruit only has a drop or two of wax. Waxes may be mixed with water or other wetting agents to ensure they are applied thinly and evenly.

The government regulates wax coatings to ensure their safety. Coatings used on fruits and vegetables must meet the food additive regulations of the U.S. Food and Drug Administration. Extensive research by governmental and scientific authorities has shown that approved waxes are safe to eat. Waxes are indigestible, which means they go through the body without breaking down or being absorbed. Produce shippers and supermarkets are required by federal law to label produce items that have been waxed so you will know whether the fruits and vegetables you buy are coated. Consumers will see signs in produce departments that say "Coated with food-grade vegetable, petroleum, beeswax, and/or shellac-based wax or resin, to maintain freshness." None of these coatings are animal-based, and they all come from natural sources. Any consumers who have questions about wax coatings should talk to their grocers. Waxes may turn white on the surface of fruits or vegetables if they have been subjected to excessive heat and/or moisture.

This whitening is safe and is similar to that of a candy bar that has been in the freezer. Consumers do have choices. Waxes generally cannot be removed by regular washing. If consumers prefer not to consume waxes-even though the waxes are safe-they can buy unwaxed commodities or can peel the fruit or vegetable, thereby removing any coating. Commodities that may have coatings applied include apples, avocados, bell peppers, cantaloupes, cucumbers, eggplants, grapefruits, lemons, limes, melons, oranges, parsnips, passion fruit, peaches, pineapples, pumpkins, rutabagas, squash, sweet potatoes, tomatoes, turnips and yucca. However, they are not always waxed.`

Storage Times for Fruits and Vegetables Food	**Refrigerator**	**Freezer**
	Fruits:	
Apples	1 month	8-12 months
Apricots	3-5 days	8-12 months
Avocados	3-5 days	8-12 months
Bananas	*	8-12 months
Berries	2-3 days	8-12 months
Cherries	2-3 days	8-12 months
Grapes	3-5 days	8-12 months
Grapefruit	2 weeks	4-6 months
Guavas	1-2 days	8-12 months
Kiwis (Chinese Gooseberry)	3-5 days	4-6 months
Lemons/limes	2 weeks	4-6 months
Mangoes	*	8-12 months

Melons	1 week	8-12 months
Nectarines	3-5 days	8-12 months
Oranges	2 weeks	4-6 months
Papayas	1-2 days	8-12 months
Peaches	3-5 days	8-12 months
Pears	3-5 days	8-12 months
Pineapples	2-3 Days	4-6 months
Plantains		* 8-12 months
Plums	3-5 days	8-12 months
Rhubarb	3-5 days	8-12 months
	Fruit Juices:	
Concentrate	*	2 years
Fresh or Reconstituted	5-7 days	8-12 months
	Vegetables:	
Artichokes	1 week	*
Asparagus	2-3 days	8-12 months
Beets	2 weeks	8-12 months
Bok Choy	2-3 days	8-12 months
Broccoli	3-5 days	8-12 months
Brussels Sprouts	3-5 days	8-12 months
Cabbage	1-2 weeks	8-12 months
Carrots	2 weeks	8-12 months
Cauliflower	1 week	8-12 months
Celery	1 week	8-12 months
Chilies	1 week	8-12 months
Cilantro	2-3 days	*
Corn	use immediately for best flavour	8-12 months
Green Beans	1 week	8-12 months
Greens (spinach, collards, swiss chard, kale,mustard, etc.)	3-5 days	8-12 months
Jicama	2-3 weeks	8-12 months
Kohlrabi (leaves)	2-3 days	8-12 months
Kohlrabi (stems)	1 week	8-12 months
Lettuce	1 week	*

Table. Storage Times for Fruits and Vegetables

Food	Refrigerator	Freezer
Lima Beans	3-5 days	8-12 months
Mushrooms	1-2 days	8-12 months
Onions, green	3-5 days	*
Okra	1-2 days	8-12 months
Parsley	2-3 days	*
Peas	3-5 days	8-12 months
Peppers	1 week	8-12 months
Radishes	2 weeks	*
Squash, hard		* 8-12 months

Squash, summer	3-5 days	8-12 months
Tomatillos	1 week	8-12 months
Tomatoes	1 week	8-12 months
Yuca (Cassava)	1-2 days	8-12 months
Zucchini	3-5 days	8-12 months

Notes:

* Storage by this method is not recommended due to safety or quality issues.

SELECTING AND STORING CEREALS AND GRAINS

WHEAT FLOUR

Definition

Flour is the product obtained by grinding then sifting wheat kernels, or berries. The kernel consists of three distinct parts: bran, the outer covering of the grain; germ, the embryo contained inside the kernel; and endosperm, the part of the kernel containing the flour.

During milling, the three parts are separated and recombined accordingly to achieve different types of flours. There are six different classes of wheat: hard red winter, hard red spring, soft red winter, hard white, soft white and durum.

The end products are determined by the wheat's characteristics, especially protein and gluten content. The harder the wheat, the higher the amount of protein in the flour. Soft, low-protein wheats are used in cakes, pastries, cookies, crackers and noodles. Hard, high protein wheats are used in breads and quick breads. Durum is used in pasta and noodles.

Storage

Flour should be stored in airtight containers in a cool, dry place. All-purpose, bread, cake and whole wheat flour will keep for six months at 90 °F, one year at 70 °F, and two years at 40 °F. Store away from foods with strong odours. Before using refrigerated or frozen flour, allow it to warm to room temperature and inspect for rancidity and taste.

Types of Flour

- White flour is the finely ground endosperm of the wheat kernel.
- All-purpose flour is a white flour milled from hard wheats or a blend of hard and soft wheats. It gives the best results for many kinds of products, including some yeast breads, quick breads, cakes, cookies, pastries and noodles. All-purpose flour is enriched and may be bleached or unbleached. Bleaching will not affect nutrient value.
- Bread flour is white flour that is a blend of hard, high-protein wheats and has greater gluten strength and protein content than all-purpose flour. Unbleached, and in some cases conditioned with ascorbic acid,

bread flour is milled primarily for commercial bakers, but is available at most grocery stores.

- Cake flour is fine-textured, silky flour milled from soft wheats with a low protein content. It is used to make cakes, cookies, crackers, quick breads and some types of pastry. Cake flour has a greater percentage of starch and less protein, which keeps cakes and pastries tender and delicate.
- Self-rising flour, also referred to as phosphated flour, is a convenience product made by adding salt and leavening to all-purpose flour. It is commonly used in biscuits and quick breads, but is not recommended for yeast breads. One cup of self-rising flour contains 1½ teaspoons of baking powder and ½ teaspoon of salt. Self-rising can be substituted for all-purpose flour by reducing salt and baking powder according to these proportions.
- Pastry flour has properties intermediate between those of all-purpose and cake flours. It is usually milled from soft wheat for pastry making, but can be used for cookies, cakes, crackers and similar products. It differs from hard wheat flour in that it has a finer texture and lighter consistency.
- Semolina is the coarsely ground endosperm of durum, a hard spring wheat with a high-gluten content and golden colour. It is hard, granular and resembles sugar. Semolina is enriched and is used to make couscous and pasta products such as spaghetti, vermicelli, macaroni and lasagna noodles. Except for some specialty products, breads are seldom made with semolina.
- Durum flour is finely ground semolina. It is enriched and used to make noodles.
- Whole wheat, stone-ground and graham flour can be used interchangeably; nutrient values differ minimally. They are produced by either grinding the whole-wheat kernel or recombining the white flour, germ and bran that have been separated during milling. Their only differences may be in coarseness and protein content. Insoluble fibre content is higher than in white flours.
- Bran is the outer layer of the wheat kernel that is removed to make white flour. It is sometimes ground into flour or it may come totally unprocessed as "miller's bran."
- Gluten flour is usually milled from spring wheat and has a high protein, low starch content. It is used primarily for diabetic breads, or mixed with other non-wheat or low-protein wheat flours to produce a stronger dough structure. Gluten flour improves baking quality and produces high-protein gluten bread.
- Wheat germ is the heart of the wheat kernel. It comes flaked or in a coarse meal, either raw or toasted. Wheat germ adds a pleasant, nutty

flavour to baked goods and increases their protein and mineral content. It is the most oil-rich and therefore the most perishable part of the wheat. At the supermarket, wheat germ is found in vacuum-packed jars that must be refrigerated after opening.

Wheat Flour Terms

The Food and Drug Administration inspects and approves the use of flour treatments and additives that are used to improve the storage, appearance and baking performance of flour. The treatments and additives are in no way harmful.

- Enriched flour is supplemented with iron and three B-vitamins and may also be supplemented with calcium. There is no change in taste, colour, texture, baking quality or caloric value of flour.
- Presifted flour is sifted at the mill, making it unnecessary to sift before measuring.
- Bromated flour is largely discontinued in the United States. Ascorbic acid is now being added to strengthen the flour for bread doughs.
- Bleached refers to flour that has been bleached chemically to whiten or improve the baking qualities. No change occurs in the nutritional value of the flour and no harmful chemical residues remain. It is only a process that speeds up the natural lightening and maturing of flour.
- Unbleached flour is aged and bleached naturally by oxygen in the air. It is more golden in colour, generally more expensive and does not have the consistency in baking qualities that bleached flour does. Unbleached is preferred for yeast breads because bleaching affects gluten strength.
- Patent flour, bleached or unbleached, is the highest grade of flour. It is lower in ash and protein with good colour. Market-wise, it is considered highest in value.
- Organic or chemical-free flour is not standardized, so its definition varies from state to state. It may be grown and stored without the use of synthetic herbicides or insecticides. It may also mean no toxic fumigants were used to kill pests in the grain, and no preservatives were added to the flour, packaging or food product.
- Gluten is a protein formed when water and wheat flours are mixed. Gluten gives bread dough elasticity, strength and gas-retaining properties. Wheat is the only grain with sufficient gluten content to make a raised or leavened loaf of bread.

CORNMEAL

- Cornmeal comes in two types, either ground from yellow corn or from white. They are virtually alike, except that yellow cornmeal contains more vitamin A. Cornmeal is an "enriched" product.

- Water-ground cornmeal still contains the fat-rich germ of the corn kernel and has a fuller flavour than degerminated cornmeal. When buying, avoid packages with a rancid, stale odour.
- Blue cornmeal, from New Mexico, has a bluish-gray tint and a stronger, toastier flavour. It is often used for tortillas and tamales.
- Corn grits are also available in white or yellow. Grits are more coarsley ground than cornmeal.

OTHER FLOUR AND GRAIN PRODUCTS

- Barley flour makes a sweet, light-textured loaf of bread. It is usually combined with white flour because it does not have gluten of its own. Barley is sold also as pearl barley to be used mainly as a soup ingredient.
- Buckwheat flour is made from the seed of the fagopyrum, an herb. This flour is suitable for making pancakes. In Russia, it is called kasha. It is popular in Jewish cooking. In Japan and Korea, buckwheat noodles, called soba, are a staple.
- Oatmeal is made by rolling the groats to form flakes. Oat bran is the envelope of the groat, composed of the outer-most pericarp. It is high in soluble fibre.
- Potato flour is sometimes called potato starch and is used in baking and as a thickener. It is made from cooked potatoes that have been dried and ground.
- Quinoa has a nutty flavour, and of all grains, it comes closest to having the "perfect" protein balance.
- Rye flour is the finely ground flour obtained by sifting rye meal. The dark and light varieties are interchangeable in recipes, but the dark does have a stronger flavour. Rye and wheat flours are the only flours containing gluten-forming proteins that are important in baked goods.
- Spelt is a grain that is native to southern Europe and has a subtle, almost hazelnut flavour.
- Soy flour has a strong flavour and must be combined with wheat flour when used in baking. It is ground from whole soybeans and sometimes called soy powder or soya. Breads and cakes made with soy flour will be moist, fine-grained, and very high in iron, calcium and protein. It has none of its own starch or gluten, so it must always be combined with another flour.
- Triticale is a combination of wheat and rye and is used mostly in multigrain flours and in cereal mixes.
- Amaranth is a tall plant similar to corn, with a large shaggy head containing thousands of tiny seeds. The seeds are milled into whole grain flour, or puffed like rice or corn.

PASTA

Definition

"Pasta," an Italian word meaning paste, describes the various shapes and sizes of products made with flour and water. Pasta products may be divided into two types, dried or commercial pasta and fresh or homemade pasta.

They may also be categorized by their shapes:

- *Long Goods*: Like spaghetti
- *Short Goods*: Like macaroni
- *Specialty Products*: Like shells and bow ties
- *Noodles:* Ribbon-like shapes, generally made with eggs. By law, egg noodle products must contain 5.5 per cent egg solids by weight.

There are at least 350 shapes available in the United States and possibly 600 shapes worldwide.

Pasta shapes can be used interchangeably in recipes. Pasta can be purchased plain or in a variety of colours and flavours such as tomato, spinach, herb and whole wheat, to name a few. Good-quality pasta is a golden colour, with a fine, even grain. Pasta that is too white or too gray indicates poor quality flour that will not cook properly and will be limp and sticky. The water will be cloudy after cooking.In the U.S. laws prohibit the use of artificial colouring and most pasta is enriched with iron and four B-vitamins.

Storage

Dry pasta can be stored almost indefinitely if kept in a tightly sealed package or a covered container in a cool, dry place. If cooked pasta is not to be used immediately, drain and rinse thoroughly with cold water.

If the pasta is left to sit in water, it will continue to absorb water and become mushy. When the pasta is cool, drain and toss lightly with salad oil to prevent it from sticking and drying out. Cover tightly and refrigerate or freeze. Refrigerate the pasta and sauce separately or the pasta will become soggy. To reheat, put pasta in a colander and immerse in rapidly boiling water just long enough to heat through. Do not allow the pasta to continue to cook. Pasta may also be reheated in a microwave.

Preparation

Bring plenty of water to a rolling boil. Add about one tablespoon of salt per gallon of water, if desired. Add the pasta in small quantities to keep the rolling boil. Stir frequently to prevent sticking. Do not cover the pan. Follow package directions for cooking time. Do not overcook. Pasta should be "al dente". It should be slightly resistant to the bite, but cooked through. Drain pasta to stop the cooking action. Do not rinse unless the recipe specifically says to do so. For salads, drain and rinse pasta with cold water.

RICE

Most U.S. rice is enriched with iron, niacin, thiamin and folic acid. Rinsing rice, or cooking rice in excess water and draining, results in loss of enrichment and other water-soluble vitamins and minerals, and is not recommended.

Types of rice:

- *Long Grain Rice:* Long, slender kernel, four times longer than it is wide. Cooked grains are separate, light and fluffy.
- *Medium Grain Rice:* Kernel is two to three times longer than it is wide. Cooked grains are moist, tender and slightly clingy.
- *Short Grain Rice*: Kernel is almost round. Cooked grains cling together.
- *Aromatic Rice*: Brown or white rice with a natural aroma and flavour similar to that of roasted nuts or popcorn. The United States grows different kinds of aromatic rice. Some cook dry and separate and some cook moist and tender.
- *Sweet Rice*: An opaque white grain. Cooked grains are very sticky.
- *Rough Rice*: The kernels are still within the hull. Before rice can be prepackaged or cooked, the outer hull or husk must be removed.
- *Brown Rice*: Kernels of rice have had only the hull removed. Brown rice may be eaten as is or milled into regular-milled white rice. Cooked brown rice has a slightly chewy texture and a nut-like flavour. The light brown colour of brown rice is caused by the presence of bran layers.
- *Parboiled Rice*: Rough rice that has gone through a steam-pressure process before milling. Parboiled rice is favoured by consumers and chefs who desire extra fluffy and separate cooked rice.
- *Precooked Rice*: White or brown rice that has been completely cooked and dehydrated after milling. The process reduces the time required for cooking.
- *Rice Flour*: Ground from either white or brown rice. The white variety has almost no fat; the brown has a considerable amount. A variety of white rice flour called "sweet" rice flour can be used only as a thickener, so read the package label to be sure of what you are getting.

Preparation

For best results, always follow package directions. When no directions are available, use one of these methods for regular white rice.

- *Top-of-the-Range Instructions*: Combine 1 cup regular white rice, 2 cups liquid, 1 teaspoon salt and 1 teaspoon butter or margarine in 2- to 3-quart saucepan. Bring to a boil; stir once or twice. Reduce heat; cover and simmer for 15 to 20 minutes or until rice is tender. If rice is not quite tender or liquid is not absorbed, replace and cook 2 to 4 minutes longer. Fluff with fork.

- *Microwave Oven Instructions*: Combine 1 cup rice, 2 cups liquid, 1 teaspoon salt and 1 teaspoon butter or margarine in 2-to 3-quart deep microwave-proof baking dish. Cover and cook on HIGH for 5 minutes or until boiling. Reduce setting to MEDIUM and cook 15 minutes. Fluff with fork.
- *Rice Cookers*: There are several reliable brands of rice cookers available. Care should be taken to follow individual manufacturer's directions. In general, all ingredients are combined using ¼ to ½ cup less liquid than the top-of-the-range method.
- *Conventional Oven:* Cooking rice in a conventional oven with other foods is an efficient way of saving energy. Use boiling liquid. Combine ingredients in a baking dish or pan; stir. Cover tightly and bake at 350 °F for 25 to 30 minutes. Fluff with fork.
- *Reheating*: For each cup of cooked rice, add 2 tablespoons liquid. Cover and heat 4 to 5 minutes on top of range or in oven. In microwave oven, cook on HIGH about 1 to 1½ minutes per cup.

Storage

Uncooked rice can be stored on the shelf in a tightly sealed container. The shelf life of brown rice is shorter than that of white rice. The bran layers contain oil that can become rancid. Refrigerator storage is recommended for longer shelf life. Washing rice is not necessary; just measure and cook. Cooked rice can be refrigerated for up to seven days or stored in the freezer for six months.

CEREALS

Corn, wheat, rice, and oats are favourite grains for making cereals. All cereals keep best in airtight containers that keep out moisture, dust and insects. At home, a tightly sealed plastic bag is sufficient protection. Always look for a "use-by" date on the package.

Crispness can be restored to ready-to-eat cereal by spreading it in a baking pan and putting it in a 350 °F oven for 5 minutes.

Instant hot cereals keep up to one year in their original box, but a tightly covered container is better. Since whole-grain cereals are rich in natural oils, purchase containers that do not have a rancid odour. Store whole-grain cereals in tightly covered containers or sealed plastic bags in the refrigerator where they should remain fresh for 5 months. When stored at room temperature, they will stay fresh one month.

KEEPING FOODS SAFE AT HOME

Of the millions of cases of food borne illness that occur each year, most can be prevented.

The U. S. Department of Agriculture (USDA) advises using these strategies to keep foods safe at home:

- Buy and use a food thermometer. It's the only way to know if meat, poultry and fish are cooked safely. You can't tell just by looking.
- Use an appliance thermometer in the refrigerator and check to make sure that the temperature is 40 °F or below. In the freezer, make sure the thermometer reads 0 °F or below. Bacteria grow rapidly at temperatures above 40 °F. If the power goes out you will know what temperatures were reached and will be able to make informed decisions about the safety of food in the refrigerator and freezer.
- Do not leave pizza sitting out on the table or a "doggie" bag in the car overnight. Foods should not be left out more than two hours at room temperature or 1 hour if it is over 90 °F. When in doubt, throw it out.
- Do not defrost a turkey in the garage or in the trunk of the car. The only safe way to defrost food is in the refrigerator, in cold water or in the microwave.
- Wash hands and all food preparation surfaces with soap and water before and after touching raw meat, poultry or fish. Bacteria on raw meat, fish or poultry can contaminate other foods such as bread or lettuce that will not be cooked.
- Do not feed "leftovers" or "take-out" food that's no longer fit for people to pets. Animals can also be stricken with food borne illnesses.
- Do not leave "take-out" or "ready-to-eat" food in the refrigerator so long that it's forgotten. You can't tell by looking at or smelling if a food is unsafe. Throw it away after three days and never taste a food when you don't know what it is or how long it has been in the refrigerator!
- Do not lick the spoon or the bowl of homemade cookie dough or cake batter made with raw eggs. Even one taste of raw dough could contain harmful Salmonella bacteria resulting in a very unpleasant and potentially dangerous illness.
- When grilling outdoors, use a clean plate for the cooked hamburgers, hot dogs or other meat or fish. Don't use the same plate that held raw meat! Juices from raw meat, poultry or fish could contaminate your cooked food.
- Separate cooked foods from uncooked foods when preparing a meal, including using separate cutting boards and knives. Cross-contamination could cause harmful bacteria from one food to be transferred to another food.
- Always put an ice pack in a child's lunch box or a lunch bag taken to the office if it includes perishable foods, such as meat, poultry, fish, milk or eggs. Foods in lunch boxes sitting in warm classrooms or offices could result in food borne illnesses. Children under the age of 10 are the most vulnerable.

- Do not "save money" by buying dented cans or cracked jars. Never use food from damaged containers. This applies to containers that are leaking, bulging or badly dented. Do not use food from cracked jars with loose or bulging lids, canned food with a foul odour or any container that spurts liquid when you open it. It's not worth taking a risk to save a few pennies.
- Put meat and poultry packages in plastic bags at the meat counter before putting them in the grocery cart. Leaking packages from meat or poultry could contaminate other foods in the cart, leading to food borne illnesses.

FOOD SAFETY MISTAKES YOU DO NOT WANT TO MAKE

USING DIRTY HANDS TO PREPARE FOODS

We all know we should wash our hands before preparing food. But, did you know that not washing your hands before and during food preparation causes most food borne illnesses? Here is how to properly wash your hands: Wet your hands under warm water. Add hand soap and scrub for 10-15 seconds before rinsing off all soap. Use a clean towel or paper towel to thoroughly dry your hands.

CROSS-CONTAMINATING

Cross-contamination is an important source of food borne illness. Cross-contamination happens when kitchen equipment is used to prepare raw meat, poultry, fish, or eggs, and then is not properly washed before preparing other foods. Harmful bacteria can transfer from these raw foods to other foods if the surface is not washed properly between uses. To prevent this, thoroughly wash any surfaces, including your hands, which come in contact with raw meat, poultry, fish or eggs.

- Clean all cutting boards, knives, utensils and counter tops with warm, soapy water before food preparation begins.
- Use one cutting board for raw meat, poultry or seafood, and a different cutting board for ready-to-eat foods, such as fresh fruits and vegetables, cheese and bread.
- Sanitize cutting boards that have been in contact with raw meat, poultry or seafood. To sanitize, put the board in a solution of 1 tablespoon liquid chlorine bleach in a gallon of warm water and leave for several minutes. Plastic cutting boards can also be sanitized in a dishwasher using the wash and dry cycle.
- To sanitize kitchen counters, first wash with hot, soapy water. Then use 1 tablespoon unscented chlorine bleach in 1 gallon of water and spread on the counter. Let sit for several minutes and dry with paper towels.
- Sanitize a non-metal kitchen sponge by heating it, while still wet, in a microwave oven for 1 to 1½ minutes. Avoid burns by allowing the sponge to cool before using it.

- Use paper towels to clean up raw meat, poultry and seafood spills on kitchen counters and other surfaces. Wash kitchen cloths and towels, which have been in contact with raw meat juices, in the hot cycle of the washing machine and dry in the dryer before reusing them.

GUESSING FOOD IS DONE

Bacteria can survive on foods that are not properly cooked. Guessing if food is done by looking at changes in the colour of meat and poultry is not a good practice.

Ground beef can turn brown and look done before it is safely cooked. The best way to know that food is done is to use a food thermometer. A metal-stem, digital thermometer is easy to use and removes the guesswork of when the food is done.

You can buy one at nearly any department store or grocery store:

- Clean the stem and insert into the thickest part of the food to get an accurate reading.
- Use your food thermometer to make sure the foods reach the internal temperatures shown in the chart.

These are minimum temperatures; if preferred, meats may be cooked more well-done.

Table. Minimum Internal Temperatures of Foods.

Temperature	Food
145 °F	Fish steaks or fillets. All cuts of beef, lamb, pork and veal. For both safety and quality, allow meat to rest for 4 minutes before carving or eating.
155 °F	Ground, mechanically tenderized or injected meats. Ground fish. Egg dishes.
165 °F	Poultry and wild game. Stuffing and casseroles.

STORING LEFTOVERS UNSAFELY

Bacteria like warm temperatures especially while foods are sitting on the countertop or when they are cooling down in the refrigerator.

Refrigerate leftovers quickly so bacteria will not grow:

- As soon as you finish a meal, refrigerate your leftovers. Make sure your refrigerator is 40 °F or colder.
- Put a piece of tape on the container and write the date on the tape. It is best to use refrigerated leftovers within 4 days. If you won't be eating your leftovers in that time, put them in the freezer where they will keep safely.
- Never put a big pot of hot food in the refrigerator—it will take too long to cool to a safe temperature. Put liquid foods like hot soup or

chili in shallow containers, no more than 2 inches deep. Refrigerate or freeze quickly.

BASICS OF SAFE FOOD HANDLING

Bacteria that contaminate food and cause food borne illnesses are everywhere.

Follow these four basic safety tips to keep your food safe:

1. Wash hands and surfaces often.
2. Don't cross-contaminate.
3. Keep foods out of the temperature "Danger Zone."
4. Cook foods thoroughly.

KEEP HANDS AND SURFACES CLEAN

Bacteria like Staphylococci are found on hair, skin, mouth, nose and throat. A cough or sneeze can transmit thousands of microorganisms that may cause disease. The best prevention is to keep yourself and your kitchen clean.

Keep your Hands Clean

Wash your hands! Hands become the most potentially dangerous when seemingly innocent acts like scratching the scalp,

Running fingers through hair, or touching a pimple become the cause for contaminating foods.

Follow the following steps to wash your hands:

- Wet hands thoroughly with warm water.
- Apply soap generously.
- Rub hands for at least 20 seconds.
- Scrub under nails with a clean nailbrush.
- Rinse hands well with warm water.
- Dry hands using a clean paper towel.

Keep Counters and Equipment Clean

Wash counters and equipment with soap and water immediately after use. Sanitize with a chlorine solution of ¾ teaspoon liquid household bleach per quart of water, especially after contact with raw meats. Use a bleach solution to sanitize the kitchen drain and disposal as well.

Food particles get trapped and the moist environment is ideal for bacterial growth. Dishes and other utensils should be washed immediately in hot, soapy water and then air-dried, or cleaned in an automatic dishwasher.

Bacteria can live in kitchen towels, sponges and cloths. Wash kitchen towels and cloths regularly and always after using them to clean up raw meat juices, or use paper towels and throw them away.

Wash kitchen cloths and towels in the hot cycle of the washing machine and dry them in the dryer before reusing them.

Sanitize a non-metal kitchen sponge by heating it, while still wet, in a microwave oven for 1 to 1½ minutes. Avoid burns by allowing the sponge to cool before using it.

Keep Cutting Boards Clean

Whether using a wooden or plastic cutting board, it is important to keep it clean and to prevent cross-contamination after cutting raw meat, poultry and seafood.

Non-porous surfaces are easier to clean than wood. It is best to keep one cutting board for fresh produce and bread and a separate one for raw meats.

This will prevent bacteria on a cutting board that is used for raw meat, poultry or seafood from contaminating a food that requires no further cooking.

Wash All Cutting Boards Thoroughly

To keep all cutting boards clean wash them with hot, soapy water after each use, then rinse and air-dry or pat dry with fresh paper towels. Non-porous acrylic, plastic or glass boards and solid wood boards can be washed in an automatic dishwasher. Laminated boards may crack and split.

Sanitize Cutting Boards Occasionally

Both wooden and plastic cutting boards can be sanitized with a solution of ¾ teaspoon liquid chlorine bleach per quart of water. Flood the surface with the bleach solution and allow it to stand for several minutes, then rinse and air dry or pat dry with fresh paper towels.

Replace Battered Cutting Boards

Even plastic boards wear out over time. Once cutting boards become excessively worn or develop hard-to-clean grooves, they should be discarded.

PREVENT CROSS-CONTAMINATION

Cross-contamination is the transportation of harmful substances to food by:

- Hands that touch raw foods, such as raw meat, then touch food that will not be cooked, like salad ingredients.
- Surfaces or cleaning cloths that touch raw foods, are not cleaned and sanitized, then touch ready-to-eat food.
- Raw meat, raw poultry and raw seafood that touch or drip fluids on cooked or ready-to-eat foods.

Keep Foods out of the "Danger Zone" Safely Store Perishable Foods

Refrigerate or freeze foods that will spoil at room temperature. Keep your refrigerator between 34 °F and 40 °F and your freezer temperature at or below 0 °F. The "Danger Zone" for most foods is between 40 °F and 140 °F. Bacteria grow most rapidly in this range of temperatures, doubling in number in as little as 20 minutes. Discard any perishable food left out at room temperature for more than two hours.

Safely Thaw Foods

Thaw and marinate foods in the refrigerator, never on the counter. If thawed at room temperature, bacteria can grow in the outer layers of the food before the inside thaws.

Proper thawing is essential to maintaining the safety, taste and texture of frozen foods.

It affects the juiciness of meats, the texture and flavour of vegetables and fruits, and moisture level of baked goods:

- Thick meat cuts should be thawed before cooking to retain juiciness. Cuts such as chops, patties and steaks that will be pre-pared by flouring or breading should be thawed before baking.
- Broccoli, cauliflower and greens are more flavourful if partially thawed before cooking.
- Thawing foods should be placed in a shallow pan to catch drippings so that other refrigerated foods will not be contaminated with raw food juices.
- Never thaw foods at or above room temperature. Remember food spoilage bacteria multiply most rapidly at temperatures between 40 °F and 140 °F.
- Thaw frozen fruits, vegetables or meat in the refrigerator overnight, in a sealed freezer container. Foods may be thawed more quickly by immersing the sealed freezer container into cold water and changing the water frequently until food is thawed. Foods may also be thawed in the microwave using the defrost setting.
- If thawed in the microwave or in cold water in the sink, food must be cooked immediately after thawing. Do Not thaw a food and then refrigerate to cook later.
- When you have defrosted food for use, keep in mind that thawed frozen food is more perishable than fresh food.
- Thawed foods that have been at room temperature for over two hours should be discarded.
- Foods thawed in the refrigerator may be refrozen IF they still contain ice crystals. Immediately remove only the amount needed from the freezer container, remove air, reseal and return remaining food to the freezer.
- Thawed meats and poultry kept in the refrigerator should be used within two to three days. Thawed seafood kept in the refrigerator should be used within one to two days.
- Thaw bread and baked goods at room temperature in sealed freezer containers or original wrapping to avoid moisture loss.

Table. Recommended Times for Refrigerator and Freezer Food Storage.

Food	Refrigerator	Freezer
Dairy		
Fresh milk	5-7 days	*
Buttermilk	1-2 weeks	*
Canned Milk (opened)	3-5 days	*
Yogurt, cottage cheese	7 days	*
Hard cheese	6-12 weeks	6-12 months
Cheese spreads	3-4 weeks	*
Ice cream	*	2 months
Eggs		
Fresh in shell	3 weeks	*
Hard-cooked	1 week	*
Meats, Fresh		
Beef roasts, steaks	3-5 days	6-12 month
Ground beef or stew	1-2 days	3-4 months
Pork roast, chops	3-5 days	4-6 months
Sausage	1-2 days	1-2 months
Chicken or turkey	1-2 days	9-12 months
Meats, Cooked		
Smoked Sausage, whole ham (fully cooked)	7 days	1-2 months
Ham slices (fully cooked)	3-4 days	1-2 months
Hotdogs, luncheon meats (unopened)	2 weeks	1-2 months
Hotdogs, luncheon meats (opened)	3-7 days	1-2 months
Leftover meat, cooked	3-4 days	2-3 months
Leftover gravy and meat broth	1-2 days	2-3 months
Leftover poultry, cooked	3-4 days	4-6 months
Seafood		
Fresh lean fish: cod, flounder, trout, haddock, halibut, pollack, perch	1-2 days	4-6 months
Fresh fatty fish: mullet, smelt, salmon, mackerel, bluefish, tuna, swordfish	1-2 days	2-3 months
Live crabs and lobster	same day purchased *	*
Live mussels and clams	2-3 days	*
Live oysters	7-10 days	*
Freshly shucked oysters	5-7 days	3-4 months
Scallops, shrimp, shucked mussels and clams	2-3 days	3-4 months
Fruits and Vegetables (Fresh)		
Apples	1 month	8-12 months
Apricots, avocados, grapes, peaches, pears, plums	3-5 days	8-12 months
Berries, cherries	2-3 days	8-12 months
Grapefruit, lemons, limes, oranges	2 weeks	4-6 months
Pineapple	2-3 days	4-6 months

Beets, carrots	2 weeks	8-12 months
Beans, broccoli, greens, peas, summer squash	3-5 days	8-12 months
Celery, cabbage, chilies, lettuce, peppers, tomatoes	1 week	8-12 months
Mushrooms	1-2 days	8-12 months
Pies		
Chiffon pie, pumpkin pie	1-2 days	1 month
Fruit pie	1-2 days	1 year

Notes:

* Storage by this method is not recommended due to safety or quality issues.

COOK FOODS THOROUGHLY

Using a thermometer is the only reliable way to ensure safety and to determine the "doneness" of meat and egg dishes. To be safe, these foods must be cooked to an internal temperature high enough to destroy any harmful bacteria that may have been in the food. Colour changes in meat are no longer considered reliable proof that all bacteria have been destroyed. Use the following minimum internal temperature chart to determine if foods have been cooked thoroughly.

MINIMUM INTERNAL TEMPERATURES

These temperatures ensure that food borne bacteria have been destroyed. For reasons of personal taste or texture preferences, consumers may choose to cook meat and poultry to higher temperatures.

Table. Minimum Internal Temperatures of Foods.

Temperature	Food
145 °F	Fish steaks or fillets. All cuts of beef, lamb, pork and veal. For both safety and quality, allow meat to rest for 4 minutes before carving or eating.
155 °F	Ground, mechanically tenderized or injected meats. Ground fish. Egg dishes.
165 °F	Poultry and wild game. Stuffing and casseroles.

SAFELY HANDLE LEFTOVERS

Divide large amounts of hot leftovers directly into small, shallow containers for quick cooling, and place directly in the refrigerator. Discard food that has been left standing at room temperature for more than two hours. Date leftovers so they can be used within a safe time. Most foods remain safe when refrigerated for three to five days. If you will not be eating the leftovers within that time, freeze them for longer storage. If in doubt, throw it out rather than risk a food borne illness. Never taste food that looks or smells strange to see if you can still use it. Even a small amount of contaminated food can cause illness.

EFFECTS OF TEMPERATURE ON FOOD

BACKGROUND

"Last night I left cooked roast beef on the counter to cool before refrigerating but fell asleep and discovered it this morning. I immediately put it in the refrigerator. Since the meat is cooked, shouldn't it be safe to eat?" The answer to this question is that the roast beef should be thrown out. Why? Because leaving food out too long at room temperature can cause bacteria-such as Staphylococcus aureus, Salmonella enteriditis, Escherichia coli 0157: H7, and Campylobacter-to grow to dangerous levels that can cause illness. Bacteria exist everywhere in nature.

They are in the soil, air, water and the foods we eat. When the bacteria have nutrients, moisture, time and favourable temperatures, they grow rapidly increasing in numbers to the point where some can cause illness. Therefore, understanding the important role temperature plays in keeping food safe is critical. If we know the temperature at which food has been handled, we can then answer the question, "Is it safe?"

THE DANGER ZONE

Bacteria grow most rapidly in the range of temperatures between 40 and 140 °F, doubling in number in as little as 20 minutes. This range of temperatures is often called the "Danger Zone." That's why perishable foods should never be left out of refrigeration over two hours. If the temperature is above 90 °F, food should not be left out more than one hour.

COOKING

Raw meat and poultry should always be cooked to a safe internal temperature. When roasting meat and poultry, an oven temperature no lower than 325 °F should be used. Use a meat thermometer to assure that meat and poultry have reached a safe internal temperature. Cook beef, lamb, pork and veal steaks, roasts and chops to a safe minimum internal temperature of at least 145 °F, then allow to rest for 4 minutes before carving or eating.

Cook longer if you prefer your meat more well-done. Cook ground meats, mechanically tenderized, or injected meats to an internal temperature of 155 °F. All poultry is safe if it reaches a minimum internal temperature of 165 °F throughout the product.

For reasons of personal taste preferences, poultry may be cooked longer. If raw meat and poultry have been handled safely, using the above preparation recommendations will make them safe to eat. If raw meats have been mishandled, bacteria may grow and produce toxins, which can cause food borne illness. Cooking does not destroy toxins that are heat-resistant. Therefore, even though cooked, meat and poultry mishandled in the raw state may not be safe to eat even after proper preparation.

STORING LEFTOVERS

One of the most common causes of food borne illness is improper cooling of cooked foods. Bacteria are everywhere, even after food is cooked to a safe internal temperature, and they can be reintroduced to the food and then reproduce. For this reason leftovers must be put in shallow containers for quick cooling, and refrigerated immediately or within two hours of preparation.

REHEATING

Foods should be reheated thoroughly until hot and steaming, and to an internal temperature of 165 °F. In the microwave oven, cover food and rotate so it heats evenly. Follow manufacturer's instructions for stand time for more thorough heating. In the absence of manufacturer's instructions, at least a two-minute stand time should be allowed.

COLD STORAGE TEMPERATURES

Properly handled food stored in a freezer at 0 °F will always be safe. Freezing keeps food safe by slowing the movement of molecules, causing bacteria to enter a dormant stage. Once thawed, these bacteria can again become active and multiply to levels that may lead to food borne illness. Because bacteria on these foods will grow at about the same rate as they would on fresh food, thawed foods should be handled as any other perishable food.

A temperature of 34 to 40 °F should be maintained in the refrigerator. In contrast to freezer storage, perishable foods will gradually spoil in the refrigerator. Spoilage bacteria will make themselves known in a variety of ways. The food may develop an uncharacteristic odour, colour and/or become sticky or slimy.

Molds may also grow and become visible. Bacteria capable of causing food borne illness either don't grow or grow very slowly at refrigerator temperatures. A refrigerator/freezer thermometer should always be used to verify that the temperature of the unit is correct. Safe food-handling practices are a good defence against food borne illness. Because we know how different temperatures affect the growth of bacteria in our food, we can protect ourselves and our families from food borne illnesses by proper handling and cooking, and by storing foods at safe temperatures.

SAFE HANDLING OF BEEF

SELECTING THE BEST

Fresh is Best

Choose beef that is bright red in colour from the fresh meat case. Vacuum packaged beef will be maroon because it has not been exposed to oxygen. Choose beef that is firm to the touch. Look for packages that are cool to the touch, have no wear or punctures, and little or no excess liquid. Always check the "sell-by" date. "Loin" and "rib" are clues that the beef is a more tender cut. "Chuck", "round" and "flank" indicate a less tender cut. Less tender cuts will require marinating or a slower, moist cooking method. Purchase raw meats last. Make sure all meats, whether raw, pre-packaged or from the deli, are refrigerated when purchased. Fresh meats may contaminate other grocery items. The best way to prevent this cross-contamination is to always keep fresh meats from other items. Put raw meat packages in a plastic bag so juices won't drip onto other foods. Pack raw meats in an ice chest if it will take you more than an hour to get home, and keep the ice chest in the passenger area of the car during warm weather. Take meats straight home to the refrigerator or freezer.

Product Dating

Product dating, applying "sell by" or "use by" dates, is not required by federal regulations. However, many stores and processors may voluntarily choose to date packages of raw beef. Use or freeze products with a "sell by" date within three to five days of purchase. If the manufacturer has determined a "use by" date, observe it. It's always best to buy a product before its date expires. It's not important if a date expires after freezing beef, because all foods stay safe while properly frozen.

Product Inspection

All beef found in retail stores is either USDA inspected for wholesomeness or inspected by state systems which have standards equal to the federal government. Each animal and its internal organs are inspected for signs of disease. The "Passed and Inspected by USDA" seal ensures that the beef is wholesome and free from disease. Although inspection is mandatory, its grading for quality is voluntary, and a plant pays to have its beef graded.

Product Grading

Quality Grade refers to the eating quality of the meat. Grades are determined by the amount of marbling, the texture of the meat and its colour and appearance.

USDA grades for beef are as follows:

- *USDA Prime:* The lean is highly marbled and usually very tender and juicy; outside fat may be excessive.
- *USDA Choice*: The lean is average in marbling and usually tender and juicy; outside fat is variable.
- *USDA Select*: The lean contains some marbling; tenderness and juiciness can be extremely variable; usually not much outside fat.
- *USDA Standard:* Little or no marbling; tenderness and juiciness extremely variable; very little outside fat.

- *USDA Commercial, Utility, Cutter and Canner*: Generally applied to older animals. This beef is most often used in processed products and is rarely cut for the freezer.

STORAGE

Refrigeration

Keep beef below 40 °F during storage. Store uncooked beef items together, separate from cooked foods. Refrigerate or freeze fresh beef Immediately after bringing it home. Never leave beef in a hot car or sitting out at room temperature. Packaged whole cuts of fresh beef may be refrigerated in their original wrappings in the coldest part of the refrigerator for three to five days after purchase, while ground beef can be stored in the refrigerator for one to two days. Keep beef refrigerated until you are ready to cook it. When transporting cooked beef to another dining site, place it in an insulated container or ice chest until ready to eat. Cooked whole cuts of beef are best when refrigerated no longer than two to three days. Cooked ground beef is best when refrigerated no longer than one to two days.

Freezing

Freeze whole cuts of fresh beef if you do not plan to cook it within three to five days after purchase. Freeze ground beef if you do not plan to cook it within one to two days after purchase. It is safe to freeze beef in its original packaging or repackage it. However, for long-term freezing, overwrap the porous store plastic with aluminum foil, freezer paper, or place in freezer bags to prevent "freezer burn", which appears as grayish brown leathery spots and is caused by air reaching the surface of food. For best quality, use steaks and roasts within 6 to 12 months, ground beef within 3 to 4 months.

PREPARATION

Cleanliness

Always wash hands thoroughly with hot soapy water before preparing foods and after handling raw beef. Don't let raw meat or juices touch ready-to-go foods, either in the refrigerator or during preparation. Don't put cooked foods on the same plate that held raw beef. Always wash utensils that have touched raw meat with hot, soapy water before using them for cooked meats. Wash counters, cutting boards and other surfaces raw meats have touched. These surfaces may be sanitized by cleaning with a solution of 1 teaspoon chlorine bleach per quart of water.

Thawing

Thaw uncooked beef in the refrigerator or in cold water. Never thaw beef at room temperature. Thawing by refrigeration requires planning ahead and most likely allowing a 24-hour thawing period. To thaw beef in cold water, leave the beef in its original wrapping or place it in a watertight plastic bag.

Change the water every 30 minutes. For quick thawing of uncooked or cooked beef, use the microwave, but plan on cooking the meat immediately after thawing because some areas of the food may become warm and begin to cook during microwaving.

Thawing time will vary according to whether you're thawing a whole roast or cuts and the number of parts frozen together. Use the Defrost or Medium-Low setting, according to the manufacturer's directions. Turn the roast and separate parts as they thaw, taking care the meat does not begin to cook. Repeat as needed. Foods defrosted by the cold water method or in the microwave should be cooked before refreezing, because they may have been held at temperatures above 40 °F.

Table. Storage Times for Beef Products.

Products	Refrigerator (40 °F)	Freezer (0 °F)
Fresh beef roast, steaks, chops, or ribs	3 to 5 days	6 to 12 months
Fresh beef liver or variety meets	1 to 2 days	3 to 4 months
Home cooked beef, soups, stews or casseroles	3 to 4 days	2 to 3 months
Store-cooked convenience meals	1 to 2 days	2 to 3 months
Cooked beef gravy or beef broth	1 to 2 days	2 to 3 months
Beef hot dogs or lunch meats, sealed in package	2 weeks (or 1 week after a "Use by" date)	1 to 2 months
Beef hot dogs, opened package	7 days	1 to 2 months
Lunch meats, opened package	3 to 5 days	1 to 2 months
TV dinners, frozen casseroles	Keep only in freezer	3 to 4 months
Canned beef products in pantry	2 to 5 years in pantry; 3 to 4 days after opening	After opening, 2 to 3 months
Jerky, commercially vacuum packaged	1 year in pantry; 2 to 3 months in refrigerator	Do not freeze

It is safe to cook frozen beef in the oven, on the stove, or grill without defrosting it first, although the cooking time may be about 50% longer. Do not cook frozen beef in a slow cooker.

Marinating

Marinate food in the refrigerator, not on the counter. If you want to use the marinade as a dip or sauce, reserve a portion before adding raw food. Discard uncooked leftover marinade, or bring to a full boil before brushing on cooked beef.

Partial Cooking or Browning

Never brown or partially cook beef, then refrigerate and finish cooking later, because any bacteria present would not have been destroyed. It is safe to partially pre-cook or microwave beef immediately before transferring it to a hot grill or oven to finish cooking.

COOKING

Importance of Kitchen Thermometers

One of the critical factors in controlling bacteria in food is controlling temperature. Pathogenic microorganisms grow very slowly at low temperatures, multiply rapidly in mid-range temperatures, and are killed at high temperatures. Cook foods thoroughly to prevent food borne illness. Using a thermometer is the only reliable way to ensure safety and to determine the "doneness" of beef and most other foods. To be safe, a product must be cooked to an internal temperature high enough to destroy any harmful bacteria that may have been in the food. Many food handlers believe that visible indicators, such as colour changes in the food, can be relied on to determine whether foods have been cooked long enough to ensure bacterial destruction. However, recent research has shown that colour and texture indicators are not reliable.

Whole Muscle Meats

When cooking whole cuts or parts of beef, the thermometer should be inserted into the thickest part of the meat, away from the bone, fat and gristle. The thermometer may be inserted sideways if necessary.

When the food being cooked is irregularly shaped, the temperature should be checked in several places. Steaks and roasts should be cooked to 145 °F followed by a 4 minute rest, 160 °F, or 170 °F.

Ground Beef

Ground beef must be cooked thoroughly to kill harmful bacteria. Unlike whole muscle meat, whose interior meat is sterile, the grinding process exposes the interior meat in ground beef to bacteria, which may be on the surface, in the air, on equipment or on people's hands. To kill these bacteria, food safety experts have one major rule of thumb—cook ground beef to at least 155 °F. This step, while very simple, offers the best protection that consumers can have for serving ground beef products safely.

Microwaving

When microwaving unequally sized pieces of beef, arrange them in a dish or on a rack so thick parts are towards the outside of the dish and thin parts are in the center, and cook on medium-high or medium power.

Place a roast in an oven-cooking bag or in a covered pot. Refer to the manufacturer's directions that accompany the microwave oven for suggested cooking times. Remove from microwave and test for doneness in several places with a meat thermometer.

SERVING

Basic Tips

Wash hands with soap and water before serving or eating food. Serve cooked products on clean plates with clean utensils and clean hands. Never put cooked foods on a dish that has held raw products unless the dish is washed with soap and hot water. Hold hot foods above 140 °F and cold foods below 40 °F. Never leave foods, raw or cooked, at room temperature longer than two hours. On a hot day with temperatures at 90 °F or warmer, this decreases to one hour.

LEFTOVERS

Basic Tips

Always use clean utensils and storage containers for safe storage. Divide large amounts of leftovers into small, shallow containers for quick cooling in the refrigerator; avoid placing large pots of gravy or stew in the refrigerator to cool since it will likely take until the next day for this amount of food to cool.

To store in the refrigerator, wrap cooked meat in plastic wrap or aluminum foil, or store it in a tightly covered cont-ainer and use within two to three days. For frozen storage, wrap meat in freezer paper, heavy aluminum foil, or place in freezer bag, and use within two to three months. Never taste food that looks or smells strange to see if you can still use it. If In Doubt Throw It Out!

Table. Approximate* Beef Cooking Times.

Type of Beef	Size	Cooking Method	Cooking Time	Internal Temperature
Rib roast, bone-in	4 to 6 lbs.	Roast 325 °F	23 to 25 min./lb.	Medium rare 145 °F
Rib roast, boneless rolled	4 to 6 lbs.	Roast 325 °F	Add 5 to 8 min./lb. to times above	Medium rare 145 °F
Chuck roast, brisket	3 to 4 lbs.	**Braise 325 °F	2 to 3 hours	Medium 160 °F
Round or rump	2½ to 4 lbs.	Roast 325 °F	30 to 35	Medium rare

roast			min./lb.	145 °F
Tenderloin, whole	4 to 6 lbs.	Roast 425 °F	45 to 60 min. total	Medium rare 145 °F
Steaks	¾" thick	Broil/Grill	4 to 5 min. per side	Medium rare 145 °F
Stew or shank cross cuts	1 to 1½" thick	Cover with liquid; simmer	2 to 3 hours	Medium 160 °F
Short ribs	4" long and 2" thick	**Braise 325 °F	1½ to 2½ hours	Medium 160 °F

Notes:

*For safety, cook hamburgers and ground beef mixtures such as meat loaf to 155 °F on a meat thermometer. However, whole muscle meats such as steaks and roasts may be cooked to 145 °F (medium rare), if that is followed by a 4 minute rest before carving or eating. The cooking times listed here are approximate for use in meal planning. Use a meat thermometer to check for safe cooking and doneness of beef.

**Braising is roasting or simmering less-tender meats with a small amount liquid in a tightly covered pan.

SAFE HANDLING OF CANNED GOODS

Canning is an important, safe method of food preservation if practiced properly.The canning process involves placing foods in jars or cans and heating them to a temperature that destroys micro-organisms that could be a health hazard or cause the food to spoil. Canning also inactivates enzymes that could cause the food to spoil. Air is driven from the jar or can during heating, and as it cools, a vacuum seal is formed. This vacuum seal prevents air from getting back into the product bringing with it microorganisms to recontaminate the food.

PURCHASING CANNED GOODS

Buy cans and jars that look perfect. Carefully check dented cans and jars for leakage and rust before buying. Cans and jars should be free of dents, cracks or bulging lids, which can indicate a serious food poisoning threat. Dusty cans or torn labels may indicate old stock. Also check for pull dates.

Product Dating

Dates on product packages recommend purchase or "use by" dates. They are not safety dates. Product dating is voluntary and not required by federal regulations. Since product dating is voluntary by federal regulations, a retailer may legally sell foods beyond the date on the package as long as the product is wholesome. However, it is not legal to alter, change or cover up a date on a product packaged under federal inspection. The product may continue to be offered for sale but the expired date must remain visible to the consumer.

Types of Dates:

- A "sell by" date tells the store how long to display the product for sale. You should buy the product before the date expires to have sufficient time to use it at best quality.
- A "best if used by" date is recommended for best flavour or quality. It is not a purchase or safety date.
- A "use by" date is the last date recommended for the use of the product while at peak quality and has been determined by the manufacturer of the product.
- "Closed or coded dates" are packing numbers for use by the manufacturer to rotate the stock as well as to locate their products in the event of a recall.

STORAGE OF CANNED GOODS

Storage does not improve the quality of any food. The quality of a food will not decrease significantly if stored properly and if the food is eaten within the recommended time frame. For best results in maintaining product quality, practice the rule, First In, First Out. This means you use the oldest products first.

A good practice in the home is to place the newly purchased cans in back of the same products already on the shelf. For best quality, use home canned foods within one year, and commercially processed cans within two years. Storage cabinets should be cool and dry. The best temperature for storing canned foods is between 50 °F and 70 °F. Avoid storing canned foods in a warm place near hot pipes, a range or furnace, or in direct sunlight. Storage time decreases significantly when temperatures are above 75 °F. Keep canned goods dry to prevent cans or metal lids from rusting, which may cause cans to leak and food to spoil.

Recommended Storage for Unopened Canned Foods in a Cool, Dry Pantry:

- *High-Acid Canned Food:* 12 to 18 months Juices, tomatoes, grapefruit, apple products, mixed fruit, berries, pickles, sauerkraut and vinegar-based products.
- *Low-acid Canned Foods:* 2 to 5 years Meat and poultry products, vegetable soups, spaghetti products, potatoes, corn, carrots, beans, beets, peas, pumpkins, etc.
- *Home-Canned Foods:* All types 1 year
- *Opened Canned Foods*: Store tightly covered in a glass or plastic storage container in refrigerator.
  - Baby food: 2 days
  - Meat, seafood, poultry: 2 days
  - Vegetables: 3 days
  - Tomato sauce, fruits: 5 to 7 days
  - Pickles and olives: 1 to 2 months

COOKING OF CANNED GOODS

Commercially canned foods can be safely eaten straight from the can as long as the container is intact. However, Do Not use home canned vegetables unless you have the means to boil them for 10 minutes before eating. Don't taste or use canned foods that show any signs of spoilage! Look closely at all cans before opening them.

A bulging lid or leaking can is a sign of spoilage. When you open the can, look for other signs such as spurting liquid, an off odour or mold. Spoiled canned foods should be discarded so they will not be eaten by humans or pets. Remember that once a can is opened, it becomes perishable and should be refrigerator-stored or cooked properly and then stored in the refrigerator if you are not going to eat it right away.

SERVING CANNED GOODS

Serve foods on clean plates, using clean utensils. Keep opened canned foods in the refrigerator until it is time to serve them. Keep cooked canned foods hot, above 140 °F, but not for more than two hours. When outside temperatures are 90 °F or warmer, hold the cooked foods no longer than one hour before reheating, refrigerating or freezing them.

Leftovers

After a meal, refrigerate or freeze uneaten food promptly, but throw it out if the food has been held too long or was a reheated leftover at this meal. Refrigerate or freeze cooked leftovers in small, covered shallow containers within two hours after cooking. Leave airspace around the containers for quick chilling. Date packages of leftovers and use them within a safe period. Cover and reheat leftovers thoroughly before serving them. Bring sauces, soups and gravies to a rolling boil; reheat all other foods to an internal temperature of 165 °F. Reheat only the amount of food needed for one meal. Never reheat a food more than once. Don't taste leftovers to determine if they are safe to eat. If in doubt, throw it out! Discard outdated, unsafe or questionable leftovers. Place them in the garbage disposal or in tightly wrapped packages that cannot be consumed by people or animals.

HANDLING OF CHEESE FOR SAFETY AND QUALITY

Cheese comes in many forms ranging from soft to hard and natural to processed. How cheese is handled for safety and best quality is dependent on the type of cheese. Natural cheese can be unripened or ripened. Unripened cheeses include cream cheese and cottage cheese. Cheeses that are ripened by bacteria include cheddar, Swiss and Parmesan. Cheeses that are ripened by mold include Blue, Roquefort and Brie.

Natural cheeses are also categorized by their degree of hardness:

- *Soft:* Brie, Camembert, cottage cheese, cream cheese, ricotta, feta
- *Semi-soft:* Blue, brick, Havarti, Monterey Jack, mozzarella, Muenster, provolone
- *Hard:* Cheddar, Colby, Edam, Gouda, Swiss
- *Very Hard:* Parmesan, Romano

Process cheese is a blend of fresh and aged natural cheese that has been melted, pasteurized and mixed with an emulsifier. Process cheese is milder in flavour and softer than the natural cheese from which it was made. It also has very good melting properties.

HOW SHOULD CHEESE BE STORED

Refrigerate all cheese between 35 and 40 °F in its original wrapping until ready to use. It is best to store cheese in a refrigerator drawer so it does not pick up off-flavours from other foods.

If cheese is removed from its original packaging, wrap it tightly with plastic film wrap or foil to prevent air pockets.

Once cheese is exposed to air, molding and dehydration might occur. To protect cheese from mold it is best to double-wrap cheese and place it in a sealed container after each use. Strong-smelling cheeses, like Limburger, should be well-wrapped and kept in a separate container to prevent odours from transferring to other foods.

HOW LONG IS IT SAFE TO KEEP CHEESE

The "best if used by" date tells you how long the product will keep its best flavour or quality. The term is not a safety date. "Best if used by" dates are general guidelines, as some foods may deteriorate more quickly and other foods may last longer than the times suggested.

A number of factors, such as improper handling and inadequate storage, can shorten the shelf-life of a food. Many foods can be eaten after the "best if used by" date if properly stored and handled.

Caution

Throw out soft cheeses that have been at room temperature for more than four hours.

NATURAL CHEESE

As a general rule, the harder the cheese, the longer its shelf-life. But remember, many types of natural cheese will continue to ripen, no matter how carefully they are stored.

Hard cheeses will generally keep for several months, whereas softer cheeses will keep from one to three weeks after opening. Large pieces of cheese tend to keep longer than shredded cheese.

PROCESS CHEESE

Unopened packages of process cheese can be used up to six months if refrigerated at 40 °F or below. Opened packages should be tightly rewrapped, refrigerated, and used within three to four weeks.

DOES CHEESE FREEZE WELL

Most hard cheeses and process cheeses can be frozen, but there will be changes in texture. For this reason, thawed cheese is best used crumbled or shredded, in salads or as toppings or in cooked dishes.

Tips for Freezing Cheeses:

- Freeze pieces of a half-pound or less.
- Use moisture-proof and airtight wrapping.
- Freeze quickly and store at 0 °F for two to six months.
- Thaw in refrigerator so cheese won't lose moisture; the slower the cheese is thawed, the better.
- Use as soon as possible after thawing

SHOULD MOLDY CHEESE BE THROWN AWAY

Molds spread through cheese by producing "hyphae," which are root-like structures. In hard cheeses, such as cheddar and many processed cheeses, these mold hyphae do not penetrate very far below the surface. Mold that is not part of the manufacturing process of a cheese should be handled.

Hard Cheese

If the block of cheese is large and molding is not extensive, remove the mold to save the remaining cheese. Remove at least 1-inch around and below the mold spot. Keep the knife out of the mold itself so it will not contaminate other parts of the cheese. Mold requires oxygen to grow, so tightly rewrap the remaining cheese. The old advice to wipe the cheese with a vinegar solution is no longer recommended and is not required to prevent further mold growth.

Semi-Soft and Soft Cheese and All Types of Crumbled, Shredded, and Sliced Cheese

Discard soft cheese, cheese that has a loose-knit curd, and shredded or sliced cheese if it contains molds that are not a part of the manufacturing process. These molds can be dangerous. Foods with high moisture content can be contaminated below the surface. Shredded, sliced, or crumbled cheese can be contaminated by the cutting instrument. Moldy soft cheese can also have bacteria growing along with the mold.

- *Caution*: Never open extremely moldy cheese in the kitchen. Do not sniff the moldy item. Wrap all moldy trimmings and moldy cheeses in plastic wrap and place in a covered trash can.

WHO SHOULD AVOID EATING CERTAIN CHEESES

Pregnant women and newborns, older adults, and people with weak immune systems due to cancer treatments, AIDS, diabetes or kidney disease are at risk for becoming seriously ill from eating foods that contain Listeria monocytogenes. People in these at-risk groups should not eat feta, Brie, Camembert, blue-veined cheeses, or Mexican-style soft cheeses such as queso blanco and queso fresco unless labeled pasteurized.

WHAT IS THE BEST WAY TO MELT CHEESE

Cheese cut into small pieces or shredded promotes more even melting in a shorter amount of time. When you add cheese to any recipe, cook on low heat, stirring constantly. High heat will toughen cheese and make it stringy. When you are making a sauce with cheese in it, add cheese as the last ingredient and heat until just melted. Process cheese melts more smoothly than natural cheese.

WHAT IS THE BEST WAY TO MICROWAVE CHEESE

Remove the wrapping and place on a microwave-safe plate. Microwave at 30 per cent until cheese reaches desired softness and/or temperature. Check every 10 seconds to prevent overheating.

Cooking times will vary among microwave ovens. Use this method to prepare cheese nachos without making the cheese tough.

WHAT IS THE BEST TEMPERATURE FOR SERVING CHEESE

The flavour of cheese is best when eaten at room temperature, so remove from refrigerator before serving time. Soft cheeses take a shorter amount of time to come to room temperature than firm and hard cheeses.

Only set out the amount of cheese you will eat to prevent the cheese from becoming dry and tough from being repeatedly warmed and chilled.

WHAT IS THE BEST WAY TO SHRED CHEESE

Cheese will shred more easily if well-chilled. It can also be placed in the freezer for 30 minutes before shredding.

SAFE HANDLING OF EGGS

SHELL EGG SAFETY

Eggs can be a part of a healthy diet. However, they are perishable just like raw meat, poultry and fish. To be safe, they must be properly stored, handled and cooked.

Concern for Egg Safety

Some unbroken fresh shell eggs may contain Salmonella enteritidis bacteria that can cause food borne illness. While the number of eggs affected is quite small, there have been some scattered outbreaks in the last few years. Currently the government, the egg industry and the scientific community are working together to solve the problem. Researchers say that if present, the Salmonella enteritidus bacteria are usually in the yolk or "yellow." But they cannot rule out the bacteria being in egg whites. So everyone is advised against eating raw or undercooked egg yolks, whites or products that contain eggs. People with health problems, the very young, the elderly and pregnant women are particularly vulnerable to Salmonella enteritidis infections. Chronic illness also weakens the immune system, making the person vulnerable to food borne illness.

STORAGE, HANDLING AND COOKING OF SHELL EGGS

Proper refrigeration, cooking and handling should prevent most egg safety problems. People can enjoy eggs and dishes containing eggs if these safe handling guidelines are followed.

Don't Eat Raw Eggs

This includes "health food" milk shakes with raw eggs, Caesar salad, hollandaise sauce and any other foods like homemade mayonnaise, ice cream or eggnog made from recipes in which the raw egg ingredients are not cooked.

These egg-based recipes should be updated to start with a cooked base or so that commercially prepared pasteurized eggs or egg substitutes are used. Use a thermometer and make sure the temperature of the cooked base reaches 160 °F.

Buy Clean Eggs from a Refrigerator Display Case

Do not purchase eggs anywhere that are not refrigerated. Any bacteria present in the egg can grow quickly if stored at room temperature. At the store, choose Grade A or AA eggs with clean, uncracked shells.

Safe Storage of Eggs at Home

Take eggs straight home and store them immediately in the refrigerator at 40 °F or slightly below. Store them in the grocery carton in the coldest part of the refrigerator, not in the door. Do not wash eggs. Washing eggs could remove the protective mineral oil coating put on at the plant and could increase the potential for bacteria on the shell to enter the egg.

Use Eggs Promptly

Use raw shell eggs within three to five weeks. When fresh eggs are hard cooked, the protective coating is washed away so hard-cooked eggs should be refrigerated within two hours of cooking and used within a week. Use leftover yolks and whites within four days. If eggs crack on the way home from the store, break them into a clean container, cover tightly, and keep refrigerated for use within two days.

Freeze Eggs for Longer Storage

Eggs should not be frozen in their shells. To freeze whole eggs, beat yolks and whites together. Egg whites and yolks can also be frozen by themselves. Use frozen eggs within a year. If eggs freeze accidentally in their shells, keep them frozen until needed. Defrost them in refrigerator. Discard any with cracked shells.

Handle Eggs Safely

Wash hands, utensils, equipment and work areas with warm, soapy water before and after contact with eggs and egg-rich foods.

Serve Immediately

Don't keep out of the refrigerator more than two hours. Serve cooked eggs and egg-rich foods immediately after cooking, or place in shallow containers for quick cooling and refrigerate at once. Use within three to four days. Recipes using raw eggs should be cooked immediately or refrigerated and cooked within 24 hours.

Cooked Eggs

Hard-cooked eggs should be safe for everyone to eat. Those at risk for food borne illness should avoid eating soft-cooked or "runny" eggs. However, healthy persons may choose to eat eggs that are less than totally firm.

Use the following cooking times:

- *Fried Eggs:* Cook 2 to 3 minutes on each side; 4 minutes in a covered pan. The yolk should begin to thicken.
- *Scrambled Eggs*: Cook until firm throughout.
- *Poached Eggs*: Cook 5 minutes over boiling water.
- *Soft-Cooked Eggs*: Cook 7 minutes in the shell in boiling water.

Use Safe Egg Recipes

Egg mixtures are safe if they reach 160 °F, so homemade ice cream and eggnog can be made safely from a cooked base. Heat the egg-milk mixture gently. Use a thermometer or be sure the mixture coats a metal spoon. Dry meringue shells are safe. So are divinity candy and seven-minute frosting, made by combining hot sugar syrup with beaten egg whites. Meringue-topped pies should be safe if baked at 350 °F for about 15 minutes. Chiffon pies and fruit whips made with raw, beaten egg whites cannot be guaranteed safe. Substitute whipped cream or whipped topping. To make key lime pie safely, heat lime juice with raw egg yolks in a pan on the stove, stirring constantly, until the mixture reaches 160 °F. Combine this mixture with sweetened condensed milk and pour it into a baked piecrust. For meringue topping. For egg dishes such as quiche and casseroles, a knife inserted in the center should come out clean.

Safety Tips for Easter Eggs:

- Wash hands before dyeing the eggs.
- Use a food-safe colouring if eggs will be eaten.
- Handle eggs carefully to prevent cracking. If the shells crack, bacteria could contaminate the inside. Do not use cracked eggs for hiding.
- After hard-cooking eggs, dye them and return them to the refrigerator immediately until ready to hide.
- Hide eggs in places protected from dirt, pets and other sources of bacteria.
- The total time for hiding and hunting eggs should not exceed two hours. Discard any Easter eggs that have been cracked. The uncracked "found" eggs should then be refrigerated until eaten.
- Eat hard-cooked eggs within one week.

Ukranian Easter Eggs

A traditional part of the Easter celebration in the Ukraine, these whole, raw eggs have their contents blown out to leave a hollow shell that is then decorated. Because some raw eggs may contain Salmonella, use caution when blowing out the contents.

Use only uncracked eggs that have been kept refrigerated. To destroy bacteria that may be present on the surface of the egg, wash the egg in hot water and then rinse in a solution of one teaspoon chlorine bleach per half cup of water. After blowing out the egg, refrigerate the contents and use within two to four days; cook thoroughly before eating.

Pickled Eggs

Pickled or brined eggs are hard-cooked eggs marinated in vinegar and pickling spices, spicy cider, or juice from pickles or pickled beets. Home-pickled eggs should be kept refrigerated. Unopened containers of commercially processed pickled eggs keep for several months on the shelf. After opening, keep refrigerated.

EGG PRODUCTS

When consumers think of an egg, most picture a pristine white, or sometimes brown, oval shell containing a completely edible, versatile food. But of the 63 billion eggs consumed in 1994, more than 25 per cent were in the form of egg products.

The term "egg products" refers to eggs that have been removed from their shells for processing. Basic egg products include whole eggs, whites, yolks and various blends with or without non-egg ingredients that are processed and pasteurized and may be available in liquid, frozen and dried forms. Egg products are widely used by the food service industry and as ingredients in other foods, such as prepared mayonnaise and ice cream.

Buying, Handling and Cooking Egg Products

Proper storage and handling is necessary for all egg products to prevent bacterial contamination:

- Buy only pasteurized egg products that bear the USDA inspection mark.
- Make sure containers are tightly sealed. Frozen products should show no signs of thawing. Refrig-erated products should be kept at 40 °F or below. Dried egg products should not be caked or hardened.
- Store frozen egg products up to one year at 0 °F or lower. After thawing, do not re-freeze.
- Thaw frozen egg products in the refrigerator or under cold running water. Do Not Thaw On The Counter.
- If the container for liquid products bears a "use by" date, observe it. Follow the storage and handling instructions provided by the manufacturer.
- For liquid products without an expiration date, store unopened containers at 40 °F or below for up to seven days. Do not freeze opened cartons of liquid egg products.
- Unopened dried egg products and egg white solids can be stored at room temperature as long as they are kept cool and dry. After opening, store in the refrigerator.
- Reconstituted egg products must be used immediately or refrigerated and used that day.
- USDA Commodity Dried Egg Mix should be stored at less than 50 °F, preferably in the refrigerator. After opening, use within seven to 10 days. Reconstitute only the amount needed at one time and use immediately or refrigerate and use within an hour.

EGG PRODUCT SAFETY

Who Inspects Egg Products

Congress passed the Egg Products Inspection Act (EPIA) in 1970. The EPIA provides for the mandatory continuous inspection of the processing of liquid, frozen and dried egg products to ensure they are wholesome and properly labeled and packaged to protect the health and welfare of consumers. USDA's Food Safety and Inspection Service (FSIS) inspects all egg products, with the exception of those products exempted under the Act that are used by food manufacturers, food service institutions and retail markets.

The Department of Health and Human Services' Food and Drug Administration (FDA) is responsible for the inspection of egg substitutes, imitation eggs and similar products that are exempted from continuous inspection under the EPIA. Currently, only Canada is exporting egg products to the United States. The EPIA specifies that egg products may not be imported into the United States except from countries that have an egg products inspection system equivalent to that in this country.

Why are Eggs Products Useful

Food manufacturers like pasteurized egg products because of their convenience and ease in handling and storing. Institutional food service operators, such as fast food chains, restaurants, hospitals and nursing homes, use egg products to ensure a high level of food safety. Consumers are starting to see more egg products in retail food stores.

How are Egg Products Made

Egg products are processed in sanitary facilities under continuous inspection by the USDA. The initial step in making egg products is breaking the eggs and separating the yolks and whites from the shells. Eggs are processed by automated equipment that moves the eggs from flats, washes and sanitizes the shells, breaks the eggs and separates the whites and yolks, and/or makes mixtures of them. The liquid egg product is filtered, mixed, and then chilled prior to additional processing.

Why and how are Egg Products Pasteurized

The law requires that all egg products distributed for consumption be pasteurized. This means that they must be rapidly heated and held at a minimum required temperature for a specified time. This destroys Salmonella, but it does not cook the eggs or affect their colour, flavour, nutritional value or use. Dried whites are pasteurized by heating in the dried form, again for a specified time and at a minimum required temperature.

Since many new and different types of egg products are now being formulated, government and industry researchers are currently evaluating the effectiveness of the pasteurization processes used for these and other products. Additional research will determine if new safety measures are needed to continue to provide safe egg products for food service, industry and consumers.

Are All Egg Products Pasteurized

Certain commodities are not presently considered egg products and are exempt from this law. These commodities include freeze-dried products, imitation egg products and egg substitutes. Inspected, pasteurized egg products are used to make these commodities and companies may elect to repasteurize these products following formulation and before packaging.

Officially inspected egg products will bear the USDA inspection mark. No-cholesterol frozen egg substitutes first became available to consumers in 1973. They consist of egg whites, artificial colour and other non-egg additives. Specific questions about egg substitutes should be directed to the manufacturer.

What Information is Provided on Egg Product Labels

In addition to nutrition information on consumer packages, other labeling information is required for egg products.

All egg products must be labeled with:

- The common or usual name;
- The ingredients listed in the order of descending proportions;
- The name and address of the packer or distributor;
- The date of pack which may be shown as a lot number or production code number;
- The net contents; and
- The official USDA inspection mark and plant number.

Can Egg Products be Used as an Ingredient in Uncooked Foods

Egg products are pasteurized and can be substituted in recipes typically made with raw eggs that won't be cooked. For optimal safety, egg products are best used in a cooked product, especially if serving high-risk persons such as the elderly, children, the chronically ill, or those with weakened immune systems. Use a food thermometer to be sure that the internal temperature of the cooked product reaches 160 °F. Egg products can also be used in baking or cooking.

What is Dried Egg Mix

USDA Dried Egg Mix is a blend of dried whole eggs, nonfat dry milk, soybean oil and a small amount of salt. There is very little moisture in it. To reconstitute, blend 2 Tablespoons of Dried Egg Mix with ¼ cup water to make the equivalent of one large whole egg. Dried Egg Mix is packaged in 6-ounce pouches, equivalent to about six eggs each. It is distributed by USDA to food banks, Indian reservations and other needy family outlets and is also used in disaster feeding. A similar product called All-Purpose Egg Mix, containing a greater proportion of eggs, is now being manufactured for USDA. It is reconstituted by mixing one part egg mix with two parts water. All-Purpose Egg Mix is available to schools as part of the School Lunch Programme. It is packaged in 10-pound bags.

SAFE HANDLING OF FISH

SELECTING THE BEST

Spotting a Safe Seafood Seller

Always purchase fish from a dealer that maintains high quality.

Based on FDA's Food Code, here are some ways of spotting a safe fish dealer:

- Employees should be in clean clothing and wearing hair coverings.
- They should not be smoking, eating or playing with their hair.
- They should not be sick or have any open wounds.

- Employees should be wearing disposable gloves when handling food and change gloves after doing nonfood tasks and after handling raw fish.
- Fish should be displayed on a thick bed of fresh—not melting—ice preferably in a case or under some type of cover. Fish should be arranged with the bellies down so that the melting ice drains away from the fish, thus reducing the chances of spoilage.

Selecting Quality Fish

Appearance is bright and shiny in quality fish, and most of the scales are intact and adhere tightly to the skin. Each species has characteristic markings and colours which fade and become less pronounced as the fish loses freshness. Eyes are bright, clear, full and often protrude. As quality goes down, the eyes often turn pink and become cloudy and sunken. This does not always apply to small-eyed fish such as salmon. Gills are red and free from slime.

With time, the colour fades to light pink, then gray and finally greenish or dull brown. Odour is fresh and mild. A fish just out of the water has practically no "fish" odour. The fishy odour develops with time, but should not be strong or objectionable. Flesh is firm, elastic and not separating from the bones.

Fresh Fillets and Steaks

Odour is fresh and mild. Flesh is moist, firm, elastic and has a fresh-cut appearance without traces of browning or drying around the edges. Pre-packaged steaks and fillets are tightly wrapped with no liquid and little or no air in the packages.

Safe Handling after Purchase

Whether you've purchased fish that is fresh or frozen, always keep it cold. Never leave perishable items in a hot car unless packed in ice or in a cooler; seafood products must be kept cold to ensure peak quality. It's always a good idea to keep your refrigerator temperature between 32 to 38 °F, and your freezer at 0 °F or colder.

STORAGE

Refrigeration

Store fresh fish in its original wrapper in the coldest part of the refrigerator, which is under the freezer or in the "meat-keeper" drawer. Plan to use your fish purchases within one to two days. If not, freeze them. However, do not refreeze previously frozen products because the quality will suffer.

Freezing

It is best to freeze fish in tightly wrapped package form. This takes less storage space and fits a family portion for one meal at a time. Fish freeze faster in tightly wrapped packages. Small whole fish, steaks or fillets are easy to prepare for packaged freezing. Prewrap them tightly and individually in cling wrap, forming a tight skin on the product. Master-bag these individually wrapped items in a good, strong polyethylene bag or foil before freezing, but never more than a pound per master bag.

Large fish have large surface areas exposed, and they are difficult to protect from oxidation. The best way to handle these fish is simply to freeze them unwrapped or temporarily bag them in plastic. After freezing, dip them in water to form a protective glaze. Then you can rebag the fish and return it to the freezer.

The glaze may need renewing every five to six weeks. Label each package with the date, kind and type of fish and the weight and number of servings or pieces.

A crayon or grease pencil is ideal for this purpose. Do not overload your freezer, and do not pack the unfrozen fish too tightly. Either of these practices can greatly extend the freezing time and reduce the quality. Most home-frozen fish should not be stored over six months, no more than three months for salmon.

PREPARATION

Cleanliness

Always wash hands thoroughly with hot, soapy water before preparing foods and after handling raw fish. Don't let raw fish or juices touch ready-to-go foods either in the refrigerator or during preparation. Don't put cooked foods on the same plate that held raw fish. Always wash utensils that have touched raw fish with hot, soapy water before using them for cooked foods. Wash counters, cutting boards and other surfaces raw fish have touched.

Thawing

While freezing fish quickly keeps more cell walls intact, the opposite is true for thawing. Defrost gradually so cells are disturbed less and fewer juices leak out. The best way to thaw is overnight in the refrigerator. Avoid thawing at room temperature.

If you must thaw fish quickly, here are safe options: seal fish in a plastic bag and immerse in cold water for about an hour, or microwave on the "defrost" setting, stopping when fish is still icy but pliable.

Marinating

Marinate fish in the refrigerator, not on the counter. Discard the marinade after use because it contains raw juices, which may harbour bacteria. If you want to use the marinade as a dip or sauce, reserve a portion before adding raw food.

COOKING

Guidelines for Cooking Fish

Cooked to perfection, fish is at its flavourful best and will be moist, tender and have a delicate flavour. In general, fish is cooked when its meat just begins to flake easily when tested with a fork and it loses its translucent or raw appearance.

Like most foods, fish should be thoroughly cooked. The U.S. Food and Drug Administration (FDA) suggests cooking fish until it reaches an internal temperature of 145 °F. One helpful guideline is the 10-minute rule for cooking fish. Apply it when baking, broiling, grilling, steaming and poaching fillets, steaks or whole fish. Practice makes perfect and cooking fish properly is all in the timing.

Here's how to use the 10-minute rule:

- Measure the seafood product at its thickest point. If the fish is stuffed or rolled, measure it after stuffing or rolling.
- At 450 °F bake for 10 minutes per inch thickness of the fish, turning the fish halfway through the cooking time. For example, a 1-inch fish steak should be cooked 5 minutes on each side for a total of 10 minutes. Pieces of fish less than half an inch thick do not have to be turned over.
- Add 5 minutes to the total cooking time if you are cooking the fish in foil or if the fish is cooked in a sauce.
- Double the cooking time for frozen fish that has not been defrosted.

Fish is the original "fast food." It cooks quickly, within minutes, because it lacks the connective tissue of red meats and poultry. Some of the best cooking methods for fish include poaching, broiling, grilling, baking and microwaving because they bring out flavour without adding fat.

Baking

Whole fish, whole stuffed fish, fillets, stuffed fillets, steaks and chunks of fish may be baked. Use pieces of similar size for even cooking. It's best to bake fish in a preheated, 450 °F oven following the 10-minute rule; bake uncovered, basting if desired.

Broiling

Steaks, whole fish, split whole fish and fillets lend themselves well to broiling. Place fish, 1-inch thick or less, 2 to 4 inches from the heat source. Place thicker pieces 5 to 6 inches away.

Baste frequently with an oil-based marinade. Using the 10-minute rule, cook on one side for half the total cooking time, basting once or twice, then turn the fish over to continue broiling and basting.

Grilling

This technique lends itself well to thick steak fish such as salmon, halibut, swordfish, tuna and whole fish. Preheat an outdoor gas or electric grill. If using a barbecue grill, start the fire about 30 minutes before cooking. Let it burn until white-hot then spread coals out in a single layer. Adjust the grill height to 4 to 6 inches above the heat. To grill fish, a moderately hot fire is best for cooking seafood.

Always start with a well-oiled grid to prevent the delicate skin of the fish from sticking. Support more delicate pieces of fish in a hinged, fish-shaped wire basket for easier turning or handling. Frequently baste steaks and fillets while grilling to prevent them from drying out.

Marinating fish an hour before grilling also helps keep it moist. Apply the 10-minute rule for proper doneness. Use indirect heat for whole fish by banking hot coals on either side of the barbecue or preheat gas or electric grill. Oil fish well and place in an oiled fish basket. Cook fish covered, 10 to 12 minutes per inch of thickness, turning halfway through cooking time.

Microwaving

Use a shallow dish to allow maximum exposure to the microwaves. Arrange fillets with the thicker parts pointing outward and the thinner parts, separated by pieces of plastic wrap, overlapping in the center of the dish. Cover dish with plastic wrap and vent by turning back one corner. Allow 3 minutes per pound of boneless fish cooked on high as a guide. Rotate the dish halfway through the cooking time. Rolled fillets microwave more evenly and are less likely to overcook than flat fillets, which may have thin edges.

SAFE HANDLING OF LAMB

SELECTING THE BEST

Fresh is Best

Select lamb that is pinkish red with a velvety texture. Dark red cuts generally indicate the meat is older and less tender.

Look for good marbling, and meat that is fine textured and firm:

- Look for packages that are cool to the touch and have no wear or punctures.
- Always remember to select meat just before checking out at the supermarket register.
- Make sure all meats, whether raw, pre-packaged or from the deli are refrigerated when purchased.
- Prevent "cross-contamination" by keeping fresh meats separate from other items. Put raw meat packages in a plastic bag so juices won't drip onto other foods.

- Pack raw meats in an ice chest if it will take more than an hour to get home. Keep ice chest in the passenger area of the car during warm weather.
- Take meats straight home to the refrigerator or freezer.

Product Dating

Product dating, applying "sell by" or "use by" dates, is not required by federal regulations.

However, many stores and processors may voluntarily choose to date packages of raw lamb.

Use or freeze products with a "sell by" date within three to five days of purchase.

If the manufacturer has determined a "use by" date, observe it. It's always best to buy a product before its date expires.

It's not important if a date expires after freezing lamb because all foods stay safe while properly frozen.

Product Inspection and Grading

All lamb found in retail stores is either USDA-inspected for wholesomeness or inspected by state systems which have standards equal to the federal government. Each animal and its internal organs are inspected for signs of disease.

The "Passed and Inspected by USDA" seal ensures that the lamb is wholesome and free from disease.

Although inspection is mandatory, its grading for quality is voluntary, and a plant pays to have its lamb graded.

USDA Lamb Quality Grades are based upon palatability-indicating characteristics of the lean and carcass conformation.

Conformation has no direct influence upon the eating quality. For lamb and yearling mutton the quality grades are Prime, Choice, Good and Utility.

Table. Safe Handling of Lamb in Cold Storage.

Food	Refrigerator (40 ºF)	Freezer (0 ºF)
Fresh Lamb		
Roast	3-5 Days	6-9 Months
Steak/Chops	3-5 Days	6-9 Months
Ground/Stew Meat	1-2 Days	3-4 Months
Cooked Lamb		
Roast	3-4 Days	2-3 Months
Steak/Chops	3-4 Days	2-3 Months
Ground/Stew Meat	1-2 Days	2-3 Months

STORING

Refrigeration

Packaged whole cuts of fresh lamb may be refrigerated in their original wrapping in the coldest part of the refrigerator up to four or five days after purchase. Ground lamb can be stored in the refrigerator for up to two days; cooked lamb is at its best refrigerated no longer than four days.

- Use an appliance thermometer and maintain a temperature of 34 to 38 °F.
- Never leave meat in a hot car or sitting out at room temperature. Refrigerate or freeze fresh lamb Immediately afer bringing it home.
- Store uncooked lamb items together, separate from cooked foods. Make sure the raw juices do not drip onto other foods.
- Keep lamb refrigerated until you are ready to cook it.
- When transporting uncooked or cooked lamb to another dining site, place it in an insulated container or ice chest until ready to cook or eat.

Freezing

Freeze whole cuts of fresh lamb if you do not plan to cook it within four days after purchase. Wrap whole cuts of lamb separately in heavy-duty foil or moisture- and vapour-proof freezer bags or wrap before freezing. Label for ease in selecting just the right number of cuts to thaw for a single meal. Be sure to press the air out of the package before freezing. If you plan to freeze lamb in its original wrapping, overwrap the porous store plastic with freezer bag or paper. Cooked lamb cuts may be frozen in the same way as fresh, unless made with a sauce or gravy. In that case, pack the meat in a rigid container with a tight-fitting lid.

PREPARATION

Cleanliness

- Always wash hands thoroughly with hot, soapy water before preparing foods and after handling raw meat.
- Don't let raw meat or juices touch ready-to-eat foods either in the refrigerator or during preparation.
- Don't put cooked foods on the same plate that held raw lamb.
- Always wash utensils that have touched raw meat with hot, soapy water before using them for cooked meats.
- Wash counters, cutting boards and other surfaces raw meats have touched.

Thawing

Thaw uncooked lamb in the refrigerator or in cold water. Never thaw meat at room temperature. Thawing by refrigeration requires planning ahead, most likely allowing a 24-hour thawing period. After defrosting raw lamb by this method, it will be safe in the refrigerator up to five days before cooking. During this time, if you decide not to use the lamb, you can safely refreeze it without cooking it first. To thaw lamb in cold water, leave the meat in its original wrapping or place it in a watertight plastic bag. Change the water every 30 minutes. For quick thawing of uncooked or cooked lamb, use the microwave, but plan on cooking the meat immediately after thawing because some areas of the food may become warm and begin to cook during microwaving. Thawing time will vary according to whether you're thawing a whole roast or cuts and the number of parts frozen together. Use the Defrost or Medium-Low setting, according to the manufacturer's directions. Turn the roast and separate parts as they thaw, taking care the meat does not begin to cook. Repeat as needed. Foods defrosted by the cold water method or in the microwave should be cooked before refreezing because they may have been held at temperatures above 40 °F.

Marinating

Marinate food in the refrigerator, not on the counter. Discard the marinade after use because it contains raw juices, which may harbour bacteria. If you want to use the marinade as a dip or sauce, reserve a portion before adding raw food.

Partial Cooking or Browning

Never brown or partially cook lamb, then refrigerate and finish cooking later, because any bacteria present would not have been destroyed. It is safe to partially pre-cook or microwave lamb immediately before transferring it to the hot grill or oven to finish cooking.

COOKING

Importance of Kitchen Thermometers

One of the critical factors in controlling bacteria in food is controlling temperature. Pathogenic microorganisms grow very slowly at low temperatures, multiply rapidly in mid-range temperatures and are killed at high temperatures. For safety, foods must be cooked thoroughly. It is essential to use a thermometer when cooking meat and poultry to prevent undercooking and, consequently, prevent food borne illness. Using a thermometer is the only reliable way to ensure safety and to determine the "doneness" of most foods. To be safe, a product must be cooked to an internal temperature high enough to destroy any harmful bacteria that may have been in the food. Recent research has shown that colour and texture indicators are not reliable.

Cooking the Meat

For safety, the USDA recommends cooking ground lamb patties and other ground mixtures to 160 °F. Whole muscle meats such as chops and roasts should be cooked to 145 °F, 160 °F or 170 °F. Remember that appliances and outdoor grills can vary in heat. Use a meat thermometer to check for safe cooking and doneness of lamb.

Cooked muscle meats can be pink even when the meat has reached a safe internal temperature. If fresh lamb has reached 160 °F throughout, even though it may still be pink in the center, it should be safe. The pink colour can be due to the cooking method or added ingredients. For approximate cooking times of lamb refer to Table.

Table. Approximate* Lamb Cooking Times (°F).

Cuts of Lamb	**Size**	**Cooking Methods**	**Cooking Times**	**Internal Temperature**
Lamb leg, bone in	5 to 7 lbs.	Roast 325 ºF	20 to 25 min./lb. 25 to 30 min./lb. 30 to 35 min./lb.	Medium-rare 145 °F Medium 160 °F Well-done 170 °F
Lamb leg, bone in	7 to 9 lbs.	Roast 325 ºF	15 to 20 min./lb. 20 to 25 min./lb. 25 to 30 min./lb.	Medium-rare 145 °F Medium 160 °F Well-done 170 °F
Lamb leg, boneless, rolled	4 to 7 lbs.	Roast 325 ºF	25 to 30 min./lb. 30 to 35 min./lb. 35 to 40 min./lb.	Medium-rare 145 °F Medium 160 °F Well-done 170 °F
Shoulder roast or Shank leg half	3 to 4 lbs.	Roast 325 ºF	30 to 35 min./lb. 40 to 45 min./lb.	Medium-rare 145 °F Medium160 °F
	45 to 50	Well-done 170 °F	min./lb.	
Cubes, for kabobs	1 to 1 ½″	Broil/grill	8 to 12 minutes	Medium 160 °F
Ground lamb patties	2" thick	Broil/grill	5 to 8 minutes	Medium 160 °F
Chops. rib or loin	1½″ to 1" thick	Broil/grill	7 to 11 minutes 15 to 19 minutes	Medium-rare 145 °F Medium 160 °F
Leg steaks	¾″ thick	Broil/grill 4"	14 to 18	Medium-rare

		From heat	minutes	145 °F Medium 160 °F
Stew meat, pieces Shanks	1 to 1½″ ¾ to 1 lb.	Cover with liquid; simmer	1½ to 2 hours	Medium 160 °F
Breast, rolled	1½ to 2 lb.	*Braise 325 °F	1½ to 2 hours	Medium 160 °F

Notes:

* Use a meat thermometer to check for proper doneness.

** Braising is roasting or simmering less-tender meat with a small amount of liquid in a tightly covered pan.

Microwaving

When microwaving unequal sizes of lamb, arrange in a dish or on a rack so thick parts are towards the outside of the dish and thin parts are in the center, and cook on medium-high or medium power. Place a roast in an oven-cooking bag or in a covered pot. Refer to the manufacturer's directions that accompany the microwave oven for suggested cooking times. Use a meat thermometer to test for doneness in several places to be sure the proper temperature.

SERVING

- Wash hands with soap and water before serving or eating food.
- Serve cooked products on clean plates with clean utensils and clean hands.
- Never put cooked foods on a dish that has held raw lamb unless the dish is washed with soap and hot water.
- Hold hot foods above 140 °F and cold foods below 40 °F.
- Never leave foods, raw or cooked, at room temperature longer than two hours. On a hot day with temperatures at 90 °F or warmer, this decreases to one hour.

SAFE HANDLING OF MILK AND DAIRY PRODUCTS

MILK

Grade A milk is carefully produced, processed and packaged in order to protect the safety of the consumer. Grade A milk must be pasteurized to be sold by retailers in interstate commerce. Raw milk is usually pasteurized either by low temperature pasteurization in which the milk is heated to 145 °F or higher for at least 30 minutes, or by high temperature pasteurization in which the milk is heated to 161 °F or higher for at least 15 seconds and then quickly cooled. Pasteurization destroys disease-causing bacteria and extends the shelf life of milk. However, pasteurized milk can readily spoil and could cause food borne illness if not properly protected and handled.

Maintaining the Safety of Milk

Refrigeration is the single most important factor in maintaining the safety of milk. By law, Grade A milk must be maintained at a temperature of 45 °F or below. Bacteria in milk will grow minimally below 45 °F. However, temperatures well below 40 °F are necessary to protect the milk's quality. It is critical that these temperatures be maintained through warehousing, distribution, delivery and storage. The cooler refrigerated milk is kept, the longer it lasts and the safer it is. As the product is allowed to warm, the bacteria grow more rapidly. Properly refrigerated, milk can withstand about two weeks' storage. Infants, pregnant women, the elderly and the chronically ill are most at risk from serious illness due to eating any unsafe food. These individuals and those who care for them must be especially careful to handle milk safely.

Fresh Fluid Milk

Fresh milk is categorized mainly by the amount of butterfat it contains. In November 1997, the FDA announced a new rule for milk labeling that helps consumers clarify the difference between 1-and 2-per cent milk and reinforces the fact that skim milk is fat-free. Under the new rule, 2-per cent milk is renamed reduced fat; 1-per cent milk is renamed low-fat; and skim milk is called fat-free or nonfat, although it may contain up to 0.5 grams of fat in a one cup serving.

Buying Fresh Fluid Milk

When selecting milk at the store, make sure it is properly displayed and pay close attention to the date on the label. All fresh fluid milks should be stored at temperatures below 40 °F and should not be stacked high in the display cases. If stored above 40 °F, milk will begin to develop signs of spoilage, including sour odour, off-flavour and curdled consistency. Remember that milk should be taken from the store and quickly placed in your refrigerator at home so that the temperature does not rise above 40 °F. Once you have purchased milk and refrigerated it promptly, it should retain its fresh taste for one to five days beyond the "sell-by" date if kept at the proper temperature. If it spoils before the date expires, this indicates it was not handled properly, and it should be returned to the store for a refund.

Storing Fresh Fluid Milk

Milk should not be left out at room temperature. Pour milk to be used into a serving container and return the original container to the refrigerator. Do not return unused milk that has been sitting out to its original container where it could contaminate the remaining milk. Milk can be stored frozen at 0 °F for up to three months and will be safe to drink if it is thawed in the refrigerator, although it does not retain its smooth texture.

Buttermilk

Originally, buttermilk was made as a by-product when making butter. Lactic acid bacteria are added to fresh, fluid pasteurized skim or part-skim milk to produce the thick, tangy buttermilk.

Buttermilk should be handled with the same precautions as regular fluid milk.

Flavoured Milk

Chocolate and other flavours-such as maple, strawberry and coffee-may be used for flavoured milks. These milks are stored and used as fresh fluid milk.

CONCENTRATED OR DRIED MILKS

Evaporated and Evaporated Skimmed Milk

This type of milk has about 60 per cent of the water removed. It may be fortified with vitamins A and/or D. Store cans of evaporated milk in a cool, dry place.

It is shelf-stable, but once opened it should be treated as fresh fluid milk, kept refrigerated and used within several days.

Sweetened Condensed Milk

This is the milk that results from the evaporation of half the water and the addition of sugar in amounts sufficient for preservation. It is stored like evaporated milk.

UHT Milk

Ultra-high temperature (UHT) milk is regular fluid milk that is packed in an airtight, sterilized, cardboard container. The product is treated by flash sterilization at 290 °F. This high temperature kills all bacteria or microorganisms.

The milk is then packed into sterilized containers and is shelf-stable for six months.

After six months, the flavour and colour begin to change and the product thickens. It is still safe, but may not produce the desired effect in a recipe. Once the package of UHT milk is opened, it is treated like fresh fluid milk and used within several days.

Nonfat Dry Milk

This dairy product is made by removing water from pasteurized, fat-free milk. Due to its low moisture content, it can be kept for long periods of time. Once reconstituted, it is handled like fresh fluid milk.

CREAM

Basic Facts

Cream has a very high fat content of between 18 and 40 per cent butterfat compared to around 3.25 per cent in whole milk. The rich, yellow colour associated with cream comes from the carotene in the fat.

The type of cream is determined by its fat content:

- Half-and-half is a combination of milk and cream with a butterfat content of about 11 per cent.
- Light cream has between 18 and 30 per cent butterfat and may be called coffee or table cream.
- Light whipping cream has between 30 and 36 per cent butterfat and can be whipped into solid form, although it tends to be less stable than heavy whipping cream.
- Heavy cream or whipping cream contains 36 to 40 per cent butterfat.
- Pressurized whipped cream is sold in aerosol cans and is made from a mixture of cream, sugar and chemical stabilizers.
- Sour cream is made by adding a lactic acid culture to sweet cream. Sour cream usually contains between 18 and 20 per cent butterfat.
- Reduced-fat sour cream has skim milk added to lower the fat content.

Storage

Store cream at 40 °F or below in its original container in the refrigerator. Do not leave cream at room temperature, and do not mix warm cream with cream that has been kept refrigerated. Use fresh, pasteurized cream within one to five days of the "sell-by" date.

NONDAIRY DESSERT TOPPINGS

Nondairy dessert toppings are made from vegetable oils but may also contain some milk products. The frozen toppings may be stored for up to one year in the freezer, or thawed and kept in the refrigerator for up to two weeks. Do not freeze dessert toppings in aerosol cans. Store the cans in the refrigerator for a maximum of two to three months.

BUTTER

Basic Facts

Butter is made from the sweet or soured cream of cow's milk by agitation or "churning." After churning, the mass of butter is washed and salted. It is worked to distribute the salt and remove extra water. To be sold in stores, butter must contain at least 80 per cent milk fat. Water and milk solids make up the other 20 per cent. Salt and colouring may be added if desired. Some unsalted butter is sold as sweet butter, but most people prefer the salted product. The USDA grade label on the butter carton or wrapper means the butter has been tested for quality by a government grader and has been produced under sanitary conditions. The highest possible grade is AA. Grade AA butter is delicate and sweet-flavoured with a creamy texture and good spreadability. Most butter sold is grade AA or A. Because of its high fat content, butter contains many calories and therefore should be used sparingly in the diet.

Storage

Storing butter properly, lengthens the shelf life so it can be used over a longer period of time. To prevent a type of spoilage called rancidity, protect butter from heat, light and air by storing it covered in the refrigerator. Rancid butter has an unpleasant taste and smell. Butter absorbs odours from other foods rapidly. To prevent flavour changes, keep butter wrapped in moisture- and vapour-proof material or in tightly covered containers. For refrigerator storage, leave butter in its original wrapper. Opened portions of butter should be refrigerated in a covered dish. Butter can be stored for up to two weeks at refrigerator temperatures.

Higher temperatures cause off-flavours and unpleasant odours to develop. Butter should not be stored in the butter keeper on the refrigerator door longer than two days. For ease in spreading, remove butter from the refrigerator 10 to 15 minutes before using it. For holding longer than two weeks, butter should be frozen.

To store butter in the freezer, wrap it in moisture-and vapour-proof freezer packaging material to keep the butter from absorbing odours from other foods and to prevent freezer burn. Butter in its original carton can be overwrapped. Butter in one-pound blocks can be cut into smaller portions, repackaged and frozen for future use. If properly wrapped and held at 0 °F or lower, butter will keep well in the freezer for six to nine months. Thaw butter in the refrigerator.

YOGURT

Basic Facts

The natural sugar in milk is converted to lactic acid by means of a bacterial culture producing the creamy, pleasantly tart yogurt. Yogurt is pasteurized to destroy disease-causing microorganisms. Fat and calorie content will differ depending on whether whole, low-fat or fat-free milk is used and whether fruit or sweeteners are added. The label will give the specific information for each yogurt.

Storage

Yogurt may be kept well covered in the refrigerator for seven to 10 days past the "sell-by" date. If it is kept longer, it will develop a stronger taste. Freezing yogurt is not recommended because of the variable results in texture.

FROZEN DAIRY PRODUCTS

Basic Facts

This category includes ice cream, ice milk, sherbet and frozen yogurt:

- Ice cream has the highest milk fat and milk solids content. The milk fat content in ice cream usually ranges between 10 and 14 per cent, but may be as high as 20 per cent in specialty ice creams.
- Ice milk often has more sugar than ice cream, but its milk fat ranges from 2 to 7 per cent.
- Sherbet also has less milk fat and milk solids than ice cream, but more sugar and usually contains fruit and fruit acid. Milk fat content of sherbet is between 1 and 2 per cent.
- Frozen yogurt is made from cultured milk and has less milk fat than ice cream and less sugar than sherbet.

Storage

When purchasing ice cream and other frozen desserts at the store, make sure they are frozen solid and that the container is not sticky or frosted which indicates it has partially thawed at some point. Request that the ice cream be placed in an insulated bag or be double bagged to reduce melting on the way home. Ice cream may be stored unopened for up to two months at 0 °F or below. However, if it will be stored longer than one month, it is best to overwrap the original container with freezer paper or wrap.

Table. Safe Cold Storage Times for Milk and Dairy Products.

Product	How to Store	Refrigerator (35-40 °F)	Freezer (0 °F)
Pasteurized Fresh Whole or Skimmed Milk	Refrigerate immediately in original container. Keep container closed.	1 to 5 days beyond "sell-by" date	3 months. Freezing may result in change in texture. Thaw in refrigerator.
Sweetened Condensed Milk(Opened)	Refrigerate tightly covered.	1 week	Do not freeze.
Evaporated Milk (Opened)	Refrigerate tightly covered.	1 week	Do not freeze.
Cultured Buttermilk	Refrigerate immediately in original container. Keep container closed.	2 weeks	Do not freeze.
Homogenized, Reconstituted Dry Nonfat and Skimmed Milk	Keep containers tightly closed. Don't return unused milk to original containers.	1 week	Do not freeze.
Sweet and Regular Cream	Refrigerate immediately in original container. Keep container closed.	1 to 5 days beyond "sell-by" date	Do not freeze. (Change of texture, body appearance. Separation of fat emulsion.)

Once the container has been opened, place plastic wrap over the surface of the ice cream to minimize the development of large ice crystals and the loss of its creamy texture. Use ice cream within seven to 10 days for best quality. Each time the ice cream is removed from the freezer, and the surface begins to thaw, the ice cream loses quality. If ice cream or other frozen dairy products thaw completely, they should be discarded because of the danger of bacterial growth.

Non-Dairy Whipped Topping	Keep covered.	3 months in aerosol can. 3 days if prepared from mix. 2 weeks if bought frozen and then thawed.	Do not freeze aerosol cans; others may be stored in freezer up to one year.
Butter	Refrigerate immediately in original container. Keep container closed.	2 weeks	Butter made from pasteurized cream: 6 to 9 months.
Sour Cream	Refrigerate immediately in original container. Keep container closed.	2 weeks	Do not freeze.
Ice Cream	Store in original container in freezer.	Do not store here.	2-3 weeks (Opened) 2 Months (Unopened)
Yogurt	Keep covered.	7-10 days	Do not freeze.
Soft Custards, Milk Puddings, Cream and	Cool cooked dishes quickly and refrigerate	5-6 days	Do not freeze.

SAFE HANDLING OF PORK

SELECTING THE BEST

Fresh is Best

When buying pork, look for cuts with a relatively small amount of fat over the outside and with meat that is firm and a grayish-pink colour. For best flavour and tenderness, meat should have a small amount of marbling. Look for packages that are cool to the touch and have no wear or punctures.

Always remember to select meat just before checking out at the supermarket register. Make sure all meats, whether raw, pre-packaged or from the deli are refrigerated when purchased. Fresh meats may contaminate other grocery items. The best way to prevent this "cross-contamination" is to always keep fresh meats separate from other items. Put raw meat packages in a plastic bag so juices won't drip onto other foods. Pack raw meats in an ice chest if it will take more than an hour to get home. Keep ice chest in the passenger area of the car during warm weather. Take meats straight home to the refrigerator or freezer.

Product Dating

Product dating, applying "sell-by" or "use-by" dates, is not required by federal regulations. However, many stores and processors may voluntarily choose to date packages of raw pork. Use or freeze products with a "sell-by" date within three to five days of purchase. If the manufacturer has determined a "use-by" date, observe it. It's always best to buy a product before its date expires. It's not important if a date expires after freezing pork because all foods stay safe while properly frozen.

Product Inspection and Grading

All pork found in retail stores is either USDA-inspected for wholesomeness or inspected by state systems which have standards equal to the federal government. Each animal and its internal organs are inspected for signs of disease.

The "Passed and Inspected by USDA" seal ensures that the pork is wholesome and free from disease. Although inspection is mandatory, its grading for quality is voluntary, and a plant pays to have its pork graded. USDA grades for pork reflect only two levels, "Acceptable" grade and "Utility" grade. Pork sold as "Acceptable" quality is the only fresh pork sold in supermarkets. It should have a high proportion of lean meat to fat and bone. Pork graded as "Utility" is mainly used in processed products and is not available in supermarkets for consumers to purchase.

STORING

Refrigeration

Keep pork below 40 °F during storage. Store uncooked pork items together, separate from cooked foods. Refrigerate or freeze fresh pork Immediately after bringing it home. Never leave meat in a hot car or sitting out at room temperature.

Packaged whole cuts of fresh pork may be refrigerated in their original wrapping in the coldest part of the refrigerator up to four or five days after purchase, while ground pork can be stored in the refrigerator for up to two days. Keep pork refrigerated until you are ready to cook it. When transporting uncooked or cooked pork to another dining site, place it in an insulated container or ice chest until ready to cook or eat. Cooked pork is at its best when refrigerated no longer than four days.

Table. Safe Handling of Pork in Cold Storage.

Food	Refrigerator (40 °F)	Freezer (0 °F)
Fresh Pork:		
Roast, chops or ribs	3-5 Days	4-6 Months
Ground pork, liver or variety meats	1-2 Days	3-4 Months

Ham (Uncured)	3-5 Days	4-6 Months
Ham (Cured)	5-7 Days	3-4 Months
Cooked Pork:		
Roast, chops, casseroles	3-4 Days	2-3 Months
Ground pork; store-cooked convenience meals	1-2 Days	2-3 Months
Ham (Uncured)	3-4 Days	3-4 Months
Ham (Cured)	3-5 Days	1-2 Months

Freezing

Freeze whole cuts of fresh pork if you do not plan to cook it within four days after purchase. Wrap whole cuts of pork separately in foil or freezer bags before freezing, and label for ease in selecting just the right number of cuts to thaw for a single meal. Be sure to press the air out of the package before freezing. If you plan to freeze pork in its original wrapping, overwrap the porous store plastic with freezer bag or paper. Cooked pork cuts may be frozen in the same way as fresh, unless made with a sauce or gravy. In that case, pack the meat in a rigid container with a tight-fitting lid.

PREPARATION

Cleanliness

Always wash hands thoroughly with hot, soapy water before preparing foods and after handling raw meat. Don't let raw meat or juices touch ready-to-go foods either in the refrigerator or during preparation. Don't put cooked foods on the same plate that held raw pork. Always wash utensils that have touched raw meat with hot, soapy water before using them for cooked meats. Wash counters, cutting boards and other surfaces raw meats have touched.

Thawing

Thaw uncooked pork in the refrigerator, in cold water or in the microwave oven. Never thaw meat at room temperature. Allow a 24-hour thawing period in the refrigerator. After defrosting raw pork by this method, it will be safe in the refrigerator up to five days before cooking or, if you decide not to use the pork, you can safely refreeze it without cooking it first. To thaw pork in cold water, leave the meat in its original wrapping or place it in a watertight plastic bag. Change the water every 30 minutes.

To thaw pork in the microwave, plan on cooking the meat immediately after thawing because some areas of the food may become warm and begin to cook during microwaving, and any bacteria present wouldn't have been destroyed. Thawing time will vary according to whether you're thawing a whole roast or cuts and the number of parts frozen together. Use the Defrost or Medium-Low setting, according to the manufacturer's directions. Turn the roast and separate parts as they thaw, taking care the meat does not begin to cook Foods defrosted by the cold water method or in the microwave should be cooked before refreezing because they potentially may have been held at temperatures above 40 °F. It is safe to cook frozen pork in the oven, or on the stove or grill without defrosting. Estimate one-third to one-half more cooking time depending upon the size of the meat. Broil frozen pork farther away from the heat source; preheat the skillet when pan-frying or pan-broiling. Do not cook frozen pork in a slow cooker.

Marinating

Marinate food in the refrigerator, not on the counter. Discard the marinade after use because it contains raw juices, which may harbour bacteria. If you want to use the marinade as a dip or sauce, reserve a portion before adding raw food, or boil used marinade before brushing on cooked pork.

Partial Cooking or Browning

Never brown or partially cook pork, then refrigerate and finish cooking later, because any bacteria present would not have been destroyed. It is safe to partially pre-cook or microwave pork and lamb immediately before transferring it to the hot grill or oven to finish cooking.

COOKING

Importance of Kitchen Thermometers

One of the critical factors in controlling bacteria in food is controlling temperature. Pathogenic microorganisms grow very slowly at low temperatures, multiply rapidly in mid-range temperatures, and are killed at high temperatures. For safety, foods must be cooked thoroughly. It is essential to use a thermometer when cooking meat and poultry to prevent undercooking and, consequently, prevent food borne illness. Using a thermometer is the only reliable way to ensure safety and to determine the "doneness" of most foods. To be safe, a product must be cooked to an internal temperature high enough to destroy any harmful bacteria that may have been in the food. Recent research has shown that colour and texture indicators are not reliable. It isn't necessary to rinse raw pork before cooking it. Any bacteria which might be present on the surface would be destroyed by cooking.

Cooking the Meat

For safety, FDA recommends cooking ground pork patties and other ground mixtures to 155 °F. Cook whole muscle meats such as chops and roasts, and fresh cured ham to 145 °F with a 4 minute rest before carving or eating, 160 °F, or 170 °F. Remember that appliances and outdoor grills can vary in heat. Use a meat thermometer to check for safe cooking and doneness of pork. Cooked muscle meats can be pink even when the meat has reached a safe internal temperature. If fresh pork has reached 145 °F throughout, and is given a 4 minute rest, even though it may still be pink in the center, it will be safe. The pink colour can be due to the cooking method or added ingredients. For approximate cooking times of pork.

Table. Fresh Pork: Safe Cooking Chart.

Internal temperature of safely cooked whole cuts of pork should reach at least 145 °F when measured with thermometer, followed by a 4 minute rest before carving or eating.

Roasting Set oven at 350 °F. Roast in a shallow pan, uncovered. Internal temperature: 145 °F (medium-rare) with a 4 minute rest, 160 °F (medium), 170 °F (well-done).

Cut Weight	Thickness or Time	Cooking
Loin Roast, bone-in or boneless	2 to 5 pounds per pound	20 to 30 min.
Crown Roast	4 to 6 pounds per pound	20 to 30 min.
Leg, (Fresh Ham) whole, bone-in	12 to 16 pounds	22 to 26 min. per pound
Leg, (Fresh Ham) half, bone in	5 to 8 pounds per pound	35 to 40 min.
Boston Butt	3 to 6 pounds per pound	45 min.
Tenderloin (Roast at 425-450 °F) minutes total	½ to 1½ pounds	20 to 30
Ribs (Back Country-style or Spareribs)	2 to 4 pounds (or until fork tender)	1½ to 2 hours
Broiling (4 inches from heat) or Grilling		
Loin Chops, bone-in or boneless	¾ inch or 1½ inch 12 to 16 min.	6 to 8 min. or
Tenderloin	½ to 1½ pounds	15 to 25 min.
Ribs (indirect heat), all types	2 to 4 pounds	1½ to 2 hours
Ground Pork Patties (direct heat) minutes—155 °F temperature	½ inch minimum for all ground	8 to 10 internal meats
In Skillet on Stove		
Loin Chops or Cutlets	¼ inch or ¾ inch 7 to 8 min.	3 to 4 min. or
Tenderloin Medallions	¼ to ½ inch	4 to 8 minutes
Ground Pork Patties minutes	½ inch	8 to 10
Braising: Cover and Simmer with a Liquid.		
Chops, Cutlets, Cubes, Medallions minutes	¼ to 1-inch	10 to 25
Boston Butt, Boneless	3 to 6 pounds	2 to 2½ hours

Ribs, all types	2 to 4 pounds	1½ to 2 hours
Stewing: Cover Pan, Simmer, Covered with Liquid.		
Rib, all types	2 to 4 pounds	2 to 2½ hours, or until tender
Cubes	1 inch minutes	45 to 60

Microwaving

When microwaving unequal sizes of pork, arrange in a dish or on a rack so thick parts are towards the outside of dish and thin parts are in the center, and cook on medium-high or medium power.

Place a roast in an oven-cooking bag or in a covered pot. Refer to the manufacturer's directions that accompany the microwave oven for suggested cooking times. Use a microwave-safe thermometer inserted before cooking, or remove meat from microwave and use a digital meat thermometer, to test for doneness in several places to be sure correct temperatures have been reached.

SAFE HANDLING OF POULTRY

SELECTING THE BEST

Fresh poultry—chicken, turkey, duck and goose—is defined by the USDA as poultry that has never been below 26 °F.

When held at temperatures ranging from 26 to 40 °F, there is minimal ice crystal formation and poultry meat is still soft and pliable. There should be no detectable odour.

The surface should not be slick nor have a shiny appearance, and should not have colour defects:

- Look for packages that are cool to the touch and have no tears, punctures, torn or missing labels.
- Always remember to select poultry just before checking out at the register.
- Make sure all poultry, whether raw, prepackaged or from the deli is refrigerated before and after it is purchased.
- Prevent cross-contamination by keeping fresh meats separate from other items. Put raw poultry packages in a plastic bag so "juices" won't drip onto other foods. If raw poultry "juices" do drip on other foods, it is best to throw these other items out and immediately wash surfaces and hands.
- Pack raw poultry in an ice chest if it will take you more than an hour to get home and keep the ice chest in the passenger area of the car during warm weather.
- Take poultry straight home to the refrigerator or freezer.

Dating of Poultry Products

Product dating is not required by federal regulations. However, many stores and processors may voluntarily date packages of poultry or poultry products. If a calendar date is shown, there must be a phrase explaining the meaning of the date. Consumers should use or freeze poultry products within one or two days of purchase.

If the manufacturer has determined a "use-by" date, observe it for peak quality and freshness.

It 's always best to buy a product before its date expires. If a date expires after the poultry is frozen, the food can still be used. However, quality begins to deteriorate after one year of frozen storage for whole poultry and nine months of frozen storage for poultry parts.

Product Inspection and Grading

All poultry found in retail stores is either USDA-inspected for wholesomeness and safety, or inspected by state systems using standards equal to the federal government.

Prior to entering the processing plant, live birds are inspected for signs of disease. Diseased birds are immediately condemned and do not enter the processing plant.

In the plant, each animal and its internal organs are again inspected for signs of disease. The "Passed and Inspected by USDA" seal ensures that the poultry is wholesome and free from disease.

Inspection is mandatory, but grading for quality is voluntary. Poultry are graded according to USDA regulations and standards for meatiness, appearance and freedom from defects. Grade A chickens, the best grade, have plump, meaty bodies and clean skin, free of bruises, broken bones, feathers, cuts and discolouration.

Prestuffed Poultry

Buying retail-stuffed whole poultry is not recommended because of the highly perishable nature of a previously stuffed item. Some USDA-inspected frozen stuffed poultry MUST be cooked from the frozen state to ensure a safely cooked product.

Many frozen entrées containing stuffed boneless poultry products may appear to be pre-cooked or browned, but they are NOT ready-to-eat and must be fully cooked by the consumer. If the label states "Cook and Serve," "Ready to Cook," or "Oven Ready" this indicates that the product is raw and must be fully cooked by the consumer.

The safest way to cook these products is in a conventional oven. If a microwave oven is used, these poultry products should be covered to allow steam to build, and then allowed to stand for the recommended time to ensure that there are no "cold spots". Check the internal temperature in several places to make sure the product has been cooked throughout to at least 165 °F

COOKING

Importance of Kitchen Thermometers

One of the critical factors for minimizing bacteria in food is controlling temperature. Most pathogenic microorganisms grow very slowly at low temperatures, multiply rapidly in mid-range temperatures and are killed at high temperatures. For safety, foods must be cooked thoroughly. It is essential to use a thermometer when cooking meat and poultry to prevent undercooking and food borne illness.

Using a thermometer is the only reliable way to ensure safety and to determine the "doneness" of most foods. To be safe, a product must be cooked to an internal temperature high enough to destroy any harmful bacteria that may have been in the food. Colour and texture changes in meat and poultry cannot be relied on to determine that foods have been safely cooked to destroy all bacteria.

All poultry and all stuffing, whether cooked alone or in the bird, must be cooked to an internal temperature of at least 165 °F. For reasons of personal taste or texture preferences, consumers may choose to cook poultry to higher temperatures.

When cooking whole turkey, the thermometer should be inserted into the thickest part of the thigh, without touching the bone. For chicken, and other smaller poultry, insert the thermometer in the thickest part of the breast. If stuffed, the center of the stuffing should be checked after the thigh or breast reaches 165 °F. If cooking poultry parts, insert the thermometer into the thickest area, avoiding the bone.

The thermometer may be inserted sideways if necessary. When the food being cooked is irregularly shaped, the temperature should be checked in several places.

Sometimes consumers will notice a pink colour in fully-cooked poultry. Commercial marinades may have a small amount of nitrites or nitrates which gives poultry a pink colour even when it is fully cooked.

Ground Chicken or Turkey

Ground meats must be cooked thoroughly to kill harmful bacteria. Unlike whole muscle meat, whose interior meat is sterile, the grinding process exposes the interior meat in ground poultry to bacteria, which may be on the surface, in the air, on equipment or on people's hands. To kill bacteria, food safety experts have one major rule of thumb: Cook ground poultry to at least 165 °F. This step, while very simple, offers the best protection that consumers can have for serving ground poultry products safely.

SERVING

Wash hands with soap and water before serving or eating food:

- Serve cooked products on clean plates with clean utensils and clean hands. Never put cooked foods on a dish that has held raw poultry unless the dish is washed with soap and hot water.
- Hold hot foods above 140 °F and cold foods below 40 °F.
- Never leave foods, raw or cooked, at room tempe-rature longer than two hours. On a hot day with temperatures at 90 °F or warmer, this decreases to one hour.

SAFE HANDLING OF SAUSAGES AND HOT DOGS

SELECTING THE BEST SAUSAGE

There are so many varieties of sausages! How long can you store them—and where? Are they fully cooked or not? The following background information will answer these questions and others. Use the storage chart as a guideline for proper handling.

Types of Sausages

Sausages are either ready to eat or not. They can be made from red meat, poultry or a combination.

Uncooked sausages include fresh and smoked sausages. Ready-to-eat sausages are dry, semi-dry and/or cooked. Dry sausages may be smoked, unsmoked or cooked. Semi-dry sausages are usually heated in the smokehouse to fully cook the product and partially dry it.

Sausage Labeling Information

Let the label be your guide to sausage selection, handling and—if applicable—cooking. It will list the safe handling and cooking instructions, the nutrient content and the ingredients. Safe handling instructions are mandatory for all raw or partially cooked meat and poultry products. The label must say "Keep Refrigerated" if the sausage is perishable. Product dating is optional but the manufacturer may have affixed a date.

All ingredients in the product must be listed in the ingredient statement in order of predominance from the one weighing the most listed first to the one weighing the least listed last.

For sausage products packaged under federal inspection, a Nutrition Facts panel is mandatory.

If sausages are made and packaged in a local store, the nutrient information on the package is voluntary. The Nutrition Facts information on the label can help consumers compare products and make more informed, healthy food choices.

SAUSAGE DEFINED

Fresh Sausages

Fresh sausages are a coarse or finely ground meat food product prepared from one or more kinds of meat, or meat and meat by-products. They may contain water not exceeding 3 per cent of the total ingredients in the product. They are usually seasoned, frequently cured and may contain binders and extenders.

They must be kept refrigerated and be thoroughly cooked before eating:

- *Fresh Pork Sausages*: May not contain pork by-products and no more than 50 per cent fat by weight.
- *Fresh Beef Sausages*: May not include beef by-products and no more than 30 per cent fat by weight.
- *Breakfast Sausages*: May contain meat and meat by-products and no more than 50 per cent fat by weight.
- *Whole Hog Sausage*: Meat from swine in such proportions as are normal to a single animal and no more than 50 per cent fat by weight.
- *Italian Sausage Products*: Cured or uncured sausages containing at least 85 per cent meat, or a combination of meat and fat, with the total fat content constituting not more than 35 per cent of the finished product. They contain salt, pepper, fennel and/or anise and no more than 3 per cent water. Optional ingredients permitted in Italian sausages are spices and flavourings, red or green peppers, onions, garlic and parsley, sugar, dextrose and corn syrup.

Cooked and/or Smoked Sausages

These products are made of one or more different kinds of chopped or ground meats that have been seasoned, cooked and/or smoked. Water can be no more than 10 per cent by weight. Meat by-products may be used.

Included in this category are:

- Salami
- Bratwurst
- Liverwurst
- Braunschweiger
- Hot Dogs
- Blood Sausage
- Bologna
- Jellied Beef Loaf
- Knockwurst
- Thuringer-Style

Cooked salami is made from fresh meats that are cured, stuffed into casings and cooked in a smokehouse at high temperature. It may be air-dried for a short time. It has a softer texture than dry and semi-dry sausages and must be refrigerated.

Meat Specialties

A ready-to-eat sausage product that is made from finely ground meats that are seasoned and usually cooked or baked rather than smoked. They are usually sliced and served cold.

Included in this category are:

- Chopped Ham Loaf
- Luncheon Meat
- Peppered Loaf
- Head Cheese
- Jellied Corned Beef
- Ham and Cheese Loaf
- Honey Loaf
- Old Fashioned Loaf
- Olive Loaf
- Pickle and Pimento Loaf
- Scrapple
- Souse
- Veal Loaf

Dry and Semi-Dry Sausages

Dry sausages may or may not be characterized by a bacterial fermentation. When fermented, the intentional encouragement of a lactic acid bacteria growth is useful as a meat preservative as well as producing the typical tangy flavour. The ingredients are mixed with spices and curing materials, stuffed into casings, and put through a carefully controlled, long, continuous air-drying process. Dry sausages require more production time than other types of sausage that results in a concentrated form of meat.

Medium-dry sausage is about 70 per cent of its "green" weight when sold. Green weight is the weight of the raw article before addition of added substances or before cooking. Less-dry and fully-dried sausages range from 80 per cent to 60 per cent of original weight at completion.

Dry sausages include:

- Chorizo
- Frizzes
- Pepperoni
- Lola or Lolita and Lyons sausage
- Genoa salami

Semi-dry sausages are usually heated in the smokehouse to fully cook the product and partially dry it. Semi-dry sausages are semi-soft sausages with good keeping qualities due to their lactic acid fermentation. "Summer Sausage" is the general classification for mildly seasoned, smoked, semi-dry sausages like Mortadella and Lebanon bologna.

WHO SHOULD AVOID EATING DRY SAUSAGES

Because dry sausages are not cooked, the elderly, very young children, pregnant women and those with weakened immune systems might want to avoid eating them. The bacterium E. coli 0157:H7 has been found to survive the process of dry fermenting, and in 1994, some children and adults became ill after eating dry cured salami containing the bacteria. This is believed to be the first time that this product has been associated with E. coli 0157:H7. These illnesses have raised some questions about the effectiveness of processes for producing dry fermented sausage free of this deadly organism. The USDA is looking at ways to identify and correct potential problems in dry sausage products, and is developing procedures for manufacturers to ensure their processing is adequate to destroy bacteria.

STORAGE OF SAUSAGE

All sausage–except dry sausage–is perishable and therefore should be brought directly home when purchased and refrigerated or frozen.

DATE ON PACKAGE OF PROCESSED MEATS

Although dating is a voluntary programme and not mandated by the federal government, if a date is used it must state what the date means. Since none is a safety date, the product can be used after the date, provided it was stored safely.

Follow the guidelines, for maximum quality in sausage products:

- "Packaging" date is the date of manufacturing, processing, or final packaging."Sell-by" date is the last day a retail store may offer the food for sale. You should buy the product before the date expires, and then use according to the guidelines in the storage chart for maximum quality and safety.
- "Sell-by" date is the last day a retail store may offer the food for sale. You should buy the product before the date expires, and then use according to the guidelines in the storage chart for maximum quality and safety.
- "Best if used by" date tells when the product should be used for best flavour and quality. It is not a purchase or safety date.
- "Use-by" date is the date after which peak quality of the product begins to decrease, but the product may still be used.
- "Expiration" date marks the end of the product's useful life or the last day to be used.

SELECTING THE BEST HOT DOGS

Types of Hot Dogs

Whether you call it a frankfurter, hot dog, wiener or bologna, it's a cooked sausage and a summertime favourite. They can be made from beef, pork, turkey or chicken–the label must specify which. All ingredients in the product must be listed in the ingredient statement in order of predominance from the one weighing the most listed first to the one weighing the least listed last. And there are federal standards for their content.

Smoking and curing ingredients contribute to flavour, colour and preservation of the product. They come in all shapes and sizes–short, long, thin and chubby. The most popular of all categories, the skinless varieties, have been stripped of their casings after cooking. Water or ice may be used to facilitate chopping or mixing or to dissolve curing ingredients. Sausages may contain no more than 10 per cent water and 30 per cent fat or a combination of 40 per cent fat and added water. Up to 3.5 per cent nonmeat binders and extenders such as nonfat dry milk, cereal, dried whole milk or 2 per cent isolated soy protein may be used, but must be shown in the ingredient statement by its common name.

By-Products, Variety Meats

Frankfurters, hot dogs, wieners or bologna "with by-products" or "with variety meats" are made according to the specifications for cooked smoked sausages except they consist of not less than 15 per cent of one or more kinds of raw skeletal muscle meat with raw meat by-products. The by-products must be accompanied by the name of the species from which it was derived and must be individually named in the ingredient statement.

Species

Beef franks or pork franks are cooked, smoked sausage products made according to the specifications above, but with meat from a single species and do not include by-products. Turkey franks or chicken franks contain turkey or chicken skin and fat in natural proportions of that found on a turkey or chicken carcass.

Mechanically Separated Meat or Poultry

Carcass parts from which most of the meat has been removed still have usable meat attached. These parts are pushed under high pressure through equipment with openings so fine that a small amount of powdered bone the size of a grain of sand may pass through along with the remaining muscle meat and other soft tissue. This is called "mechanically separated" meat, and if used in a product, the label must state it. If a serving contains 20 mg or more of calcium from the finely powdered bone, the label must give the calcium content as a percentage of the US RDAs.

Mechanically Deboned Poultry

This does not have the same requirements as mechanically separated meat and is simply listed in the ingredients statement as "chicken" or "turkey."

Handling of Hot Dogs

When you leave the grocery store with any kind of sausage, head straight home and refrigerate or freeze it immediately. If there is a date on the package, follow those guidelines for use. If there is no date, hot dogs can be safely stored unopened in the refrigerator for up to two weeks. Once opened, they are safe in the refrigerator for only one week.

For maximum quality, freeze hot dogs no longer than one to two months. Never leave hot dogs at room temperature for more than two hours, or in the hot summer months when the temperature rises to 90 °F or above, for more than one hour. Finally, even though hot dogs are fully cooked, if you choose to reheat them

Table. Sausage and Hot Dog Storage Chart (for Products with a "Sell-By" date or no date).

Type of Sausage	Refrigerator Storage-Unopened	Refrigerator Storage-after Opening
Fresh Sausage, uncooked	1 to 2 Days	1 to 2 Days
Fresh Sausage, after cooking by the consumer	(Not Applicable)	3 to 4 Days
Hard/Dry Sausage	Indefinitely in Refrigerator; 6 Weeks in Pantry	3 Weeks in Refrigerator, or Until It Turns Rancid
Hot Dogs and Other Cooked Sausage	2 Weeks but No Longer than 1 Week After the "Sell-by" Date	7 Days
Summer Sausage (Semi-dry)	3 Months	3 Weeks

Freeze the product if you cannot use it within the times recommended above for refrigerator storage. Once frozen, it does not matter if the date expires, because all foods kept frozen continuously are safe indefinitely. However, for best quality, use within 1 to 2 months.

SAFE HANDLING OF VEAL

WHAT IS VEAL

Veal is the meat from a calf or young beef animal. A veal calf is raised until about 16 to 18 weeks of age, weighing up to 450 pounds. Male dairy calves are used in the veal industry. Dairy cows must give birth to continue producing milk, but male dairy calves are of little or no value to the dairy farmer. A small percentage are raised to maturity and used for breeding. A calf is a young bovine of either sex that has not reached puberty and has a maximum live weight of 750 pounds. "Bob" veal is a veal calf marketed up to 3 weeks of age or at a weight of 150 pounds. "Special-Fed" veal is usually fed nutritionally balanced milk or soy based diets. These specially controlled diets contain iron and 40 other essential nutrients. The majority of veal calves are "special-fed".

SELECTING THE BEST

Choose veal in the fresh meat case that is grayish pink in colour and firm to the touch. Vacuum packaged veal in the self-serve case will be more maroon in colour because it has not been exposed to oxygen. Look for packages that are cool to the touch, have no wear or punctures, and little or no excess liquid. Always check the "sell-by" date. Purchase raw meats last. Make sure all meats- whether raw, pre-packaged or from the deli are kept refrigerated. Fresh meats may contaminate other grocery items. The best way to prevent this cross-contamination is to always keep fresh meats from other items. Put raw meat packages in a plastic bag so juices won't drip onto other foods. Pack raw meats in an ice chest if it will take more than an hour to get home. Keep ice chest in the passenger area of the car during warm weather. Take meats straight home to the refrigerator or freezer.

Product Dating

Product dating, applying "sell-by" or "use-by" dates, is not required by federal regulations. However, many stores and processors may voluntarily choose to date packages of raw veal or processed veal products. Use or freeze products with a "sell-by" date within three to five days of purchase. If the manufacturer has determined a "use-by" date, observe it. It's always best to buy a product before its date expires. It's not important if a date expires after freezing veal, because all foods stay safe while properly frozen.

Product Inspection and Grading

All veal found in retail stores is either USDA-inspected for wholesomeness or inspected by state systems which have standards equal to the federal government. Each animal and its internal organs are inspected for signs of disease. The "Passed and Inspected by USDA" seal ensures that the veal is wholesome and free from disease. Although inspection is mandatory, its grading for quality is voluntary, and a plant pays to have its veal graded. Quality grade refers to the eating quality of the meat.

Veal and calf carcasses are graded on a composite evaluation of two general grade factors: conformation and quality of the lean. In addition, the colour of the lean carcasses is key in differentiating between veal, calf and beef carcasses. The five grades for veal are as follows: prime, choice, good, standard and utility.

Retail Cuts

There are seven basic major cuts into which veal is separated: leg, sirloin, loin, rib, shoulder, foreshank and breast. When examining a package of veal, the label can help the purchaser identify the meat in the package. For example, a label stating "veal rib chop" identifies the packaged meat as "veal", the primal or large wholesale cut from the "rib", and the name of the retail cut as "chop". This information helps consumers know what type of preparation method to use. The most readily available cuts of veal today include rib chops, loin chops, veal for stew, cutlets, arm steak, blade steak, rib roast, breast, shanks and round steak.

STORAGE

Refrigeration

Keep veal below 40 °F during storage. Store uncooked veal items together, separate from cooked foods. Refrigerate or freeze fresh veal Immediately after bringing it home. Never leave veal in a hot car or sitting out at room temperature.

Packaged whole cuts of fresh veal may be refrigerated in their original wrappings in the coldest part of the refrigerator for three to five days after purchase, while ground veal can be stored in the refrigerator for one or two days. Keep veal refrigerated until you are ready to cook it. When transporting cooked veal to another dining site, place it in an insulated container or ice chest until ready to eat. Cooked whole cuts of veal are at their best when refrigerated no longer than two to three days. Cooked ground veal is best when refrigerated no longer than one or two days.

Freezing

Freeze whole cuts of fresh veal if you do not plan to cook it within three to five days after purchase. Freeze ground veal if you do not plan to cook it within one to two days after purchase. Wrap veal parts separately in aluminum foil or freezer paper before freezing, and label for ease in selecting just the right number of parts to thaw for a single meal. Be sure to press the air out of the package before freezing. If you plan to freeze veal in its original wrapping, overwrap with freezer bag or paper. Cooked parts may be frozen in the same way as fresh, unless made with a sauce or gravy; in that case, pack in a rigid container with a tightfitting lid.

PREPARATION

Cleanliness

Always wash hands thoroughly with hot soapy water before preparing foods and after handling raw veal. Don't let raw meat or juices touch ready-to-go foods either in the refrigerator or during preparation. Don't put cooked foods on the same plate that held raw veal. Always wash utensils that have touched raw meat with hot, soapy water before using them for cooked meats. Wash counters, cutting boards and other surfaces raw meats have touched.

Thawing

Thaw uncooked veal in the refrigerator or in cold water. Never thaw veal at room temperature. Allow a 24-hour thawing period. After defrosting raw veal by this method, it will be safe in the refrigerator for up to five days before cooking, or, if you decide not to use the veal, you can safely refreeze it without cooking it first. To thaw veal in cold water, leave the veal in its original wrapping or place it in a watertight plastic bag. Change the water every 30 minutes. For quick thawing of uncooked or cooked veal, use the microwave, but plan on cooking the meat immediately after thawing, because some areas of the food may become warm and begin to cook during microwaving. Thawing time will vary according to whether you're thawing a whole roast or cuts and the number of parts frozen together. Use the Defrost or Medium-Low setting, according to the manufacturer's directions. Turn the roast and separate parts as they thaw, taking care the meat does not begin to cook. Repeat as needed. Foods defrosted by the cold water method or in the microwave should be cooked before refreezing, because they may have been held at temperatures above 40 °F.

Table. Safe Handling of Veal in Cold Storage.

Product	Refrigerator (40°F)	Freezer (0°F)
Raw Whole Cuts of Veal: Chops, roasts and steaks	3-5 Days	4-6 Months
Raw Ground Veal and Stew	1-2 Days	3-4 Months
Broiled, Fried, Grilled or Roasted Veal	2-3 Days	2-3 Months
Cooked Ground Veal and Gravies Made From Veal	1-2 Days	2-3 Months

It is safe to cook frozen veal in the oven, or on the stove or grill without defrosting. Estimate one-third to one-half more cooking time depending upon the size of the meat. Broil frozen veal farther away from the heat source; preheat the skillet when pan-frying or pan-broiling. Do not cook frozen veal in a slow cooker.

Marinating

Marinate food in the refrigerator, not on the counter. Boil used marinade before brushing on cooked veal. Discard any uncooked, leftover marinade after use because it contains raw juices, which may harbour bacteria.

Rinsing

There is no need to rinse raw veal before cooking. Any bacteria that might be present on the surface would be destroyed by cooking.

Partial Cooking or Browning

Never brown or partially cook veal, then refrigerate and finish cooking later, because any bacteria present would not have been destroyed. It is safe to partially precook or microwave veal IMMEDIATELY before transferring it to a hot grill or oven to finish cooking.

COOKING

Importance of Kitchen Thermometers

One of the critical factors in controlling bacteria in food is controlling temperature. Pathogenic microorganisms grow very slowly at low temperatures multiply rapidly in mid-range temperatures, and are killed at high temperatures. For safety, foods must be cooked thoroughly. It is essential to use a meat thermometer when cooking veal to prevent undercooking and, consequently, prevent food borne illness. Using a thermometer is the only reliable way to ensure safety and to determine the "doneness" of most foods. To be safe, a product must be cooked to an internal temperature high enough to destroy any harmful bacteria that may have been in the food. Recent research has shown that colour and texture indicators are not reliable. When cooking whole cuts or parts of veal, the thermometer should be inserted into the thickest part of the meat, away from the bone, fat and gristle. The thermometer may be inserted sideways if necessary. When the food being cooked is irregularly shaped, the temperature should be checked in several places.

Table. Approximate Veal Cooking Times.

Types of Veal	Size	Cooking Method	Cooking Times	Internal Temperature
Rib Roast	4 to 5 lbs.	Roast 325 °F	25 to 27 min/lb. 29 to 31 min/lb.	Cook at least to an internal
Loin	3 to 4 lbs. 38 to 40 min/lb.	Roast 325 °F 145 °F with a	34 to 36 min/lb. 4 minute rest	temperature of
Loin/Rib Chops	1" thick or 8 oz.	Broil/Grill	7 min. per side 8 to 9 min per side	
Cutlets	1/8" thick ¼" thick	*Pan Fry	3 to 4 min. 5 to 6 min.	
Arm/Blade Steak	¾"thick 16 oz.	Broil/Grill	7 min per side 8 min. per side	
Cross Cut Shanks	1½" thick	Cover with liquid; simmer	1 to 1¼ hrs.	
Stew Meat	1 to 1½" cubes/pieces	Cover with liquid; simmer	45 to 60 min	
Round Steak	¼" thick ½" thick	**Braise	30 min 45 min.	

Notes:

*Pan frying, which is often called "sautéing," is a quick cooking method. Meat is placed in small amount of heated oil and cooked on medium-high heat.

**Braising is roasting or simmering less tender meats with a small amount of liquid in a tightly covered pan.

Whole Muscle Meats

Cook whole cuts of meat to a minimum internal temperature of 145 °F for medium-rare, with a 4 minute rest before carving or eating or 160 °F for medium-cooked whole cuts of meat, and 170 °F for well-done cuts.

Ground Veal

Ground veal must be cooked thoroughly to kill harmful bacteria. Unlike whole muscle meat that is sterile inside, the grinding process exposes the interior meat in ground veal to bacteria that may be on the surface, in the air, on equipment or on people's hands. To kill these bacteria, food safety experts have one major rule of thumb—cook ground veal to at least 155 °F. This step, while very simple, offers the best protection that consumers have to serve ground veal safely.

Microwaving

When microwaving unequal size pieces of veal, arrange in a dish or on a rack so thick parts are towards the outside of the dish and thin parts are in the center, and cook on medium-high or medium power. Place a roast in an oven-cooking bag or in a covered pot. Refer to the manufacturer's directions that accompany the microwave oven for suggested cooking times. Use a microwave-safe thermometer inserted before cooking, or removes meat from microwave oven and use a digital meat thermometer in several places to be sure correct temperatures have been reached. Meats cooked in the microwave oven must be cooked to a minimum internal temperature of 165 °F and allowed to stand covered at least 2 minutes. Follow standing or rest times given.

4

Catering and Food Service

Catering is the business of providing food service at a remote site. Mobile catering is the business of selling prepared food from some sort of vehicle. It is a feature of urban culture in many countries.

The food service generally encompasses those places, institutions, and companies responsible for any meal eaten away from home. This industry includes restaurants, school and hospital cafeterias, catering operations, and many other formats. The companies that supply food service operators are called food service distributors. Food service hard goods like ovens and refrigerators are often sold by large buying groups.

Some companies manufacture products in both consumer and food service versions. The consumer version usually comes in individual-sized packages with elaborate label design for retail sale. The food service version is packaged in a much larger industrial size and often lacks the colourful label designs of the consumer version. Food service sales to restaurants and institutions are estimated to be approximately $400 Billion, about equal with consumer sales of foods through grocery outlets. A food cart is a motorless trailer that can be hauled by automobile, bicycle, or hand to the point of sale, often a public sidewalk or park. Carts typically have an onboard heating or refrigeration system to keep the food ready for consumption. Foods and beverages often served from carts include...

- Halal food such as lamb or chicken over rice, or in a gyro
- Ice cream and other frozen treats
- Coffee, bagels, donuts, Egg sandwichs (*i.e.* bacon, egg, and cheese) and other breakfast items

Food Truck is a mobile kitchen, known colliqually in some regions as a "X" Truck, is a mobile venue that sells food. Some, including ice cream trucks, sell mostly frozen or prepackaged food; others are more like restaurants-on-wheels. Food trucks make frequent appearances at carnivals, construction sites, and other temporary venues where large numbers of people gather.

Some college campuses and surrounding areas boast many food trucks with loyal followings; for example, visitors to Harvard University or MIT in

Cambridge, Massachusetts or the campus of the University of Pennsylvania in Philadelphia may see some very popular trucks parked outside the main entrances to buildings at lunchtime. At Rutgers University, the Grease Trucks serve "fat sandwiches" that contain an ensemble of ingredients such as steak, cheese, chicken fingers, french fries, mozzarella sticks, jalapeño poppers, and more.

In the United Kingdom, these are known as burger vans and can be found on nearly all major trunk roads at the side of the road selling their food. A 1/4lb burger can be purchased for about £2 (approx. $3.5USD). Many people prefer to stop at one of these Burger vans when travelling due to the cheap price, rather than stop at a motorway service station where prices can be extremely high. Sometimes also called "maggot wagon," "roach coach," or "gut truck," these rolling restaurants can frequently be found at or near construction sites.

An early version of the food truck was the US Army's mobile canteen and before that the old West's chuckwagon. A mobile kitchen is a modified van with a built-in grill, deep fryer, or other cooking equipment.

It offers more flexibility in the menu since the vendor can prepare food to order. A vendor can choose to park the van in one place, as with a cart, or to broaden the business's reach by driving the van to several customer locations. Examples of mobile kitchens include taco trucks on the west coast of the United States, especially Southern California, and fish and chips vans in the United Kingdom.

A concession trailer has preparation equipment like a mobile kitchen, but it cannot move on its own. As such it is suited for events lasting several days, such as funfairs.

In addition to being operated as private businesses, mobile catering vehicles are also used after natural disasters to feed people in areas with damaged infrastructure. The Salvation Army has several mobile kitchens that it uses for this purpose. An event caterer serves food with waiting staff at dining tables or sets up a self-serve buffet. The food may be prepared on site, made completely at the event, or the caterer may choose to bring prepared food and put the finishing touches on once they arrive. The event caterer staff isn't responsible for preparing the food but often help set up the dining area. This service is typically provided at banquets, conventions, and weddings. Any event where all the attenders are provided with food and drinks or sometimes only hors d'oeuvres is often called a catered event.

A catering company or specialist is expected to know not just food preparation, but how to make it attractive. Many events require working with the entire theme or colour scheme. Catering companies have moved towards full-service taking charge of not only food preparation but also decorations, such as table settings or lighting. It's not that food is no longer a focal point, but rather that it is part of a broader mission. Many suggest that catering is about satisfying all the senses. A caterer and his or her staff should be friendly and cooperative because, after all, they are in the food service industry and should follow the motto "the customer is always right".

Catering is typically sold on a per-person basis, where adding additional people is a flat price per person. Keeping the cost of the food and supplies below this is required to make a profit on the catering. With the correct atmosphere, professional event caterers experience can bring clients satisfaction of all the senses in a way that makes an event special and memorable. Of course, beautifully prepared food can appeal to your sense of taste, smell and sight - perhaps even touch, but the decorations and ambiance should play a significant part in the clients enjoyment as well.

Industrial catering includes providing food for airline passengers, schools, prisons and other institutional settings. It can include contract management of client food service facilities. Airlines often have divisions or hire third parties to provide food for passengers. Catering is covered by two different groups. "Independent caterers and companies with a catering business on the side" is a phrase that could be combined with the previous sentence.

CATERING TIPS AND TRICKS

CHOOSING RIGHT CATERING SERVICE

Food is an integral part of any party so one must choose a catering service wisely. But how does one choose the right caterer for an event? It is important to do a lot of research, check references, and often request a sampling to make your final decision.

List your catering needs In order for a caterer to provide an accurate estimate for your party or event, you must communicate your needs clearly. Do you have a location for your party/event reserved and is there a kitchen on site? How many guests are coming to your event? Find out if the potential caterer has a minimum guest requirement. Take into consideration that some of your guests may have special dietary needs and be certain to communicate this with your caterer. A great caterer will be ready for any surprise that may surface, but at what cost to you? Discuss your budget with your caterer and what options are available. Ask yourself, do you prefer a buffet style or a silver-service sit down dinner for your guests? Be clear about your proposed menu, do you have a theme or style at the event that will be reflected in the cuisine? Your budget may or may not determine how flexible your caterer is to meet your needs. Keep in mind; it is the type of food that often determines the bulk price of the catering job. Find out, and possibly request, if the caterer will provide a detailed contract of service and outline what the payment terms will be.

Does the caterer use fresh or frozen food for recipes? Is the produce grown locally? Is it organic? Will any of the dishes be pre-made and then frozen until the party/event? Does anything come from a can? Does the potential caterer supply decorations, linens, tables and chairs? Very often there will be a brochure catering services supply with examples of past event and table decorations. It is important to be very clear in what your event needs and what the caterer will be supplying. Is a menu board provided for the guests that describes the ingredients of the dishes being served?

Will the catering company provide a wait-staff? What is their required dress code? What is the ratio of servers to guests? A rule of thumb is one server for every 10 guests. Be certain to ask your potential caterer if taxes and gratuities are included in the final bid.

What happens to the leftovers? Often, upon request, a catering service will compile a food basket at no additional charge for the host or hostess of the event. Remember, it is critical that you communicate with your potential caterer exactly you want; the result, you get what you want and the caterer can provide an accurate bid for the job as well as the exceptional service your event deserves.

SERVING ALCOHOL AT YOUR EVENT

When one commits to planning an event or party, one must decide whether or not to serve alcohol to the guests. There are a few considerations to keep in mind and discuss with your caterer. Where will your event or party be taking place? It is important to confirm that your event or party site will allow alcohol on its premises. Once you have made certain that you can serve alcohol at your chosen site, ask your caterer if he or she holds a liquor license. He or she must have a valid liquor license. If he or she does not hold a liquor license, then you must contact a liquor-licensed dealer. Prepare to provide a guest estimate for your caterer to work with. The caterer in turn will supply you with a quote for the number of bartenders that must attend bar and the quantity of ice, glasses, and mixers necessary. The amount of bartenders depends on the number of guests. Your caterer or licensed liquor dealer will be responsible for setting up the bar.

You must now determine what you wish to be served from the bar as well as if you require your guests to pay for alcohol themselves. A cash bar requires the guest to pay for their drinks. Guests tend to consume less alcohol when it isn't free. This is a basic bar with all the works and at no charge to the guests. The open bar includes hard liquor for mixing drinks, wine, beer, and soft drinks.

A limited bar will set boundaries on what will be served and in what moderation. An example of a limited bar is an event in which beer and wine is offered to the guests at no charge and hard liquor is offered at a pre-determined price. Whatever you decide in regards to serving alcohol at your event or party is up to you. Be certain to discuss all the beverage details with your caterer beforehand. Cheers.

WEDDING CATERING

After watching the happy couple exchange vows and begin their married life together, your guests will be hungry. Many of the guests may have scaled back on eating in order to look good for pictures or just because they were so busy during the day.

When you're putting together such a large assortment of people, there are bound to be those that have certain ways or preferences of eating. You may find that there are vegetarians or those that can not eat dairy. You might have a diabetic in the crowd or some other health restriction.

You should certainly try to have options for any sort of eating arrangement. In the case of those that don't eat meat, you might want to have a cheese lasagne available or other pasta dish. This is becoming widely popular to have two options anyways, so why not offer them?

Another way to cope with varied needs is to serve dinner in a buffet style. This allows each person to pick only what they want or what they can eat. A lot of wedding caterers rely on word of mouth (no pun intended) to get their services recognized. If you can, talk to other people that have gotten married in your town to see who they recommend. Of course, you will still want to see them for yourself, but this list can be a great starting point.

Another way to find good catering is to talk to the reception hall coordinators. Many times they will either require the use of a particular caterer or they have a list of those that they recommend. Of course, you will want to schedule an appointment with all of the catering candidates in order to do a taste test of their menu options. At that point, you can pick what you think your guests will enjoy.

A good meal is a great way to send your thanks to your guests for coming to your wedding. This is the part that shouldn't be skimped on for any reason. Of course, that doesn't mean that you can't find moderately priced options. Try your favourite restaurant, for example. If they're able to cater, then you may be able to get a better deal because you're buying food in bulk.

Having a friend who is a cook is even better—so long as they don't mind working through the wedding. So you've tasted the offerings of the caterer and you've selected your main menu options. What about drinks?

Much like selecting the menu options, you will need to factor in what kinds of drinks everyone would like to drink. The easiest way to take care of this is to offer a full service bar. In this way, guests can have mixed drinks of all varieties or they can stick to wine and beer.

You want to plan this option out carefully as you may end up paying more than you would like. Check with the provider as to how many drinks each guest can have, or can expect from the supply that will be brought. In most cases, there is no limit.

A word of advice: Don't ever have a cash bar. Making your guests pay for their drinks when they may also have paid for their outfits and transportation is just a lot to ask. In terms of wine and beer, tastes and varieties are enormous—how does someone choose?

The best advice is to select four to five different kinds of beer with each one having enough to fill everyone's glass. This may surprise you, but sometimes all of your guests will like the same thing and you may want to make sure that they can have it. As for wine, you may want to have at least one of each a red varietal and a white varietal. This ensures a milder and more acidic selection. A way to make sure that everyone is happy is to find blends of each of these wines. By blends, this means to find a red that includes a merlot, syrah, and pinot noir, while the white might include a chardonnay, reisling, and zinfandel. These can be tricky to find, but they are crowd pleasers.

Toasts are just not toasts without a little glass (or two) of champagne. It's common sense to make sure that the new couple and their wedding party have the very finest in champagne (as determined by the budget), while the rest of the guests have another variety. In many reception halls or catering services, the champagne for the wedding party is provided. Of course, there will also be designated drivers at the wedding, so you will also want to have water, sodas, coffee, and juices available as well. When you're planned it thoroughly, everyone will be well-watered throughout the evening.

HOW TO START A CATERING BUSINESS

The catering industry in the United States is estimated to be worth $5 billion a year. Caterers are hired to perform an assorted number of jobs-everything from cooking to serving, mixing drinks, and whipping up delicious desserts. Functions range from dinner parties that serve a handful of guests to enormous events that serve thousands of guests. Normally a caterer will define their niche, meaning a caterer will choose what type of functions to specialize in as well as their job description. For example, you may offer the best fondue table for up to 100 guests, perhaps you would rather prepare meals for business catering parties that are held within banker's hours. There really are no limits in regards to catering styles.

Once you have arrived to the idea stage it is great to begin a business catering plan. Be meticulous when you detail how the catering business will be operated, managed and capitalized.

The following checklist can help you organize your ideas into the beginning of a business catering plan:

- What services will your catering business offer? Will you run a full service catering business, corporate catering service, custom event catering service, or a scheduled events catering business?
- Research necessary permits and requirements your local government imposes on a catering business.
- Determine your start up costs of your catering business. Remember to include everything-permit fees, catering equipment, marketing, uniforms, catering supplies etc.

- Construct a budget, forecast and projection.
- How will you finance the start up of your catering business?
- Research liability insurance needed to protect your catering business.
- Where will you house your catering business office and how will you manage your business? Prepare to think about cancellations, payment policies, consultations, menu-planning as well as samples, contracts and the transportation of food.
- What food suppliers do you intend to work with?
- Will your catering service rent equipment for special requests?
- What will you name your catering business?

Owning a catering service not only includes cooking but also be prepared to wear many hats such as: accountant, manager, marketer, sales representative, and bill collector.

Additional questions to consider when constructing your catering business plan:

- Is my business idea practical and is it in demand?
- What is my competition?
- What is my advantage over existing services?
- Can I deliver a better quality service?
- Can I create a demand for my business?
- What will be my legal structure?
- How will I compensate myself?

Your answers to these questions will help you create a focused, well-researched catering business plan that can serve as a blueprint for your new catering service. Whatever you choose to specialize in, running a catering business offers creativity, flexibility, and growing opportunities.

Maybe you've got the details of the actual wedding ceremony worked out, but what about the reception? One of the major costs of the wedding reception will definitely be the food, so you'll want to make sure you'll have enough food for everyone without spending too much money. Here are some top ways to cut on your catering bill that will ensure that your guests enjoy your reception—and you save money.

Most couples want to order an extra tray or two of hors d'oeuvres in case extra guests show up. This is fine (and usually a smart idea), but you should still make sure that you're not order more appetizers than you actually need; use your discretion based on the guest list.

For instance, if you know a number of your guests are vegetarian, you may not need to order as many appetizers with meat. Also, ordering two or three types of hors d'oeuvres will help to reduce your catering bill. If you buy more of the same dish, you can usually save money with most catering companies—different kinds of foods will increase the bill, so it's important to keep it classy but simple at the wedding—even when it comes to food.

Caterers will also try to encourage you to spend more than you may need to on the actual meal as well. You may not need a five course meal if you've already purchased three types of appetizers and a salad, or three extra desserts if you already have a pretty large wedding cake. The time of day that you hold your wedding will give you a good indication of how much food to serve; if you're having the ceremony in the afternoon or early evening, you may want to serve more food. There are some foods that are always going to be expensive, even if you only order small amounts. So, since you have to order a considerable amount of food, ordering dishes that aren't so costly will help you to keep your catering bill reasonable. Certain seafood, like shrimp, lobster and salmon will definitely make your catering bill higher, so if you have to have them, try to use them as only one of the course choices for dinner, or purchase these foods as appetizers to save on costs.

Food stations are a unique way to serve a variety of foods at your wedding reception, and you can be sure that everyone will find something they like to eat. This way, you won't have to worry about people changing their minds about their meal choices once they arrive at the reception. A food station with different types of pasta is usually a hit with most guests, and can be very economical. You can also include food stations with other types of the ethnic foods, such as Mexican or Indian fare, to celebrate the cultures of the people who will be attending your wedding, or to acknowledge your backgrounds.

You may also be able to cut your catering bill by not requesting an elaborate setup for your food stations and tables. Using a single colour for tablecloths, usually white, will cut down on labour costs.

OFF-PREMISE CATERING

OFF-PREMISE CATERING MANAGEMENT

Off-Premise Catering Management fills you in on all crucial legal and financial aspects of the subject, including catering contracts, legal requirements, finding and working with a lawyer, preparing income statements, cost control, and much more. Off-premise catering is serving food at a location away from the caterer's food production facility. One example of a food production facility is a freestanding commissary, which is a kitchen facility used exclusively for the preparation of foods to be served at other locations.

Other examples of production facilities include, but are not limited to, hotel, restaurant, and club kitchens. In most cases there is no existing kitchen facility at the location where the food is served. Caterers provide single-event food service, but not all caterers are created equal.

They generally fall into one of three categories:

- Party food caterers supply only the food for an event. They drop off cold foods and leave any last-minute preparation, plus service and cleanup, to others.

- Hot buffet caterers provide hot foods that are delivered from their commissaries in insulated containers. They sometimes provide serving personnel at an additional charge.
- Full-service caterers not only provide food, but frequently cook it to order on-site. They also provide service personnel at the event, plus all the necessary food-related equipment—china, glassware, flatware, tables and chairs, tents, and so forth. They can arrange for other services, like decor and music, as well. In short, a full-service caterer can plan an entire event, not just the food for it.

Off-premise catering can mean serving thousands of box lunches to a group of conventioneers; barbecuing chicken and ribs for fans before a big college game, serving an elegant dinner for two aboard a luxury yacht, or providing food, staff, and equipment for an upscale fundraiser with hundreds of guests. On a "degree of difficulty" scale from one to ten—one meaning "easy" and ten meaning "most challenging"—on-premise catering is a two, and off-premise would rank a ten!

Off-premise caterers meet the needs of all market segments, from the low-budget customer who looks for the greatest quantity and quality for the least amount of money, to the upscale client with an unlimited budget who wants the highest level of service, the ultimate in food quality, and the finest in appointments—crystal stemware, silver-plated flatware, and luxurious linens. Between these two extremes is the mid scale market segment, which requires more quality than the low-budget sector, but less than the upscale.

Off-premise catering is an art and a science. The art is creating foods and moods, as the caterer and client together turn a vision into reality. The science is the business of measuring money, manpower, and material. Successful off-premise caterers recognize the importance of both aspects—art and science—and are able to work at both the creative and the financial levels. In off-premise catering, there is only one chance to get it right.

Many events, such as wedding receptions, occur only once in a lifetime. Other events are scheduled annually, quarterly, or on a regular basis, and the caterer who fails to execute all details of such an event to the satisfaction of the client will seldom have another chance. Unfortunately for some, off-premise catering can be like living on the brink of disaster unless they are experienced.

Uninitiated amateurs may not recognize a volatile situation until it becomes a problem, later realizing they should have recognized it earlier. Catering off-premise is very similar to a sports team playing all of its games away from home, in unfamiliar surroundings, with none of the comforts of home to ease the way. There is no home field advantage, but there is a minefield disadvantage!

As caterers plod their way towards the completion of a catered event, there are thousands of potential "land mines" that can ruin an otherwise successful affair.

Some examples follow:

- Already running late for a catering delivery, the catering van driver discovers that all vehicle traffic around the party site is in gridlock. The traffic has been at a standstill for more than an hour, the police say it will be hours before the congestion can be eliminated, and the clients and their guests are anxiously awaiting dinner.
- The only freight elevator in a high-rise office building has been commandeered for the evening by moving and cleaning people, thus preventing access to the floor where a caterer is to stage an event scheduled to start in two hours.
- The wrong hot food truck is dispatched to a wedding reception. The error is not discovered until the truck has reached the reception and the bride and groom are ready for their guests to be served. It will take more than an hour to send the correct truck with the food that was ordered.
- A cook wheels a container filled with cooked prime ribs down a pier towards a yacht where the meat will be served to a group of 80 conventioneers in half an hour. Suddenly, the cook is distracted, and the prime rib container tumbles over the edge of the pier into 40 feet of water.
- The table numbers have vanished, and the guests are ready to be seated for dinner.
- The fire marshal arrives at a party site 20 minutes before a catered event and refuses to allow guests access to the party site because the space had not been authorized for party use.
- The catering crew arrives at the party site with a van full of food, cooked to order—exactly one week early.
- A new customer places an order and asks that the caterer deliver to a home where family members and guests will have gathered prior to a funeral service. The caterer sends the food and, upon arrival, is told that the person with the checkbook is at the funeral home and is asked to please stop back in an hour for the money. The delivery person leaves without obtaining a signature. Upon returning, there is no one home and no one from whom to collect payment.
- While using a garbage disposal in a client's home, the caterer suddenly hears a terrible noise and watches in horror as water and garbage spew from the disposal all over the floor. The irate customer refuses to pay the caterer and threatens to sue for the cost of replacing the garbage disposal that was ruined because of (in the customer's words) the caterer's "negligence."
- After catering a flawless party at a client's home and loading the catering truck to capacity, the caterer is shocked to learn from the

client that all 15 bags of trash must be removed from the client's property because of the neighbourhood's zoning ordinances.

- The caterer's rental company representative calls the caterer the morning after an event and advises the caterer that the $600 rented chafing dish is missing.

It was there the night before, when the caterer left the client's home. Get the picture? We could tell horror stories all day! Seasoned off-premise caterers agree, these are only a few of the thousands of obstacles that stand in the way of completing a catered event.

This book addresses the various ways to professionally and successfully deal with difficult situations. With all of these very real potential problems, why are there more than 50,000 off-premise caterers in the United States? Why are more young people studying catering at two-year and four-year colleges and universities? Why are thousands of people starting their own catering companies, risking their savings on their dreams of future success? The reasons are numerous. They may love the adventure of working in new and exciting places.

They look forward to the peaks and valleys of the business cycle. They love the intense feeling of satisfaction that comes after successfully catering a spectacular party. They love the myriad challenges of this very difficult profession. Many are their own bosses, with no one to answer to but the client. Many pick and choose the parties they wish to cater. Many make six-figure incomes each year, and others cater occasionally, just for the fun of it.

What are the differences between off-premise catering and on-premise catering? Let's examine these differences, from both the client's and the caterer's viewpoints. Most clients fail to consider the cost of the rental equipment such as tables, chairs, linens, china, glassware, and flatware when they consider engaging an off-premise caterer. They think it will be less expensive to entertain in their homes, or at unique off-premise sites, than in hotels.

In fact, it can be more expensive, considering not only the cost of the rental equipment, but also other costs such as transportation of food and supplies to the site, the costs of special labour and décor, the need for tenting, air-conditioning and/or heating, and other expenses. Clients may save some money by buying their own liquor, but this can be insignificant as compared with the added costs. For many clients, the additional costs are far outweighed by the benefits of entertaining in the privacy of their own homes or the uniqueness of a special off-premise location such as a museum, state-of-the-art aquarium, antique car dealership, or historical site. From the Caterer's Viewpoint Off-premise caterers must plan menus that can be prepared successfully at the client's location.

For example, foods to be fried should not be cooked in unventilated spaces, like small kitchens in high-rise office buildings. On-premise caterers are not as limited in this regard, and they are generally supported by built-in equipment that can support a wider variety of menus. On-premise party personnel are more familiar with the party facilities than those who work at a variety of unfamiliar locations. Off-premise catering generally has greater seasonal and day-to-day swings in personnel needs, which can create a greater challenge for the off-premise caterer, who is constantly recruiting and training staff; turnover is usually high because such work is on an "as-needed basis."

There is definitely a greater potential for oversights in off-premise catering. Backup supplies, food, and equipment can be miles away or even inaccessible when catering, for instance, aboard a yacht miles from shore. In spite of the uncertainties, off-premise catering offers the opportunity to work in a greater variety of interesting locations. The work is more likely to be different each day, resulting in less boredom and more excitement. For those looking for unlimited challenges and rewards, off-premise catering may be the answer.

ADVANTAGES AND DISADVANTAGES OF OFF-PREMISE CATERING

Advance deposits Limited start-up investment Limited inventories Controllable costs G Additional revenues Business by contract Direct payment Advance forecasting Free word-of-mouth advertising Selectivity Let's discuss a few of these items in more detail. First, most off-premise caterers require some form of advance deposit prior to an event.

This deposit provides the caterer with some security if the event is cancelled and also can be used to purchase some or all of the food and supplies for the party. There is no need for large amounts of capital to get started, since most off premise catering operations begin by using the existing kitchen facilities of a restaurant, club, hotel, church, or other licensed food service business. (It is common knowledge that many start their catering businesses in their home kitchens, but it is imperative to state that this is in direct violation of most local zoning ordinances.)

In addition, all of the necessary catering food service equipment such as china, glassware, flatware, tables, chairs, and linens can usually be rented, thus avoiding having to invest in expensive equipment inventories. Food and supply inventories, as well as operating costs, are much more easily controlled, because clients must advise the caterer in advance as to the number of guests that are expected. Off-premise caterers need buy only the amounts necessary to serve the event, unlike a restaurant where there is a large variation from day to day regarding the number of patrons and their menu selections.

Off-premise catering generates additional revenues for existing operations like hotels, clubs, and restaurants. They can generate even more profit by providing other services—rental equipment, flowers, décor, music, entertainment, and other accessory services. Both the client and the caterer have expectations regarding the outcome of the party. These expectations should be clearly spelled out in a written contract. Payment for an event is normally made directly to a manager or owner, eliminating a middleman, whether it's a wedding planner, on-site food and beverage director, or one of the caterer's own staff members. This form of direct payment provides for better cash control and fewer folks to share the profit. Advance forecasting is more accurate for off-premise caterers, because parties are generally booked weeks, months, or years in advance.

Moreover, each part of the country has seasonal swings, which make revenue forecasting somewhat easier. For example, in the South the summer months are generally less busy, but in the North these are the busy months. Off-premise events generate tremendous amounts of free word-of-mouth advertising, which can produce future business without the necessity of advertising. Many off-premise caterers feel that satisfied guests at one party will either directly or indirectly book another party by speaking favourably to friends and co-workers about the event and the caterer. In other words, one party can create future parties.

Caterers also have the advantage of being somewhat selective about their clients. There are no laws that require you to accept every request to cater. If the job doesn't Advantages and Disadvantages of Off-Premise Catering meet your standards, politely decline. In sticky situations where you've already begun to work with a client but find that your communication styles just don't mesh—or, as sometimes happens with weddings, the client is not heeding your advice and you can't even decide who's really in charge—you can walk away, as long as you do so within the terms of your written agreement.

Off-premise catering does have some disadvantages too: Catering managers, owners, and staff undergo periods of high stress during very busy periods. Deadlines must be met. There are no excuses for missing a catering deadline. Stress is compounded because the workload is not evenly spread throughout the year. For most off-premise caterers, 80 per cent of the events are scheduled in 20 per cent of the time. For most, weekends are generally busier than weekdays.

Certain seasons, including Christmas, are normally busier than others. Of course, caterers must maintain general business hours too! Many have left the catering field, burned out by the constant stress and high energy demands. The seasonality of the business makes it difficult to find staff at certain times. Revenues are inconsistent, making cash management very difficult, particularly during the slower periods when expenses continue yet revenues do not.

For those caterers who operate hotels, restaurants, clubs, and other businesses, the time away from the main business—spent on the off-premise business—can hurt. It is difficult for even the well-organized person to be in two places at the same time. Many hoteliers and restaurateurs find the rigours of off-premise catering too great. Some quit after realizing the difficulty of catering away from their operations. They feel that the financial benefits are insufficient compared with the effort required to cater off-premise events.

ELEMENTS OF SUCCESSFUL OFF-PREMISE CATERING

What does it take to become a successful off-premise caterer? What experience is necessary, and what personality traits are desirable? Work Experience. Prior experience in the catering profession or the food service industry is important. Experience in food preparation and food service (both back of- the-house and front-of-the-house) helps caterers understand the procedures and problems in both areas and how the two areas interface. Those with a strong kitchen background, for example, would be wise to gain some front-of-house experience, and front-of-house personnel should learn the kitchen routine. Many successful off-premise caterers began by working as accommodators.

Accommodators are private chefs who are hired to prepare food for parties. Many assist the client with planning the menu, purchasing the food, and even arranging for kitchen and service staff. The food is prepared and served in the client's home or facility, eliminating the need for a catering commissary. Accommodators receive a fee for their services. The party staff is paid directly by the client.

PASSION

Successful professionals are passionate about their work, and caterers are no exception. They love what they do! Clients and staff members will quickly detect a lack of passion, and it will cost you business and good workers. If you don't love what you do, move on and try something else. The desire to be an entrepreneur is a trait that is highly desirable for off-premise caterers. An entrepreneur must be willing to spend extraordinary amounts of time and energy to make the off-premise catering business successful, possess an inherent sense of what is right for the business, have the ability to view all aspects of the business at once rather than focusing only on one or two parts, and demonstrate a strong, incessant desire to be his or her own boss and become financially independent.

Accounting and bookkeeping skills are necessary to understand the financial aspects of operating a catering business.

The ability to prepare and interpret financial statements is essential:

- Learn as much about computers as you can. You'll be amazed at how much you can accomplish by using e-mail, having a website, and using specialized programmes for everything from budgeting to menu planning.
- It's also important to understand the legal aspects of catering. Laws that affect caterers include regulation of licensing, contracts, liability,

labour, and alcoholic beverage service. _ A caterer, like any other businessperson, must have some human resource skills. Knowing how to recruit, train, motivate, and manage personnel is critical.

- Off-premise caterers should be knowledgeable about how to develop and implement a marketing plan. Ability to Plan, Organize, Execute, and Control. These are the four basic functions of management. To plan, a caterer must visualize in advance all of the aspects of a catered event and document the plans so they are readily understood by the client and easily executed by the staff.

Organizing is simply breaking down the party plans into groups of functions that can be executed in an efficient manner. Execution is the implementation of the organized plans by the party staff. Controlling is the supervisory aspect of the event. All well-organized and well-executed plans require control and supervision. The adage is, "It is not what you expect, but what you inspect." The premier off-premise catering firms in the United States insist on excellent supervision at each event. Ability to Communicate with Clients and Staff. Listening is the key to good communication with clients and prospective clients. Off-premise caterers must listen carefully and attentively to determine what the client needs.

A client who calls and asks, "Are you able to cater a party next Friday?" should be dealt with differently from one who calls and asks, "How much will it cost for a wedding reception?" The first caller is ready to buy your services, whereas the second caller is shopping. Astute caterers must be able to respond to client requests in such a manner that the client will immediately gain confidence in the caterer.

Communicating with staff is a complex issue. In simple terms, it can be reduced to the ability to tell staff what is expected so that they understand, and the ability to receive their feedback regarding problems, both actual and potential. The result of effective communication is an off-premise catering staff that professionally executes a well-planned party that meets or exceeds the client's expectations. Off-premise catering is a very risky business. It is not for the fainthearted who are afraid of the unknown. For example, it is more risky catering a corporate fund-raiser at the local zoo under a tent than serving the same group in a hotel ballroom. Off-premise caterers must know when the risk outweighs the gain. In this particular example, catering the event at the zoo without adequate cover in case of rain would probably be too risky. The event could be ruined. The tent makes the risk of rain a calculated one.

Off-premise catering requires working long hours without rest or sleep, lifting and moving heavy objects, intense pressure as deadlines near, and even long periods of little or no business, which can cause concern.

Successful caterers should be in good physical shape, have a high energy level, and be able to mentally deal with seasonal business cycles that range from non-stop activity to slow periods with little or no business.

Off-premise caterers must be self-confident, but at the same time realize that they must always find ways to improve the quality of their food and services. In this profession a fondness for people and feeling comfortable in crowds is important. A "cool head" when under pressure will keep both staff and client calm while potential problems are resolved professionally and efficiently.

This is the benchmark of all outstanding caterers. Creative caterers are able to turn a client's vision into reality by creating the appropriate look, feel, menu, service, and ambiance. Those who are not very creative can learn to be, or they can employ those who are creative.

Dependability is a major cornerstone of success in off-premise catering. When a caterer fails to deliver what was promised, the negative word of mouth travels fast among clients and potential clients.

Even in those situations where circumstances change, making it more difficult to perform as promised, the outstanding caterer will find a way to deliver rather than use the changed circumstances as an excuse not to deliver.

OPEN-MINDEDNESS

Open-minded caterers read up on catering trends and try new recipes and menus. They are willing to prepare unfamiliar dishes requested by clients, after thoroughly testing and understanding the recipes. They discover and try new dishes. They are always learning better ways to run their businesses. The needs of the client must always come first. Success in this business comes from identifying these needs and satisfying them. Unsuccessful off-premise caterers are those who get lost in trying to satisfy their own needs for money, equipment, and greater self-esteem. They forget that the primary goal is to serve the needs of the client. When a client's needs are met, the caterer's needs for revenues, profits, and positive feedback will automatically be met.

Prospective clients hire caterers based on their perceived image of the caterer and what the caterer will provide. In some sense, then, caterers are selling themselves more than their food. Off-premise caterers must be able to project a favourable image to the client, one that is in accord with the client's expectations. For example, a caterer whose image is sophisticated and upscale will be hard-pressed to sell a Little League banquet with a low budget. Successful caterers understand their projected images and target their marketing efforts at those clients who desire that image.

In this pressure-packed, deadline-oriented, and stressful business, it is easy to get carried away with the magnitude of the undertakings and become so tense and uptight that work ceases to be fun. Laughter at the right time can relieve that tension and stress, putting a renewed sense of fun into the work at hand. How do caterers serve shrimps? They bend down! Managing an Off-Premise Catering Operation Even those who possess the qualities that indicate off-premise catering success must know how to put these talents to use effectively. Off-premise caterers should be hands-on managers who are constantly customer focused. They must be able to lead staff and clients alike, while conducting business in a professional manner. They must be able to make timely, ethical decisions, while understanding what makes for a successful event. They must also avoid those situations that cause a business to fail. Developing a Strategic Plan Yogi Berra, the zany former New York Yankee catcher, is famous for his many witticisms, such as, "Nobody goes there anymore—it's too crowded."

But his best quote may be this one: "If you don't know where you're going, you will wind up somewhere else." That's the reason you need a strategic plan—a roadmap to help you determine the direction in which you wish to go, and the specific goals you'll need to accomplish to get there. A strategic plan starts with a statement of core values, which may include things like client satisfaction; ethical business practices; staff satisfaction, training, and motivation; community service; and operating an environmentally conscious business. G

From these core values, a caterer can develop a Mission Statement—a succinct sentence that sums up the company's mission. Here's an example: "To meet the catering needs of the corporate community, providing high levels of service and food quality that result in repeat business and vital growth." After the Mission Statement comes the Vision Statement—a concise summary of where you want to be in the future.

Again, an example: "Within five years, our company will be the top-ranked catering firm in our area, with continuing sales and profit growth, while giving back to our community." It's not enough to brainstorm about these statements. Writing them down is the first step to making a commitment—to make them a reality. Only after they are put in writing can you develop more specific objectives to increase sales and profits, measure customer satisfaction, size up your competitors, and plan the ways in which you will give back to the community. Your Mission and Vision Statements lead naturally to the next step—to establish goals for the operation. You may have heard time management experts use the term "SMART" when describing goals.

The acronym stands for:

- *Specific:* The goals to be accomplished must be easily understood, concise, and unambiguous.
- *Measurable:* There should be no question about whether one attains, or falls short of, a goal. It may be measured in terms of quality, cost, quantity, or time.
- *Attainable:* The goals may be just out of reach, but they're not out of sight! The best goal challenges and motivates you and your team. If it's practically impossible, it may be too frustrating.
- *Relevant:* The goals must fit well with your long-term mission and vision, your objectives, and the results you expect.

- *Time-bound:* There must be a specific deadline for completion of each goal. An example of a SMART goal might be to increase sales and profits by 20 per cent each year for the next five years. Once a caterer has set goals, there must be certain trade-offs.

To increase sales, for instance, may require raising prices, hiring more staff to be able to cater more events, or spending money on advertising. The major goals can be broken into smaller, intermediate steps, with a time line to keep the company on track. And remember, goals are not just for the owner of a company. The staff and other professionals employed by the company—tax preparer, banker, attorney—should also be well aware of the goals. You'll need their help to achieve them, and you want them on your side, committed to your goals.

Too often, caterers believe they can do everything themselves. They fail to ask for or accept advice from outside consultants and colleagues. It is far more intelligent to ask for assistance when you need it. Someone familiar with your plans and your passion for them is far more likely to be helpful. Finally, as soon as a goal is set, take some action on it. The last part of a strategic management process is to re-evaluate your mission, vision, and goals periodically. Times change, trends change, and you become aware of new information. Let's say a caterer's sales year showed a 50 per cent increase, when he or she had set a 20 per cent annual goal. In this case, the next year's goal might be more realistically revised to a 30 per cent increase.

HANDS-ON ATTENTION TO DETAIL MANAGEMENT

The devil is in the details. Have you ever heard that old saying? Another way to put it: We've all been bitten by a mosquito or stung by a bee, but how many of us have been bitten by an elephant? It's always the little things that get us! In catering, the details are virtually endless, a stream of tiny elements that might go wrong and result in a catastrophe. One thing forgotten, misheard, or misplaced can ruin an event. So it's important to check and recheck and to be prepared for last-minute emergencies. It is simply not possible to run this kind of business from behind a desk, reading computer printouts and delegating all tasks.

Off-premise catering companies must be managed from the centre of the action, whether that is with the guests or preparing foods in the kitchen. It comes from checking and rechecking every detail to ensure that it meets the highest of standards. It comes from inspecting for the best and expecting the best. Some call this management style "management by walking around." In one sense that is true, but there is more to it than walking around.

Astute offpremise caterers must:

- Obtain feedback from clients and guests regarding the food and service.

- Oversee the catering staff to ensure they are performing as directed and as expected.
- Help out when a table needs to be cleared or when the bar suddenly becomes very busy.

Help in the kitchen during critical times such as hot food dish-up, and even help scrape, stack, and wash dirty dishes if that's what is necessary. It's a roll-up-your-sleeves kind of profession, and you should never be totally satisfied with the way things are. Always look for new ways to present food and make it more flavourful, and for better and more efficient ways to do things. Customer-Focused Management An off-premise caterer's full-time mission must be to satisfy the needs of clients.

Mike DeLuca, editor of Restaurant Hospitality, puts it this way: Companies that are 100 per cent customer focused make the customer's satisfaction their only goal. They do not have as goals, increasing sales by a certain percentage, raising a profit margin, or reducing debt. They believe... that if you strive to sell only the highest quality product and strive to please every customer, sales, profit and success will follow.

This is a difficult concept for many of us to grasp. It means letting go of a financial accounting structure passed down from generation to generation of Harvard MBAs who've instilled in us that the only way to build your bottom line is to raise your top line and squeeze the middle.... That can work... but wouldn't you rather make the quality of your food, the dining experience and your customer's satisfaction your primary concern? The moral is simple: If you satisfy your customers while charging a fair price and controlling costs, profits will follow.

Managerial Decision Making Off-premise catering managers must make decisions that keep their operations running smoothly. They realize that some decisions will be better than others, that there is no perfect solution to every problem, and that the best decision-making goal is to find the best possible solution with the least number of drawbacks. Connie Sitterly, a management consultant and author, states that to be a good decision maker you should "plan ahead so when problems crop up, you're prepared to act, not react.

Control circumstances, instead of allowing them to control you. Take the initiative by anticipating and solving business problems." Although hundreds of books have been written about decision making, the following tips from Ms. Sitterly should be helpful.

They're paraphrased from an article she wrote back in 1990 in The Meeting Manager, but they are still up-to-the-minute when it comes to making tough decisions successfully:

- Remember that there's seldom only one acceptable solution to the problem. Choose the best alternative.
- Make decisions that help achieve the company objectives.

- You need to consider feelings whenever people are involved. Even if you must make an unpopular decision, you can minimize repercussions... if workers know you have taken their feelings into account.
- Allow quality time for planning and decision making... pick a time when you are energetic and your mind is fresh.
- Realize that you'll never please everyone. Few decisions meet with unanimous approval... the appointed authority, not the majority, rules.
- Make time for making decisions... in business, delaying a decision can cost thousands of dollars.
- Put decision making in perspective. Every executive feels overwhelmed at times by either the enormity or the number of decisions made during a business day.... For peace of mind accept that you are doing the best job you can with the time, talent, and resources you have.
- Don't wait for a popular vote. Rallying your colleagues around your decision before you take action or waiting for their vote of confidence before deciding anything may cost too much in time. There are times when you just have to do something.

LEADERSHIP

There are major differences between those who lead and those who manage. Catering companies need both types of executives, and some who can do both. If a catering company is earning seven- and eight-figure annual revenues, it is most definitely being led by people with leadership skills. Leaders are able to get people to do things they don't necessarily like to do, but they do them and even enjoy them. You might say: Maintains Develops Administers Innovates Relies on systems Relies on people Counts on controls Counts on trust Does things right Does the right things Works within the system Works on the system Manages things Leads people A leader is more like a thermostat than a thermometre. A thermostat sets the standard temperature for the space it's in.

A thermometre simply records the temperature; it can't change anything. And one more important trait: Leaders take a little more than their share of the blame and a little less than their share of the credit.

Professionalism and Common Business Courtesy Off-premise caterers who are not professional in their business practices will never reach the pinnacle of success in the field.

Before we address the technical aspects of catering in the succeeding chapters, it is of utmost importance that we define professionalism.

The following guidelines are adapted from an article by Carol McKibben in Special Events magazine:

- Become known for doing what you say you are going to do.
- Give price quotes and commitments only when you know everything about the event.
- Treat clients and staff members with respect.
- Build relationships with clients. Do not look at them as accounts or projects.
- Be on time, or a bit early, for appointments. Be prepared for an appointment.
- Be honest; don't play games.
- Stand behind your work. If it is wrong, make it right.
- In the face of abuse from others, don't respond by becoming abusive. Try to detach yourself from it emotionally and handle it logically. Of course, do not use your position of power to abuse others.
- Dress professionally.
- Enjoy your work as an off-premise caterer. When work ceases to be enjoyable, it is time to quit and find a new career.

ETHICS IN MANAGEMENT

The Roman philosopher Publilius Syrus said, "A good reputation is more valuable than money." This is as true today as it was in ancient times. And yet, lack of ethics is perhaps the most widely discussed topic in today's business world. We read and hear of illegalities, scandals, and other forms of questionable behaviour bringing down some of the nation's largest corporations. Off-premise caterers are in no way exempt from ethical concerns.

Even the smallest caterers deal in issues of fairness, legal requirements, and honesty on a daily basis. Examples include truth in menu, misleading advertising, unexpected and unjustified last-minute add-ons to the party price, and even underbidding a competitor when the client has disclosed your competitor's price.

The truly ethical caterer will assume responsibility for the host to ensure that the host plans an event in the best interest of the guests. A host who wishes to serve alcohol to underage guests or barbecued ribs to a group of elderly people (tough to eat with dentures) is out of line and needs to be advised that this will not work. In fact, an ethical caterer will refuse to cater an event that is clearly not being planned in the best interest of the host or guests.

There are times when a caterer is given a free hand in planning a menu. Perhaps a grieving client calls for food after the funeral of a loved one, saying, "Please send over food for 50 guests tomorrow night. You know what we like!" The ethical caterer will not take advantage of this situation by either providing too much food or overcharging the client. Another temptation arises when the caterer is pressed to cater more events on a certain day or evening than he or she can reasonably accommodate. The extra money looks good.

Unethical caterers will rationalize that they can handle all the events, even if an inexperienced supervisor or staff must oversee these events, or even if the kitchen staff will not be able to prepare the caterer's usual high-quality food because of lack of time and personnel. Caterers who take on more work than they can reasonably accommodate are greedy and are considered by many observers to be unethical.

In the foregoing situation the caterer should decline the work and perhaps recommend another caterer. Some caterers refuse to recommend another catering firm because they feel that if the client is not pleased with the other firm, the caterer who turned down the business will be blamed for the recommendation. Other caterers freely recommend one or more companies when unable to cater events. There are times when it is very hard not to bad-mouth a competitor, but this is considered unethical as well as rude.

Those who are ethical would rather point out their own strengths than downgrade the competition. It can be very tempting for self-employed caterers to underreport income or overstate expenses. They rationalize that no one will know if they accept cash for a party, then fail to report it as income and pay the associated tax, or that no one will know if they happen to charge personal expenses now and then to the business. Some caterers who are licensed to sell liquor by the drink or by the bottle are tempted to bill clients for beverages that were not consumed.

These practices are not only unethical—they are illegal. Other ethical violations occur when caterers receive under-the-table cash "kickbacks" from suppliers, misrepresent their services to potential clients, or bid on party plans or ideas stolen from other caterers. Caterers also soon learn that some clients are unethical. A few are masterful at finding fault with a wedding or other important event, then demanding a "discount" based on whatever flaw they feel they have uncovered. Some will refuse to pay for linens that were damaged by candles they lit on them! You'll find people who, mid- party, will ask you to stay "a couple hours of overtime, just to wrap things up"— then not show up to pay you for the extra time the next day, as agreed.

Others will haggle over the tiniest details on an invoice or try to engage more than one caterer in a bidding war to lower prices. Caterers who deal with "middleman" organizations, like destination management firms or production companies, may find that a client of one of these companies will come back later to try to deal directly with you, thus cutting out the middleman who recommended you! As a catering professional, you need to expect a certain amount of this behaviour and must protect yourself if you suspect an ethical question may arise.

Insisting on security deposits, having a valid and authorized credit card number on file for unforeseen charges, refusing to look at other caterers' written bids, and standing firm on your own invoice prices are just a few ways ethical problems can be avoided. And rather than cut out a legitimate middleman-type of vendor, you can either refuse to deal directly with a client who tries such a manoeuvre or suggest a commission be paid to the middleman. You will also be put in some sticky situations as—during tough times, and even good times—certain clients will make unrealistic requests.

They've often been good, regular clients too! But they'll promise you future business if you'll cater their party "at cost," or defer payment for them, or ask some other special favour "just this once." These requests are unfair, and you're right to be squeamish about them. Offpremise caterers should be extremely wary when approached in this fashion. As a general rule, clients who do not pay their bills in a professional manner, or who are not willing to pay a fair price for catering services, are not worth the headaches they cause.

The Jefferson Centre of Character Education has set forth a list of ten "universal values": honesty, integrity, promise keeping, fidelity, fairness, caring for others, respect for others, responsible citizenship, pursuit of excellence, and accountability. These values should provide some solid guidance for any businessperson who considers him- or herself a true professional. Separating yourself from the Competition Great caterers do more than imitate—they innovate. There are distinct advantages for those who offer a unique menu, a unique service, or perhaps a unique location.

They may build and improve on someone else's concept, but they strive to take the idea to the next level. Rather than mimicking another's success, they imprint their own signature on their menus.

To illustrate, let's take a look at two simple, self-service mashed potato bars. Mashed potatoes Sweet potatoes Sour cream Crème fraiche Bacon bits Canadian bacon Chopped chives Chopped fresh basil Shredded cheddar cheese Crumbled Stilton The "Unique" bar may include all the traditional accompaniments too—but what a difference a little imagination makes! There might even be a bit of caviar to top the mashers at the Unique bar, and perhaps they'll be served in martini glasses. Why not have fun with it? One of America's top chefs, Charlie Trotter, looks at food trends differently in his book Lessons in Excellence.

Says Trotter, "It's important that you foster a company culture that spurs you and your employees to search for innovative opportunities. Innovations can satisfy needs that are unmet or offer solutions to time-worn problems, or they can be new ways of saving time, space and money." Trotter says he and his staff use input from their travels, readings, television, radio, and even hobbies to hit upon trends. They keep up on the latest changes in public opinion and demographics to search for interesting, potentially high-growth markets.

Currently, they've identified ethnic cuisines such as Pan-Asian and Nuevo Latino as hot areas for menu innovation. The bottom line is that they create their own trends. Similarly, as with any career, catering professionals need to reexamine their business strategies from time to time. Some caterers do what they do best, are well known for it, and never vary their formulas. Their clients love them and get exactly what they expect. Other caterers blindly copy everybody else. They ricochet from one recipe to the other, never bothering to see if it meets their clients' needs.

If they read about it in Food Arts magazine, they feel they have to serve it! But most caterers lie somewhere between these two extremes, blending the successful ideas of the past with new twists. Great caterers also separate themselves from competitors by using the resources around them to build their businesses. In South Florida, for example, one caterer specializes in event planning for doctors, through his hospital food service management job.

Another has an exclusive off-premise contract for a sports facility; a third was the on-premise caterer for a city club, which resulted in off-premise jobs for the club members. Capitalize on the audience you have—they're (almost) already yours! Personal Management Off-premise caterers must learn how to deal with principles of stress management, time management, and personal organization if they are to manage at peak efficiency.

Time is our most precious commodity, and to waste it because of being overstressed or disorganized will inevitably result in less-than-desirable results. Stress Management Stress comes from interaction with others, and from having to meet deadlines.

A certain amount of stress and tension is necessary to achieve the best results—those who are too laid back generally do not maximize their potential—but too much stress causes chronic fatigue, irritability, cynicism, hostility, inflexibility, and difficulty in thinking clearly. Catering managers who are overstressed are unable to perform at maximum capability.

Stress can often be controlled through:

- Daily exercise such as brisk walking, running, or other aerobic pursuits that increase the pulse rate. Some folks purposefully take their minds off work when they exercise; for others, the daily walk or run is a time to get their day mentally organized.
- Relaxation techniques, including meditation and yoga.
- Writing down the issues that cause stress. Identify those issues in your life that can be controlled, and simply decide to make the best of those that cannot. List ways to deal with the controllable stress factors.
- Reading articles and books on stress reduction. It is important to remember that some stress in catering is good. An arrow would not be propelled from a bow if the bow was not stressed.

However, too much stress can break the bow, as well as ruin catered events. Time Management There are only 168 hours in each week, and the greatest rewards come to those who accomplish the most meaningful things during this fixed amount of time. Offpremise caterers realize that if they can accomplish more meaningful production in less time, they will have more time for things other than work. They also realize that working smarter, not harder, through the effective use of time will produce greater results.

The key to effective time management is to set goals for a lifetime, for five years, and for each year, month, week, and day. (Use some of the tips for putting SMART goals in writing—not just for "big picture" goals, but as part of your daily business.) Without written goals, off-premise caterers cannot effectively manage their time. Because time management involves choosing how to spend time, it is impossible to make proper choices without knowing your desired goals.

The captain of a ship without a destination cannot choose the proper course. He will cruise aimlessly at sea, never reaching his port of call. It is equally important to schedule "downtime" for yourself—for family, friends, hobbies, and interests other than work. You are guarding against burnout when you insist on some personal time.

Off-premise caterers can choose from an array of time-saving techniques and technical advances to help them in the quest to efficiently manage time:

- Make those daily, detailed lists of goals and objectives.
- Use technical advances to speed up paper handling, such as fax machines and computers with word processing, accounting, and menu-planning software.
- For heaven's sake, if you don't have a computer, get one! You can purchase one nowadays for a monthly payment of less than $40. You can take classes to learn how to use it or hire someone to teach you individually.
- Use cellular phones to stay in touch while away from the office. These are lifesavers at off-premise catering locations when emergency and other calls are necessary, and if you have downtime, a cellular phone can make it easy for you to use this time to return phone calls.
- Handle incoming papers only once. Here's the rule: Do it, delegate it, discard it, or file it. (Better yet, hire someone else to file it!)
- Do your most important work at times when you happen to be most alert. Most of us know whether we are "morning people" or "night owls." Take advantage of your peak energy periods to handle your most challenging tasks.
- Sign up for a seminar or course in time management to learn more tips.

One of the biggest time wasters for a caterer is also the source of much business— the prospective client who calls to ask questions—so it's an interruption that cannot be ignored, but can be controlled.

Whoever answers the phone at your business should always qualify the incoming call by asking:

- The date of the event
- The location of the event
- The number of guests
- The budget for the event Why?

First of all, time can be wasted talking about an event before you ask the date and discover you're not able to do it in the first place because of a scheduling conflict. Perhaps the number of guests is too small or too large for your particular company, the budget is insufficient, or the proposed location is already booked for another event. Always focus on results by asking yourself, "Will this activity help me achieve any of my goals?" Prioritize tasks in order of their importance and know when to delegate them to others.

Most people waste countless hours, days, weeks, and years chitchatting on the phone, shuffling papers, running errands, and doing other things that are easy enough but offer little or no payoff. Learn to delegate these types of tasks whenever possible. Pay other people to do them, and don't tell yourself you can't afford it—you can always make more money, but you have only so much time. The true achievers—in catering and in other fields—minimize their time on low priority, low-payoff tasks and turn their attention to those things that will bring the greatest rewards. These tasks are often difficult to accomplish, take a great deal of time, and involve at least some risk.

For example, a caterer could spend the entire day showing prospective clients numerous suitable locations for a major event. The caterer would then spend the next three days preparing a written proposal for an event at each of the locations, with no guarantee that the event will even take place. However, if the caterer is hired, there's a five-figure profit to be made. Worth the risk? Certainly! Another high-payoff task might be to write a new catering menu.

Both this and the aforementioned task require large chunks of time and involve some risk, but more than likely will produce major rewards in increased revenues and profits. In summary, off-premise caterers who best manage their time in the long run will be the most successful. They become the leading caterers in their communities, in their states, and in the country. Getting Organized When projects, tasks, catering kitchens, and offices are organized, things run much more smoothly and efficiently. The time spent looking for things and jumping from job to job is wasted time that could be put to much better use.

Many off-premise caterers have found various methods that work for them:

- Establish a filing system using hanging folders and manila folders. Categories can include upcoming events, projects to do, and projects pending. Files should be stored vertically, rather than stacked atop one another, for greater accessibility.
- Take a tip from event planners who start a separate notebook for each event they are working on. Into this three-ring binder go all

notes, contracts, sketches, colour samples—anything for that particular job.

- Consider hiring a professional organizer to come to your office and set up a filing and record-keeping system that works for your business.
- Keep those items that are used frequently close by.
- Focus on one project at a time, rather than jumping from one thing to another. This can be easily accomplished by blocking out some time during the day to work on major projects and arranging for no interruptions.
- Whenever possible, try to schedule time to return phone calls and/or e-mail messages. That way, you can handle them all at once, instead of scattering them (and your thoughts) in five-minute intervals throughout the day.
- Either at the end of each day or first thing in the morning, prepare a list of things to do for the day.

Those off-premise caterers who can effectively deal with stress, who properly manage their time, who learn to delegate and keep things organized will lead their peers into the future. They will set the standards for others to follow. They will accomplish more and will be in a position to receive the greatest rewards as a result.

LOOKING AHEAD—CATERING IN THE FUTURE

What does the future hold for caterers in this new century? First of all, we know that catering is neither rocket science nor brain surgery. Change is inevitable in this business, but not at the same rate as, say, in molecular theory or medical technology. In fact, in catering, rediscovering foods of the previous century is trendy! Many caterers still feature the signature dishes—honey coconut shrimp, beef tenderloin, Caesar salad—that they've served for decades. Why? The customers demand, and enjoy, them.

This certainly doesn't mean things stay stagnant in our industry. Innovative buffet and food station décor will continue to evolve. Most catering companies will continue to build their reputations on elegant, "over-the-top" food presentations, and the healthy competition shows no signs of abating. Other caterers prize research, developing cutting-edge menu items to set them apart from the pack.

More women are entering the off-premise catering field. Paula LeDuc in the San Francisco Bay area, Katherine Farrell in Ann Arbor, Abigail Kirsch in New York, Mary Micucci in Los Angeles, and Joy Wallace in Miami are but a handful of enterprising women who have grown their companies into catering's elite. Staffing woes will continue to be monumental, as hiring, training, and retraining get tougher. Food service has always been a somewhat transient industry.

Astute caterers will use pre-employment aptitude and personality testing, master online staff scheduling systems, and develop their own training programmes. They will also realize, if they haven't already, that they must treat their employees at least as well as they treat their clients. Along the same lines, in a top-tier catering operation, the employees treat each other as well as they treat their clients. Caterers of the future will come to realize that bigger is not necessarily better.

Having a large volume of business is admirable—but only when the quality of your work rises to the same level. A company can grow to the point where quality slips, gross profit margins lag, more equipment is needed, overhead costs expand, and the bottom line shrinks proportionately. The intelligent caterer will downsize, watch margins and profits grow—and overall stress levels diminish—as they become more selective about the clientele they service. Caterers are realizing that "high tech" will never replace personalized service, or "high touch"—but without high tech, they'll limit their potential for high touch.

In an industry where, amazingly, some caterers still don't accept credit cards, the savvy businessperson is learning to embrace new technology, launching interactive websites and e-mail marketing campaigns. They're creating improved computer generated proposals, rental orders, packing lists, staffing schedules, and instant financial statements. And they're realizing that computer-savvy business owners have more time to do what they love—which is run their business! Competition will continue to increase.

Sales will grow, but not without some dips, because economic woes, terrorist attacks, and the resulting fears cannot help but impact the catering profession. More caterers were hurt financially by the recession at the beginning of this century than by the September 11 terrorist attacks, but both left their marks on the industry. An increased use of security cameras at high profile events (and in some cases, to thwart theft) is one result of the heightened awareness. Mega-event catering is acknowledged as an excellent way to grow business—at golf and tennis tournaments, NASCAR races, air shows, boat shows, and more.

In addition to being profitable events, they expose the caterer to a wider range of potential clients. Then again, a caterer from Augusta, Georgia, generates enough revenue from serving sandwiches and beverages at the Masters' Golf Tournament that he need not cater at all the rest of the year! The pressure experienced in servicing huge, multiday events is as big as the events themselves, but the rewards can be significant. At the end of the 1900s, B. Joseph Pine II wrote The Experience Economy, a primer about the "new rules of engagement" for businesses.

Pine asserts that a new economic model is taking shape as we move from a service-based economy into an experience-based economy, where successful vendors literally create an "experience" for clients by using props and services to engage them in an "inherently personal way." Pine claims that Walt Disney was the founding father of the "Experience Economy," and in today's restaurant industry there are plenty of examples—Rainforest Cafe, Planet Hollywood, Hard Rock Cafes, and other themed eateries that combine food, service, and atmosphere to create a more "complete" dining experience. This kind of trend is adaptable for off-premise caterers too, with elaborate themes, staff members who double as costumed performers, team-building events, and imaginative menu items presented in wild new ways to delight and entertain the crowd as well as feed them!

For those who love to have fun, and who are as adventurous as they are practical, it's a great time to be an off-premise caterer. The Seven Habits of Highly Successful Caterers Let's examine some additional techniques, philosophies, and real-life ways to be successful in the challenging field of off-premise catering. Habits are things we do automatically, like brushing our teeth, combing our hair, or straightening a tablecloth that's uneven. We hardly think about them, we just do them. Stephen R. Covey wrote The Seven Habits of Highly Effective People, which has been a bestseller for years—you should read it if you haven't already. But what are some habits that mark successful caterers? What separates star performers from the rest of the crowd? With a nod to Mr. Covey, here are seven key traits.

One of our favourite sayings is, "A turtle goes nowhere until it sticks its neck out." In order to succeed, we must be continually growing and improving, and the only way to do this is to leave our comfort zones—and stick our necks out! If you're right-handed, you feel quite comfortable writing with your right hand. Try writing with your left hand. You're definitely out of your comfort zone. But after a while, you'll find you can actually write with either hand.

Successful caterers make things happen by taking calculated risks, whether it is trying new menu items, new buffet display concepts, or accepting a job in a new and challenging off-premise location. Caterers who refuse to take risks fail to grow and learn are left behind. Sincere Concern for Others Nobody cares how much you know until they know how much you care. Empathy and genuine concern for your clients and staff are paramount to long-term success. What are their needs, wishes, and desires? What are their concerns and their "hot buttons"? By putting ourselves in their positions, we can begin to show concern for others and understand them.

When we do this, we develop meaningful relationships and, not coincidentally, loyalty. We give them what they want, and we get what we want. Keeping Up with Current Trends It's not just a matter of food and presentation and theme trends. Caterers who are not wired to do business online through the Internet and e-mail are missing out on huge opportunities. The online catering referral service, Leading Caterers of America (founded by the book's co-author Bill Hansen), receives 5 to 20 enquiries per day from clients looking for catering services coast to coast, in Alaska, Hawaii, and occasionally overseas. People do shop for catering online, and the companies that lead the way have high quality websites and diligently reply to e-mailed requests in a timely manner.

Caterers need to get in the habit of responding to e-mail correspondence as soon as possible, as well as providing e-mailed proposals to those clients who prefer to do business via their computers. Event planners who book caterers for their clients love receiving e-mailed proposals, because they are easy to copy-and-paste into their own proposals. If you're not in the habit of working online, you're behind the times. Excellent Priorities and Time Management You get 20 per cent of your sales and profits from 80 per cent of your clients, and 80 per cent of your sales and profits from 20 per cent of your clients. None of us ever go home at night thinking that all the work is done—it never is. It's simply a question of what's most important, as well as what's most urgent. Urgent things are never really an issue. There's no question that if you have a catered event today, it will get done. But what's most urgent is not necessarily what's most important. You must understand the difference.

For example, you could spend a day catering three small parties for 25 guests each, but fall behind on preparing a proposal for another job, in three months, for 500 guests—and lose it to a competitor whose proposal was simply submitted on time. Successful caterers spend their time in those areas that generate the biggest paybacks in terms of money, quality, and other rewards. They make a habit of planning their days, leaving time for the most important, as well as the most urgent.

At the start of each day they prepare an agenda that details both short-term objectives and long-term goals. If you're a student, you should already be using this technique to accomplish as much as you can in school. Quality before Quantity Bigger is not necessarily better. Still, many of us get caught up in that way of thinking.

If our sales are $1 million, let's go for $2 million. If they're $2 million, what's wrong with $4 million? And if $4 million is good... There's nothing wrong with building sales if quality does not suffer. However, when the quality of our products and services suffers so does the quality of our lifestyle. More business means more hours at work. And doctors will tell you they've never met a man or woman who, on a deathbed, expressed a wish that he or she had spent more time at work.

If we can grow our businesses with no adverse effects on the quality of our lives or our products, then we should go for it! But if we find profits slipping and clients complaining, and we need a letter of introduction when we stumble home at 3:00 A.M., then something's very wrong. We need to make of habit of continually asking ourselves whether we might be better off with less business and more time for ourselves and for our families.

We need to continually examine the quality of our work to ensure that it's not slipping because we've allowed ourselves to take on too much. Being Detail Oriented A baseball player who bats.250 gets three hits for every 12 times at bat. One who bats. 333 gets four hits for every 12 times at bat. The difference—one more hit for every 12 times at bat—means the difference between an average major league ball player and a Hall of Fame inductee. Do you make it a habit to continually look for the little things?

A good caterer isn't nitpicky, but is forever finding something that needs to be tweaked, adjusted, redone, or improved—little things that most customers won't notice, but that greatly impact the overall professionalism of an event. Being aware of the details in flavours, looks, aromas, and tidiness separates the average caterers from the superstars. And, by all means, check the spelling, grammar, and punctuation in all your written materials, from brochures to contracts—or hire someone to do it.

Again, the goal is to present a professional image. Remember? The devil is in the details. Setting High Standards If you refuse to accept anything but the very best, you very often get the best.

Successful caterers set their standards high and expect excellence from themselves and their staff members. They're never happy with the status quo, always striving to make each party, wedding, or event better than the last.

They debrief after an event, asking staff for input and improvements. They know that if they fail to improve, they're leaving the door open for their competitors to capture a good customer or a larger share of the market. Successful caterers also make a habit of lifelong learning.

They're forever reading, attending trade shows, and exploring areas that will help them improve their own businesses with new ideas. They challenge and reward their staff members for having the same attitude. Vince Lombardi, the late NFL coach, who during his career coached the first team to ever win the Super Bowl, put it this way: "The quality of a person's life is in direct proportion to their commitment to excellence, regardless of their chosen field of endeavor." How Does an Off-Premise Caterer Gauge Success? There are a number of signs to look for when evaluating an existing off-premise catering business. Healthy companies rate highly in all of these areas.

Those that are unhealthy, or even on the brink of failure, will not rate nearly as well:

- Management thoroughly plans, organizes, executes, and controls each catered event.
- Proper controls are in place for costs, accounts receivable and payable, and liquid assets such as cash and inventories. Theft prevention is also a priority.
- Food and service quality is well-controlled and meets or exceeds clients' approval.

- Pricing for food and services is fair and competitive with other firms in the marketplace. There is a spirit of healthy competition.
- The catering firm enjoys good working relationships with both clients and suppliers.
- Time and attention are given to food safety in storage, preparation, and display. Employees know the local health codes and follow them.
- There is sufficient working capital to operate the business. The firm can make loan payments as they become due. Excessive credit is not extended to clients.
- Budgets are prepared and followed. Business records, insurance coverage, and licenses are kept up to date. The information derived from these records is used to provide data to help manage the business.
- Sales growth is controlled. There are sufficient financial and personnel resources to operate as business steadily grows.
- Market trends are anticipated.
- Management and staff have a good working knowledge of the off-premise catering field.
- There are solid, trusting relationships between management and staff. Staff members are well trained and feel truly appreciated—because they are.
- Management works closely with a qualified accountant to plan for payment of taxes.
- And, finally, management is willing to seek qualified professional assistance if problems arise.

The Off-Premise Catering Model is the factors that enter into the off-premise catering arena. It shows how managerial philosophies and techniques, as well as laws regarding personnel, business, alcoholic beverage service, and sanitation and safety, must all be interrelated to guide the company. It then depicts how marketing efforts produce clients, which in turn creates needs for site inspections and logistical plans, including planning in these specific areas: menus, beverages, equipment, personnel, and any other related services.

Once the planning is complete, it is possible to provide clients with written proposals, which include all the aforementioned plans along with pricing. Normally, proposals are modified somewhat. Once modification is complete and all provisions meet with the approval of both caterer and client, a contract is prepared that contains all the conditions outlined in the proposal.

As the party date approaches, certain operational elements are addressed, such as:

- Hiring and scheduling staff
- Purchasing and pre-preparation of menu items

- Ordering equipment as needed from party rental companies
- Obtaining licenses and permits, as needed, for use of the site, serving alcohol, etc.
- Preparing a "pull sheet" that details all items supplied by the commissary to produce the party.
- Coordinating all beverage and accessory services with the client and the vendors.

All the preplanning elements culminate on the day or night of "The Show." That's when staff, equipment, food, and other services arrive at the party site, and the event is executed. After the event, there are certain outcomes, which include: Positive and/or negative word of mouth about the event Revenues, expenses, profits, and cash Accounting records.

SOCIABILITY AND MODELS OF CATERING MULTI-LAYERED MORALS

Picnicking is eating in the open, and thus being seen by others. In interpreting the behaviour of people eating in the open, it is crucial to consider frames of interpretation and connotation, grounds for moral and legal judgements. Places where alcohol was being served, especially, proved prone to moralizing and comments.

Results of new research on everyday and festive eating and drinking yield an interesting variation on the debate, launched by Peter Burke in the 1970s, about the growing divergence between elite and popular cultures. Differentiation is a key concept here, next to appropriation and demarcation. In this book Christoph Guggenbiihl makes use of emic interpretations of elite groups in Switzerland. He emphasizes that from the end of the eighteenth century a differentiation of catering businesses established itself.

Guggenbiihl discusses the many functions of inns and shows how they were decanted into moral issues. The moralizing gaze was also present in middle-class observations of the (eating) habits of French labourers in the nineteenth century, as Anne Lhuissier demonstrates. Oliver Haid adds to this debate the case of Meran, where the introduction of a beer culture in a wine region did not pass unnoticed.

Beat Kumin discusses gastronomic culture in early modern inns. He questions the sharp cut-off before and after the 'modern' restaurant, with enhanced consumer choice, flexible dining times and menus with different dishes. Sources for early-modern Central Europe, in particular the Swiss republic of Bern and the principality of Bavaria, reveal variety, both in dining options and catering quality, a la carte selection options and table *d'hote* menus. The major towns provided exquisite dining contexts. Kumin launches the thesis that what was crucial was not the invention of individualized service, but the creation of establishments exclusively dedicated to customer choice. Restaurants built on earlier practices but wrapped the eating experience in a special context, promoted an environment of leisurely and quality time consuming indulgence and bourgeois ostentation. In contrast to inns, they gradually moved away from the table d'hote system and the offer of accommodation facilities.

Maja Godina-Golija provides a case study of food available in catering establishments in the city and the countryside in Slovenia at the end of the nineteenth century and the first half of the twentieth century. The distribution of specific institutions of inns and then restaurants gives an insight into the kind of food potentially within reach.

It is clear that a wideranging virtual menu of food and dining arrangements was available in Slovenia. Inhabitants and travellers in the region had access to many sorts of dishes, if they had the means.

BENEATH THE PAYING CUSTOMERS, THE CUSTOMS

There is a relation between eating out and having a home. Soup kitchens or charity meals in the open air, in city streets or squares, are not addressed here. People invited to a feast usually do not pay (but bring gifts and invite their hosts on another occasion). This is often embedded in what Pierre Bourdieu called an economy of symbolic goods.

Eszter Kisban emphasizes that in nineteenth- and early twentieth century Hungary wedding meals were the opposite of everyday meals, having their own rules and norms. Alexander Fenton describes how, in mid-twentieth-century Scotland, employers had to provide meals free of charge to children granted exemption from school attendance for helping in the harvest. In a number of chapters of this book, 'cash' is suspended. Food can be carried to the field but it is not paid for there; it is distributed. Paying at the picnic is also not customary, although, as noted above, pooling was organized or people brought their own food. Nevertheless, the carrying has its price: a time investment at home, an effort to keep and store food on the way (and money is more economical, it takes up less space, volume and weight).

We may discover a number of occasions of eating and drinking out where the food or drinks are not paid for by the diners themselves. Marc Jacobs explores a tip of the iceberg of eating food for free (but, on a closer look, with social strings attached).

Reciprocity and unwritten rules are important topics in the history of semi-public wining and dining. Eating in public is also a way to communicate with other groups or individuals. The concept of the tournee generale, when someone pays for all the clientele at an inn, is not usual in a restaurant. It is possible to invite a whole group to a restaurant, on the occasion of a wedding or a funeral, but at the time a number of the normal rules change (no menu, no open access for outsiders). Rituals involving eating out, or in front of other households, remind us of alternative needs, codes and expectations and bring to mind a broad range of possibilities and repertoires. Symbolic violence often accompanied rites of passage or forms of collective action, resulting in free meals or in conspicuous food consumption.

Most chapters of the book show how menus gradually changed over time. Special occasions of eating in public functioned as a serving-hatch for innovations on the menu of everyday life. Kisban suggests that public occasions of hospitality, traditional feasts and the liminal zone of rites de passages in the country were important for the process of food innovation. Fenton emphasizes that eating out in peripheral areas is not frozen in time. He identifies a process of endogenous development: slowly, almost imperceptibly, but cumulatively, eating habits change.

Specific attempts at intervention, central direction, do not necessarily have a lasting effect on eating habits. However, eating landscapes do change. New objects are introduced (picnic baskets, hamburger packs ...). New settings are created. New dealers operate. New distribution lines are organized. New words are developed. This is far from just a contribution to 'oral history': the history of eating out involves all senses, it is a total experience. Seeing the food, seeing the other eaters, the people serving, smelling the food, hearing the food and the other eaters, and the people serving, touching the food ... Eating out is also about reflecting on the food and the situation. The context evokes (or is the result of) all kinds of strings attached to the food: incentives of perception, being conscious of, or alert to, implication and obligations when eating the food (to pay, to shift to a ritual mode of etiquette, to be polite...).

This book reopens an old but never concluded debate of the 1980s: a discussion on popular and elite culture about the relations, actions, perceptions and interventions of elite groups seeking distinction and distance, on the one hand, and the vast majority of the population, on the other.

Next to Roger Chartier, who discussed the concept of appropriation, E. P. Thompson temporarily closed the debate in his Customs in Common. He pointed to the definition that was propagated by Peter Burke, who approached culture as a system of shared meaning, attitudes and values, and the symbolic forms (performances, artefacts) in which they are embodied. Thompson added an agonistic view to this consensual view:

But a culture is also a pool of diverse resources, in which traffic passes between the literate and the oral, the super-ordinate and the subordinate, the village and the metropolis; it is an arena of elements full of conflict, which requires some compelling pressure - as, for example, nationalism or prevalent religious orthodoxy or class consciousness-to take form as 'system' [...]. The plebeian culture which clothed itself in the rhetoric of 'custom' [...] was not self-defining or independent of external influences. It had taken form defensively, in opposition to the constraints and controls of the patrician rulers.

Thompson emphasizes the relations of power, which are masked by the rituals of paternalism and deference. The history of the restaurant in the transition from early-modern to modern society and in the nineteenth and twentieth centuries is also the history of service. Rituals of deference and service are available in eating-out situations, when money is exchanged. E. P. Thompson formulated a programme of research that requires attention today in the study of popular culture, peripheral 1/or traditional communities. Needs and expectations should be major themes:

The industrial revolution and accompanying demographic revolution were the backgrounds to the greatest transformation in history, in revolutionizing 'needs' and in destroying the authority of customary expectations. This is what most marks the 'pre-industrial' or the 'traditional' from the modern world this transformation, this remodelling of 'need' and this raising of the threshold of material expectations (along with the devaluation of traditional cultural satisfactions) continues with irreversible pressure today, accelerated everywhere by universally available means of communication.

This is precisely a central problem in the book we present here, in particular in the contributions by Beat Kumin, Julia Csergo and Stephen Mennell.

Tradition and the dissolving or reoriented opposition between popular and elite culture, and the mediation between the two, is very present in the chapter by Virginie Amilien. Taking Norway in the last decade as her case, she investigates the confrontation between a traditional way of eating and thinking about food, on the one hand, and the very (post)modern style of eating in restaurants, on the other.

She stresses the still prevalent traditional values of eating (in), observes the clamorous discourse on dining out in restaurants, and opposes both to the marginal success of eating out in restaurants. She emphasizes the fracture with traditional, indoor-eating Norway. In doing so, she accurately embodies the bridge as well as the tensions between Part I and Part II of this book.

One may directly connect today's elegant brasseries to the taverns of the seventeenth and eighteenth centuries, and to the restaurants and grand hotels of the nineteenth and the twentieth centuries. The main feature of the history of this particular type of eating out would then be the democratization of a once rather elitist practice. Eating out in semi-public places, therefore, would testify to a key element of the history of the West during the past three centuries.

Yet the difference between eating out in preindustrial, industrial and post-industrial times is not only a mere matter of scale, meaning that more people would be able to visit restaurants more regularly, and spend more money, crucial though this is. It is equally necessary to study the characteristics of eating places in that past and present, as well as how they were perceived, labelled, classified and represented. It then becomes clear that 'democratization' does not refer to question of access of the exquisite restaurant to all people, but that democratization of the restaurant involves the search for identification, status, distinction and pleasure for all. In the twenty-first century, there are 'restaurant' accommodations for every purse and budget.

Nowadays, Europeans are eating out on a larger scale than ever before, but definitely when they do so they purchase prepared food instead of bringing it with them. Norway may be an exception, but in most European countries since 1950, many individuals and households have started to increase their expenditure on 'eating out'. This growth has been accompanied by the multiplication of culinary columns and tips in the media.

Part II deals with this history of numerous innovations related to outdoors eating in Europe since the late eighteenth century and up to today. It focuses on the culinary capital, Paris, and on a number of neighbouring countries in Western Europe, in particular on France, on the United Kingdom, on Germany and the Netherlands. Adel den Hartog discusses technological innovations in an international perspective, while Stephen Mennell touches upon the public sphere of the modern era.

COOKERY WRITING AND CULINARY ZENITHS

The perception, denotation, classification and representation of semi-public eating places may be explained by three intimately related phenomena, namely food, eaters and writers. 'Culinary zeniths', or places in certain periods that are generally viewed as successful with regard to food (in terms of gastronomy and sales), necessitate innovative supply, high demand and extensive discourse. An example of a successful culinary epoch would be the surrounding of the Parisian Jardin du Palais Royal in the 1800s, with great chefs, affluent eaters and culinary commentators.

Another example, suggesting that the gourmet connotation is not required, would be the global burger-culture in the 1990s, with the setting up of thousands of similar restaurants, a desirous public and extensive, albeit often hostile, writing (and action). The role of writing cultivating culinary zeniths has already been assessed, but it has primarily been limited to the culinary criticism of professionals like Grimod, Curnonsky or Gault and Millau. 'Culinary discourse' is understood here as the bundle of all written accounts dealing with food.

The discourse actually contributed to the shaping of a new culture, for which it was a requirement. Such is a central point made by Karin Becker and Alan Warde in this book, and by Stephen Mennell, who attributes to gastronomic writing a cardinal place in the forming of 'public opinion'. All three authors stress the importance of writing with regard to the construction of gastronomy, gourmets and taste, and they explore further the information provided by culinary discourse. Writers reported on food, prices, dishes and, perhaps above all, on places. Atmospheres were depicted, the clientele was discussed, the service and staff were valued, the decoration was commented on, and the general environment (music, conviviality...) was described. Particularly the new-style restaurant (a la carte, lavishly, expensive and elitist) enticed many to write.

RESTAURANTS IN ALL FORMS, DISHES OF ALL TASTES

Luxury food was, of course, not only prepared in fancy restaurants. Long before and after 1800, the rich and famous used professional cooks. Also, domestic caterers brought and served fine food at home. Against Kiimin's assertion, several authors suggest here and elsewhere that the emergence of the modern restaurant around 1800 marked an important qualitative leap in many respects.

First, restaurants were open luxurious places, in principle accessible to everyone (but totally different from the openness of a picnic!). Surely, the salle (or dining room) was a restricted area, only accessible to an elite. Their privacy was brought into the public: the ambiguity between private and public is nicely illustrated by the placing of individual ('own') tables in one room (opposed to the 'collective' table d'hote).

Hence, our classification of 'semi-public' (or 'semi-private'). In this, Hans-Jiirgen Teuteberg stresses the emergence of the 'private' table, while Stephen Mennell addresses the issue of the 'bourgeois public sphere' of eating. Adel den Hartog, in turn, addresses a crucial condition of the restaurant's selective accessibility, namely technology. Among other things, he demonstrates the importance of subsequent types of lighting to create special effects, new gimmicks and prolonged opening hours. Second, this 'private eating in public' entailed new rules and prescriptions. The eater could be recognized as a gourmet or a connoisseur by other eaters, the staff and - when talked and written about - the wider public, only if certain (invisible, subtle, discrete) rules had been met. Such rules did change over time (again, here was a crucial role for writers in judging and creating 'good' and 'bad' taste, places and manners). Social codes in restaurants were used to exclude and include, but they could also be acquired, interpreted and applied for transgression. In a way, the temperance movement (restriction and self-control) may be seen, mutatis mutandis, as an example of severe but clear rules and prescriptions.

Third, a restaurant offered a choice of dishes, thus leaving the decision of what to eat to the individual - a theme addressed by Teuteberg and Warde. The change of the menu card reflected this innovation: before the breakthrough of the restaurant (and still today at weddings or private parties) a menu was mostly a card that informed the eater what he or she would eat, but with the restaurant a menu became a card that informed the eater about the choice and the price.

It was a key element that allowed the marking of boundaries, the stressing of preferences, the construction of good taste, and distinguished the connoisseur from the parvenu. Fourth, restaurants were enterprises, confronted with market rules of price setting, production cost, sale figures, workforce turnover, productivity and competitiveness.

Equally, wage demands, unions, strikes, apprenticeship, working conditions and schooling were part of a restaurant's daily life. Such matters have hardly been studied, except perhaps for businesses and businessmen if they had names like Escoffier, Bocuse and other stars. Alain Drouard explores the covert world of (French) cooks, stressing their search for status, recognition and professionalism.

Elements of coping with this, as well as with competition, were specialization, innovation and increasing of choice, a process that was bound to be incessantly renewed. This creation and retention of a niche in the bourgeois public sphere existed right from the start of the modern restaurant, and perhaps formed the most obvious - and surely the most commented upon - difference with regard to the traditional inn or tavern. Adel den Hartog shows how the use of technological devices contributed to such a creation.

Fifth, individual and collective pleasures were also of great importance, with fine food being one element among many to enjoy alongside conversation, flirting, joking, laughing, etcetera. Hans-Jiirgen Teuteberg and Virginie Amilien stress this element of pleasure. The combination of these five features resulted in a semi-public place that soon became the locus of nineteenth-century bourgeois culture in the entire world. The plot between chefs, eaters and writers consisted of a non-stop search for distinction, innovation, novelties, surprise and amazement with new tastes, new dishes, new drinks, new tastes, new experiences, new forms, new chefs, new everything... Amilien demonstrates that this plot is still very active nowadays.

FAST, FASTER AND FASTEST FOOD

Accessibility, choice, expanding supply and pleasure are characteristics of fancy and tourist restaurants; it may be argued that the same goes for fast-food restaurants. The accessibility of such restaurants is general, though, in 1970s Europe, for various reasons (such as relatively high prices and a type of eating experience and an image that were culturally unfamiliar) there was some reluctance to enter a Burger King. Today, these places are wide open to a diverse clientele, with particular focus on youngsters.

The matter of choice and expanding supply seems more difficult to deal with. Whether a sandwich bar, a fish-and-chip shop or a burger restaurant, the supplied food is very similar in each type of restaurant all over the globe. Nevertheless, choice increases, adapting to custom and taste, with an enlarging supply of cheeseburgers, chicken burgers, nuggets or hulaburgers. Moreover, a local touch is added to the burger culture: in France during the summer of 2001, for example, 'a regional touch to your hamburger' was advertised, while sandwiches with daily changing regional sorts of cheese were sold. Such innovations are linked to the 'Happy Meal', which intends to make the food in this type of restaurant into a total experience of fun.

Sure, this is marketing talk. For many (young) children, however, eating out in a burger restaurant represents their very first 'restaurant experience', often during the celebration of a birthday party: a double rite of passage indeed. Quite clearly, eating in a fast-food restaurant may be a very enjoyable event. It remains to be seen whether 'shortorder cooking' arrangements provide as much pleasure to those preparing the meals.

This kind of eating out provoked the most sturdy reactions related to pureness, authenticity, identity, taste, gourmandise, and so on, brought together in the slow-food movement and erupting sometimes in assaults on burger restaurants. The intensity of this movement may be linked to globalization processes that conflict with national agriculture, the local restaurant industry and 'authentic' taste. Here, globalization and regionalization come together.

Yet fast-food businesses have long existed and can hardly be viewed as a pure US import. John Burnett shows that fish-and-chip shops, charcutiers, tea-shops?, coffee and sandwich bars and food stalls of various sorts were set up in cities and places with crowds long before the coming of the US-style hamburger restaurant. Two chapters address the history of the snack restaurant. Derek Oddy surveys the British fastfood industry since the 1880s, linking its development to work, shopping and leisure, and thus underlining once more the mixture between coercion and pleasure.

He surveys the development of various forms of eating out in the fast way, seeing a period of transition in the 1970s, and ends up trying to define the fast-food eater in the UK in the 1990s. Anneke van Otterloo and Adri Albert de la Bruheze discuss the Dutch variant of the snack restaurant, with special emphasis on 'eating out of the wall'. They detect a clear break around 1960, when the snacking started to reshape the traditional meal pattern. Van Otterloo and Albert de la Bruheze link these developments to broad social and economic changes, like the increase of purchasing power and leisure time, individualization and technological breakthroughs. They stress the implication of the food system, meaning that consumption of snacks cannot be studied without looking at production and distribution.

DIFFUSING PUBLIC PLACES OF DISCIPLINE

It would be wrong to conceive the modern history of eating out solely from the angle of fancy and popular restaurants, taverns, snack bars or inns. If it is accepted that 'innovation' is an important feature of the modern eating-out industry, then innovative places were also to be found elsewhere. Evidently, the luxury Parisian Cafe Riche had a totally different aura than a school canteen of the neighbouring arrondissement, but such canteens were also places of innovation with enormous influence. This opens up the wide field of eating (out) in schools, factories, army and police barracks (and indeed aeroplanes).

It is a mistake to think of these public-eating places wholly in terms of coercion, control and the sphere of grimy barracks. In many such communities, eating was a cherished moment to which special meaning was attributed. It could be a source of joy when a particular dish was served, a special desert was put on the table, or an extra bottle of beer was allowed. However, discipline was more at stake. In this book Anne Lhuissier uses the investigation of the Le Play group into eating habits of workers in nineteenth-century France, which was conducted with a sheer moralizing end. The workers' lunch was frugal, prodigal or totally excessive (each time with a plausible reason). Control, however, was complete when workers (or students, policemen ...) were fed by the institution.

Feeding a larger group necessitated financial control, and administrators have long calculated the daily price per person. Efficiency was high on the agenda. One consequence was that technological devices were first introduced in larger kitchens, a point well made by Adel den Hartog. Second, feeding a larger group necessitated social control involving strict rules, hierarchy and organization. In many schools, for example, food was used as a means to punish or reward.

Third, 'mass feeding' permitted a contribution to the construction and spreading of ideology. In this book, Isabelle Techouyeres illustrates this by looking at the 'republican' debate on the educational aspect of school meals in the long twentieth century. In doing so, she also demonstrates the importance and interest France (be it teachers, parents, politicians, children...) has in taste and gastronomy.

This leads to the fourth point: according to the development and perception of nutritional science, administrators of larger kitchens considered the energetic values of food (often linking this to the cost), as well as hygienic rules. Ulrike Thorns considers here industrial canteens in Germany between 1850 and 1950, stressing the influence of nutritionists who promoted 'rational' feeding. In particular, she looks at the building of new canteens and kitchens, the technology of this type of food serving, and, again, social and ideological implications. Through the controlling of eaters in public eating and drinking places, many innovations were introduced. In this respect, the distance between the Parisian Cafe Riche and the army canteen of the adjacent district was not that big.

This introduction merely echoes the richness of all chapters of this book. It presents just one plat dujour of a kitchen that in facts serves many appetizing tapas with new approaches, questions and insights. Thus, the history of the cooks, the fast-food bars, the industrial canteens, the tourist restaurants, the writing on taste or the technology of eating out is highlighted. Other aspects, such as demographic pressure, the history of businesses, the influencing of eaters and eating, foreign restaurants or cooking techniques are present in this book and deserve equally to be discussed. We hope that the reader has found a nice carte dujour for many days here.

UP THE COST OF A MEAL

Of little-known origin, the term, unheard of in the sixteenth century, seems to have been used for the first time in the seventeenth century, more precisely by LaBruyere in Les Caracteres written between 1687 and 1688 and continued until 1694: If he has a picnic at home, he puts aside part of what was brought to him. This date is confirmed by Bloch and von Wartburg, who note the first appearance of the term in 1694 without giving a precise reference.

If we refer to the dictionaries of the period, the term appears neither in the Dictionnaire Universel by Furetiere (1690), although it is true that it precedes the first usage of the term by four years, nor in the Richelet (1719). The first time the word is mentioned is in the third edition of the Dictionnaire de I'Academie, which appeared in 1740. Therefore it was only officially introduced into the French language in the middle of the eighteenth century, when it is defined as an adverbial way of speaking that is only used in phrases such as a 'picnic supper', 'to have a picnic meal'. It is used to say, 'to have a meal where each person pays his or her share'.

That form fell out of use, pushed aside by its noun form, 'a picnic', which was used in the elliptical form of a meal in the picnic style, which later led to the simplified use of 'picnic'. How did this term come into being? Who invented it and what was the intention that could not be expressed in the existing vocabulary? None of these questions have any reliable answers. According to Bloch and von Wartburg, the expression comes from the wordpiquer (pick or to pinch/ swipe) but with the meaning of picorer (peck at or pinch food) (as in piquer les tables for someone who lives as a parasite) and from nique with the meaning moquerie ou chose sans valeur (mockery or something without value). According to them, the term, of French origin, was adopted throughout the rest of Europe, ending with 'picnic' in English in 1748 and picknick in German in 1753. That etymology is not universally accepted.

The Littre of 1869 and La Grande Encyclopedic of 1885 consider it of English origin, coming from 'to pick' (grasp) and 'nick' (an instant), and proposes the spelling pikenike, piquenique or picnic. One of the hypotheses proposed and later rejected by the Larousse universel of the nineteenth century (1866–79) shows the extent of the confusion: 'Pique-nique', says Larousse, 'aurait pu s'etre dit originairement d'un repas fait dans un village nomme "Pique-nique"' (Picnic could have come originally from a meal eaten in a village named 'Picnic'). He suggests another hypothesis, just as eccentric, according to which the term comes from a deformation of es beicktet nicht (sic), a phrase which a German traveller might have said after a satisfying meal eaten at a Parisian caterer's.

According to another hypothesis proposed by Larousse, it comes from the expression you offend me, I mock you this expression itself coming from the German nicken (to wink at someone in mockery) - an expression close in meaning to 'get back at someone'. The dominant idea here is both of revenge and a balancing out where 'each person will get his or her own'.

The term could then be used in all sorts of situations: one could love or hate 'in picnic', an expression used by Alphonse Karr, for example. Applied to a meal, the expression would therefore justify the definition 'repas ou chacun paye son ecot' (have a meal where each person pays his or her share), 'ou apporte son plat' (or brings their own dish), or a meal where no one owes anything to anyone else because participants all pay their share, paying in kind or with money.

Payment could be of diverse nature: by paying money, by bringing one's own meal or by providing dishes for the group. In this way the term originated to express a practice that was not covered by any other term. In 1870, Bescherelle's Dictionnaire National endorses that same meaning even if he suggests another etymology: the expression could come from the verb piquer (pick) and the term nique, an ancient small coin. Picnic would then express a meal where each person picks at a dish for their coin - for their money.

According to different publications, the definition of picnic as a meal where each person brings a contribution grows in three dimensions; spatial, hedonistic and convivial: 'a meal for two or several people, 'repas de plaisir ou chacun paye son ecot et qui se fait soil en payant sa quote-part d'une depense de plaisir, soil en apportant chacun son plat dans la maison ou on se reunit' (a pleasurable meal where people pay their part either by paying their share or by bringing a dish to the house where everyone meets), 'repas de societe [..., diner improvise' (a social meal [...] improvised dinner), 'repas, partie de plaisir' (a pleasurable meal or party).

Originally, then, 'to picnic' would be to eat together away from one's home, at someone else's home, but not necessarily outdoors. It would be to spend pleasurable time together and share expenses by contributing financially to the meal or by bringing something to eat. This definition is confirmed by the use of the term in literature. In his Essai sur la peinture (1766), Diderot, when addressing Boucher, mentions the convivial dimension of a picnic: 'Quand je suis en pique-nique avec mes amis et que la tete s'est un peu echauffee de vin blanc, je cite sans rougir une epigramme de Ferrand' (When I am 'picnicking' with my friends and I have been warmed by white wine, I quote without blushing an epigram by Ferrand). It is also used by Flaubert with the meaning of a meal in which everyone shares the expenses.

In Lucien Leuwen (1825–39), d'Antin and his gambling friends organize a picnic for which Mme d'Hocquincourt declares: 'Je vais m'occuper au nom du pique-nique d'avoir du vin et de le faire frapper' (In honour of the picnic, I will take care of the wine and make sure it is cooled).

Used as a meal eaten 'together' 'away from home', but in various and private places, it is mentioned by Flaubert or George Sand, for example in Sand's

L'Histoire de ma vie, published in 1855: 'Everard venait me chercher vers six heures pour diner dans un petit restaurant, avec nos habitues, en pique-nique' (Everard came to get me around six o'clock to dine in a little restaurant, with our regular companions, 'in picnic'). Again in Le Pieton de Paris (1932), L. P. Fargue mentions a Curiosity shop where 'des pique-niques s'improvisaient le dimanche' (picnics are improvised on Sundays).

Frederic Le Play's monographs about the working classes illustrate the colloquial and popular use of the term 'picnic' with this meaning. Among the twenty monographs about workmen in Paris (or in the near suburbs), it is used twice for meals where the expenses are shared. The first time is in an 1857 study of a shawl weaver from Gentilly where the term is used by poor families when they 'have a picnic meal' during a wedding 'payant' (where guests are charged):

Les invites sont alors avertis a 1'avance, et, au moment de se separer, apres les rejouissances, on fixe le chiffre de la cotisation qui doit etre fournie par chaque menage. [...] Cet usage a cela d'avantageux qu'il permet de conserver, dans les families les plus pauvres, 1'ancienne habitude des fetes celebrees au moment du mariage. (The guests are warned in advance and when it is time to go home at the end of the festivities, the cost is determined that must be provided by each family group.

This custom has the advantage of allowing the poorest families to maintain the age-old custom of a celebration at the time of a wedding.) The second time it is mentioned is in a study carried out in 1891 concerning a Parisian cabinet maker who, during the summer, was accustomed to having 'picnics' at his friends' home in the suburb of Ivry: 'On se rend chez des amis et Ton paie son ecot sans fa?on, a litre de revanche' (We go to our friends' home and we bear the cost for our share without any fuss, to pay them back).

When they are referring to a meal eaten outdoors during a Sunday, the authors of monographs never use the term 'picnic', but expressions such as dejeuner (luncheon), diner sur I'herbe (luncheon on the grass), or dans la campagne (in the country), or even gouter ('snack'), which refers to a meal that the peasants eat in the fields. In this way, this form of a meal that can be improvised at anyone's home, at any time, and where everyone pays their share, this use of 'picnic', which can be defined as a way of sharing expenses of a meal, has lasted for a long time. Yet the term has become, in our imagination, a rural or rustic meal eaten outdoors, a dejeuner sur I'herbe (luncheon on the grass).

It is worth noting that the last edition of Dictionnaire de I'Academie (1931–5) still gives the definition of 'repas ou chacun paye son ecot' (a meal where everyone pays their share), while only the contemporary supplements of famous dictionaries like the Larousse the Littre or the Robert mention a country meal. For the origin of this modern definition of 'meal with a group of people eaten in the countryside', Alain Rey reports in the Dictionnaire historique de la langue francaise (1992) that the word was borrowed from English probably before 1870, and that the English 'picnic' was itself a French loan word that had developed that meaning (1748, Chesterfield). We will now consider the reasons for this mutation and the steps leading up toil.

NECESSITY AND AN EXCEPTIONAL PLEASURE

First, it must be remembered that in spite of the importance and the prominence of the representations of which it is the object, starting from the last third of the nineteenth century, a meal eaten in the open air was a common practice during the pre-industrial era. There is frequent evidence of this practice ranging from an everyday necessity to an exceptional pleasure.

For field labourers, a meal eaten outdoors was a practice linked to their working conditions and to their meal break. According to the period, countries or regions, it goes by different names, but until the middle of the twentieth century nothing was written and no pictorial representation termed this meal eaten in a field a 'picnic'. These practices, born of necessity, were often seen in paintings or engravings of the seventeenth and eighteenth centuries, showing pastoral or romantic practices. Here, these images must be considered in the light of their depiction of a rural scene close to charitable Mother Nature. They would have the connotation of disgrace if they were situated in an urban setting where the act of 'eating outside', in the open air, was associated for a long time with a practice of the destitute and homeless.

However, both in town and in the countryside since the Renaissance, probably following Italian fashion, and later, when verdure and gardens were customary, dinners and light meals eaten out doors became part of the aristocratic way of life. Put aside hunting meals, which are a particular type of meal, and look at pictorial representations of outdoors meals in gardens of Eden where paradisiacal happiness reigns, such as in the works of Lancret or Vernet.

Written evidence is abundant too. For example, we can read about the distinct taste of Catherine de Medici for improvised meals in the Tuileries Gardens. During the seventeenth century, elite Parisians liked to 'manger du jambon le matin aux Tuileries' (eat some ham in the morning in the Tuileries Gardens), where Anne of Austria herself 'joue la collation' (enjoys a light meal). Finally, what can be said about the revolutionary banquets organized in the streets, where everyone brought the food that was to be placed on the common table, and which led to the commemoration ceremony in France in the year 2000, with I'incroyablepique-nique (the unbelievable picnic) as a meal of fraternity?

Travelling was also a pretext for outdoor meals. During King Charles IX 's tour of France (1564–6), ambassadors tell of the taste of Catherine de Medici for meals in the countryside: as she travelled, she was followed by two beasts of burden carrying 'fruits et confitures' (fruit and jam) and a horse laden with 'la malette ou Ton meet la collation de ladite dame allant par pays' (the chest that contained the meal of the lady going through the country). Other sovereigns too appreciated these improvised meals during their travels: Saint-Simon reports that for his journeys, Louis XIV required that his carriage be supplied with meat, pastries and fruit and that he would often stop on his way to 'diner sans sortir de son carrosse' (dine without getting out of his carriage).

Other types of evidence testify to this taste of the aristocracy for rustic meals. For example, MarieAntoinette's travelling chest, a masterpiece of cabinet-making filled with choice porcelain, silverware and crystal glassware, gives us a foretaste of the picnic chests made by the most famous accoutrement makers in the era of the car.

During the first third of the nineteenth century, the Prince of Faucigny-Lucinge reports the special fondness of the Duchess of Berry for the brilliant entertainment obtained from meals eaten unceremoniously in a carriage. It wasn't something that happened every day and was out of the ordinary. It was therefore a real pleasure.

For this, the butler would set up a table covered with a tablecloth made up of little boards folded one into the other, but once unfolded would be attached by little screws so that they would be stable. He would set the silver, the pitcher, the silver cups, pull the ivory spools from the armrests for the salt and pepper, and serve the meal of a perfect picnic: salami, prosciutto from Bologna, mortadella cold tongue, and chicken with the pieces which had been separated and then carefully put back and held in place with silk threads, fruit, and wine from Cyprus. These few references show that taking meals in the open air, only for pleasure, was a common activity among the elite, who were not obliged to do it for financial reasons.

COUNTRY PARTIES AND RUSTIC MEALS

During the nineteenth century several factors contributed to the practice of rustic meals: urbanization and industrialization, and at the same time the development of the hygienist trend, progress in the means of transportation, and new legislation on the duration of the working week. Some brief reminders.

While the hygienist trend was gaining momentum in the name of public health, and leading to improvement in medicalization and sanitation in the country, representations of urban pathologies, previously based on demographic pressure, anarchical urbanization, deadly epidemics, pollution and physical and moral disorders (alcoholism and debauchery), were supplemented by a new imagery linked to the confusion caused by new technology and to an acceleration of the tempo of modern life. Surrounded by the pathologies of the modern world, including nervous fatigue, exhaustion and anemia, the hygienist trend favoured representations, extensively depicted since the seventeenth century, of nature as a healthy haven and a source of physical and moral rest.

At the same time the extension of the railway system and the rapid improvement of the speed of traveling, leading to a decrease in the price of railway tickets, prompted the growth of the social and geographical counter-urban phenomenon, the recreational day trip to the country called partie de campagne? A lot of evidence shows an increasing trend of Sunday invasions in the summer of the outskirts of a city like Paris to a distance that varied between 4 and 50 km.

In 1878, Zola mentioned 500,000 Parisians, almost a quarter of the population of the city, who 'par certains dimanches de soleil [...] prennent d'assaut les voitures et les wagons pour se rendre a la campagne' (on certain sunny Sundays [...] storm the carriages and trains to get out to the countryside). Finally, the progressive and concomitant compression of work time brought about the 'profanation' of the values of Sunday free time.

This day was traditionally dedicated to religion, but from then on it was (also) used for rest, recreation and family sociability, especially during days spent outside of the cities in a natural setting that became a place of regenerating leisure. In spite of the increase in these recreational day trips and the generalization of rustic meals, the term 'picnic' to describe these countryside meals remains absent from our sources. For example, it never appears in the guidebooks of the outskirts of Paris printed in the eighteenth and nineteenth centuries.

It is worth noting that this meal on the grass itself was rarely given as a model. For each site mentioned, the guidebooks pointed out restaurants, caterers, guinguettes and cafes where food could be obtained. The Cuchet and Lagaranciere's Almanack des plaisirs of 1815, a classical guidebook which enumerates the pleasures and amusements offered by the towns surrounding the capital, only mentioned the possibility of a 'meal out of doors' for one of the twenty-nine sites proposed, and without reference to 'picnic': it is Saint-Germain en Laye and its forest that offers this possibility to the Parisian bourgeoisie

Some people loaded their car with excellent rouget pate, boned fowl and bottles of Chambertin, others brought a big basket with beef stew, salad with dressing, and are obliged to make do with the local wine. Everyone eats with a hearty appetite, enjoying the beauty of the site, the freshness of the air and that precious liberty so rarely found in the city. Later Promenades aux environs de Paris pointed out only for Romainville, which attracted Parisians on holidays, that a great many groups dine in the woods, in the grass, and what cannot be brought along such as bread, wine, etc., is obtained from the game keeper or a caterer. It was not until the Guide Tinnenbrock of the outskirts of Paris that, when codifying the rules for an excursion in the chapter entitled 'Conseils donnes aux touristes pour une partie de campagne' (Advice given to tourists for a country party), the equipment and the menu of a 'country buffet' were specified without ever using the term 'picnic'.

However, a meal out of doors, as an amusing activity, seems for a time to have been an unavoidable activity for children in Promenades aux environs de Paris. In some of these works published between 1838 and 1850, engravings portrayed scenes on the lawns of Versailles, on the Island of Sevres or in the woods of Meudon. These scenes were called diner sur I'herbe, or diner de campagne (dinner in the countryside) - in Charonne, with a roast and a salad.

It is worth noting that the term 'picnic' was almost never mentioned in travel journals or chronicles. Here are a few examples chosen from a large sampling. When visiting in Paris in 1834, the naturalist Alfred MoquinTandon went to see the usual tourist sites in the capital and participated in the inevitable partie de campagne (party in the countryside) in SaintCloud, without mentioning a 'picnic'. Flaubert, although using the term in his novels, in his Garnets de voyages (1847) mentioned his supplies for the road several times and, after long and tiring hikes, his meals out of doors, which he calls casse-croute. A hand-written document like the Journal kept between 1854 and 1874 by Alexandre Bruyer, a Parisian employee who loved Sunday outings, never mentioned a 'picnic'. In the summer season, accompanied by his wife, he went on outings loaded with 'filets remplis de victuailles' (string bags full of food).

This custom did not come from a deliberate choice or from the desire for an entertaining meal, but was adopted because their modest financial situation only allowed them to eat occasionally in restaurants. So at the edge of a wood or forest, the couple would take a break 'sur le gazon, a 1'ombre' (on the grass, in the shade), and pull their meagre lunch our of their bag, to savour it 'avec la lenteur des gens qui ont envie de se reposer' (slowly like others at leisure) or 'garment' (joyfully) because they were 'heureux de se sentir libre' (happy to feel free). However, a rapid examination of journals or correspondence of foreigners travelling in France shows that for the same period the term 'picnic' is used by Anglo-Saxon travellers to describe a rustic meal. Mrs Trollope, an English woman who stayed in Paris during the spring of 1835, tells of an excursion to Montmorency to visit the Hermitage, where a 'picnic' on the grass is followed by a walk on the paths of the foresters.

Robert Louis Stevenson, who travelled on foot through the Cevennes in 1878, never used this term for the meals that he ate alone in the outdoors, which he was forced to do because of hunger and the absence of any inn. However, in a short text, 'An Autumn Effect' (1875), he tells of an outing in a cart above High Wycombe and notes: 'The fields were busy with people ploughing and sowing; every here and there a jug of ale stood in the angle of the hedge [...]. There was a spirit of picnic.'

It is a term that he associated with the pleasure of a social occasion. It was also the American Mark Twain who set sail on 8 June 1867 on the Quaker City for the famous first organized trip in the history of tourism. He gave the following subtitle to his travel journal 'A picnic in the Old World' because 'this book is a record of a pleasure trip [not] a record of a solemn scientific expedition'.

AN OUTDOOR SOCIAL OCCASION OR AN INEXPENSIVE MEAL

Unlike its use in France, the term seems to have become a customary part of English as early as the beginning of the nineteenth century, used to designate a 'rustic meal' and not a way to share the expenses of a meal. In her Journal dated 1803, Dorothy Wordsworth uses the word to designate the custom of certain upper-class young people to eat on the grass on the banks of the Thames. In his 1806 issue of L'Almanack des Gourmands, Grimod de la Reyniere subscribes to that definition of the term. Presenting the way to organize 'Parties de campagne erotiques et gourmandes' (erotic and gourmet countryside parties), he explains: 'Nous voulons trailer aujourd'hui de ces pique-niques a la campagne que Ton fait parfois entre amis pour tromper le temps, amuser son loisir' (Today we want to deal with picnics in the country that are sometimes organized among friends to pass the time, for entertainment in their leisure hours). The following model differs from the Anglo-Saxon:

On forme une societe d'hommes et de femmes bien apparies, mais qui ne doivent pas exceder douze personnes. On nomme un pourvoyeur qui doit etre choisi connaisseur, intelligent, probe, sachant bien acheter [...]; on lui remet les fonds pour lesquels chacun s' est cotise par egale portion, selon les depenses qu'on a voulu faire, et on le charge de tous les details nutritifs (A group of wellmatched men and women is formed, but not more than twelve people. A purveyor is nominated who must be chosen because he is a connoisseur, intelligent, honest, knowing how to buy. [...] He is given the funds to which everyone has contributed in equal shares, according to the purchases desired, and he is charged with all the culinary details.)

A gastronomic meal follows, carried in large baskets: fattened chicken fricassee served in bread, galantine of beef tongue, galantine of rabbit, cold roast turkey, ham from Mayence or Bayonne, boned pullet pate surrounded by some quail or larks, timbale of partridge, frangipane tart, Savoy cake, salad, seasonal fruit, petit fours, biscuits, macaroons, jams, without forgetting, for the men, Swiss or Roquefort cheese, all of which is served with table wine, wine from Juranfon, wine from Champagne, from Malaga, from Frontingnan, liqueurs and coffee. After having specified the order of the dishes, because Grimod's picnic is not an informal meal, he concludes: Nous ne parlerons point des joyeux propos, des couplets erotiques et des tendres discours qui auront assaisonne les mets de cette agape champetre. II suffit de dire que les femmes sont jeunes et jolies et que les hommes aimables et gourmands, le reste, on le devine (We will not talk about the happy remarks, the erotic verses and the tender speeches that will have spiced the dishes of this rural feast. We will only say that the women are young and beautiful and the men appreciate good food and are friendly, the rest we can guess.)

Is the above the reason why picnics in France have long been tainted with a certain immorality, considered as a practice of artists, students and grisettes, and bohemians of easy virtue? Is this why it was little used, at least under this terminology, in good company? The scandal caused by Manet's Dejeuner sur I'herbe could therefore be explained by the dramatic contrast between half-dressed women and well-dressed men because a gourmet sharing of food and women could be implied.

In prudish Victorian England, picnics have a prominent place in the bible for young women published in 1861 by Mrs Beaton, The Book of Household Management, which specifies in detail the art of organizing a picnic and a model menu similar to that of Grimod. This is in sharp contrast to the oracles of French manners, which are very reserved in respect to picnics.

In 1889, Baronne Staffe notes that Pique-niques and Cagnottes, a term that has today fallen into desuetude, are 'caisse commune a un groupe de personnes, alimentee par des cotisations ou des dons' (a common fund of a group of people which is financed by contributions or gifts), which goes back to the first definition of picnic:

Il faut eviter les pique-niques. II regne en ces parties un laisser-aller qui mene vite aux inconvenances. Chacun est chez soi et les gens de nature un peu grossiere ne se sentent pas obliges a la retenue qui existe quand il n'y a qu'un seul amphitryon. Et puis, ces repas a frais communs donnent lieu a toutes sortes de remarques peu charitables, peu aimables, peu convenables: Mme une telle a apporte deux poulets et a amene six personnes. Mile X a donne un plat de fraises et elle a mange toutes les peches, etc. (Picnics must be avoided.

Casualness prevails in these parties, which leads to impropriety. Each person feels at home, and people who are a little uncivilized do not feel obliged to keep up the reserve that is maintained when there is only one host. And then, these meals with shared expenses lead to all sorts of uncharitable, unfriendly and improper remarks: 'Mrs. Y brought two chickens and invited six people. Miss X brought a dish of strawberries and ate all the peaches', etc.)

A little further she adds: 'Les cagnottes ne me plaisent pas davantage. Au plus, pourrait-on admettre la cagnotte pour les pauvres' (Putting money in a common fund does not please me more. At the most, a money pool would be acceptable for the poor). To finish she concludes: 'Pique-niques et cagnottes ne sont pas en faveur dans le monde chic ni aupres des personnes dedicates' (Picnics and money pools are popular neither with stylish people nor with refined people). For Baronne Staffe, Garden parties, Lunch and Parties de campagne (country parties) are acceptable in good company with one exception, a recommendation for women:

On part souvent en bande pour faire une excursion et dejeuner ou luncher sur 1'herbe. Les femmes prendront garde de ne donner lieu a aucune interpretation facheuse dans ces parties ou regne un certain laisser-aller; elles doivent s'y monter tres reservees, ne pas s'isoler, enfin, pour tout dire, on ferait bien de s'abstenir de ces excursions qui ne sont possibles qu'entre hommes ou en famille (We often go out in a group, to go on an outing and to dine or have lunch on the grass. The women must be careful not to allow any misinterpretation in these parties, which are very casual; they must be very reserved and not go off alone, and finally, in a nutshell, it would better not to go on these outings, which are only possible among men or with a family.)

The Countess of Gence moderates this judgement of her Savoir vivre et usages mondains, dedicated to repas champetres (rural meals), she notes: Les pique-niques sont generalement organises par la collectivite des jeunes gens ou des families qui en prennent 1'initiative. On a proteste centre la liberte un peu large de ces reunions tres gaies, sous pretexte que les convenances n'y etaient pas toujours parfaitement respectees.

Entre gens bien eleves, tout est permis et les ecarts ne sauraient etre redoutes (Picnics are generally organized by a group of young people or families who take the initiative. There have been protests against the relative freedom of these gay gatherings, under the pretext that etiquette was not always respected. Among well-mannered people, everything is allowed and there should be no fear of lapses of conduct.)

The menu follows, which is almost invariable, with its cold meat, hot and cold pates and galantines, and the recommended financial organization refers directly to the first meaning of the term, still used in France: 'Quand on organise un pique-nique, les frais sont repartis sur chaque cavalier d'apres le nombre de dames presentes' (When a picnic is organized, the expenses are shared by each escort according to the number of women present).

SUCCESS OF OUTINGS AND RECOGNITION OF THE PICNIC AS A COUNTRY MEAL

By the end of the nineteenth century the spectacular growth of various means of transportation and the henceforth-recognized success of tourism enabled 'picnic' to gain social recognition and become a standard term used to designate the practice of eating a meal in the outdoors. From now on, the term 'picnic' was to be associated with a meal eaten during a trip and just as often with one eaten during an outing or a country party. It was now considered a pleasurable meal and could even be a recreational objective. In effect, the arrival, then the slow popularization, of the bicycle, which, a little later, was followed by the automobile, considerably reinforced the geographical displacement and transposition already induced by the railways, allowing a growing number of people to participate in various outings. At the end of the century, the new series of portable guidebooks that were printed reveal the substantial extension of the road network and the future of new transportation techniques. The Cyclo-guide Miran, the Guide Baroncelli or the Guide Michelin, written for cyclists 1/or motorists, indicate for the outskirts of Paris, for example, itineraries for day trips or longer, organized around natural or monumental, picturesque or imposing sites. At the same time, excursion company publications were becoming more numerous.

With the ease and increase in individual transportation, a pause for refreshment in the open air became for the 'sportsman' an indispensable part of the experience of a site. It added eating pleasure to the sensual and intellectual pleasures that came with the perception of a landscape from the point of view of its sounds, smells and sights. Integrated into the travelling experience, the word 'picnic' gradually took over as the generic term designating 'a packed lunch', formerly a necessity carried along during a trip but which has become a meal that is deliberately eaten in the outdoors, in order to savour the site visited, relish the pleasure of change that comes with travelling, nourish the physical activity enjoyed in nature, and reward the effort. The automobile particularly favoured the birth of the nomadic picnic. On the eve of World War I, a motorist like Marius Carle who drove the roads of the Alps recommended that one should always have a supply of food in one's car in order to be able to stop to eat anywhere as soon as one found a pleasing location.

The most spectacular expression of this justification of the distinctive practice of 'picnics' is found in the increase in the number of new objects such as the punier Niniche, a chest equipped with plates, forks, tinware goblets, a coffee pot with a hot plate, and a rubber flask, the last accessory being recommended by the already mentioned Guide Tinnenbrock des Environs de Paris, which for the first time established the rules of an outing. They specified Tinvariable menu d'un dejeuner sur 1'herbe' (the usual menu of a luncheon on the grass): cold chicken and pates. This guide further provided a list of addresses where it was possible to obtain the first 'boites de conserves a chauffoir indispensables a toute partie de campagne' (heatable tinned goods indispensable for any country party). These tinned goods, which were still used by campers during the first half of the twentieth century, contained full meals of meat and vegetables. The lower part of these tins had a small sealed container with a wick soaked in spirits of wine, which enabled the heating of the contents of the tin to boiling point.

It must be remembered that tinned goods, which were not popular in France until after World War II, remained, for a long time, a luxury item: in other words, through advertisements for trips and outings in automobiles, they become a symbol of picnics for the well-to-do. For example, Amieux Frere put a 'Pic-nic' box on the market containing

Une assiette, deux serviettes japonaises, un tire bouchon renferme dans le manche de la fourchette, une fourchette, un cure dent, un verre a boire, une boite de sardines a cle, une boite de pate de foie gras truffe a cle, une bouteille de Medoc, une fiole de fine Champagne, une tablette de chocolat (a plate, two Japanese napkins, a corkscrew folded into the handle of a fork, a fork, a toothpick, a glass for drinking, a tin of sardines with a key, a tin with a key of foie gras pate with truffles, a bottle of Medoc, a small bottle of Champagne liqueur and a chocolate bar).

During the 1920s, the number of luxury accessories continued to increase: chests, suitcases, kits, food boxes equipped with china, silver and crystal, and portable hot plates made by the most stylish accoutrement makers following the tradition of the royal chests that we have already mentioned. Around 1925, Hermes began selling a malette a picnic (picnic chest) - English spelling - containing all the necessary items: a platter for presenting dishes, thermos flasks, plates, goblets, closed cases, cups and folding tableware.

In 1931 Hermes launched a new model that was a cloth case with a washable liner containing, for example, knives that could also be used as corkscrews and spoons as openers. In 1933 the chest was further improved as a folding table designed to be used for dining. Vuitton created other luxury items: folding tables and chairs, portable hot plates and even tents under which one could eat sheltered from the sun or unpleasant weather. All of these were proposed as picnic objects. To picnic now meant to eat in the open air but not necessarily on the grass. The practice was beginning to resemble 'camping', which was originally a sporty and elegant practice. This was how the term was used by Proust, for example, but with paid holidays, it later represented inexpensive and popular holidays.

Henceforth freed from the awkward notion of saving money or sharing the expenses of a meal, which was unacceptable to the customs, the savoirvivre and the conception of dining of the bourgeoisie, the Anglo-Saxon definition of 'picnic' was to prevail. Picnics came to be represented as a hedonistic pastime — a moment of shared pleasure centring on a meal eaten in a natural setting.

5

Tasting and Hospitality Service for Food Lovers

The concept of Hospitality Services, also known as "accommodation sharing", "hospitality exchange", and "home stay networks", refers to centrally organized social networks of individuals who trade accommodation without monetary exchange. While this concept could also include house swapping or even time share plans, it has come to be associated mostly with travellers and tourists staying with one another free of charge. Since the 1990s, these services have increasingly moved away from using printed catalogs and phone trees to connect users towards Internet web sites. These have grown exponentially since 2000 and today it is estimated that well over 100,000 people are registered users of these networks. These vary in operational structure, place different emphasis on graphical vs. textual formatting, and cater disproportionately to specific geographic regions.

HOTEL

A hotel is an establishment that provides paid lodging, usually on a short-term basis. Hotels often provide a number of additional guest services such as a restaurant, a swimming pool or childcare. Some hotels have conference services and meeting rooms and encourage groups to hold conventions and meetings at their location. Hotels differ from motels in that most motels have drive-up, exterior entrances to the rooms, while hotels tend to have interior entrances to the rooms, which may increase guests' safety and present a more upmarket image.

In Australia, a hotel may also be an establishment that serves alcoholic drinks, and usually meals in a casual setting but which does not necessarily provide accommodation. This type of establishment would more usually be called a pub or bar in other countries. In general use in Australia the terms '"hotel" and *pub* are usually taken to be synonymous. In India, the word may also refer to a restaurant since the best restaurants were always situated next to a good hotel.

The word *hotel* derives from the French *hôtel,* which referred to a French version of a townhouse, not a place offering accommodation (in contemporary usage, *hôtel* has the meaning of "hotel", and *hôtel particulier* is used for the old meaning). The French spelling (with the circumflex) was once also used in English, but is now rare. The circumflex replaces the 's' once preceding the 't' in the earlier *hostel* spelling, which over time received a new, but closely related meaning.

Basic accommodation of a room with only a bed, a cupboard, a small table and a washstand has largely been replaced by rooms with en-suite bathrooms and climate control. Other features found may be a telephone, an alarm clock, a TV, and broadband Internet connectivity. Food and drink may be supplied by a mini-bar (which often includes a small refrigerator) containing snacks and drinks (to be paid for on departure), and tea and coffee making facilities (cups, spoons, an electric kettle and sachets containing instant coffee, tea bags, sugar, and creamer or milk). In the United Kingdom a hotel is required by law to serve food and drinks to all comers within certain stated hours; to avoid this requirement it is not uncommon to come across "private hotels" which are not subject to this requirement. However, in Japan the capsule hotel supplies minimal facilities and room space.

CLASSIFICATION

The cost and quality of hotels are usually indicative of the range and type of services available. Due to the enormous increase in tourism worldwide during the last decades of the 20th century, standards, especially those of smaller establishments, have improved considerably. For the sake of greater comparability, rating systems have been introduced, with the one to five stars classification being most common.

Boutique Hotels

"Boutique Hotel" is a term originating in North America to describe intimate, usually luxurious or quirky hotel environments. Boutique hotels differentiate themselves from larger chain or branded hotels by providing an exceptional and personalized level of accommodation, services and facilities. Boutique hotels are furnished in a themed, stylish and/or aspirational manner. Although usually considerably smaller than a mainstream hotel (ranging from 3 to 100 guest rooms) boutique hotels are generally fitted with telephone and wi-fi Internet connections, honesty bars and often cable/pay TV. Guest services are attended to by 24 hour hotel staff. Many boutique hotels have on site dining facilities, and the majority offer bars and lounges which may also be open to the general public.

Of the total travel market a small percentage are discerning travellers, who place a high importance on privacy, luxury and service delivery. As this market is typically corporate travellers, the market segment is non-seasonal, high-yielding and repeat, and therefore one which boutique hotel operators target as their primary source of income.

Famous Hotels

Some hotels have gained their renown through tradition, by hosting significant events or persons, such as Schloss Cecilienhof in Potsdam, Germany, which derives its fame from the so-called Potsdam Conference of the World War II allies Winston Churchill, Harry Truman and Joseph Stalin in 1945. Other establishments have given name to a particular meal or beverage, as is the case with the Waldorf Astoria in New York City, USA, known for its *Waldorf Salad* or the Raffles Hotel in Singapore, where the drink *Singapore Sling* was invented.

Another example is the Hotel Sacher in Vienna Austria, home of the *Sachertorte*. There are also hotels which became much more popular through films like the Grand Hotel Europe in Saint Petersburg, Russia when James Bond stayed there in the Blockbuster, Goldeneye. Cannes hotels such as the Carlton or the Martinez become the center of the world during Cannes Film Festival (France).

A number of hotels have entered the public consciousness through popular culture, such as the Ritz Hotel in London, UK ('Putting on The Ritz') and Hotel Chelsea in New York City, subject of a number of songs and also the scene of the alleged stabbing of Nancy Spungen by her boyfriend Sid Vicious. Hotels that enter folklore like these two are also often frequented by celebrities, as is the case both with the Ritz and the Chelsea. Other famous hotels include the Beverly Hills Hotel, the Hotel Bel-Air and the Chateau Marmont, in California, Watergate complex in Washington DC, the Hotel Astoria in Saint Petersburg, Russia, the Hotel George V and Hôtel Ritz in Paris, Palazzo Versace hotel on the Gold Coast, Queensland, Australia, Hotel Hermitage and Hotel de Paris in Monaco (in the French Riviera) and Hotel Leningradskaya in Moscow.

Unusual Hotels

Many hotels can be considered destinations in themselves, by dent of unusual features of the lodging and/or its immediate environment:

Treehouse hotels

Some hotels, such as the Costa Rica Tree House in the Gandoca-Manzanillo Wildlife Refuge, Costa Rica, or Treetops Hotel in Aberdare National Park, Kenya, are built with living trees as structural elements, making them treehouses. The Ariau Towers near Manaus, Brazil is in the middle of the Amazon, on the Rio Negro. Bill Gates even invested and had a suite built there with satellite internet/phone. Another hotel with treehouse units is Bayram's Tree Houses in Olympos, Turkey.

Cave hotels

Desert Cave Hotel in Coober Pedy, South Australia and the Cuevas Pedro Antonio de Alarcón (named after the author) in Guadix, Spain, as well as several hotels in Cappadocia, Turkey, are notable for being built into natural cave formations, some with rooms underground.

Capsule hotels

Capsule hotels are a type of economical hotels that are quite common in Japan.

Ice hotels

Ice hotels, such as the Ice Hotel in Jukkasjärvi, Sweden, melt every spring and are rebuilt out of ice and snow each winter.

Snow hotels

The Mammut Snow Hotel in Finland is located within the walls of the Kemi snow castle, which is the biggest in the world. It includes The Mammut Snow Hotel, The Castle Courtyard, The Snow Restaurant and a chapel for weddings, etc. Its furnishings and its decorations, such as sculptures, are made of snow and ice. There is snow accommodation also in Lainio Snow Hotel in Lapland (near Ylläs), Finland.

Garden hotels

Garden hotels, famous for their gardens before they became hotels, includes Gravetye Manor, the home of William Robinson and Cliveden, designed by Charles Barry with a rose garden by Geoffrey Jellicoe.

Underwater hotels

As of 2005, the only hotel with an underwater room that can be reached without Scuba diving is Utter Inn in Lake Mälaren, Sweden. It only has one room, however, and Jules' Undersea Lodge in Key Largo, Florida, which requires scuba diving, is not much bigger. Hydropolis is an ambitious project to build a luxury hotel in Dubai, UAE, with 220 suites, all on the bottom of the Persian Gulf, 20 meters (66 feet) below the surface. Its architecture will feature two domes that break the surface and an underwater train tunnel, all made of transparent materials such as glass and acrylic.

Other unusual hotels

The Library Hotel in New York City is unique in that its ten floors are arranged according to the Dewey Decimal System. The Rogers Centre, formerly SkyDome, in Toronto, Canada is the only stadium to have a hotel connected to it, with 70 rooms overlooking the field. The Burj al-Arab hotel in Dubai, United

Arab Emirates, built on an artificial island, is structured in the shape of a sail of a boat.

World-record Setting hotels

Tallest: The tallest hotel in the world is the Burj al-Arab in Dubai, United Arab Emirates at 321 meters (1,053 feet). However, this title may be taken by the less illustrious Ryugyong Hotel in Pyongyang at 330 meters (1,083 feet), pending its (perhaps unlikely) completion; it has been under construction since 1987 and was abandoned in 1992.

Largest: The current largest hotel in the world is First World Hotel[4] in Genting Highlands, Malaysia. It has a total of 6,118 rooms, and is part of the Genting Highlands Resort and Casino.

The First World Plaza which is adjoined to the two hotel towers boasts 500,000 square feet of indoor theme park, shopping centres, casino gaming areas, and eateries. Previously, the largest hotel in the world was the MGM Grand Las Vegas in Las Vegas, Nevada, USA with 5,044 rooms in the main building and a total of 6,276 rooms.

Oldest: According to the Guinness Book of World Records, the oldest hotel still in operation is the Hoshi Ryokan, in Awazu, Japan. It opened in 717 CE, and features ot springs.

Hotel Occupations

The owner, chairman, or CEO of a hotel or hotel group is known as a *hotelier*. The American billionaire Howard Hughes lived much of his life in hotels. He moved with his entourage from hotel to hotel and from Beverly Hills to Boston before deciding to move to Las Vegas and become a casino baron. Less than a month after his November 27, 1966 arrival, Hughes made a public offer to buy the Desert Inn. The hotel's 8th floor became the nerve center of his empire and the 9th floor penthouse became Hughes's personal residence. Hughes moved to the Bahamas, Vancouver, London and several other locations — always taking up residence in the top floor penthouse of the hotel. Between 1966 and 1968, he also purchased several other hotel-casinos from the Mafia: Castaways, New Frontier, The Landmark Hotel and Casino, Sands and Silver Slipper.

Coco Chanel made the Hôtel Ritz in Paris her home for more than thirty years, until the day of her death, at 87, in a suite now named "Coco Chanel Suite". King Peter II of Yugoslavia spent much of the Second World War at Claridge's, a hotel in London. His son, Aleksandar Karaðorðeviæ, was born in the hotel.

Prince Felix Yusupov lived in the Hotel Vendôme in Paris. Alois Brunner, Austrian Nazi war criminal, is believed to have lived in the Meridian Hotel in Damascus, Syria, under the name Georg Fischer.

Sultan Said Bin Taimur of Muscat lived at Dorchester Hotel in London after he was deposed by Qaboos of Oman in 1970, He died in the hotel in 1972. Eleftherios Venizelos, Greek statesman and diplomat, lived in the Hôtel Ritz Paris while he was in exile in France from 1935-1936.

History of Hospitality Service

In 1949, Bob Luitweiler founded the first hospitality service called Servas Open Doors as a cross national, non-profit, volunteer run organization advocating interracial and international peace. The next earliest began in 1965 when John Wilcock set up the Traveller's Directory, originally as a listing of his mutual friends willing to host each other when traveling. This later became the Hospitality Exchange in 1988 when Joy Lily rescued the organization from imminent demise.

Hospitality Club is the direct successor Hospex, the first Internet-based service, operating out of Poland since 1992. It is currently the largest hospitality exchange network, growing rapidly. CouchSurfing is a newer but also rapidly growing hospitality exchange organization founded in 2004. Just as all the individual services have their own individual creation stories and organizational histories (often including demise and resurrection), many also have specific niche markets that they cater to including students, activists, religious pilgrims, and even occupational groups like police officers. However, the trend in recent years points to a greater consolidation of users in networks without a specific group, value, or lifestyle affiliation.

How They Work

In essence, these systems employ reciprocity – users gain access to other users' information only by posting their own. Required fields normally include name and contact information, though newer services encourage users to include more detailed personal material, including likes and dislikes, hopes and dreams, and even photographs. Of course, more information included tends to improve the chances that someone will find them trustworthy enough to host or stay with while traveling. It is very much akin to online dating services.

A comfortable room, good food, and a helpful staff can make being away from home an enjoyable experience for both vacationing families and business travellers. While most lodging managers work in traditional hotels and motels, some work in other lodging establishments, such as camps, inns, boardinghouses, dude ranches, and recreational resorts.

In full-service hotels, lodging managers help their guests have a pleasant stay by providing many of the comforts of home, including cable television, fitness equipment, and voice mail, as well as specialized services such as health spas. For business travellers, lodging managers often schedule available meeting rooms and electronic equipment, including slide projectors and fax machines.

Lodging managers are responsible for keeping their establishments efficient and profitable. In a small establishment with a limited staff, the manager may oversee all aspects of operations. However, large hotels may employ hundreds of workers, and the general manager usually is aided by a number of assistant managers assigned to the various departments of the operation. In hotels of every size, managerial duties vary significantly by job title.

General managers have overall responsibility for the operation of the hotel. Within guidelines established by the owners of the hotel or executives of the hotel chain, the general manager sets room rates, allocates funds to departments, approves expenditures, and ensures expected standards for guest service, decor, housekeeping, food quality, and banquet operations. Managers who work for chains also may organize and staff a newly built hotel, refurbish an older hotel, or reorganize a hotel or motel that is not operating successfully. In order to fill entry-level service and clerical jobs in hotels, some managers attend career fairs.

Resident or hotel managers are responsible for the day-to-day operations of the property. In larger properties, more than one of these managers may assist the general manager, frequently dividing responsibilities between the food and beverage operations and the rooms or lodging services. At least one manager, either the general manager or a hotel manager, is on call 24 hours a day to resolve problems or emergencies.

Assistant managers help run the day-to-day operations of the hotel. In large hotels, they may be responsible for activities such as personnel, accounting, office administration, marketing and sales, purchasing, security, maintenance, and pool, spa, or recreational facilities. In smaller hotels, these duties may be combined into one position. Assistant managers may adjust charges on a hotel guest's bill when a manager is unavailable.

An Executive Committee made up of a hotel's senior managers advises the general manager, assists in setting hotel policy, coordinates services that cross departmental boundaries, and collaborates on efforts to ensure consistent and efficient guest services throughout the hotel. The Committee may be comprised of the department heads for housekeeping, front office, food and beverage, security, sales and public relations, meetings and conventions, engineering and building maintenance, and human resources. Executive committee members bring a different perspective of guest service to the total management objective reflecting the unique expertise and training of their positions. Executive housekeepers ensure that guest rooms, meeting and banquet rooms, and public areas are clean, orderly, and well maintained. They also train, schedule, and supervise the work of housekeepers, inspect rooms, and order cleaning supplies.

Front office managers coordinate reservations and room assignments, as well as train and direct the hotel's front desk staff. They ensure that guests are treated courteously, complaints and problems are resolved, and requests for special services are carried out. Front office managers may adjust charges posted on a customer's bill.

Convention services managers coordinate the activities of various departments in larger hotels to accommodate meetings, conventions, and special events. They meet with representatives of groups or organizations to plan the number of rooms to reserve, the desired configuration of the meeting space, and banquet services. During the meeting or event, they resolve unexpected problems and monitor activities to ensure that hotel operations conform to the expectations of the group.

Food and beverage managers oversee all food service operations maintained by the hotel. They coordinate menus with the Executive Chef for the hotel's restaurants, lounges, and room service operations. They supervise the ordering of food and supplies, direct service and maintenance contracts within the kitchens and dining areas, and manage food service budgets.

Catering managers arrange for food service in a hotel's meeting and convention rooms. They coordinate menus and costs for banquets, parties, and events with meeting and convention planners or individual clients. They coordinate staffing needs and arrange schedules with kitchen personnel to ensure appropriate food service.

Sales or marketing directors and public relations directors oversee the advertising and promotion of hotel operations and functions, including lodging and dining specials and special events, such as holiday or seasonal specials. They direct the efforts of their staff to purchase advertising and market their property to organizations or groups seeking a venue for conferences, conventions, business meetings, trade shows, and special events. They also coordinate media relations and answer questions from the press.

Human resources directors manage the personnel functions of a hotel, ensuring that all accounting, payroll, and employee relations matters are handled in compliance with hotel policy and applicable laws. They also oversee hiring practices and standards and ensure that training and promotion programmes reflect appropriate employee development guidelines. Finance (or revenue) directors monitor room sales and reservations. In addition to overseeing accounting and cash-flow matters at the hotel, they also project occupancy levels, decide which rooms to discount and when to offer rate specials.

Computers are used extensively by lodging managers and their assistants to keep track of guests' bills, reservations, room assignments, meetings, and special events. In addition, computers are used to order food, beverages, and supplies, as well as to prepare reports for hotel owners and top-level managers. Managers work with computer specialists to ensure that the hotel's computer system functions properly. Should the hotel's computer system fail, managers must continue to meet the needs of hotel guests and staff.

The Nature of Services

Along with the growth in services, an appreciation for the ways in which services are different from products has developed. The traditional ways of marketing tangible products are not equally effective in services marketing. In many industries, marketing involves tangible manufactured products, such as automobiles, washing machines, and clothing, whereas service industries focus on intangible products such as travel and foodservice. However, before we can explore how services get successfully marketed, we need to examine the ways services differ from products.

Nine key differences:

No ownership by customers

A customer does not take ownership when purchasing a service. There is no transfer of assets.

Service Products

The value of owning a highperformance car or the latest computer lies in the physical characteristics of the product and to some extent the brand image it conveys. The value of purchasing services lies in the nature of the performance. For example, if you decide to celebrate a birthday or anniversary by dining at an expensive restaurant, the value lies in the way in which the service actors perform. When servers come to the table and present all the entrees simultaneously, the choreographed presentation appears in the same manner as a choreographed play or performance.

Involvement of Customers in the Production

Because consumers tend to be present when receiving service within a hospitality operation, they remain involved in the service production. In many instances, they are directly involved through the element of self-service. Examples of this can be seen in fast-food restaurants as well as in hotels that provide automated check-in and checkout by means of either a machine or a video connection through the television. Airlines have greatly expanded self-service within their operations as a means of reducing labour costs. In any case, the customer's level of satisfaction depends on the nature of the interaction with the service provider, the nature of the physical facilities in which the service gets provided, and the nature of the interaction with other guests present in the facility at the time the service is provided.

People as part of the Product

People or firms that purchase services come in contact with other consumers as well as the service employees. For example, a hotel guest waits in line at the front desk or the concierge desk with other guests. In addition, the guests share facilities such as the pool, the restaurant, and the fitness center.

Therefore, service firms must also manage consumer interactions to the best of their abilities to ensure customer satisfaction. For example, a hotel's sales office would not want to book group business with a nondrinking religious group at the same time as a reunion of military veterans. The two groups are significantly different in behaviour, and the expectation is that they would not mix well within the facilities at the same time. Similarly, restaurants separate smokers and nonsmokers, and they should try to separate other patrons that show some potential for conflict.

Variability in operational inputs and outputs

In a manufacturing setting, the operational production can be controlled very carefully. For example, staff carefully manage inventory and precisely calculate production times. Services, however, are delivered in real time, with many variables not being fully under the control of managers. For example, if a guest has been promised an early check-in but all of the guests from the preceding night are late in checking out, it becomes more difficult for the hotel to honour the arriving guest's request.

A service setting remains a more difficult site in which to control quality and offer a consistent service experience. Service firms try to minimize the amount of variability between service encounters, but much of the final product stays situational. There are many uncontrollable aspects of the delivery process, such as weather, the number of consumers present, the attitudes of the consumers, and the attitudes of the employees. Therefore, it becomes impossible to consistently control the quality for services in the same manner as the quality of manufactured products.

Consumers to Evaluate

Consumers can receive considerable information regarding the purchase of products; however, they often do not obtain it for services. Prior to buying a product, a consumer can research the product attributes and performance and use this information when making a purchase decision, especially an important one.

No Inventories for Services

Due to the intangible nature of services, they cannot be inventoried for future use. Therefore, a lost sale can never be recaptured. When a seat remains empty on a flight, a hotel room stays vacant, or a table stays unoccupied in a restaurant, the potential revenue for these services at that point in time becomes lost forever.

In other words, services are perishable, much like produce in a supermarket or items in a bakery. It remains critical for hospitality and tourism firms to manage supply and demand in an attempt to minimize unused capacity. For example, restaurants offer early-bird specials and airlines offer deeply discounted fares in an attempt to shift demand from peak periods to nonpeak periods, thereby increasing revenue and profits.

Importance of Time

Hospitality services are generally produced and consumed simultaneously, unlike tangible products, which are manufactured, inventoried, and then sold at a later date. Customers must be present to receive the service. There are real limits to the amount of time that customers are willing to wait to receive service. Service firms study the phenomenon of service queues, or the maximum amount of time a customer will wait for a service before it has a significant (negative) impact on his or her perception of service quality. Airline companies offer curbside check-in for the most time-conscious passengers, and restaurants have devised practices such as providing guests with pagers and expanding the bar area in order to reduce the negative effect that results from waiting for service.

Different Distribution Channels

The distribution channel for services is usually more direct than the traditional channel (*i.e.*, manufacturer-wholesaler retailer- consumer) used by many product firms. The simultaneous production and consumption normally associated with service delivery limits the use of intermediaries. The service firm usually comprises both the manufacturer and the retailer, with no need for a wholesaler to inventory its products. Consumers are present to consume the meals prepared in a restaurant, to take advantage of the amenities in a hotel, and to travel between cities by plane.

Benefits

Monetary Savings

Staying in private homes means that travellers can save lots of money on accommodation that they would usually be spending on hotels or hostels. Used over a long period of time (2 to 4 weeks), this strategy can cut overall travel budgets in half, or even more combined with hitchhiking. These savings can then be passed on towards more generously patronizing local establishments or simply staying abroad for longer periods of time.

Local Economic Sustainability

Many tourist vacations today are sold in package form, often including flights, hotels, rental cars, sightseeing tours, and coupons for chain restaurants and bars. While this makes purchasing more convenient, it also puts more money in the hands of large multinational corporations exploiting the synergy strategy of marketing their products in the context of their subsidiary companies operating in other markets. Many years ago, this might have been termed *collusion*; today, however, it is the norm. This comes at the expense of locally owned independent businesses. Accommodation sharing helps to break apart this monopoly and hopefully redirects some of the tourist revenue back to the local or national economy.

Ecological Sustainability

While this is especially important in more rural travel venues where hotels are often built in very picturesque, though fragile environments, every night stayed at a local's home means that much less demand for such hotel rooms. Also, if accommodation sharing does in fact increase the length of average stays, it may reduce the amount of trips to and from different locations and back home again, thus reducing the overall fuel expenditures in the process.

Local Contact

Ostensibly, one of the primary reasons we travel is to experience what life is like for people living in other countries. Making interpersonal connections and fostering understanding of different cultures may in the long run also be important to international relations. However, even in our increasingly globalized world supposedly rife with diversity, in many popular travel destinations we find tourists milling around "tourist enclaves" where the companies they patronize back home have set up shop to cater to their desires while they are abroad.

Sociologist George Ritzer has referred to this phenomenon as the "McDonaldisation of society" and the more recently, the "globalization of nothing". The location of hotels near these centers only fosters more convenient envelopment of the tourist dollar. During hospitality exchanges, hosts want to show off their local knowledge and exciting "off the map" venues. Not only may travellers get a distinctly different experience, but they will also get a feel for the everyday lives of local residents.

Reciprocity

These systems foster richer and more convenient travel experiences not so much on the premise of altruism, but on the basis of social exchange theory. Implicit in the agreement to host travellers is the ability to ask to be hosted by them in the future. If one enjoys having interesting guests in their home, this works out well for both parties. It works comparatively better if you are visited by travellers from a locale you find particularly attractive. Thus, hosting someone from New York City in Gainesville, FL seems to be an unbelievable opportunity. Moreover, if you are a Westerner visiting someone in a developing nation, your stay might be the only way that this individual or family could afford a trip to a rich nation. This may mean more than just a relaxing vacation for such disadvantaged parties.

Authenticity and Adventure

Tourism has always searched for these two qualities, but much like Midas and his golden touch, the reach of tourism has to a large extent destroyed the opportunity to encounter them in most places. Unluckily, the experience has been thoroughly commodified by everyone who wanted to secure their opportunity to make a buck in the process. Accommodation sharing offers a way out of this bind and a viable alternative to having one's desires manipulated by corporate conglomerates who never had the best interests of the place or the people foremost in their minds.

Drawbacks

Lack of Guarantee

There is no contractual agreement between users in these systems. Reservations are made, but if they are for some reason broken, there is no higher authority to which one could plead for a refund or other compensation. The only repercussion will be the poor rating you give that user and your only consolation will be that your warning will deter others from visiting or hosting them.

For those who feel insecure unless their travel arrangements are written in stone before departure, this system will not be comforting.

Potential Interpersonal

There is a chance that guest and host will not get along. Perhaps there will be scheduling or ideological conflicts. Maybe you will find that hosts or visitors have misrepresented themselves. Perhaps the experience will not live up to your expectations.

Intense interpersonal communications in advance and a flexibility once you have arrived is your best bet.

These experiences require additional planning and courtesy towards the demands of your host. Thus, your living conditions, length of stay, and overall experience will be circumscribed by the living conditions you enter into.

Demographic Segregation

The average user is a young white person who speaks English and lives in a developed nation. While there are many users who do not fit this description, the more different they are, the less likely they will be involved. This is especially true for persons living in the developing world who likely do not have easy access to the fundamental prerequisite for using these services: computers and the Internet.

Thus, the sample population found in searches of these databases are really much less diverse than a geographical representation of worldwide users might suggest.

Security

There is a distinct possibility that someone will abuse the system and that innocent users (especially women) will get hurt. All services include disclaimers that require users to waive their rights to hold anyone but themselves responsible for any harm that may come to them in using the system. They advise that the best Defence mechanism is to only involve oneself with users that have extensive personal information and interpersonal networks within the system that have been verified by others. It does seem entirely plausible that someone clever and patient enough might be able to invent an entire group of complex user identities and build histories convincing enough to fool even more cautious patrons.

Still, the difference between these systems and the other social networking platforms popular nowadays on the web (such as MySpace, Tribe, Orkut, LiveJournal and Ebay) is that any agreement reached through the accommodation sharing medium is contingent on actually meeting other people face-to-face. Other web scams are easier because interpersonal interactions rely so much on putative identities that are never actually verified in the real world. However, this does not diminish the greater risk to physical well being that this kind of traveling by definition must entertain. The best advice is to meet unknown persons in public spaces first, and try to meet some of their acquaintances in person before agreeing to a hospitality exchange.

Food and Beverage Department

Because of the diversity of services provided, the food and beverage department is typically split into subunits. The executive chef, a person of considerable importance and authority in any full-service hotel, runs the food production, or kitchen, department. A variety of culinary specialists who are responsible for different aspects of food preparation report to the executive chef.

The actual serving of food in a large hotel's restaurants is usually the responsibility of a separate department, headed by the assistant food and beverage director. The food service department is composed of the individual restaurant and outlet managers, maitre d's, waiters, waitresses, and bus help.

Because of their special duties and concerns, many large hotels have a separate subunit that is responsible only for room service. Because of the high value and profit margins associated with the sale of alcoholic beverages, some hotels have a separate department that assumes responsibility for all outlets where alcoholic beverages are sold. The person responsible for this department is the beverage manager.

Most full-service hotels also do a considerable convention and catering business. The typical convention uses small function rooms for meetings and larger rooms for general sessions, trade shows, exhibits, and banquets. As a hotel or lodging business increases the use of its facilities for conventions and meetings, it may form a separate convention services department. The convention services department and its personnel are introduced to the client, a meeting planner, or an association executive by the marketing and sales department. The convention services department then handles all of the client's meeting and catering requirements.

Individually catered events include parties, wedding receptions, business meetings, and other functions held by groups. To provide for the unique needs of these types of customers, hotels often organize separate catering and convention departments. Depending on the size of the hotel, the job of cleaning the food and beverage outlets themselves as well as of washing pots and pans, dishes, glasses, and utensils is often delegated to a subunit known as the stewarding department.

It is only through continuous cooperation and coordination that a hotel's food service function can be carried out effectively. A guest who is dining in a hotel restaurant requires the joint efforts of the kitchen, food service, beverage, and stewarding departments. A convention banquet cannot be held without the efforts of the convention and catering department along with the food production, beverage, and stewarding departments. The sequence of events and cooperation required among the food and beverage staff is even more important than in the rooms department, thus increasing the importance of communication between managers and employees alike.

Another challenge faced by management is the diversity of the employees in the food and beverage department; the dishwasher in the stewarding department is at a dramatically different level than the sous chef in the kitchen. Coordination is not as important an issue in the marketing and sales department, which is generally much smaller than the food and beverage department. The primary responsibility of the sales managers who make up the marketing and sales department is sales, or the selling of the hotel facilities and services to individuals and groups. Sales managers sell rooms, food, and beverages to potential clients through advertising, attendance at association and conference meetings, and direct contacts.

The marketing and sales department is also removed from most of the day-to-day operational problems faced by other departments. The division of work among the sales managers is based on the type of customers a hotel is attempting to attract. Individual sales managers often specialize in corporate accounts, conventions, or tour and travel markets. Sales managers' accounts are sometimes subdivided along geographical lines into regional or national accounts. The sales staff of the largest full-service hotels usually does not exceed a dozen or so. These sales managers work more or less independently in their particular market segments. The human resources department serves no customers, books no business, and prepares no meals, yet it plays a vital role in a hotel's efficient operation. The three functions of the human resources department are employee recruitment, benefits administration, and training. The director of human resources is also expected to be an expert on federal and state labour laws and to advise managers in other departments on these topics. The human resources department's major challenge is in its interactions with other hotel departments.

Although the human resources department recruits, interviews, and screens prospective employees, the final hiring decision rests within the department in which the potential employee will be working. The same is true of promotion and disciplinary decisions; the human resources department's input is, in most cases, limited to advice and interpretation of legal questions. The human resources department's effectiveness depends on its manager's ability to form effective working relationships with managers of other departments. In many hotels, the accounting department combines staff functions and line functions, or those functions directly responsible for servicing guests. The accounting department's traditional role is recording financial transactions, preparing and interpreting financial statements.

6

Food and Beverage Management

The past few decades have wrought great changes on the functions of management and the way in which business is conducted. No generic function has been left untouched and it would be surprising if a specialist vocation role such as food and beverage management had escaped the march of progress – it has not. The changes in generic management that have been brought about by information technology and globalisation have created whole new ways of marketing, financing distributing and organising work. Although it is almost automatic to assume the influence of progress, in this changing milieu, it is still worth asking the question: how different is change?

In other words, to assess the extent of change it is necessary to understand what change actually implies. Often, in changing situations there is a tension between the remains of the old and the new. The function of food and beverage management is an interesting case of tension between change and that which remains constant – the fine distinction between genuine change and the accommodation of the new within the traditional. What we see from the outside is an area of management where the new and the old have to live and develop together.

Although not exclusively so, food and beverage management generally sits under the hospitality management umbrella and as such reflects the changes of recent times in hospitality management. Here, change has emphasised the business aspects of profitability and marketing over the more, for want of a better word, romantic issues of food as a cultural entity and hospitality as a human propensity. In a very real sense, change has brought technological innovation and conceptual creativity.

If Escoffier doesn't live here any more and instead we have celebrity chefs and global branded restaurants then all that really reflects is that society has changed and that new modes of management in the food and restaurant industry have popularised the notion of eating out to levels not previously known. This expansion has been propelled by the application of two tenets of modern marketing: specialisation and branding. Any conceptual specialisation automatically brings with it a specialisation of skill. However, once this specialism is forced to change then the skill base changes with it. This is the case with modern food and beverage management. It has broken up its original skills and knowledge base in cuisine and re-tooled with marketing and productivity knowledge on the assumption that while the old adage that a good restaurant sold itself has proved durable, it may just have outlived its time.

Food and beverage management as an activity resides in many roles and carries various labels across different sectors of the industry: a restaurateur, a banqueting manger, a ship's purser could be food and beverage managers of one type or another.

If food and beverage management has a generic heart of its own then that must be "catering" – at its simplest the cooking and serving of food. The word catering has fairly low status in the prestige hierarchy of activities yet it is not only an essential role in society but it is also a complex one requiring particular organising skills that can transformperishable materials in short time frames. Catering is about having knowledge of food and cooking and having the skills of timing and of sequencing to organise a production process within a compressed time frame. The basic process of buying storing, costing, processing and serving food is, even without adding creative and marketing elements, a complex process.

It is a process that has to be controlled and managed and what makes it so central to the notion of food and beverage management is that it remains essentially the same in all circumstances and irrespective of size or quality be they industrial canteen, grand hotel or smart restaurant. Whoever is in charge has to make many decisions, most of which require them to be part quantity surveyor, part cost accountant and part cook, all rolled into one activity – and all this, despite the undoubted effects of modern changes throughout the basic process. However, in all this talk of change the question that is worth asking is has the body of knowledge required to fulfil the role of managing a food and beverage operation, in whatever guise, really changed or has it just added some more sophisticated ingredients?

The basic process has changed. The buying process, for one thing, has developed models beyond the simple price comparing market operation. In one respect, we see development along the lines of supply chain management, where the hospitality industry works with primary producers to improve quality. This development has been assisted by the use of the internet. In another, we see the growth of horizontal integration in supply companies which supply a complete range of products, including food and beverage, on contract. Such companies have the power of economies of scale to exert a deflationary pressure on prices. It is not uncommon to find the purchasing function subcontracted to outside organizations. However, notwithstanding the purchasing model applied, there is still at the heart of the process a requirement for product knowledge. Specifications have to be drawn up and deliveries checked which makes any system dependent on human expertise.

Information technology has, for a long time, made stock management easier with stronger connections to accounting systems and forecasting systems. However, they have not replaced the need to actually physically take stock. Similarly, the use of standard recipes, with costings applied, has, with computerisation, become a budgetary control process. Again, performance against budget is determined by the willingness of cooks to actually use standard recipes. The perennial problem of food production and cost control is that it always needs vigilance by management, irrespective of the sophistication of information systems.

The cooking process too has been invaded by modern technology in the form of microwave, cook chill methods, induction ovens and many other labour-saving mechanical innovations. It has also been invaded by that emblem of modern business – outsourcing.

In cooking terms this comes in the form of buying-in food instead of making it on the premises. This has a long tradition behind it but has accelerated in recent years because its transactional cost value has simply led towards subcontracting. The consequences of buying-in manufactured food products are, on the one hand savings in labour cost but on the other, a reduction of skill and training opportunity. The balancingperformancefor food outlets is whether to surrender freshness and skill for bought-in products that are attractive in themselves but also save labour costs. This equation is at the heart of food and beverage management because it always has to control labour costs. What is important to the future of cuisine is that the decisions on maintaining skilled labour in each unit accumulate for the industry.

The industry versus the individual establishment dimension is a crucial one for food and beverage and the most important issue is that of skill development versus de-skilling. If everybody goes in for fabricated products then cooking skills become confined to factory-like production units. In all fairness, this idea of fabrication versus freshly cooked food by skilled labour denies the grades of skill/technology combinations that lie between the two poles. The advances in cook chill and in the ability of yeasts to be reactivated after freezing have changed approaches to the preparation of food. Certainly, shift systems have declined due to the ability of technology to maintain freshly prepared food for longer periods.

It is no longer necessary to start making bread in the middle of the night for breakfast – there is now a choice. Kitchens are now designed to be productive and the organisation of production has become more systematic, in that it is designed around standardised final products.

This does not mean that it is time to bury the old "partie system", far from it. Over the years this system has evolved in a manner which collapsed the original division of labour into less areas of specialisation and in high standard a' la carte kitchens it remain, to this day, the basis of the division of labour and productivity in the kitchen.

Notwithstanding these technological changes the real impact of change has come through the market itself. Not only are more people eating out but they are also demanding greater variety. In food and beverage management, marketing and operations share the same dilemmas. The marketing problem for food and beverage management is whether to meet the demand for variety through a market structure of specialised and possibly branded restaurants or to offer a wider choice within the restaurant menu. How much choice do we give customers? The initial dilemma here is – is wide choice attractive? If wide choice is deemed to be an attractive attribute, then another dilemma follows, that wide choice leaves open the opportunity for products and service to be provided but not consumed.

For example, a large range of dishes on a menu may entice the customers to dine but if they choose narrowly then the avoidance of waste becomes a managerial objective. In these circumstances, the ideal solution would be that everything be cooked to order. The problem is that the very attractions of cuisine work against cooking to order – some dishes require long cooking times. The solutions lie in the technology of food production, storage and regeneration. The alternative to wide choice is specialisation – offering to produce a small variety at a controlled level of quality. This would be more productive but would segment the market. In a sense the width of choice dilemma is about appeal versus productivity.

One concept, which straddles both these ideas, is that of branding, whereby although the choices on offer can be wide or narrow, specifying the choices within the overall concept of the brand reduces some of the uncertainty for the customer. It does not remove the issue of range of choice versus productivity but takes it into the identity of the product and by so doing handles the attractiveness issue separately from the production issues. An example would be helpful here. Compare a restaurant that has a large range of French dishes on the menu with a hamburger bar – they are different markets and the latter will be more productive than the former. Compare these extremes with a branded Bistro chain that offers choice but not as much as the French restaurant but increases its attractiveness by offering not just a range of dishes but also the reassurance of quality control through standardisation.

Similarly, an American restaurant concept might expand choice beyond the hamburger but still maintain productivity and attractiveness. In both cases, reducing uncertainty is seen as a form of attractiveness. But, this too has a sting in the tail because the more specialist the restaurant the quicker will be its redundancy. Familiar can easily become too familiar and the system will demand more novelty. Modern thinking says "keep it simple" even at the higher level. This was not always the case– in earlier times the great compendium of French cuisine–La Repertoire de la Cuisine based on Escoffier's Guide to Modern Cookery encouraged large a la carte menus. Whether French cuisine, as the fundamental corpus of knowledge for the development of skill, is relevant to modern food and beverage is a point worth debating. The value of such a corpus of knowledge be it French or Chinese or any national based cuisine is that it always has embedded within it a set of physical or craft skills that form the performance and motivational basis of the occupation chef or cook. While the principles of cookery can be taught outside the expensive teaching of French cuisine they are nevertheless essential for any level of cooking, even the hybrid versions of the French repertoire so beloved of celebrity chefs. Within vocational education there are serious issues of resourcing chef training that are the subject of much debate.

What is clear, however, is that despite the onset of technological intervention the demand for skilled chefs continues to increase. To an extent this demand is fed by the evolution of national cuisine into international cuisine. This is an ill-defined concept but nevertheless one which is easily recognisable on menus around the world. Food and beverage management used to be dominated by French cuisine and proscribed forms of table service – these were the defining skills and knowledge of the area. They stem from the hegemony of continental European of what constitutes "haute cuisine". If, in matters of taste, Europe no longer rules the roost then all the formality and rigourous training no longer matter. Such an extreme position does not seem tenable because for one thing haute cuisine is still alive and well and for another it appears to have made a pact with our postmodernist world and become more accessible, both in terms of knowledge and price, without losing its soul. The biggest enemy of haute cuisine is not public taste but specialisation simply because of its assault on training.

At this juncture it would be appropriate to return the discussion to the notion of food and beverage management as a role and its place within hospitality management. The traditional view of food and beverage management was that the skills and knowledge it required were the defining corpus of knowledge of the hotel manager – not the sum of knowledge, not even the most valuable but definitely the part which defined the occupation as distinct from other forms of management. In other words, food and beverage management, in whatever guise it appears, is the special knowledge, the unique bit. What is more it could be said the food and beverage is the "rock n' roll" of hospitality management – complex, risky, creative, glamorous, dirty and messy but definitely a challenge. The antipathy of this view is that as most profit is made on the sale of rooms, food and beverage therefore is a subservient set of skills to those of accommodation management.

In the move towards hotel management as a pure business rooms have won the day and this has led to the subcontracting of the food and beverage functions in hotels. To an extent this is an understandable reaction to the perennial dilemma of making any hotel restaurant profitable. Yet this argument is not complete until the value of food and beverage, first as a contributor to hotel image, second, as constant source of business and finally, as the bedrock of cash-flow. Managing food and beverage is more complex than managing rooms and it demands a greater range of knowledge and a degree of creativity, which room management does not. It is for this reason that traditionally the career paths of hotel managers have been strewn with food and beverage experience.

Yet this again is changing as financial and marketing skills come to the fore. Certainly, the modern food and beverage manager has to take on board more marketing skills and graft them on to the old skills of menu engineering based on knowledge of cuisine. Food and beverage management is a creative management activity and, to an extent, the creative end of marketing, namely the designers, have invaded this creative space. Designers and chefs have come together with entrepreneurs to innovate in the industry, adding a level of creativity to the "catering process" that lies beneath. It may well be that the need to innovate has added more to the role of food and beverage manager that it can be expected to carry and therefore subcontracting and specialisation is only natural.

In all this talk of specialisation and corporate brands it is time to hear it for the small independents which are, after all, the majority of establishments. The romantic idea of opening a restaurant still has its appeal and people succeed and fail in a way that is still mysterious to rational thinking. If there is one message from the small business sector it is that the feasibility study can be defied – people succeed against the odds by their drive and commitment and people fail when they should succeed. It is, however, worth saying that the old idea of opening a restaurant motivated by romantic optimism is suffering from diminishing returns. Basic business acumen and some training are definitely an advantage. Success, however, is never permanent and restaurant and bar concepts need to be refreshed regularly asmarkets shift and public taste changes. Here again the influence of strategic thinking has entered the world of small restaurants, which are being encouraged to "cluster" in close proximity to form mini-destinations that can be marketed.

It is easy to undervalue the obvious and to an extent food and beverage is suffering from this trait. National cuisine, however, is now being recognised as being part of the attraction of a destination and given its rightful place in tourism destination marketing campaigns. Furthermore, the quality of experience of holidays has now to take on board the quality of food and drink. This is boost for the prestige of this activity.

Has the function of food and beverage management really changed? The answer is yes and no. It is an example of were manual skills are closely connected to creative intellectuals skills. The chef, the accountant, the marketier and the designer were never closer. In educational terms, what does it mean to study food and beverage management? It means having a deep understanding of food and wine and other beverages in order to be able to engineer menus, being able to cook to a degree that would facilitate designing production systems, being able to cost and control food – an activity that looks easy but which is hard in practice. On top of this would come the skills of hospitality and the commercial skills of marketing. Whether vocational education had grasped this particular problem is a matter of conjecture.

In education, food and beverage training sits very uncomfortably at the intersections between generic and vocational, education and on-job training and public and private funding. It is this position that is a threat to skills and makes it hard to modernise.

MARKET ORIENTATION AND NEW PRODUCT DEVELOPMENT

Market orientation is a construct that has received much attention in the literature over the past 17 years. Several articles have comprehensively reviewed the literature, and more recently Lafferty and Hult and Kirca, Jayachandran, and Bearden. The fundamental premise that market orientation leads to superior performance has also been examined in conjunction with constructs such as learning orientation and product innovation.

This research has used the conceptualisation of market orientation posited by in which market orientation as consists of five dimensions; customer orientation, competitive orientation, inter-functional coordination, profit emphasis and responsiveness. Although other studies have used the Kohli and Jaworski approach to measuring market orientation, the more comprehensive conceptualisation by Gray *et al.*, is consistent with recent literature and the Gray perspective has been shown to be more valid in the Australasian context.

Baker provides a comprehensive review of the extant literature examining the relationship between market orientation and new product success. It is argued that given the market sensing activities that are inherent in a firm with a market orientation these firms will be more likely to introduce new products that meet the needs of consumers and thus be successful.

METHODOLOGY

The data for this research were gathered using self-administered questionnaires. The sample frame was drawn from a commercial database composing a significant number of Australian food manufacturers. 1000 questionnaires were mailed to marketing managers throughout Australia with a reminder letter following two weeks later. In total, 232 fully completed useable questionnaires were returned representing a response rate of 25.8 per cent. The relatively moderate response rate was a combination of a number of factors likely including time of the year and size of the questionnaire. Of the 232 respondents, 173 indicated that they undertook significant NPD related activities. It is these 173 responses which form the basis for this analysis. A single item was also used to assess how well respondents understood NPD management in the organisation.

RESULTS

The respondents identified that their business focus was divided equally between food service and FMCG markets. Both are volatile marketing environments with significant competitive pressures. There was a slight over-representation in the sample from the beverages industry possibly reflecting increased emphasis on marketing in this industry at the time of data collection. Company ownership was mostly private and is likely to be a reflection of the relatively small size of many Australian food manufacturers. Firm size was well distributed with 38 per cent of firms reporting sales between \$1m and \$4m dollars and 27 per cent reporting sales of \$20 million and above. Respondents reported that product development efforts to be focused on improvements to existing products, product line extensions the development of new product lines, and radical innovation. The food industry is not one in which major radical or disruptive change to products and product use occurs very often. Prior to structural equation analysis, the internal validity of constructs was evaluated using Cronbach's alpha. The measures used appear to perform adequately, apart from NPD culture. This construct was retained for exploratory and theoretical reasons.

DISCUSSION

Interestingly, this analysis indicates that market orientation does not appear to have a direct and positive association with new product development performance. This finding is counter to results found in much of the past research but supports a finding by Langerak *et al.,* who also found no significant direct relationship.. This result may be a function of the use of the Gray *et al* conceptualisation based on Naver and Slater and Deng and Dart rather than the often used Jaworski and Kohli approach. The Jaworski and Kohli conceptualisation of market orientation did not have sufficient validity to warrant its inclusion in the analysis. The strength of the associations between Market orientation, NPD process execution proficiency and NPD programme performance does suggest that significant and positive indirect effect exists. Further analysis to examine the individual components of market orientation in this model is also warranted.

The Organisation of NPD has a direct and positive influence on the execution proficiency of the actual NPD process. This association is important and has not been fully examined in much of the existing literature. A significant indirect effect exists between Organisation of NPD, NPD process execution proficiency, and new product programme performance. In summary, market orientation plays a significant role in NPD programme performance in the food and beverage industry, particularly in terms of its influence on the Organisation for NPD and in terms of the execution proficiency of the NPD process. Market Orientation was found to have an indirect rather direct influence on NPD programme performance. The limitations of this research and thus the opportunities for further research include a relatively small sample size, a focus solely on the food and beverage industry, and possible respondent bias through use of a sole informant from each firm. Nevertheless the results are both interesting and useful for practitioners and academics.

RESPONSIBILITY

The Food and Beverage Management Industry is the emerging service industry in India today. It promises to offer individuals with specialised training a great and promising career. It is this context that Food and Beverage Management Courses *in India* are becoming increasingly popular. The food and beverage management programme prepares graduates to enter a restaurant, club or food service management as a trainee or assistant manager. Individuals who are considering this field should enjoy a very active environment and a lot of contact with people.

There are some other courses in supervisory management, hospitality accounting, hospitality law, food management, design techniques and advanced hospitality management which also provide a comprehensive food and beverage management background in India. Students also learn food preparation skills through courses in basic and intermediate food preparation, menu planning, and purchasing, nutrition and beverage control.

Food and Beverage Management generally involves overlooking of meals that are being served on behalf of the client. The Food and Beverage Management Company is responsible for the successful execution of management contracts for food and beverage accounts. Food and Beverage Management companies often manage both housing and food and beverage operations for clients. In such cases, an area or regional director assumes broader responsibility for the overall management account and the director of food and beverage operations works with him or her in a support capacity.

ECONOMICS OF THE FOOD AND BEVERAGE INDUSTRY

Much like any other product, the economics of the food and beverage industry is characterised by demand, supply and price dynamics. Hotels and restaurants that supply food and beverage base the level of supply on market demand. Consumer demand is determined through its various determinants. Consumers differ in their motivations to consume at a given time so that there are only generic determinants and managers have to recognise which determinants apply to their particular food and beverage market.

Generally, demand for food and beverage is captured by this equation:

$$Qd = f(P, M, PR, T, \ldots)$$

where:

Qd = Quantity demanded of food and beverages
P = Price of food and beverages

M = Per capita income
PR = Price of related goods
T = Tastes and preferences of consumers

Simply put, the equation provides that the demand or the amount of food and beverage consumed by customers is determined by price, income, price of related goods, and tastes and preferences. The letter 'f' denotes a summary of demand determinants. Based on this formula, decision-makers in the food and beverage industry determine specific data represented by the formula. In the food and beverage industry price determines consumption so that in menu pricing managers consider acceptable price based on costs, ability to pay of consumers and competition prices. Depending upon the market segment targeted by the food and beverage company price has to be adjusted to the purchasing power of the segment. If the target market is the high end sector of the market, then the firm can adjust the price up to a level acceptable to this segment. Pricing is also made relative to close competitors so that it is equivalent or more competitive than the price of food and beverage establishment offering products and services similar to the firm. Tastes and preferences of consumers are determined by the socio-demographic characteristics of the targeted market segment. Food and beverage companies utilise these demographic characteristics to determine the food and drinks menu.

PREPARATION OF STARTER CULTURE

The traditional catalyzing agent used in the preparation of fermented food and beverage is called balam in Kumaon and balma in Garhwal region, which is not prepared by all villagers in the society. The alpine grazers called as anwals have specialized knowledge to prepare this starter culture. It is made up of wheat by mixing a number of herbs and spices. First, the raw wheat is washed in water and sun dried, later this is grinded into flour, and then it is roasted over fire and removed before it becomes brown in colour.

The roasted flour is then mixed with spices like long, elachi, kalimirch, leaves of mirchi-ghash, and seeds of pipal. In this mixture, powder of old balam is also added. The addition of old balam powder is a must, without this production of fresh balam is not possible. The mixture so prepared is then thoroughly mixed up with the required quantity of water, and is rolled into a thick paste. This mixture is then pressed between palms to make balam balls of the required size. These balls are then dried in shade and stored for future use for an indefinite period of time.

PREPARATION OF LOCAL BEER

Jann is a traditional soft drink of the Bhotiyas, and contains very low concentration of alcohol. It is commonly prepared out of rice; however, it can also be made out of a good number of substrates of both cereals and fruits. Some of the common cereals from which jaan can be made are rice, wheat, jau, koni, china, oowa, and chuwa. Similarly, amongst the fruits, apple is most desired and is also very delicious.

But jann prepared from koni is considered to be the best in quality. The quality of jann is best judged by its taste, smell and strength. Mostly rice jann is commonly used and is prepared almost in every household in this society, but now its preparation and consumption has declined. In the making of rice jaan, first rice is cooked or boiled for about half an hour or until it becomes soft and edible.

The cooked rice is drained off the excess of water and spread on a flat container allowing to be cooled quickly. The cooked rice is then thoroughly mixed with balam powder.

The quantity of the balam powder required is proportionate to the quantity of rice to be fermented. This mixture is then kept in an airtight container and is kept in a dark and warm place for fermentation. In cold conditions, the rate of fermentation is slow as compared to warm. But for a good quality jann slow fermentation at low temperature is a required condition. The process of fermentation takes place in the absence of oxygen, and usually after a week of fermentation jann is prepared.

However, for a better quality of jann the fermentation period is extended as long as possible but not more than a year. Longer the period of fermentation the less is the undigested remains of rice, and in that case the quantity of jann produce is more.

It has been proved that longer the period of fermentation, there is more and significant reduction in phytic acid content while the availability of in-vitro minerals increases. After the completion of fermentation, the jann so produced is filtered with the help of a sieve. The filtrate is a whitish liquid, which is abandoned or used as animal fodder. Earlier, when Bhotiyas migrated to their winter settlement in lower valleys, before their migration they prepared jaan material and left them for fermentation.

For six months of winter, their entire settlement got submerged under snow, and as result of the internal heat generated due to the external pressure of ice from the top, the jaan fermentation was slow but steady. On their return to the place again in summer the people found their jann ready for drink, and jann produced in this way is considered to be the best in quality.

Similarly, the preparation of jann is same from other cereals like koni, wheat, jaw, oowa, chuwa and cheena. Like rice, first the seeds of any of these cereals are boiled in water until they become soft and edible. Then they are mixed with balam powder and the rest of the stages of storing and fermentation, and finally yielding of jann is the same. Only in the case of jaw the seeds are partially grinned before boiling, which enables quick fermentation and optimum yielding. Jann is also prepared from fruits like apple, banana, pumpkin and orange. Apples are first cut into pieces and then are mixed with balam powder for fermentation. The rest of the method is the same, except in case of orange, where either the juice or the complete fruit after peeling is mixed with balam powder and fermented for yielding jann. Banana is used without removing its outer skin. The preparation of jann from pumpkin is slightly different, where a small cut is made in a large sized pumpkin in such a way that the cut piece is again fitted back to its place.

First, the seeds and loose tissues contents of the fruit is removed through the opening, and boiled rice or other substrate mixed with balam powder as usual is poured into the empty space of the fruit. It is then sealed again by placing back the cut piece in its place. The process of fermentation takes place inside as a result of which along with rice the inner soft tissue of the fruit also gets digested, and thus yields jann in due course of time.

PREPARATION OF ALCOHOLIC DRINK

Wine is the distilled liquor containing ethyl alcohol at a much higher concentration than other alcoholic beverages. Rice and jaggery are the common substrate used for preparation of wine. Apart from rice, the cereals like koni, chuwa, oowa and wheat are used in the preparation of wine. However, unlike in the case of jann the taste of the wine does not vary just as to the type of substrate used.

Therefore, choice of substrate does not matter in the preparation of wine. The most commonly available and cost effective materials used in the preparation of wine, is rice and jaggary. Cooked rice on becoming cool is mixed with the powder of balam, the proportion of balam powder required in preparation of wine is much more than what is required in jann preparation. This mixture is then kept in an airtight container for fermentation, and is kept in preferably a warmer place.

To ensure the warmth, either the fermentation container is covered with woolen cloth or else it is kept near the cooking hearth, direct heating is, however, avoided. After about a week of fermentation, when the mixture is in a semi liquid condition, it is distilled in a distillation vessel. The distillate substance is the wine, which is collected in bottles. The undigested residue is called chak, is dirty white in colour, this can be used again for preparation of wine by fortification with jaggary and fresh balam powder. This way chak is recycled or reused in wine preparation. However, this is not used for more than three times, and is given to animals to eat.

DISTILLATION AND COLOURING OF WINE

The traditional distillation method is still practiced in this region, the indigenous set, which is quite simple has three parts parar, jokhal and tal, as called in the local dialect. The parar is a big saucepan like container with flat bottom, and jokhal is a flat wooden device like a dish having an elongated channel with a hole at the centre, and is indigenously prepared by the people. The tal is a simple cooking vessel, but the neck of tal and the bottom of parar is of such a size that they hold the jokhal perfectly.

This whole system is put on fire, on being heated the alcoholic vapour first evapourate and come through the central hole of the jokhal. But on coming in contact with cold bottom of parar the vapour gets condensed into liquid. This liquid is collected in a container, and this distillate is the alcohol or wine. The wine collected in first three to four bottles during the process of distillation contains very high percentage of alcohol, and is always diluted before consumption.

The alcohol content gradually reduces and finally only water evapourates. Traditionally wine is graded into three categories the initial few bottles containing high percentage of alcohol is called paileful; the final few bottles containing very low contents of alcohol is called piskani, and a few bottles in between them containing moderate contents of alcohol is rated good for consumption. For making the wine attractive in appearance, a small quantity of turmeric is hanged right at the mouth of the distillation set through which the distillate is collected. This makes the liquid a light but brilliantly shining yellow in colour.

SEZ (SEMI-FERMENTED FOOD)

The traditional semi-fermented food used by the Bhotiyas is called sez, it is made from rice, and is mostly used as a snacks. Earlier, it was a delicacy and was prepared only during certain festivals. In most cases, sez is extracted while preparation of rice jann. In the case of wine preparation the intermediate stage yielding sez is very unstable. The quantity of balam powder added is the determinant factor for the rate of fermentation.

In wine preparation quantity of balam used is maximum. Thus whenever extraction of sez is required the fermentation process has to be slowed down. To that effect a small quantity of balam powder is mixed with the substrate. Under a slow fermentation it becomes easy to intervene into the process removing the sez easily. Once sez has been removed fresh balam powder is added to hasten the process of fermentation so that jann or wine could be yielded.

PRODUCTION OF JANN, SEZ AND WINE FROM A COMMON CYCLE OF FERMENTATION

All the three different categories of fermented beverage and foods can be prepared from a common fermentation cycle, only when rice is used as substrate. Rice is first cooked or boiled in water for half an hour or until become soft and edible. This is then kept in a flat container to be drained off excess water and also to be cooled down. This boiled rice is mixed with balam powder.

The mixture is kept in an airtight container preferably in a dark and cool place. The container nowadays even plastic vessel is also used. After one or two days of fermentation, the sez is ready for consumption. The required quantity of sez could be removed at this stage. After that the container is again kept airtight for another five to ten days for further fermentation, then jann is produced. Jann is removed by filtration, *i.e.* by passing the content through a sieve or a piece of cloth. In the remaining mixture, jaggary and fresh balls of balam at a ratio of one ball per kg jaggary is added for the preparation of wine. The jaggary is boiled and cooled, and is mixed with balam powder. This is then added to the mixture and kept for fermentation in a tin container. Earthen ware is not used in wine preparation. The container set for fermentation is made air tight and kept in a warmer condition. Wine is produced within three to four days of fermentation. The emergence of this indigenous knowledge system in this part of high altitudes of the Himalaya was due to the cold climatic conditions of the Bhotiya dominated areas.

The way this society carved a niche in the making and living on the surrounding natural resources for adaptation to the emerging circumstances in the region. However, there is a shift in livings due to the intervention of outside forces, which have been damaging the traditional and self- sustaining systems in the name of development through introducing the outside made products. The indigenous knowledge of making fermented food and beverages developed over a long period of time. However, due to the expansion of road network and market forces, the availability of prepared yeast and modern liquor has changed the quality and quantity of indigenous fermented food and beverages. The age-old indigenous fermentation techniques should be encouraged as it led to the development of nutritious food items, which can cope up the inhospitable climatic conditions of high altitude areas.

7

Tasting Tourist Motivation

INTRODUCTION

Various studies have dealt with tourist motivations and market segmentation. Factors that motivate tourists for leisure travel are classified into two types, *i.e.* "push" and "pull" factors. An analysis on tourist motivation and activities is important for destinations to understand leisure tourist destination choice; it can also enhance destination image and its interplay with tourist satisfaction and loyalty. The analysis of tourist motivation can focus on one destination; or it can be conducted by a comparative study by nationality and destination.

The motivation study can also focus on one type of target group such as on senior travellers and on backpackers. This object focuses on the tourist motivation and activities related to the destinations in Denmark. Different criteria can be applied for analyzing destinations with their market segments, for example, a geographic criterion that can identify a destination as an urban or a rural/peripheral area. Destination attributes, such as cultural/historical heritage versus natural/beach is another criterion that "pulls" tourists into the local areas.

Market segmentation can also apply demographic, psychographic and personal behaviour criteria, for example, segments can be divided by tourist markets, tourist choice on type of accommodation, or active tourists versus more relaxed, nonactive tourists. Two main types of destination, *i.e.* city versus rural/beach destinations in Denmark are investigated and compared, and they are also compared with the other destinations. The tourists who choose to visit big cities are called "city-breaker" and tourists who choose to take their holiday at beaches are called "nature-beach" tourists. The analysis for the tourist characteristics within these two types of segments shows that they are significantly different from each other in term of age, household type and length of stay. It is also different in which activities tourists participate and patterns of their spending. The purpose of analyzing tourist motivation and activities is to explore visitors' desire, wants and needs. The analysis results will assist destination developers to understand target markets and improve the products, services and activities arranged to the tourists. Tourist motivation studies are useful in developing products, promotion, and marketing strategies. Destination marketing and development become important issues in both theoretical and practical tourism business. As global tourism markets become more and more competitive, many tourism destinations put efforts on improving quality of their products and services and enhancing the competitiveness.

TOURIST MOTIVATIONS AND MARKET SEGMENTATION

Each destination offers a variety of products and services to attract tourists. From the destinations' point of view, it is very important to know why tourists choose this destination and how the tourists feel about the place they visited. Analysis of tourist motivation attempts to extend the theoretical and empirical evidence on the causal relationship among the push and pull motivations, satisfaction, and destination loyalty. Motivation has been referred to as psychological/biological/social needs and wants, including internal and external forces.

Uysal and Hagan, these forces describe how individuals are pushed by motivation variables into making travel decisions and how they are pulled or attracted by destination attributes. "Push" factors are defined as origin-related and refer the intangible, intrinsic desires of the individual traveller, such as desire to escape, rest and relaxation, adventure, health and prestige. "Pull" factors are defined mainly related to the attractiveness of a given destination and tangible characteristics such as beaches, accommodation and recreation facilities and cultural and historical resources. Quite a number of literatures have studied tourist motivation from biological, psychological, sociological and anthropological aspects.

Tourism motivation is a multi-motive dimensional. Tourists often have more than one motive for choosing a certain destination, for example, people can choose one destination with a motive of relaxation in a pleasant safe place combined with visiting a local historical heritage. Motivation is also a dynamic and flexible variable. The design of a motivation list 'must be flexible enough to incorporate individual changes across the life-span and consider the effects of broad cultural force on tourist motivation'.

For example, a person may change his travel preferences as he moves through the family life cycle from a single-career person to a more family-oriented person, his motives for choosing destinations may be changed accordingly. The travel market is often divided into four types of markets: personal business travel, government or corporate business travel, visiting friends and family, and leisure travel. Each type of market can be sub-divided further into segments. Market segmentation is based on the profiles of target groups and measuring the attractiveness of the market. Destinations select one or a few segments as their target markets and develop the products and marketing strategies accordingly.

Effective market segmentation must exhibit the following characteristics:

- *Measurability*: The degree to which the size and purchasing power of the segments can be measured. Certain segmentation variables are difficult to measure;
- *Accessibility*: The degree to which the segment can be effectively reached and served;
- *Substantiality*: The degree to which the segments are large and/or profitable enough;
- *Action ability*: The degree to which effective programmes can be designed for attracting and serving the segments.

There are a number of objects dealing with tourism motivation, tourist perception and market positioning. Positioning involves identifying potential visitors' perception of the strong attributes of a destination, comparing them with their perceptions of the attributes of competitive destinations, and selecting those which differentiate a destination from its competitors. These features are then emphasized and form the cornerstone of marketing strategy.

Calantone point out that multinational tourism research requires researchers to investigate the problem of multinational origin, multinational destination, and multi-attribute criteria. Tourism planners should have a sound understanding of tourist perceptions and how they may differ across countries. Chen and Uysal use a new approach that could be applied to market positioning studies from a regional perspective. Different criteria are applied in this research.

- First, a regional perspective can identify a destination as an urban or a rural/peripheral area.
- Second, types of accommodation distinguish the same 'desires' and 'needs' of tourists, therefore, it can identify the market segments.
- Third, tourism markets show the potential directions for marketing, the same origins might have the same personal behaviours.
- Fourth, after the above three criteria, the markets can be further segmented by tourist motivation and activities in order to understand what kind of products, services and experiences tourists really desire, then the market planners can have a deep understanding of tourists needs, so that they can make appropriate marketing strategies for the segments.

Kozak gives an analysis of tourist motivations by comparing British and German tourists who have visited Mallorca and Turkey. The analysis uses cross-tabulation, factor analysis and a series of independent t-tests to evaluate quantitative data. The findings show that personal motivation and destination attributes should be used for destination positioning studies.

Efforts to understand the factors motivating tourists to visit a particular destination and how likely it is to be different from those of others visiting other destinations could help destination planners to set marketing strategies. It will also help the destination to build a self image for marketing and differentiating its own products and services from those of competing destinations.

DATA AND TOURISM PROFILE

The data for this study are based on a large survey that Danish Tourism Organization undertook in 2004. Visit Denmark conducted a survey of approximately 7,600 leisure tourists in all regions of Denmark, which covered both domestic and foreign tourists, and five different accommodation types, *i.e.* all types except yachting. The questionnaire was designed with the purposes of both economic analysis and tourism marketing analysis. Apart from the tourist profile, such as age, gender, household types, income level, party sizes and length of stay, tourist motivation and activities that tourists made at the destination and their satisfaction are also included in the questionnaire. Bornholm and Copenhagen are chosen amongst 14 destinations for further investigation in this study.

From the sample analysis, it is seen that the tourist characteristics within these two types of segments are significant different from each other. Families with children tend to come to Bornholm, as shown that the party size with more than 3-4 persons accounted for 44% at Bornholm, while tourists in Copenhagen are relatively younger, single or couples without children. 39% of tourists stayed one week and 37% stayed for more than one week at Bornholm.

Only 7% of tourists at Bornholm stayed for 1-3 nights, while in Copenhagen 64% of tourists stayed for 1-3 nights. From Statistics Denmark's tourism information it is seen that 91% of all tourist nights in Copenhagen are spent at hotels, while the nature-beach tourists stay at summer cottages and camping sites. The spending patterns of these two segments show that tourism spend more in big cities than rural/peripheral destination; hotel guests spend more than those staying at camping sites and holiday cottages. In the Danish survey 22 motives are included in a list of things that may affect tourists to choose the destinations.

These motives are grouped into seven factors by a rotated component matrix analysis:

- Nature (beach, forest, clean environment, safe place to stay and few tourists);
- local ways of life (people in general, enjoying local food, shopping and other motives);
- attractions (children friendly, attraction/amusement, possibility of activities);

- value for money (good/cheap transport, price level/inexpensive, possibility for spa, health and fitness)
- physical activities (golfing, bicycle, fishing, sailing);
- cultural and museum (museum/cultural, historical heritage, special events, theatre, musical festival;
- visit family and friends and possibility of playing golf.

STATISTICAL RESULTS AND EXPLANATION

A variety of analytical tools are applied in the analysis, including correlation and multivariate statistical techniques such as a factor analysis and multiple regression analysis. The point of departure is to check the differences in tourist motivation between the different types of destination, different types of accommodation and different tourism markets. Statistic tests show that tourist motivations have no direct relation with their satisfaction; it is found that activities that tourists made at destinations have influence on the tourist satisfaction. The activities like long walks or hikes and relaxation contribute positively to satisfaction. Those tourists who were less active in participating in activities are less satisfied than those who are very active participants.

DIFFERENCE IN MOTIVATION BY DESTINATIONS

An analysis of variance shows that motives for visiting Denmark are significantly different depending on destination. The tests are carried out for each of 22 different motives; it can identify tourism motivation for choosing different destinations, *i.e.* different county regions in Denmark. Tourist motive for nature shows the greatest difference between the various destinations.

The motive for good/cheap transport is the least difference between 16 destinations in Denmark, which is followed by motive of possibility for yachting. The differences in motivation by destination Copenhagen, Bornholm, rest of Denmark, and Denmark as whole. It is seen that most tourists choose to visit Bornholm because of nature, clean country and safety place, however, tourists also come with motivation of attraction, possibility of activities, children friends, possibility for bicycling and cultural, historical heritage.

Copenhagen attracts tourists by attractions and amusement many museums, cultural and historical heritage, many shopping possibilities and many restaurants. The main motives for tourists choosing Denmark as destination are nature, clean country, and safety place; also people in general, children friendly, attractions and amusement and possibility for activities. All these factors are scored by more than 40% of tourists.

DIFFERENCE IN MOTIVATION BY TYPES OF ACCOMMODATION

A second analysis of variance shows that motives for visiting Denmark are also significantly different depending on type of accommodation. The tests are conducted again for each of the 22 different motives. Tourists' motive for nature shows the greatest difference between the various accommodations. The tourists come to enjoy the nature, they are more likely to choose summer cottages, camping sites and holiday centres.

Tourists with motives for cultural, historical and special events, are more likely to stay at hotels and youth hostels. Sport-active tourists more likely choose camping sites; and tourists focusing more on value for money more likely choose to stay in holiday centres.

DIFFERENCE IN MOTIVATION BY TOURISM MARKETS

A third analysis of variance shows that motives for visiting Denmark are also significantly different depending on market. The difference in motivation by tourist markets. A high proportion of tourists from all nationalities think nature, clean country and safety are important influencing factors for the destination choice.

However, there are significant differences between nationalities with respect to the proportion of tourists who think these attributes are important. It is shown that German tourists are more likely motivated by possibilities of angling and bicycling than other tourists; Swedish/Norwegian tourists are more likely motivated by short distance to destination, inexpensive and attraction and amusement. In the analysis of variance with destination as the dependent variable, the average F-value for the 22 motives was 25.

For type of accommodation, the average F-value was 80, and for market it was also very large, namely 72. Therefore when segmenting the market for potential holiday visitors to Denmark, both market and types of accommodation are relevant criteria.

TOURIST SATISFACTION BY PARTICIPATION IN ACTIVITIES AT DESTINATIONS

Tourists are more satisfied with their holidays at Bornholm than those who visit Copenhagen or the rest of Denmark in term of overall satisfaction. For Denmark as a destination as a whole overall satisfaction among leisure tourists was 4.48 on a scale from 1 to 5, with a 95% confidence interval ranging from a low of 4.47 and a high of 4.50.

Average satisfaction for tourists who visit Bornholm is 4.63, for those who visit Copenhagen it is 4.39. Average scores in satisfaction at Bornholm for all types of accommodation are higher than those corresponding types of accommodation in Copenhagen and the rest of Denmark. Tourist satisfaction by their participation in activities at destinations. The level of participation in each activity is scaled from 1 – 5, representing from no participation, a lower level to a higher level of participation. NO represents non-participation in the category of activities. LOW represents for answers 2-4 and HIGH shows a higher level of participation in activity.

The weighted average scores for satisfaction on a scale from 1 to 5 for these three types of tourists, namely 'nonparticipation', 'lower level of participation' and 'higher level of participation'. For nearly all activities, tourists at Bornholm are more satisfied than the tourists who visited Copenhagen and the rest of Denmark.

Tourists at Bornholm are more satisfied with 'long walks or hikes', 'visiting attractions', 'swimming', 'cultural events', 'relax' and 'sunbathe' with relative higher percentage of respondents.. Tourists in Copenhagen are relatively more satisfied with 'shopping', 'cultural events', 'meeting new friends' and 'eating at restaurants' with also higher percentage of respondents, etc. In most cases at all regions the tourists with a higher level of participation are more satisfied than those with lower level of participation in activities.

MARKETING STRATEGIES FOR CITY-BREAKER AND NATURE-BEACHES TOURISM

Tourism markets are characterized by multinational origin, multinational or multi-regional destinations and multiple motives. Segmentation criteria should consider the points concerning measurability, accessibilities, substantiality of market segments. Destination planners should be aware of its comparative and competitive advantage in relation to other destinations. Comparative advantage involves the resources available to a destination, while competitive advantage relates to a destination's ability to use these resources.

Demographical trends in the main tourism markets and the changes in tourist motives should also be considered, as individual choice and tourism satisfaction do have influence on the destination development. Demographical trends in most western countries show growing shares of senior people and decreasing shares of young people in the population. This has been observed from the destinations in Denmark that tourist arrivals have decreased from the German families with small children and young people. The purpose of analyzing the target markets and motivations for destination choice is to understand the needs and desire of tourists better. Destinations can use the analysis to make appropriate strategies for tourism products and marketing mix.

The object uses two typical destinations as case studies to show the difference both in destination attributes and tourism motives for visiting the destination. The marketing strategies discussed here are focused also on these two types of destination. It should be noticed that some destinations have both features, such as one destination could be a rural-coastal area that is also close to a large city; or a destination has both cultural heritage, and at the same time it has an attractive natural environment.

It really depends on how large the destination area is defined. Another notice is that the authors do not suggest that each destination should only make their own marketing efforts; instead it is suggested to have a cooperative strategy between the different regions, coordinated by a national or regional tourism organization. Each accommodation would need to find the right balance between marketing through destination marketing organizations and accommodation brand marketing. Many hotels in Denmark and in Europe in general are unbranded, and therefore the booking platform may to some extent take on the role of a brand.

MARKETING STRATEGY FOR CITY-BREAKER TOURISM

City-breakers have a diversified background related to age, nationality, family types and income. They stay on average 4-5 days, but they stay at genuine hotels and spend much more than the nature-beach tourists, who generally stay at lower cost forms of accommodation. City-breakers are also relatively more interested in activities and culture attraction. It is suggested that marketing strategies for city destinations should concentrate on the attractions, activities development and event arrangement. Tourists from far away countries typically fly to the destination and are attracted by seeing the city and experience the activities happening in the city, however they are also interested in people in general, to experience every day life in the cities, including shopping.

For the repeat or domestic visitors, they are attracted to the city by the variety of activities, such as new shows in the theatres and opera houses or music festivals, new exhibitions, sport arrangements.

It is suggested that destinations like large cities continuously focus on the needs of relatively widely covered tourists, such as events tourism and cultural tourism. Destination planners should follow the new trends in the tourism development, such as more and more tourists prefer prolonged weekend holidays to the large cities to be relaxed or enjoy some cultural experience.

City marketing planners can accordingly make some effective activities to attract this type of tourists. City destinations have possibilities to explore new markets, such as Eastern European countries, Asian and South American countries. Following the rapid economic development in recent years in some developing countries, residents in these countries can afford to have long-haul travel 16 experience. The large cities are often the first choice when they are going abroad. Therefore city destinations should make appropriate products and marketing strategies for the target markets. A large city like Copenhagen should market itself with the unique attractions and diversified services in the city. The attractions, such as Tivoli and new Opera House, can be flagships for marketing.

The survey shows that 53% of those visiting Copenhagen sited the attractions/amusements as an important motive for coming. Besides the wide selection and variety of restaurants and shopping opportunities, good and cheap transport facilities to and at the destination are favourable attributes for Copenhagen to attract tourists.

MARKETING STRATEGY FOR NATURE-BEACHES TOURISM

Nature-beach tourists are more family-types with more emphasis on relaxation. The average length of stay for this kind of tourists is around 8-9 days. They enjoy beach or forest, few tourists at destination, clean environment, children friendly and possibilities of different activities, such as golfing, bicycling, fishing and most likely swimming. The destination at rural and peripheral areas should have the quality of providing good, clean environment to attract tourists coming again.

Certain facilities, such as possibilities for tourists to play golf, bicycling, fishing, should be available at destinations. Provincial destinations can also arrange children friendly activities, like mini-Tivoli and other small-scale amusement parks to attract tourists with children. At the same time destinations are facing the challenge of decreasing share of tourists with children, it is worthwhile starting to investigate the senior tourist markets to attract more retired people to visit the nature-beach destinations. The wonderful island of Bornholm should emphasize its unique nature, sited by a whopping 93% of visitors, including its rocky cliffs on the north coast and its white sandy beaches on the south coast. Also in the area of cycling possibilities the island is far ahead of the rest of the country.

Also the island has a strong cultural and historical heritage, which is mentioned by 44% of visitors, which is a higher percentage even than those visiting the capital of Denmark. Bornholm is the only place in Denmark with round churches, and there are five of them, and also there is an ancient castle ruin. The rest of Denmark, as most of them have attributes of nature and rural or coastal features, could also use nature or unspoiled environment to attract tourists. Nature, for one: 80% site Nature as an important reason for visiting other provinces.

Also the facts that these other provinces are child friendly and the price level is relatively low. Angling is quite popular at mainland provinces of Denmark, sited by 15%. But actually, the Baltic Sea along the coasts of Bornholm has got tremendous amounts and sizes of salmon, and one weekend in the spring there is a huge trolling competition, an event which should perhaps be emphasized even more by Destination Bornholm. Analyzing tourist satisfaction shows that more active tourists are more satisfied with destinations.

The results reflect the fact that tourists desire for experiences at destination. Destination marketing planners should investigate the possibilities of arranging more tourism activities. The regional cooperation needs to be further coordinated and more marketing efforts and investment is required. For the national marketing organization of Denmark it would be better to emphasize the variety of accommodation offers rather than the different regions, since motives vary more between different types of accommodation than between different regions. However, there is also great variation in motives between regions.

IN INDIA

Tourism is the largest service industry in India, with a contribution of 6.23% to the national GDP and 8.78% of the total employment in India. India witnesses more than 5 million annual foreign tourist arrivals and 562 million domestic tourism visits. The tourism industry in India generated about US$100 billion in 2008 and that is expected to increase to US$275.5 billion by 2018 at a 9.4% annual growth rate.

The Ministry of Tourism is the nodal agency for the development and promotion of tourism in India and maintains the "Incredible India" campaign. World Travel and Tourism Council, India will be a tourism hotspot from 2009-2018, having the highest 10-year growth potential. The Travel and Tourism Competitiveness Report 2007 ranked tourism in India 6th in terms of price competitiveness and 39th in terms of safety and security.

Despite short- and medium-term setbacks, such as shortage of hotel rooms, tourism revenues are expected to surge by 42% from 2007 to 2017. India has a growing medical tourism sector. The 2010 Commonwealth Games in Delhi are expected to significantly boost tourism in India.

BY STATE

ANDHRA PRADESH

Andhra Pradesh has a rich cultural heritage and a variety of tourist attractions. The state of Andhra Pradesh comprises scenic hills, forests, beaches and temples. Also known as The City of Nizams and The City of Pearls, Hyderabad is today one of the most developed cities in the country and a modern hub of information technology, ITES, and biotechnology. Hyderabad is known for its rich history, culture and architecture representing its unique character as a meeting point for North and South India, and also its multilingual culture.

Andhra Pradesh is the home of many religious pilgrim centres. Tirupati, the abode of Lord Venkateswara, is the richest and most visited religious centre in the world. Srisailam, the abode of Sri Mallikarjuna, is one of twelve Jyothirlingalu in India, Amaravati's Siva temple is one of the Pancharamams, and Yadagirigutta, the abode of an avatara of Vishnu, Sri Lakshmi Narasimha.

The Ramappa temple and Thousand Pillars temple in Warangal are famous for some fine temple carvings. The state has numerous Buddhist centres at Amaravati, Nagarjuna Konda, Bhattiprolu, Ghantasala, Nelakondapalli, Dhulikatta, Bavikonda, Thotlakonda, Shalihundam, Pavuralakonda, Sankaram, Phanigiri and Kolanpaka.

The golden beaches at Visakhapatnam, the one-million-year old limestone caves at Borra, picturesque Araku Valley, hill resorts of Horsley Hills, river Godavari racing through a narrow gorge at Papi Kondalu, waterfalls at Ettipotala, Kuntala and rich bio-diversity at Talakona, are some of the natural attractions of the state. Visakhapatnam is home to many tourist attactions such as the INS Karasura Submarine museum, Yarada Beach, Araku Valley, VUDA Park, Indira Gandhi Zoological Gardens. The weather in Andhra Pradesh is mostly tropical and the best time to visit is in November through to January. The monsoon season commences in June and ends in September, so travel would not be advisable during this period. Also worth visiting, the only Indian Buddhism Based Theme Park and Resorts on the Vijayawada-Guntur Highway-Agrigold Haailand.

ARUNACHAL PRADESH

Arunachal Pradesh attracts tourists from many parts of the world. Tourist attractions include Tawang, a beautiful town famous for its Buddhist monastery, Ziro, famous for cultural festivals, the Namdapha tiger project in Changlang district and Sela lake near Bomdila with its bamboo bridges overhanging the river. Religious places of interest include Malinithan in Lekhabali, Rukhmininagar near Roing and Parshuram Kund in Lohit district. Rafting and trekking are common activities. A visitor's permit from the tourism department is required. Places like Tuting have wonderful, undiscovered scenic beauty.

ASSAM

Assam is the central state in the North-East Region of India and serves as the gateway to the rest of the Seven Sister States. Assam boasts of famous wildlife preserves - the Kaziranga National Park, which is home to the Great Indian One-Horned Rhinoceros and the Manas National Park, the largest river island Majuli, historic Sivasagar, famous for the ancient monuments of Ahom Kingdom, the city of eternal romance, Tezpur and tea-estates dating back to time of British Raj. The weather is mostly sub-tropical.

Assam experiences the Indian monsoon and has one of the highest forest densities in India. The winter months are the best time to visit. Assam has a rich cultural heritage going back to the Ahom Kingdom, which governed the region for many centuries before the British occupation. Other notable features include the Brahmaputra River, the mystery of the bird suicides in Jatinga, numerous temples including Kamakhya of Tantric sect.

'Gurdwara Sri Guru Tegh Bahadur also known as Damdama Sahib at Dhubri '. This famous Gurudwara is situated in the heart of the Dhubri Town on the bank of the mighty Brahmaputra river in far north-east India. Guru Nanak the first Sikh Guru visited this place in 1505 and met Srimanta Sankardeva as the Guru travelled from Dhaka to Assam, ruins of palaces, etc. Guwahati, the capital city of Assam, boasts many bazaars, temples, and wildlife sanctuaries.

BIHAR

Bihar is one of the oldest continuously inhabited places in the world with history of 3000 years. The rich culture and heritage of Bihar is evident from the innumerable ancient monuments that are dotted all over this state in eastern

India. This is the Place of Aryabhata, Great Ashoka, Chanakya and many more. Bihar is one of the most sacred places of various religions such as Hinduism, Buddhism, Jainism, Sikhism and Islam. Famous Attraction includes Mahabodhi Temple, a Buddhist shrine and UNESCO World Heritage Site is also situated in Bihar, Barabar Caves the oldest rockcut caves in India, Khuda Bakhsh Oriental Library the Oldest Library of India.

DELHI

Delhi is the capital city of India. A fine blend of old and new, ancient and modern, Delhi is a melting pot of cultures, religions. Delhi has been the capital of numerous empires that ruled India, making it rich in history. The rulers left behind their trademark architectural styles. Delhi currently has many renowned historic monuments and landmarks such as the Tughlaqabad fort, Qutub Minar, Purana Quila, Lodhi Gardens, Jama Masjid, Humayun's tomb, Red Fort, and Safdarjung's Tomb.

Modern monuments include Jantar Mantar, India Gate, Rashtrapati Bhavan, Laxminarayan Temple, Lotus temple and Akshardham Temple. New Delhi is famous for its British colonial architecture, wide roads, and tree-lined boulevards. Delhi is home to numerous political landmarks, national museums, Islamic shrines, Hindu temples, green parks, and trendy malls.

GOA

Goa is one of the most famous tourist destinations in India. A former colony of Portugal, Goa is famous for its excellent beaches, Portuguese churches, Hindu temples, and wildlife sanctuaries. The Basilica of Bom Jesus, Mangueshi Temple, Dudhsagar Falls, and Shantadurga are famous attractions in Goa. Recently a Wax Museum has also opened in Old Goa housing a number of wax personalities of Indian history, culture and heritage. The Goa Carnival is a world famous event, with colourful masks and floats, drums and reverberating music, and dance performances. The celebrations run three days culminating in a carnival parade on fat Tuesday.

HIMACHAL PRADESH

Himachal Pradesh is famous for its Himalayan landscapes and popular hill-stations. Many outdoor activities such as rock climbing, mountain biking, paragliding, ice-skating, and heli-skiing are popular tourist attractions in Himachal Pradesh. Shimla, the state capital, is very popular among tourists. The Kalka-Shimla Railway is a Mountain railway which is a UNESCO World Heritage Site. Shimla is also a famous skiing attraction in India. Other popular hill stations include Manali and Kasauli. Dharamshala, home of the Dalai Lama, is known for its Tibetan monasteries and Buddhist temples. Many trekking expeditions also begin here.

JAMMU AND KASHMIR

Jammu and Kashmir is the northernmost state of India. Jammu is noted for its scenic landscape, ancient temples, Hindu shrines, castles, gardens and forts. The Hindu holy shrines of Amarnath in kashmir attracts about. 4 million Hindu devotees every year. Vaishno Devi alsoattract tens of thousands of Hindu devotees every year. Jammu's historic monuments feature a unique blend of Islamic and Hindu architecture styles.

Tourism forms an integral part of the Kashmiri economy. Often dubbed "Paradise on Earth", Kashmir's mountainous landscape has attracted tourists for centuries. Notable places are Dal Lake, Srinagar Phalagam, Gulmarg, Yeusmarg and Mughal Gardens etc.

Kashmir's natural landscape has made it one of the popular destinations for adventure tourism in South Asia.Marked by four distinct seasons,Ski enthusiasts can enjoy the exotic himalayan powder during winters. 7000000 tourists arrived in kashmir in the months of April,May and June alone In recent years, Ladakh has emerged as a major hub for adventure tourism. This part of Greater Himalaya called "moon on earth" comprising of naked peaks and deep gorges was once known for the silk route to High Asia from the subcontinent. Leh is also a growing tourist spot.

KARNATAKA

Karnataka has been ranked as fourth most popular destination for tourism among states of India. It has the second highest number of protected monuments in India, at 507.

Kannada dynasties like Kadambas, Western Gangas, Chalukyas, Rashtrakutas, Hoysalas and Vijayanagaras, ruled Karnataka particularly North Karnataka. They built great monuments to Buddhism, Jainism, Shaivism.

The monuments are still present at Badami, Aihole, Pattadakal, Hampi, Lakshmeshwar, Sudi, Hooli, Mahadeva Temple, Dambal, Lakkundi, Gadag, Hangal, Halasi, Galaganatha, Chaudayyadanapura, Banavasi, Belur, Halebidu, Shravanabelagola, Sannati and many more. Notable Islamic monuments are present at Bijapur, Bidar, Gulbarga, Raichur and other part of the state. Gol Gumbaz at Bijapur, has the second largest pre-modern dome in the world after the Byzantine Hagia Sophia. Karnataka has two World heritage sites, at Hampi and Pattadakal, both are in North Karnataka. Karnataka is famous for its waterfalls.

Jog falls of Shimoga District is one of the highest waterfalls in Asia. This state has 21 wildlife sanctuaries and five National parks and is home to more than 500 species of birds. Karnataka has many beaches at Karwar, Gokarna, Murdeshwara, Surathkal. Karnataka is a rock climbers paradise. Yana in Uttara Kannada, Fort in Chitradurga, Ramnagara near Bangalore district, Shivagange in Tumkur district and tekal in Kolar district are a rock climbers heaven.

KERALA

Kerala is a state on the tropical Malabar Coast of southwestern India. Nicknamed as one of the "10 paradises of the world" by National Geographic, Kerala is famous especially for its ecotourism initiatives. Its unique culture and traditions, coupled with its varied demography, has made it one of the most popular tourist destinations in India. Growing at a rate of 13.31%, the tourism industry significantly contributes to the state's economy. Kerala is known for its tropical backwaters and pristine beaches such as Kovalam.

MADHYA PRADESH

Madhya Pradesh is called the "Heart of India" because of its location in the centre of the country. It has been home to the cultural heritage of Hinduism, Islam, Buddhism, Sikhism, Jainism. Innumerable monuments, exquisitely carved temples, stupas, forts and palaces are dotted all over the State. The temples of Khajuraho are world-famous for their erotic sculptures, and are a UNESCO World Heritage Site.

Gwalior is famous for its forts, the Tomb of Rani Lakshmibai, and the Palace of Tansen. Madhya Pradesh is also known as Tiger State because of the tiger population. Famous national parks like Kanha, Bandhavgadh, Shivpuri, Sanjay, Pench are located in MP. Spectacular mountain ranges, meandering rivers and miles and miles of dense forests offering a unique and exciting panorama of wildlife in sylvan surroundings.

MAHARASHTRA

Maharashtra is the second most visited state in India by foreign tourists, with more than 2 million foreign tourists arrivals annually. Maharashtra boasts of a large number of popular and revered religious venues that are heavily frequented by locals as well as out-of-state visitors. Ajanta Caves, Ellora Caves and Chhatrapati Shivaji Terminus are the three UNESCO World Heritage sites in Maharashtra and are highly responsible for the development of Tourism in the state. Mumbai is the most cosmopolitan city in India, and a great place to experience modern India.

Mumbai famous for Bollywood, the world's largest film industry. In addition, Mumbai is famous for its clubs, shopping, and upscale gastronomy. The city is known for its architecture, from the ancient Elephanta Caves, to the Islamic Haji Ali Mosque, to the colonial architecture of Bombay High Court and Chhatrapati Shivaji Terminus. Maharashtra also has numerous adventure tourism destinations, including paragliding, rock climbing, canoeing, kayaking, snorkeling, and scuba diving in places like Kolad, Tarkarli, Koyna, Manor. Maharashtra also has several pristine national parks and reserves, some of the best ones are Tadoba with excellent accommodation and safari experiences besides little known by amazing wildlife destinations like Koyna, Nagzira,

Melghat, Dajipur, Radhanagari and of course the only national park within metropolic city limits in the world-Sanjay Gandhi National Park.

The Bibi Ka Maqbara at Aurangabad the Mahalakshmi temple at Kolhapur, the cities of Nashik, Trimbak famous for religious importance and the city of Pune the seat of the Maratha Empire and the fantastic Ganesh Chaturthi celebrations together contribute for the Tourism sector of Mahrashtra.

MANIPUR

Manipur as the name suggest is a land of jewels. Its rich culture excels in every aspects as in martial arts, dance, theater and sculpture. The charm of the place is the greenery with the moderate climate making it a tourists' heaven. The beautiful and seasonal Shirui Lily at Ukhrul, Sangai and the floating islands at Loktak Lake are few of the rare things found in Manipur. Polo, which can be called a royal game, also originated from Manipur.

MEGHALAYA

Meghalaya has some of the thickest surviving forests in the country and therefore constitutes one of the most important ecotourism circuits in the country today. The Meghalayan subtropical forests support a vast variety of flora and fauna. Meghalaya has 2 National Parks and 3 Wildlife Sanctuaries. Meghalaya also offers many adventure tourism opportunities in the form of mountaineering, rock climbing, trekking and hiking, water sports etc. The state offers several trekking routes some of which also afford and opportunity to encounter some rare animals such as the slow loris, assorted deer and bear. The Umiam Lake has a water sports complex with facilities such as rowboats, paddleboats, sailing boats, cruise-boats, water-scooters and speedboats.

Cherrapunjee is one of the most popular tourist spots in North East of India. It lies to the south of the capital Shillong. The town is very well known and needs little publicity. A rather scenic, 50 kilometer long road, connects Cherrapunjee with Shillong. The popular waterfalls in the state are the Elephant Falls, Shadthum Falls, Weinia falls, Bishop Falls, Nohkalikai Falls, Langshiang Falls and Sweet Falls. The hot springs at Jakrem near Mawsynram are believed to have curative and medicinal properties.

ORISSA

Orissa has been a preferred destination from ancient days for people who have an interest in spirituality, religion, culture, art and natural beauty. Ancient and medieval architecture, pristine sea beaches, the classical and ethnic dance forms and a variety of festivals. Orissa has kept the religion of Buddhism alive. Rock-edicts that have challenged time stand huge and over-powering by the banks of the river Daya. The torch of Buddhism is still ablaze in the sublime triangle at Udayagiri, Lalitagiri and Ratnagiri, on the banks of river Birupa. Precious fragments of a glorious past come alive in the shape of stupas, rockcut caves, rock-edicts, excavated monasteries, viharas, chaityas and sacred relics in caskets and the Rock-edicts of Ashoka. Orissa is also famous for its well-preserved Hindu Temples, especially the Konark Sun Temple and The Leaning Temple of Huma. Orissa is the home for various tribal communities who have contributed uniquely to the multicultural and multilingual character of the state. Their handicrafts, different dance forms, jungle products and their unique life style blended with their healing practices have got world wide attention. The Sitalsasthi Carnival is a must see for everyone who wants to see a glimpse of the art and culture of Odisha at one place.

PUDUCHERRY

The Union Territory of Puducherry comprises four coastal regions viz-Puducherry, Karaikal, Mahe and Yanam. Puducherry is the Capital of this Union Territory and one of the most popular tourist destinations in South India. Puducherry has been described by National Geographic as "a glowing highlight of subcontinental sojourn". The city has many beautiful colonial buildings, churches, temples, and statues, which, combined with the systematic town planning and the well planned French style avenues, still preserve much of the colonial ambience.

PUNJAB

The state of Punjab is renowned for its cuisine, culture and history. Punjab has a vast public transportation and communication network. Some of the main cities in Punjab are Amritsar, Chandigarh, and Ludhiana. Punjab also has a rich religious history incorporating Sikhism and Hinduism. Tourism in Punjab is principally suited for the tourists interested in culture, ancient civilization, spirituality and epic history.

Some of the villages in Punjab are also a must see for the person who wants to see the true Punjab, with their beautiful traditional Indian homes, farms and temples, this is a must see for any visitor that goes to Punjab. India-Pakistan border at Wagha is also a popular tourist attraction.

RAJASTHAN

Rajasthan, literally meaning "Land of the Kings", is one of the most attractive tourist destinations in Northern India. The vast sand dunes of the Thar Desert attract millions of tourists from around the globe every year.

SIKKIM

Originally known as Suk-Heem, which in the local language means "peaceful home", Sikkim was an independent kingdom till the year 1974, when it became a part of the Republic of India. The capital of Sikkim is Gangtok, located approximately 105 kilometers from New alpaiguri, the nearest railway station to Sikkim. Although, an airport is under construction at Dekiling in East Sikkim, the nearest airport to Sikkim would be Bagdogra. Sikkim is considered as the land of Orchids and mystic cultures and colourful traditions. Sikkim is well known among trekkers and adventure lovers, as West Sikkim has a lot to give them. Places near Sikkim include Darjeeling also known as the Queen of hills and Kalimpong. Darjeeling, other than its world famous "Darjeeling tea" is also famous for its refined "Prep schools" founded during the British Raj. Kalimpong is also famous for its flora cultivation and is home to many internationally known Nurseries.

TAMIL NADU

Tamil Nadu is the top state in attracting the maximum number of foreign tourists in India. Tamil Nadu. Marina Beach, Carnatic music, Bharata Natyam dance and country's largest Shopping locality. This city is also famous for Medical tourism and houses Asia's largest hospital. Archaeological sites with civilization dating back to 3800 years are found in Tamil Nadu. With more than 34000 temples this state also holds the credit of having maximum number of UNESCO heritage sites in India which includes Great Living Chola Temples and Mahabalipuram.

Country's largest temple srirangam and Pichavaram the world's Second largest Mangrove forest are located in this state. Tamilnadu has some great temples like Madurai Meenakshi Amman Temple, Tanjore Brihadeeswarar Temple, Srirangam Ranganathaswamy Temple and all the mentioned temples has world class architecture that really mesmerize everyone.

Kanyakumari is the southernmost tip of India provides sceneic view of sunset and sunshine over the Indian ocean.Hill stations like Yercaud, Kodaikanal, Ooty, Valparai, Yelagiri are widely visited. Velankanni Church and Nagoor Dharga are visited by people of all religion.Water Falls and Wildlife sanctuaries are located across the state.

UTTARAKHAND

Uttarakhand, the 27th state of the Republic of India, is called "the abode of the Gods". It contains glaciers, snow-clad mountains, valley of flowers, skiing slopes and dense forests, and many shrines and places of pilgrimage. Char-dhams, the four most sacred and revered Hindu temples: Badrinath, Kedarnath, Gangotri and Yamunotri are nestled in the Himalayas.

Haridwar which means Gateway to God is the only place on the plains. It holds the watershed for Gangetic River System spanning 300 km from Satluj in the west to Kali river in the east. Nanda Devi is the second highest peak in India after Kanchenjunga.

Dunagiri, Neelkanth, Chaukhamba, Panchachuli, Trisul are other peaks above 23000 Ft. It is considered the abode of Devtas, Yakashyas, Kinners, Fairies and Sages. It boasts of some old hill-stations developed during British era like Mussoorie, Almora and Nainital.

UTTAR PRADESH

Situated in the northern part of India, Uttar Pradesh is important with its wealth of monuments and religious fervour. Geographically, Uttar Pradesh is very diverse, with Himalayan foothills in the extreme north and the Gangetic Plain in the centre. It is also home of India's most visited site, the Taj Mahal, and Hinduism's holiest city, Varanasi. The most populous state of the Indian Union also has a rich cultural heritage, and at the heart of North India, Uttar Pradesh has much to offer. Places of interest include Varanasi, Agra, Kanpur, Lucknow, Mathura, Jhansi, Prayag, Sarnath, Ayodhya, Dudhwa National Park and Fatehpur Sikri.

WEST BENGAL

Kolkata, one of the many cities in the state of West Bengal has been nicknamed the City of Palaces. This comes from the numerous palatial mansions built all over the city. Unlike many north Indian cities, whose construction stresses minimalism, the layout of much of the architectural variety in Kolkata owes its origins to European styles and tastes imported by the British and, to a much lesser extent, the Portuguese and French. The buildings were designed and inspired by the tastes of the English gentleman around and the aspiring Bengali Babu. Today, many of these structures are in various stages of decay.

Some of the major buildings of this period are well maintained and several buildings have been declared as heritage structures. From historical point of view, the story of West Bengal begins from Gour and Pandua situated close to the present district town of Malda. The twin medieval cities had been sacked at least once by changing powers in the 15th century.

However, ruins from the period still remain, and several architectural specimens still retain the glory and shin of those times. The Hindu architecture of Bishnupur in terracotta and laterite sandstone are renowned world over. Towards the British colonial period came the architecture of Murshidabad and Coochbehar.

NATURE TOURISM

India has geographical diversity, which resulted in varieties of nature tourism.

- Water falls in Western Ghats including Jog falls.
- Western Ghats
- Hill Stations
- Wildlife reserves
- Deserts

WILDLIFE IN INDIA

India is home to several well known large mammals including the Asian Elephant, Bengal Tiger, Asiatic Lion, Leopard and Indian Rhinoceros, often engrained culturally and religiously often being associated with deities. Other well known large Indian mammals include ungulates such as the domestic Asian Water buffalo, wild Asian Water buffalo, Nilgai, Gaur and several species of deer and antelope. Some members of the dog family such as the Indian Wolf, Bengal Fox, Golden Jackal and the Dhole or Wild Dogs are also widely distributed. It is also home to the Striped Hyaena, Macaques, Langurs and Mongoose species. India also has a large variety of protected wildlife. The country's protected forest consists of 75 National parks of India and 421 Sanctuaries, of which 19 fall under the purview of Project Tiger. Its climatic and geographic diversity makes it the home of over 350 mammals and 1200 bird species, many of which are unique to the subcontinent. Some well known national wildlife sanctuaries include Bharatpur, Corbett, Kanha, Kaziranga, Periyar, Ranthambore, Manas and Sariska. The world's largest mangrove forest Sundarbans is located in southern West Bengal. The Kaziranga National Park,Manas National Park, Sundarbans and Keoladeo National Park is UNESCO World Heritage Site.

HILL STATIONS

Several hill stations served as summer capitals of Indian provinces, princely states, or, in the case of Shimla, of British India itself. Since Indian Independence, the role of these hill stations as summer capitals has largely ended, but many hill stations remain popular summer resorts.

Most famous hill stations are:

- Mount Abu, Rajasthan
- Pachmarhi, Madhya Pradesh-It is also known as The Queen of Satpura.
- Araku, Andhra Pradesh
- Gulmarg, Srinagar and Ladakh in Jammu and Kashmir
- Darjeeling in West Bengal
- Munnar in Kerala
- Ooty, Yercaud and Kodaikanal in Tamil Nadu
- Shillong in Meghalaya
- Shimla, Kullu in Himachal Pradesh
- Nainital in Uttarakhand
- Gangtok in Sikkim
- Mussoorie in Uttarakhand
- Manali in Himachal Pradesh
- Tawang in Arunachal Pradesh
- Mahabaleshwar in Maharashtra
- Haflong in Assam

In addition to the bustling hill stations and summer capitals of yore, there are several serene and peaceful nature retreats and places of interest to visit for a nature lover. These range from the stunning moonscapes of Leh and Ladhak, to small, exclusive nature retreats such as Dunagiri, Binsar,

Mukteshwar in the Himalayas, to rolling vistas of Western Ghats to numerous private retreats in the rolling hills of Kerala.

BEACHES

India offers a wide range of tropical beaches with silver/golden sand to coral beaches of Lakshadweep. States like Kerala and Goa have exploited the potential of beaches to the fullest. However, there are a lot many unexploited beaches in the states of Andhra Pradesh, Gujarat, Maharastra, Tamil Nadu and Karnataka. These states have very high potential to be develop them as future destinations for prospective tourists.

Some of the famous tourist beaches are:

- Beaches of Vizag, Andhra Pradesh
- Beaches of Puri, Orissa
- Beaches of Digha, West Bengal
- Beaches of Goa
- Kovalam Beach, Kerala
- Marina Beach, Chennai
- City Beach, Puducherry
- Beaches of Mahabalipuram
- Beaches in Mumbai
- Beaches of Diu
- Beaches of Midnapore, West Bengal
- Beaches of Andaman and Nicobar Islands
- Beaches of Lakshadweep Islands

ADVENTURE TOURISM

- River rafting and kayaking in Himalayas
- Mountain climbing in Himalayas
- Rock climbing in Madhya Pradesh
- Skiing in Gulmarg or Auli
- Boat racing in Bhopal
- Paragliding in Maharashtra

8

Wine Tasting and Tourism

INTRODUCTION

Wine tasting is the sensory examination and evaluation of wine. While the practice of wine tasting is as ancient as its production, a more formalized methodology has slowly become established from the 14th century onwards. Modern, professional wine tasters use a constantly-evolving formal terminology which is used to describe the range of perceived flavors, aromas and general characteristics of a wine. More informal, recreational tasting may use similar terminology, usually involving a much less analytical process for a more general, personal appreciation.

Tasting Stages

The results of the four recognized stages to wine tasting:

- Appearance.
- "In glass" the aroma of the wine.
- "In mouth" sensations.
- "Finish".

The combined in order to establish the following properties of a wine:

- Complexity and character.
- Potential.
- Possible faults.

A wine's overall quality assessment, based on this examination, follows further careful description and comparison with recognized standards, both with respect to other wines in its price; if it is typical of the region or diverges in style; if it uses certain wine-making techniques, such as barrel fermentation or malolactic fermentation, or any other remarkable or unusual characteristics.

Whereas wines are regularly tasted in isolation, a wine's quality assessment is more objective when performed alongside several other wines, in what are known as tasting "flights". Wines may be deliberately selected for their vintage or proceed from a single winery to better compare vineyard and vintages, respectively. Alternatively, in order to promote an unbiased analysis, bottles and even glasses may be disguised in a "blind" tasting, to rule out any prejudicial awareness of either vintage or winery.

Blind Tasting

To ensure impartial judgement of a wine, it should be served *blind* — that is, without the taster(s) having seen the label or bottle shape. Blind tasting may also involve serving the wine from a black wine glass to mask the colour of the wine. A taster's judgement can be prejudiced by knowing of a wine, such as geographic origin, price, reputation, colour, or other considerations.

Scientific research has long demonstrated the power of suggestion in perception as well as the strong effects of expectancies. For example, people expect more expensive wine to have more desirable characteristics than less expensive wine. When given wine that they are falsely told is expensive they virtually always report it as tasting better than the very same wine when they are told that it is inexpensive. French researcher Frédéric Brochet "submitted a mid-range Bordeaux in two different bottles, one labeled as a cheap table wine, the other bearing a grand cru etiquette" and obtained predictable results. Tasters described the supposed grand cru as "woody, complex, and round" and the supposed cheap wine as "short, light, and faulty."

Similarly, people have expectations about wines because of their geographic origin, producer, vintage, colour, and many other factors. For example, when Brochet served a white wine he received all the usual descriptions: "fresh, dry, honeyed, lively." Later he served the same wine dyed red and received the usual red terms: "intense, spicy, supple, deep."

Vertical and Horizontal Tasting

Vertical and horizontal wine tastings are wine tasting events that are arranged to highlight differences between similar wines.

- In a vertical tasting, different vintages of the same wine type from the same winery are tasted. This emphasizes differences between various vintages.
- In a horizontal tasting, the wines are all from the same vintage but are from different wineries. Keeping wine variety or type and wine region the same helps emphasize differences in winery styles.

Tasting Flights

Tasting flight is a term used by wine tasters to describe a selection of wines, usually between three and eight glasses, but sometimes as many as fifty, presented for the purpose of sampling and comparison.

Tasting Notes

A tasting note refers to a taster's written testimony about the aroma, taste identification, acidity, structure, texture, and balance of a wine.

Serving Temperature

The temperature that a wine is served at can greatly affect the way it tastes and smells. Lower temperatures will emphasize acidity and tannins while muting the aromatics.

Higher temperatures will minimize acidity and tannins while increasing the aromatics. Master of Wine Jancis Robinson recommends the following temperature range for different styles of wine.

- Light bodied sweet dessert wines: *(Ex: Trockenbeerenauslese, Sauternes)* 41-50°F (5-10°C).
- White sparkling wines: *(Ex: Champagne)* 43-50°F (6-10°C).
- Aromatic, light bodied white: *(Ex: Riesling, Sauvignon blanc)* 46-54°F (8-12°C).
- Red sparkling wines: *(Ex: Sparkling Shiraz, some frizzante Lambrusco)* 50-54°F (10-12°C).
- Medium bodied whites: *(Ex: Chablis, Semillon)* 50-54°F (10-12°C).
- Full bodied dessert wines: *(Ex: Oloroso Sherry, Madeira)* 46-54°F (8-12°C).
- Light bodied red wines: *(Ex: Beaujolais, Provence rosé)* 50-54°F (10-12°C).
- Full bodied white wines: *(Ex: Oaked Chardonnay, Rhone whites)* 54-61°F (12-16°C).
- Medium bodied red wines: *(Ex: Grand Cru Burgundy, Sangiovese)* 57-63°F (14-17°C).
- Full bodied red wines: *(Ex: Cabernet Sauvignon, Nebbiolo based wines)* 59-64°F (15-18°C).

Glassware

The shape of a wineglass can have a subtle impact on the perception of wine, especially its bouquet.

Typically, the ideal shape is considered to be wider towards the bottom, with a narrower aperture at the top. Glasses which are widest at the top are considered the least ideal. Many wine tastings use ISO XL5 glasses, which are 'egg'-shaped. Interestingly, the effect of glass shape does not appear to be related to whether the glass is pleasing to look at.

Wine Colour

Without having tasted the wines, one does not know if, for example, a white is heavy or light. Before taking a sip, the taster tries to determine the order in which the wines should be assessed by appearance and nose alone. Heavy wines will be deeper in colour and generally more intense on the nose. Sweeter wines, being denser, will leave thick, viscous streaks down the inside of the glass when swirled.

The Wine Tasting Process

There are five basic steps in tasting wine: colour, swirl, smell, taste, and savour. This is also known as the five Ss. During this process, a taster must look for clarity, varietal character, integration, expressiveness, complexity, and connectedness.

A wine's colour is better judged by putting it against a white background. The wine glass is put at an angle in order to see the colours. Colours can give the taster clues to the grape variety, and whether the wine was aged in wood.

Characteristics Assessed During Tasting

Varietal character describes how much a wine presents its inherent grape aromas. A wine taster also looks for integration, which is a state in which none of the components of the wine is out of balance with the other components. When a wine is well balanced, the wine is said to have achieved a harmonious fusion. Another important quality of the wine to look for is its expressiveness. Expressiveness is the quality the "wine possesses when its aromas and flavors are well-defined and clearly projected. The complexity of the wine is affected by many factors, one of which may be the multiplicity of its flavors. The connectedness of the wine, a rather abstract and difficult to ascertain quality, describes the bond between the wine and its land of origin.

Connoisseur Wine Tasting

A wine's quality can be judged by its bouquet and taste. The bouquet is the total aromatic experience of the wine. Assessing a wine's bouquet can also reveal faults such as cork taint, oxidation due to age, overexposure to oxygen, or lack of preservatives and wild yeast contamination due to *Brettanomyces* or acetobacter yeasts. Although low levels of *Brettanomyces* aromatic characteristics can be a positive attribute, giving the wine a distinctive character, generally it is considered a wine spoilage yeast.

The bouquet of wine is best revealed by gently swirling the wine in a wine glass to expose it to more oxygen and release more aromatic etheric, ester, and aldehyde molecules that comprise the essential components of a wine's bouquet. However, sparkling wine is not swirled, as this speeds the release of the bubbles.

Pausing to experience a wine's bouquet aids the wine taster in anticipating the wine's flavors. The "nose" of a wine - its bouquet or aroma - is the major determinate of perceived flavor in the mouth. Once inside the mouth, the aromatics are further liberated by exposure to body heat, and transferred retronasally to the olfactory receptor site. It is here that the complex taste experience characteristic of a wine actually commences.

Thoroughly tasting a wine involves perception of its array of taste and mouthfeel attributes, which involve the combination of textures, flavors, weight, and overall "structure". Following appreciation of its olfactory characteristics, the wine taster savors a wine by holding it in the mouth for a few seconds to saturate the taste buds.

By pursing ones lips and breathing through that small opening oxygen will pass over the wine and release even more esters. When the wine is allowed to pass slowly through the mouth it presents the connoisseur with the fullest gustatory profile available to the human palate.

The acts of pausing and focusing through each step distinguishes wine tasting from simple quaffing.

Through this process, the full array of aromatic molecules is captured and interpreted by approximately 15 million olfactory receptors, comprising a few hundred olfactory receptor classes. When tasting several wines in succession, however, key aspects of this fuller experience must necessarily be sacrificed through expectoration.

Although taste qualities are known to be widely distributed throughout the oral cavity, the concept of an anatomical "tongue map" yet persists in the wine tasting arena, in which different tastes are believed to map to different areas of the tongue. A widely accepted example is the misperception that the tip of the tongue uniquely tells how sweet a wine is and the upper edges tell its acidity.

Scoring Wine

As part of the tasting process, and as a way of comparing the merits of the various wines, wines are given scores behalf of a relatively set system. This may be either by explicitly weighting different aspects, or by global judegement.

These aspects are:

- The appearance of the wine,
- The nose or smell,
- The palate or taste, and
- Overall.

Different systems weight these differently. Typically, no modern wine would score less than half on any scale. It is more common for wines to be scored out of 20 in Europe and parts of Australasia, and out of 100 in the US. However, different critics tend to have their own preferred system, and some gradings are also given out of 5.

Expectoration

As an alcoholic drink, wine can affect the consumer's judegement. As such, at formal tastings, where dozens of wines may be assessed, wine tasters generally spit the wine out after they have assessed its quality. However, since wine is absorbed through the skin inside the mouth, tasting from twenty to twenty-five samplings can produce an intoxicating effect, depending on the alcoholic content of the wine.

Visiting Wineries

Traveling to wine regions is another way of increasing skill in tasting. Many wine producers in wine regions all over the world offer tastings of their wine. Depending on the country or region, tasting at the winery may incur a small charge to allow the producer to cover costs. It is not considered rude to spit out wine at a winery, even in the presence of the wine maker or owner. Generally, a spittoon will be provided. In some regions of the world, tasters simply spit on the floor or onto gravel surrounding barrels. It is polite to enquire about where to spit before beginning tasting.

Attending Wine Schools

A growing number of wine schools can be found, offering wine tasting classes to the public. These programmes often help a wine taster hone and develop their abilities in a controlled setting. Some also offer professional training for sommeliers and winemakers. It is even possible to learn how to assess wine methodically via e-learning.

THE BASIC OF WINE TASTING

Learning how to taste wines is a straightforward adventure that will deepen your appreciation for both wines and winemakers. Look, smell, taste - starting with your basic senses and expanding from there you will learn how to taste wines like the pros in no time! Keep in mind that you can smell thousands of unique scents, but your taste perception is limited to salty, sweet, sour and bitter. It is the combination of smell and taste that allows you to discern flavor.

- *Look*: Check out the Colour and Clarity.
- *Pour a glass of wine into a suitable wine glass*: Then take a good look at the wine. Tilt the glass away from you and check out the colour of the wine from the rim edges to the middle of the glass.
- What colour is it? Look beyond red, white or blush. If it's a red wine is the colour maroon, purple, ruby, garnet, red, brick or even brownish? If it's a white wine is it clear, pale yellow, straw-like, light green, golden, amber or brown in appearance?
- *Still Looking*: Move on to the wine's opacity. Is the wine watery or dark, translucent or opaque, dull or brilliant, cloudy or clear? Tilt your glass a bit, give it a little swirl - look again, is there sediment, bits of cork or any other floaters? An older red wine will often have more orange tinges on the edges of colour than younger red wines. Older white wines are darker, than younger white wines when comparing the same varietal at different ages.
- *Smell*:
- Our sense of smell is critical in properly analyzing a glass of wine.
- *Still Smelling*: Now stick your nose down into the glass and take a deep inhale through your nose. What are your second impressions?

Do you smell oak, berry, flowers, vanilla or citrus? A wine's aroma is an excellent indicator of its quality and unique characteristics. Swirl the wine and let the aromas mix and mingle, and sniff again.

- *Taste*:
- *Finally, take a taste*: Start with a small sip and let it roll around your mouth. There are three stages of taste: the Attack phase, the Evolution phase and the Finish.
- The Attack Phase, is the initial impression that the wine makes on your palate. The Attack is comprised of four pieces of the wine puzzle: alcohol content, tannin levels, acidity and residual sugar. These four puzzle pieces display initial sensations on the palate. Ideally these components will be well-balanced one piece will not be more prominent than the others. These four pieces do not display a specific flavor per se, they meld together to offer impressions in intensity and complexity, soft or firm, light or heavy, crisp or creamy, sweet or dry, but not necessarily true flavors like fruit or spice.
- The Evolution Phase is next, also called the mid-palate or middle range phase, this is the wine's actual taste on the palate. In this phase you are looking to discern the flavor profile of the wine. If it's a red wine you may start noting fruit - berry, plum, prune or fig; perhaps some spice - pepper, clove, cinnamon, or maybe a woody flavor like oak, cedar, or a detectable smokiness. If you are in the Evolution Phase of a white wine you may taste apple, pear, tropical or citrus fruits, or the taste may be more floral in nature or consist of honey, butter, herbs or a bit of earthiness.
- The Finish is appropriately labeled as the final phase. The wine's finish is how long the flavor impression lasts after it is swallowed. This is where the wine culminates, where the aftertaste comes into play. Did it last several seconds? Was it light-bodied, medium-bodied or full-bodied? Can you taste the remnant of the wine on the back of your mouth and throat? Do you want another sip or was the wine too bitter at the end? What was your last flavor impression – fruit, butter, oak? Does the taste persist or is it short-lived?
- After you have taken the time to taste your wine, you might record some of your impressions. Did you like the wine overall? Was it sweet, sour or bitter? How was the wine's acidity? Was it well balanced? Does it taste better with cheese, bread or a heavy meal? Will you buy it again?

VISUAL PERCEPTION

Visual perception is one of the senses of the body which allows the brain to intercept and interpret visible light. Sight is regarded as a critical sense by many people, as the world contains a great deal of important visual information.

Many organisms have developed some form of visual perception, and there are a number of different systems animals employ in the process of interpreting visual stimuli.

Visual perception is provided courtesy of a light-sensitive organ known as the eye. A number of structures within the eye contribute to visual perception, with the most important being the rods and cones in the back of the eye which respond to light, sending signals along the optic nerve to the brain so that the brain can interpret them. Another structure of interest in the eye is the pupil, which dilates and contracts to control the amount of light which enters the eye.

Several different processes are involved in visual perception. Some are physiological, caused by the reaction of the eye to light, which converts light into signals which can be understood. The Gestalt theory in psychology explains how the brain deals with visual input, and the ways in which the brain smooths out and normalizes images to make sense of them.

In a classic example of Gestalt theory, when someone opens the newspaper and sees a photograph, the brain interprets the photograph as a smooth. Yet, when inspected closely, the photograph is actually a series of tiny dots of ink. The brain blends these dots together to create the appearance of a crisp image, and it is also capable of blending dots of different colours to create new ones, allowing a newspaper to use relatively crude printing techniques to produce images which will be recognizable to readers. The same process is allowed in the perception of images on a computer screen, which are presented in the form of pixels of information.

A number of things can interfere with visual perception. Sometimes these abnormalities can be addressed or corrected, as when someone dons a pair of glasses to see clearly because the structure of his or her eye creates myopia. People can also have problems in their brains which interfere with vision, in which case the eye functions perfectly, but the brain is unable to interpret or understand the signals sent by the eye.

Sight is deemed an important sense, so doctors may administer visual perception tests to their patients to confirm that their eyesight is in good condition, and to identify problems and issues which should be addressed. Problems with visual perception, in addition to being frustrating, can also be a sign that a patient has a more serious underlying medical condition.

COLOUR

Wine Colour

The colour of wine is one of the most easily recognizable characteristics of wines. Colour is also an element in wine tasting since heavy wines generally have a deeper colour. The accessory used to judge the wine colour is the tastevin, a shallow cup allowing to see the colour of the liquid in the dim light of a cellar. The colour is an element in the classification of wines.

Colour Origins

The colour of the wine mainly depends on the colour of the drupe of the grape variety. Since pigments are localized in the exocarp of the grape drupe, not in the juice, the colour of the wine depends on the method of vinification and the time the must is in contact with those skins, process called maceration. The blending of two or more varieties of grapes can explain for the colour of certain wines, like the use of Australian Rubired.

Red drupe grapes can produce white wine if they are quickly pressed and the juice not allowed to be in contact with the skins. The colour is mainly due to plant pigments notably phenolic compounds. The colour depends on the presence of acids in the wine. It is altered with the wine aging by reaction between the different active molecules present in the wine, these reactions generally giving rise to a browning of the wine, leading from red to a more tawny colour. The use of a wooden barrel in aging also affects the colour of the wine. Presence of complex mixture of anthocyanins with procyanidins can increase the stability of colour in wine.

Colours

Main colours of wine are :

- Red
- White
- Rosé
- Yellow
- Orange wine, a white wine that has spent some time in contact with its skin, giving it a slightly darker hue

Other :

- Burgundy, a shade of purplish red
- Sangria, a colour that resembles Sangría wine

Colour Perception

Colour perception is a fascinating series of physical and chemical reactions which allow some organisms to see in colour. The process of colour perception is literally all in the mind, with the eye containing the equipment which responds to light so that the brain can process it. The number of colours an organism can distinguish can vary considerably, from animals that can see a very wide array of millions of colours to animals that see in a much more limited range.

Two types of cells in the eye are responsible for vision: rods and cones. Both cells are located in the retina, and they respond to light when it enters the eye. Rods are highly light-sensitive, allowing for vision in a range of light levels, while cones are sensitized to colours of particular wavelength ranges. Humans have three different types of cones sensitized to short, medium, and long wavelengths, and they are especially sensitive to yellow and green light.

Organisms with three types of cones are known as trichromatic, and other animals may have two types of cones, while others have up to five.

Until 2005, researchers assumed that the number of cones in the eye was roughly the same for all people. However, when imaging technology which could be used to look into a living eye and distinguish between the different types of cones present was developed, researchers learned that people actually have very irregular distributions of cones. 40% of one person's cones might be sensitive to medium wavelength light, while someone else might only have half that number, but both people would perceive colour in the same way, which strongly suggests that the key aspects of colour perception happen in the brain, not the eye.

When light enters the eye and hits the cones, certain cones fire in response to the wavelength they are sensitized to. The response is sent along the optic nerve to the brain, and the brain processes the information. Colour perception is important for many animals because it can be used to distinguish more of the natural environment, and because colours are often used as cues. Poisonous mushrooms, for example, are sometimes brightly coloured as a warning.

The process of visual perception happens so quickly that people feel like it is instant. The eyes also constantly return new information, allowing people to detect changes such as movement. Although the basic mechanics of how vision and colour perception work are understood, the processes are still a little bit mysterious to researchers. The mechanisms behind colour blindness, for example, are not fully understood.

CLARITY

Identify Clarity in Wine Tasting

- *Step* 1: The very first step in testing the clarity of wine is to make sure that the wine glasses that you are using are very clean. Any dingy areas, water spots and so forth might cloud the wine from the glass and have no bearing on the clarity of the wine. This is a step that is often skipped but makes a huge difference with clean glasses versus water spotted one.
- *Step* 2: Pour the wine into a wine clean wine glass. A simple step, but it is too hard to see the clarity from inside the wine bottle. Most wine bottles are often coloured and make it so we can not judge the clarity of the wine through the bottle.
- *Step* 3: Clarity of the wine is completely dependant on the appearance of the wine. Clarity is the first step in judging a wine since it is the first thing that people will be able to see about the wine.
- *Step* 4: Look at the wine through the wine glass. The easiest thing to spot is if the wine is cloudy, murky or even dirty looking. These are signs that the wine has poor wine clarity. Even if the wine has aged, there should not be a cloudy or murky feel to the wine itself.

- *Step* 5: Check to see if there is something in the wine. Anything floating in the wine such as cork gives the wine a poor clarity rating. Also is often a sign that something may have gone off with the wine or that it is not the best quality. Unless when opening the wine bottle, the cork was shoved into the bottle. Once this occurs it is difficult to see if the bits were there before the cork entered the wine or if it was something there only afterwards. In testing clarity this needs to be avoided if possible.
- *Step* 6: While judging for clarity is making sure the wine is basically clear and without anything in the liquid. This shows that the wine has good clarity.

Crystals

Sediments occasionally occur in bottled wine, and wine crystals are a type of sediment. The crystals are potassium tartrate which is found naturally in wine, and it will precipitate under certain conditions, such as prolonged storage at cold temperatures. The processing required to guarantee that these crystals will never form is generally considered to diminish the quality of the wine.

Wine crystals come in various shapes and sizes. Sometimes they resemble tiny grapenuts. Sometimes they resemble diamonds or tiny pieces of amber or ruby glass. Unlike glass, they will dissolve in warm or hot water.

Some wines may contain crystals when you buy them. Others may develop crystals after being stored in an unheated room during cold weather or simply refrigerated for a few days. The ideal serving temperature for wine is 50° - 70° F depending on the wine. From season to season, the proper serving temperature will be achieved by different methods. However, a wine should rarely need more than one hour in the refrigerator or 20 minutes in an ice bucket. If crystals *are* present in the wine, you might prefer to decant the bottle before serving.

Sediment

Sediment during Wine Production

The initial sediment which forms in wine appears during the fermentation process and is called "lees." The lees sediment consists of dead yeast cells, proteins, stems, bits of skin, and other solid matter that has settled to the bottom of the fermentation tanks. Wine is left with the lees for a while so it can develop more character and complexity, but if the mixture is handled incorrectly some bad flavors can develop.

The initial lees sediment is separated from the wine during a process called "clarification," when the wine is filtered during the transfer from fermentation tanks to aging casks or tanks. In the aging casks more lees sediment can form, so it's not only common for wine to be siphoned out of this first aging cask and into a second to separate it from the second lees sediment, but this process might occur two or three times depending on the wine.

Siphoning and clarification can occur quickly or very slowly depending on what the wine maker is trying to achieve. The more a wine is left in contact with the lees sediment at each stage, the more character and complexity it will acquire. Today, won't find lees sediments in any bottles of wine except among sparkling wines and champagnes made to traditional methods where secondary fermentation occurs in the bottle itself.

Sediment in Your Wine Bottle

When people think about sediment in wine, they probably think about the formation of sediment in wine bottles that you have to take care to remove before serving. Most people probably don't ever have to deal with that, however, because this kind of sediment only forms in red wines that have been aging for at least eight years, but probably ten years or more. A bottle of wine that you bought a couple of months ago, even if it's a red wine, won't have this kind of sediment.

The sediment which develops in red wine bottles and which you need to carefully remove is formed from tannins and other solid matter that gradually falls to the bottom. The presence of this material helps give the wine character and complexity, but you don't want to leave it in the wine when you serve it. First, this kind of sediment can give a nasty, bitter flavor to the wine. Even if the sediment is very mild, it will at the very least interfere with any of the subtle nuances that have developed during the aging process. Second, it's simply not pleasant to look down at red or dark bits in your wine glass.

If you're serving a red wine that's been aging for several years, you'll want to hold it up to the light to see if a sediment has formed. If so, set the wine bottle upright for a few days before serving so all the sediment collects in small area at the bottom of the bottle. When you open the bottle, you'll want to decant it first before serving and possibly aerate the wine as well.

Crystalline Sediment in Your Wine Glass

The tiny crystals you find in your wine glass, and sometimes first in the wine bottle. Fortunately, these crystalline sediments are not only the least likely to taste bad, but are treated by some as a sign of a better wine. So if you find crystal sediment in your wine glass, there's no reason to worry or fret.

The crystal sediment you might find in a wine glass is called tartrate and forms from tartaric acid in grapes. Not all fruit has tartaric acid and its presence in grapes is what allows us to make better wines from grapes than can we can from any other fruit. Because tartaric acid doesn't remain dissolved in alcohol as easily as it does in grape juice, it binds to potassium after fermentation and forms potassium acid tartrates — the crystalline solids creating the sediment in your wine glass. Because red wines have probably been exposed to cold temperatures less than white wines, they are more likely form tartrate crystals.

In theory all wines should probably form tartrate sediment, but modern wine production has introduced cold stabilization and fine filtration which remove most to all tartrates. More expensive wines that have been created to more traditional methods, thus eschewing cold stabilization and filtration, are more likely to produce tartrate sediment. People who prefer the traditional methods of wine production, which includes a lot of wine drinkers in France and Italy, will treat the presence of tartrate sediment as a sign of quality.

The tartrate sediment in your wine glass or wine bottle won't hurt you if you consume it and it isn't going to ruin the flavor of your wine, so you don't need to worry about separating the crystals from your wine before serving and drinking. However, there is also no value in consuming this sediment so don't go out of your way to doso.

Proteinaceous Haze

Proteins are typically present in wines in low concentrations, contributing little to their nutritive value. However, they assume a considerable technological and economical importance because they greatly affect the clarity and stability of wines. Although exhibiting a large diversity, the majority of the wine proteins are structurally related and have been identified as pathogenesis related (PR) proteins. Thus, different wines are essentially composed by identical sets of polypeptides.

They derive from the grape pulp, and survive the vinification process simply because they are highly resistant to proteolysis and to the low pH characteristic of wines. There is increasing evidence suggesting that although protein-dependent, the development of turbidity in wines is controlled by a number of factors of non-protein origin, such as polyphenols, the wine pH and the presence of polysaccharides. A variety of procedures has been developed and tested for the specific removal of proteins from wines. Even though bentonite fining is nonspecific and can impair the quality of wine, it remains the only effective method to stabilize wines.

The mechanism responsible for protein haze formation in wines remains essentially to be elucidated. Current knowledge suggests the absolute requirement of one or more as yet unknown non-proteinaceous wine components for protein precipitation in wines. Using the single grape variety Arinto wine, naturally containing 280 mg protein/l, a series of heat stability tests were performed over a range of wine-relevant pH values. The results obtained indicate the existence of at least two different mechanisms responsible for the heat-induced precipitation of the Arinto wine proteins: one occurring only at the higher pH values, that appears to result from isoelectric precipitation of the proteins; another prevailing at the lower pH values, but possibly operating also at other pH values, that depends on the presence of the X factor.

Therefore, conclusive evidence is provided for the existence of the X factor, here defined as one or more low molecular mass wine components that sensitise proteins for heat-induced denaturation at low wine pH values and whose presence is a pre requisite for the precipitation of proteins in wines under these circumstances.

The chemical nature of protein aggregation was further analysed as a function of pH. Neither of the two proposed mechanisms responsible for the heat-induced precipitation of the wine proteins is electrostatic in nature, lectin-mediated or divalent cation-dependent. Both mechanisms show minimum turbidity at pH 7, but increased turbidity towards lower and higher pH values.

Microbial Spoilage

Depending on oxygen availability, meat spoilage by micro-organisms can manifest itself as follows

Oxygen	Microbial agent	Symptoms	
Present	Aerobic bacteria	•	Surface slime
		•	Discoloration
		•	Gas production
		•	Change in odor
		•	Fat decomposition
Present	Yeasts	•	Surface slime
		•	Discoloration
		•	Change in odor
and			taste
		•	Fat decomposition
Present	Molds	•	Sticky and
"whiskery"			surface
		•	Discoloration
		•	Change in odor
		•	Fat decomposition
Absent	Anaerobic bacteria	•	Putrefaction and
foul			odors
		•	Gas production
		•	Souring

VISCOSITY

This is one of the areas of greatest misconception in wine tasting. Many newbies will always that a wine has great "legs" as if that proves the quality of the wine. The wine legs are the stripes of wine that slowly roll down the sides of your glass after swirling the wine.

The reason that this is a misleading characteristic of a wine's appearance is that there are several things that influence how pronounced a wine's legs will be. Basically, the legs are a measure of the viscosity of the liquid in your wine glass. The more viscous, the more pronounced legs. But do an experiment, pour some honey in your glass and roll it around to coat the sides before standing your glass up on the table. This doesn't mean your honey is a good wine, what it means is that your honey has a high sugar content. Sugar concentration is one of the several things that can influence the wine legs.

The more sugar, the more viscous. Therefore, sweeter wines such as dessert wines will always have much more pronounced legs. Another thing that increases the viscosity of wine is the alcohol content. Alcohol is more viscous than water so wines with more alcohol will have more legs. For both of these reasons, fortified dessert wines, like Port or Madeira, tend to have the most profound legs of any wines, because they have both high sugar and high alcohol. Finally, the wine legs can be influenced by other things such as the concentration of solutes dissolved in the wine. In other words, a wine with more concentration of compounds dissolved into it will have a slightly higher viscosity and thus more legs. For this reason, big, dark, heavily extracted red wines tend to have more legs than lighter wines.

SPRITZ

The Spritz is a wine-based cocktail commonly served as an aperitif in northern Italy, especially in the Veneto region and surrounding areas. The drink is prepared with white wine or Prosecco wine, a dash of some bitter liqueur such as Aperol, Campari, Select or Cynar. The glass is then topped off with sparkling mineral water. It is usually served over ice in a lowball glass and garnished a slice of orange, or sometimes an olive, depending on the liqueur. The drink originated in Venice while it was part of the Austrian Empire, and is based on the Austrian Spritzer, a combination of equal parts white wine and soda water.

TEARS OF WINES

The phenomenon called tears of wine is manifested as a ring of clear liquid, near the top of a glass of wine, from which droplets continuously form and drop back into the wine. It is most readily observed in a wine which has a high alcohol content. It is also referred to as wine legs, curtains, and church windows.

Cause

The effect is a consequence of the fact that alcohol has a lower surface tension than water. If alcohol is mixed with water inhomogeneously, a region with a lower concentration of alcohol will pull on the surrounding fluid more strongly than a region with a higher alcohol concentration. The result is that the liquid tends to flow away from regions with higher alcohol concentration. This can be easily and strikingly demonstrated by spreading a thin film of water on a smooth surface and then allowing a drop of alcohol to fall on the center of the film. The liquid will rush out of the region where the drop of alcohol fell.

Wine is mostly a mixture of alcohol and water, with dissolved sugars, acids, colourants and flavourants. Where the surface of the wine meets the side of the glass, capillary action makes the liquid climb the side of the glass. As it does so, both alcohol and water evaporate from the rising film, but the alcohol evaporates faster, due to its higher vapor pressure and lower boiling point. This change in the composition of the film causes its surface tension to increase - this in turn causes more liquid to be drawn up from the bulk of the wine, which has a lower surface tension because of its higher alcohol content. The wine which moves up the side of the glass then forms droplets which fall back under their weight.

The phenomenon was first correctly explained by physicist James Thomson, the elder brother of Lord Kelvin, in 1855. It is an instance of what is today called the Marangoni effect: the flow of liquid caused by surface tension gradients. It is sometimes claimed incorrectly that wine with "lots of legs" is sweeter or of a better quality. In fact the intensity of this phenomenon depends only on alcohol content, and it can be eliminated completely by covering the wine glass. British physicist C. V. Boys argues that the biblical injunction refers to this effect. Since the "tears of wine" are most noticeable in wine which has a high alcohol content, the author may be suggesting this as a way to identify wines which should be avoided in the interest of sobriety.

"Look not thou upon the wine when it is red, when it giveth his colour in the cup, when it moveth itself aright."

Related Phenomena

Other fluid phenomenon that arise in alcohol-water mixtures are *beading* and *viscimetry*. These are more pronounced in liquor than in wine, and both phenomena are more pronounced in stronger liquor. Beading refers to the formation of stable bubbles when liquor is shaken. This occurs only in liquor that contains more than 46% alcohol. It is an example of the Marangoni effect. Shaking a whisky bottle to form bubbles is referred to as "beating the whisky". Viscimetry is the formation of whorls when water is added to a high-alcohol mixture.

OLFACTORY (SENSE) SENSATIONS

Sense

Senses are the physiological methods of perception. The senses and their operation, classification, and theory are overlapping topics studied by a variety of fields, most notably neuroscience, cognitive psychology and philosophy of perception. The nervous system has a specific sensory system, or organ, dedicated to each sense.

There is no firm agreement among neurologists as to the number of senses because of differing definitions of what constitutes a sense. One definition states that an exteroceptive sense is a faculty by which outside stimuli are perceived. The traditional five senses are sight, hearing, touch, smell and taste, a classification attributed to Aristotle. Humans are considered to have at least five additional senses that include: nociception; equilibrioception; proprioception and kinaesthesia; sense of time; thermoception; and possibly an additional weak magnetoception, and six more if interoceptive senses are also considered.

One commonly recognized categorisation for human senses is as follows: chemoreception; photoreception; mechanoreception; and thermoception. This categorisation has been criticized as too restrictive, however, as it does not include categories for accepted senses such as the sense of time and sense of pain. Non-human animals may possess senses that are absent in humans, such as electroreception and detection of polarized light.

A broadly acceptable definition of a sense would be "A system that consists of a group of sensory cell types that responds to a specific physical phenomenon, and that corresponds to a particular group of regions within the brain where the signals are received and interpreted." Disputes about the number of senses typically arise around the classification of the various cell types and their mapping to regions of the brain.

Senses

Sight

Sight or vision is the ability of the brain and eye to detect electromagnetic waves within the visible range which is why people see interpreting the image as "sight." There is disagreement as to whether this constitutes one, two or three senses. Neuroanatomists generally regard it as two senses, given that different receptors are responsible for the perception of colour and brightness. Some argue that stereopsis, the perception of depth, also constitutes a sense, but it is generally regarded as a cognitive function of brain to interpret sensory input and to derive new information. The inability to see is called blindness.

Hearing

Hearing or audition is the sense of sound perception. Since sound is vibrations propagating through a medium such as air, the detection of these vibrations, that is the sense of the hearing, is a mechanical sense because these vibrations are mechanically conducted from the eardrum through a series of tiny bones to hair-like fibres in the inner ear which detect mechanical motion of the fibres within a range of about 20 to 20,000 hertz, with substantial variation between individuals. Hearing at high frequencies declines with age. Sound can also be detected as vibrations conducted through the body by tactition. Lower frequencies than that can be heard are detected this way. The inability to hear is called deafness.

Taste

Taste or gustation is one of the two main "chemical" senses. There are at least four types of tastes that "buds" on the tongue detect, and hence there are anatomists who argue that these constitute five or more different senses, given that each receptor conveys information to a slightly different region of the brain. The inability to taste is called ageusia.

The four well-known receptors detect sweet, salt, sour, and bitter, although the receptors for sweet and bitter have not been conclusively identified. A fifth receptor, for a sensation called *umami*, was first theorised in 1908 and its existence confirmed in 2000. The umami receptor detects the amino acid glutamate, a flavour commonly found in meat and in artificial flavourings such as monosodium glutamate.

Note: that taste is not the same as flavour; flavour includes the smell of a food as well as its taste.

Smell

Smell or olfaction is the other "chemical" sense. Unlike taste, there are hundreds of olfactory receptors, each binding to a particular molecular feature. Odour molecules possess a variety of features and thus excite specific receptors more or less strongly.

This combination of excitatory signals from different receptors makes up what we perceive as the molecule's smell. In the brain, olfaction is processed by the olfactory system. Olfactory receptor neurons in the nose differ from most other neurons in that they die and regenerate on a regular basis. The inability to smell is called anosmia. Some neurons in the nose are specialized to detect pheromones.

Touch

Touch, also called tactition or mechanoreception, is a perception resulting from activation of neural receptors, generally in the skin including hair follicles, but also in the tongue, throat, and mucosa. A variety of pressure receptors respond to variations in pressure. The touch sense of itching caused by insect bites or allergies involves special itch-specific neurons in the skin and spinal cord. The loss or impairment of the ability to feel anything touched is called tactile anesthesia. Paresthesia is a sensation of tingling, pricking, or numbness of the skin that may result from nerve damage and may be permanent or temporary.

Balance and Acceleration

Balance, equilibrioception, or vestibular sense is the sense which allows an organism to sense body movement, direction, and acceleration, and to attain and maintain postural equilibrium and balance.

The organ of equilibrioception is the vestibular labyrinthine system found in both of the inner ears. Technically this organ is responsible for two senses of angular momentum and linear acceleration, but they are known together as equilibrioception.

The vestibular nerve conducts information from sensory receptors in three ampulla that sense motion of fluid in three semicircular canals caused by three-dimensional rotation of the head.

The vestibular nerve also conducts information from the utricle and the saccule which contain hair-like sensory receptors that bend under the weight of otoliths that provide the inertia needed to detect head rotation, linear acceleration, and the direction of gravitational force.

Temperature

Thermoception is the sense of heat and the absence of heat by the skin and including internal skin passages, or rather, the heat flux in these areas. There are specialized receptors for cold and to heat. The cold receptors play an important part in the dogs sense of smell, telling wind direction, the heat receptors are sensitive to infrared radiation and can occur in specialized organs for instance in pit vipers. The thermoceptors in the skin are quite different from the homeostatic thermoceptors in the brain which provide feedback on internal body temperature.

Kinesthetic Sense

Proprioception, the kinesthetic sense, provides the parietal cortex of the brain with information on the relative positions of the parts of the body. Neurologists test this sense by telling patients to close their eyes and touch the tip of a finger to their nose. Assuming proper proprioceptive function, at no time will the person lose awareness of where the hand actually is, even though it is not being detected by any of the other senses. Proprioception and touch are related in subtle ways, and their impairment results in surprising and deep deficits in perception and action.

Pain

Nociception signals near-damage or damage to tissue. The three types of pain receptors are cutaneous, somatic and visceral. It was believed that pain was simply the overloading of pressure receptors, but research in the first half of the 20th century indicated that pain is a distinct phenomenon that intertwines with all of the other senses, including touch. Pain was once considered an entirely subjective experience, but recent studies show that pain is registered in the anterior cingulate gyrus of the brain.

Direction

Magnetoception is the ability to detect the direction one is facing based on the Earth's magnetic field. Directional awareness is most commonly observed in birds, though it is also present to a limited extent in humans. It has also been observed in insects such as bees. Although there is no dispute that this sense exists in many avians, it is not a well-understood phenomenon.

One study has found that cattle make use of magnetoception, as they tend to align themselves in a north-south direction. Magnetotactic bacteria build miniature magnets inside themselves and use them to determine their orientation relative to the Earth's magnetic field.

Other Internal Senses

An internal sense or interoception is "any sense that is normally stimulated from within the body". These involve numerous sensory receptors in internal organs, such as stretch receptors that are neurologically linked to the brain.

- Pulmonary stretch receptors are found in the lungs and control the respiratory rate.
- The chemoreceptor trigger zone is an area of the medulla in the brain that receives inputs from blood-borne drugs or hormones, and communicates with the vomiting center.
- Cutaneous receptors in the skin not only respond to touch, pressure, and temperature, but also respond to vasodilation in the skin such as blushing.
- Stretch receptors in the gastrointestinal tract sense gas distension that may result in colic pain.
- Stimulation of sensory receptors in the esophagus result in sensations felt in the throat when swallowing, vomiting, or during acid reflux.
- Sensory receptors in pharynx mucosa, similar to touch receptors in the skin, sense foreign objects such as food that may result in a gag reflex and corresponding gagging sensation.
- Stimulation of sensory receptors in the urinary bladder and rectum may result in sensations of fullness.
- Stimulation of stretch sensors that sense dilation of various blood vessels may result in pain, for example headache caused by vasodilation of brain arteries.

Olfactory System

The olfactory system is the part of the brain which allows people to interpret smells. It converts chemical signals in the form of odours into perception by the brain. A number of separate structures are part of the olfactory system, including the olfactory epithelium, which collects chemical signals, and the olfactory bulb, which sends those signals to the brain. The olfactory system is part of the larger limbic system in the brain which is involved in memories, emotional responses, and behavior. When smells reach the olfactory epithelium, cells within this structure respond to them. Different cells are sensitized to different odours, sending messages to microregions in the olfactory bulb known as glomeruli. Each glomerulus can pass signals on to different areas of the brain. The brain's perception of an odour will be influenced by which microregions are activated, and where they send their signals.

Different smells route to different areas of the brain because different responses may be required. For example, a smell which triggers a memory would be routed to one location, while a smell which requires immediate physical reaction, such as the scent of burning, would go to another area of the brain.

The human brain can distinguish between a number of types of smells and related smells, although it is far less sensitive than the olfactory systems of many other animals. In addition to the main olfactory system which processes odours in the environment, many organisms also have an accessory olfactory system which responds to pheromones. People do not perceive pheromones as specific odours, but they do react to them, because they reach various areas of the brain which can trigger responses such as sexual interest or the urge to flee. Often, responses to pheromones are subtle, and people may not realize that these chemicals are involved in their reaction to a person or situation.

The olfactory system is believed to be one of the oldest sensory systems. A sense of smell is critical to a wide variety of organisms, from rabbits which need to be able to smell approaching predators to scavengers which need to be able to detect whether or not meat is safe to eat. Damage to the olfactory system can be caused by congenital birth defects, exposure to harsh chemicals, brain damage, or damage to the nose which interferes with the delicate olfactory epithelium. Individuals with a disabled sense of smell can be a social and personal disadvantage.

Nasal Passages

Smell is often considered to be the least important of all the senses, but it may be one of the oldest, and probably acts on the subconscious more than the other senses.

There is little doubt that scents have important roles in human behavior. The body is provided with glands to produce specific odours, many of which appear to be associated with sexual attraction and excitement, and others that have considerable significance as well.

The bond between a baby and its mother is thought to be tightened by a form of "scent imprinting." In it, a baby which is suckling at the mother's breast pushes his or her face into a bank of scent organs that surround the nipple. A further sign of the importance of the sense of smell is the way it becomes a major source of information when other senses are not working, especially sight.

Only a small part of the nose and nasal cavity is taken up by the organs of smell; the rest of it is mainly concerned with processing the airflow on its way through to the lungs. The walls of the nasal cavity, and particularly the flaplike middle and inferior conchae, are coated with respiratory mucous membranes which incorporate a vast number of tiny hairlike cells which act to move waves of mucus towards the throat. Dust, bacteria, and chemical particles which are inhaled from the air are trapped by the mucus, carried back and swallowed; they are then taken care of by gastric juices to nullify any potential harm.

The sense organs themselves are made up of two yellowish-gray patches of tissue, called the olfactory membranes, each about the size of a postage stamp. They are located in a pair of clefts just under the bridge of the nose and at the top of the nasal cavity. The reasons for the coloration are not completely clear, but it seems to be necessary for the membrane to work. During normal breathing, most of the air flows through the nose, with only a small part reaching the olfactory clefts, but this is enough to get a response to a new smell.

When a person "sniffs the air" to detect smells, the air moves through the nose much faster, increasing the flow that makes its way to the olfactory clefts and so carrying more odour to those sensors. If you "follow your nose," you are taking a route that lies straight ahead and is obvious or else you are going ahead without a plan, that is, following wherever instinct leads.

Olfactory Epithelium

The olfactory epithelium is an area inside the nose which is responsible for intercepting odours and passing them on to the brain. The mechanics of the olfactory epithelium are not fully understood; this structure contains a huge number of neurons, but the exact way in which they interact with and distinguish between smells is a bit of a mystery. The larger the area covered by the olfactory epithelium, the more neurons, and the better the sense of smell.

Like other layers of epithelial tissue in the body, the olfactory epithelium contains a number of layers of cells. These cells include specialized neurons which communicate with the olfactory bulb via long axons, and olfactory hair cells which have highly sensitive receptors which pick up odours. The olfactory epithelium is also quite delicate, and it can be damaged by exposure to chemicals, strong odours, and head injuries.

The olfactory epithelium is located inside the back of the nose. As people breathe in through the nose, fine hairs and mucus near the opening of the nose trap particles which could be harmful, and the rest of the air passes over the olfactory epithelium. The neurons in the epithelium respond to specific odours and send a signal to the brain to tell it what the nose knows. Essentially, the olfactory epithelium is like a laboratory: when people are exposed to odours, they don't smell them instantly, but rather wait for them to be processed and for their brains to return the results.

Different animals have varying degrees of sensitivity to smell. Animals rely on their olfactory epithelium to alert them to the presence of predators, potential food sources, or contamination which could make food or water dangerous to consume. Certain odours appear to trigger stronger responses than others; sour milk, for example, is often very easy to detect, because it can be dangerous to drink, while people and animals are less sensitive to more benign odours. Some people can train themselves to have an excellent sense of smell, a skill achieved in part with the olfactory epithelium someone was born with, and in part with patient training. Wine experts, for example, may smell wines while blindfolded to learn to identify specific scents, and perfume "noses" use similar techniques in their training. People who rely on their sense of smell for a living also take steps to protect it, such as avoiding harsh chemicals and strong odours. Damage resulting in loss of odour sensitivity isn't just unfortunate because people can't stop and smell the roses any more. Anosmia, as the loss of the sense of smell is known, can actually be quite dangerous, because people miss important cues to danger, such as the smell of a gas leak, when they can't smell.

Receptor Neuron

An olfactory receptor neuron, also called an olfactory sensory neuron is the primary transduction cell in the olfactory system.

In Vertebrates

Humans have about 40 million olfactory receptor neurons. In vertebrates, olfactory receptor neurons reside on the olfactory epithelium in the nasal cavity. These cells are bipolar neurons with a dendrite facing the interior space of the nasal cavity and an axon that travels along the olfactory nerve to the olfactory bulb.

Structure

Many tiny hair-like cilia protrude from the olfactory receptor cell's dendrite into the mucus covering the surface of the olfactory epithelium. The surface of these cilia is covered with olfactory receptors, a type of G protein-coupled receptor. Each olfactory receptor cell expresses only one type of olfactory receptor, but many separate olfactory receptor cells express olfactory receptors which bind the same set of odours. The axons of olfactory receptor cells which bind the same odours converge to form glomeruli in the olfactory bulb. *Function*

A given olfactory receptor can bind to a variety of odour molecules with varying affinities. The activated olfactory receptor in turn activates the intracellular G-protein GOLF and adenylate cyclase and production of Cyclic AMP opens ion channels in the cell membrane, resulting in an influx of sodium and calcium ions into the cell.

This influx of positive ions causes the neuron to depolarize, generating an action potential. *Regeneration* Individual olfactory receptor neurons are replaced approximately every 40 days by neural stem cells residing in the olfactory epithelium. The regeneration of olfactory receptor cells, as one of the only few instances of adult neurogenesis in the central nervous system, has raised considerable interest in dissecting the pathways for neural development and differentiation in adult organisms.

In Insects

In insects, olfactory receptor neurons typically reside on the antenna. Much like in vertebrates, axons from the sensory neurons converge into glomeruli in the antennal lobe.

Cerebal Palsy

Cerebral palsy is a disorder of muscle control which results from some damage to part of the brain. The term cerebral palsy is used when the problem has occurred to the developing brain either before birth, around birth or in early life. Children can have problems such as weakness, stiffness, awkwardness, slowness, shakiness and difficulty with balance. These problems can range from mild to severe. In mild cerebral palsy, the child may be slightly clumsy in one arm or leg, and the problem may be barely noticeable. In severe cerebral palsy, the child may have a lot of difficulties, with the whole body affected.

Various Types of Cerebral Palsy

There are several different types of cerebral palsy:

- *Spastic Cerebral Palsy*: This is the most common type of cerebral palsy. Spasticity means stiffness or tightness of muscles. The muscles are stiff because the message to the muscles is relayed incorrectly through the damaged part of the brain. When people without cerebral palsy perform a movement, some groups of muscles become tighter and some groups of muscles relax. In children with spastic cerebral palsy, both groups of muscles may become tighter. This makes the movement difficult.
- *Athetoid Cerebral Palsy*: Athetosis is the word used for the uncontrolled movements that occur in this type of cerebral palsy. This lack of control is often most noticeable when the child starts to make a movement. In addition, children with athetoid cerebral palsy often have very weak muscles or feel floppy when carried.
- *Ataxic Cerebral Palsy*: This is the least common type of cerebral palsy. Ataxia is the word used for unsteady shaky movements or tremor. Children with ataxia also have problems with balance.
- *Mixed Types*: Many children do not have just one type, but a mixture of several of these movement patterns.

Cause of Cerebal Palsy

Damage to the brain can occur:

- In the early months of pregnancy .eg. if the mother is exposed to certain infections such as German measles;
- During labour or at birth, for example, when there is lack of oxygen supplied to the baby;

- In the period shortly after birth.eg. where an infant develops a severe infection in the first few days or weeks of life.

CHEMICAL COMPOUNDS INVOLVED

Acids

The acids in wine are an important component in both winemaking and the finished product of wine. They are present in both grapes and wine, having direct influences on the colour, balance and taste of the wine as well as the growth and vitality of yeasts during fermentation and protecting the wine from bacteria. The measure of the amount of acidity in wine is known as the "Titratable Acidity" or "Total acidity", which refers to the test that yields the total of all acids present, while strength of acidity is measured to pH with most wines having a pH between 2.9–3.9. Generally, the lower the pH, the higher the acidity in the wine.

However, there is no direct connection between total acidity and pH. In wine tasting, the term "acidity" refers to the fresh, tart and sour attributes of the wine which is evaluated in relation to how well the acidity balances out the sweetness and bitter components of the wine.

There are three primary acids found in wine grapes: tartaric, malic and citric. During the course of winemaking and in the finished wines, acetic, butyric, lactic and succinic acid can play significant roles. Most of the acids involved with wine are fixed acids with the notable exception of acetic acid, mostly found in vinegar, which is volatile and can contribute to the wine fault known as volatile acidity. Sometimes additional acids are used in winemaking such as ascorbic, sorbic and sulfurous acids.

Tartaric Acid

Tartaric acid is, from a winemaking perspective, the most important in wine due to the prominent role it plays in maintaining the chemical stability of the wine and its colour and finally in influencing the taste of the finished wine. In most plants, this organic acid is rare but it is found in significant concentrations in grape vines. Along with malic acid, and to a lesser extent citric acid, tartaric is one of the fixed acids found in wine grapes.

The concentration varies depending on grape variety and the soil content of the vineyard. Some varieties, such as Palomino, are naturally deposed to having high levels of tartaric acids while Malbec and Pinot noir generally have lower levels. During flowering, there are high levels of tartaric acid concentrated in the grape flowers and then young berries. As the vine progresses through ripening, tartaric does not get metabolized through respiration like malic acid so that the levels of tartaric acid in the grape vines remains relatively consistent throughout the ripening process.

Less than half of the tartaric acid found grape is free standing, with the majority of the concentration present as potassium acid salt. During fermentation, these tartrates bind with the lees, pulp debris and precipitated tannins and pigments. While there is some variance among grape varieties and wine regions, generally about half of the deposits are soluble in the alcoholic mixture of wine. The crystallization of these tartrates can happen at unpredictable times and in a wine bottle appear like broken glass though they are in fact harmless. Winemakers will often put the wine through cold stabilization where it is exposed temperatures below freezing to encourage the tartrates to crystallize and precipitate out of the wine.

Malic Acid

Malic acid, along with tartaric acid, is one of the principal organic acids found in wine grapes. It is found in nearly every fruit and berry plant but its most often associated with green apples from which flavor it most readily projects in wine. Its name comes from the Latin *malum* meaning "apple". In the grape vine, malic acid is involved in several processes which are essential for the health and sustainability of the vine.

Its chemical structure allows it to participate in enzymatic reactions that transport energy throughout the vine. The concentration of malic acids varies depending on the grape variety with some varieties, like Barbera, Carignan and Sylvaner being naturally deposed to high levels. The levels of malic acid in grape berries are at their peak just before *veraison* when they can be found in concentrations as high as 20 g/L.

As the vine progresses through the ripening stage, malic acid is metabolized in the process of respiration and by harvest could be as low as 1 to 9 g/L. The respiratory loss of malic acid is more pronounced in warmer climates. When all the malic acid is used up in the grape it is considered "over-ripe" or senescent. Winemakers must compensate for this loss by manually adding acid at the winery in a process known as acidification.

Malic acid can be further reduced during the winemaking process through malolactic fermentation or MLF. In this process bacteria convert the stronger malic acid into the softer lactic acid: formally, malic acid is polyprotic, while lactic acid is monoprotic and thus has only half the effect on acidity; also, the first acidity constant of malic acid is lower than the acidity constant of lactic acid indicating stronger acidity. Thus after MLF, wine has higher pH and different mouthfeel.

The bacteria behind this process can be found naturally in the winery, in cooperages which make oak wine barrels that will house a population of the bacteria or it can be manually introduced by the winemaker with a cultured specimen. For some wines, the conversion of malic into lactic acid can be beneficial, especially if the wine has excessive levels of malic. For other wines, such as Chenin blanc and Riesling, it produce off flavors in the wine that would not be appealing for that variety. In general, red wines are more often put through MLF than whites which means that there is a higher likelihood of finding malic acid in white wines.

Lactic Acid

A much milder acid than tartaric and malic, lactic acid is often associated with "milky" flavors in wine and is the primary acid of yogurt and sauerkraut. It is produced during winemaking by lactic acid bacteria which includes three genera: *Oenococcus, Pediococcus* and *Lactobacillus*. These bacterium convert both sugar and malic acid into lactic acid, the later through a process known as malolactic fermentation or MLF. The process of converting malic into lactic acid can be beneficial for some wines, adding complexity and softening the harshness of malic acidity but it can generate off flavors and turbidity in others.

Some strains of LAB can produce biogenic amines like histamine, tyramine and putrescine which may be a cause of red wine headaches in some wine drinkers. Winemakers wishing to control or prevent MLF can use sulfur dioxide to stun the bacteria. Racking the wine quickly off its lees will also help control the bacteria since lees are a vital food source for them. They must also be very careful of what wine barrels and winemaking equipment that the wine is exposed to because of the bacteria's ability to deeply embed themselves within wood fibres. A wine barrel that has completed one successful malolactic fermentation will almost always induce MLF in every wine that gets stored in it from then on.

Citric Acid

While very common in citrus fruits, such as limes, citric acid is found only in very minute quantities in wine grapes. It often has a concentration about 1/20 that of tartaric acid. The citric acid most commonly found in wine are commercially produced acid supplements derived from fermenting sucrose solutions. These inexpensive supplements can be used by winemakers in acidification to boost the total acidity of the wine.

It is used less frequently than tartaric and malic due to aggressive citric flavors that it can add to the wine. When citric acid is added, it is always done after primary alcohol fermentation has been completed due to the tendency of yeast to convert citric into acetic acid. In the European Union, use of citric acid for acidification is prohibited but limited use of citric acid is permitted for removing excess iron and copper from the wine if potassium ferrocyanide is not available.

Other Acids

Acetic acid is a two-carbon fatty acid produced in wine during or after the fermentation period. It is the most volatile of the primary acids associated with wine and is responsible for the sour taste of vinegar. During fermentation, activity by yeast cells naturally produce a small amount of acetic acid. If the wine is exposed to oxygen, acetobacter bacteria will convert the ethanol alcohol into acetic acid.

This process is known as the "acetification" of wine and is the primary process behind wine degradation into vinegar. Excessive amounts of acetic acid is also considered a wine fault. A taster's sensitivity to acetic acid will vary but most people can detect excessive amounts at around 600 mg/L.

Ascorbic acid, also known as vitamin C, is found in young wine grapes prior to *veraison* but is rapidly lost throughout the ripening process. In winemaking it is used with sulfur dioxide as an anti-oxidant to prevent oxidation, often added during the bottling process for white wines. In the European Union, use of ascorbic acid as an additive is limited to 150 mg/L. Butyric acid is a bacteria-induced wine fault that can cause a wine to smell of spoiled Camembert or rancid butter. Sorbic acid is a winemaking additive used often in sweet wines as a preservative against fungi, bacteria and yeast growth. Unlike sulfur dioxide, it does not hinder the growth of the lactic acid bacteria. In the European Union there is a limitation on the amount of sorbic acid that can be added — no more than 200 mg/L.

Most humans have a detection threshold of 135 mg/L, with some having a sensitivity to detect its presence at 50 mg/L. Sorbic acid can produce off-flavors and aromas which can be described as "rancid". When lactic acid bacteria metabolizes sorbates in the wine, it creates a wine fault that is most recognizable by an aroma of crushed *Pelargonium* geranium leaves. Succinic acid is most commonly found in wine but can also be present in trace amounts in ripened grapes. While concentration varies amount grape varieties, it is usually found in higher levels with red wine grapes. The acid is created as a by-product of the metabolization of nitrogen by yeast cells during fermentation. The combination of succinic acid with one molecule of ethanol will create the ester mono-ethyl succinate that is responsible for a mild, fruit aroma in wines.

In Winemaking

Acidity is highest in wine grapes just before the start of *veraison*, which ushers in the ripening period of the annual cycle of grape vines. As the grapes ripen, their sugars level increase and their acidity decreases. Through the process of respiration, malic acid is metabolized by the grape vine. Grapes from cooler climate wine regions, generally have a higher level of acidity due to the slower ripening process which is accelerated by warmer temperatures. The levels of acidity still present in the grape is an important consideration for winemakers in deciding when to begin harvest. For wines, like Champagne and other sparklers, having high levels of acidity is even more vital to the winemaking process and so grapes are often picked under-ripe and at higher acid levels. In the winemaking process, acids aid in enhancing the effectiveness of sulfur dioxide to protect the wines from spoilage and can also protect the wine from bacteria due to the inability of most bacteria to survive in an acidic solution. Two notable exceptions to this are acetobacter and the lactic acid bacteria. In red wines, acidity helps preserve and stabilize the colour of the wine. The ionization of anthocyanins is affected by pH so wines with lower pH have redder colours that are more stable. Wines with higher pH have more blue pigments that are less stable, eventually taking on a muddy grey hue. These wines can also develop a brownish tinge. In white wines, higher pH cause the phenolics in the wine to darken and eventually polymerize as brown deposits.

Winemakers will sometimes add additional acids to the wine, known as acidification, in order to increase the acidity level of the wine. This is most common in warm climate regions where grapes are often harvested at advanced stages of ripeness with high levels of sugars but very low levels of acid. Tartaric acid is most often added but winemakers will sometimes add citric or malic acid. Acids can be added either before or after primary fermentation. It can be added during blending or aging but the increase acidity will become more noticeable to wine tasters if added at this point.

In Wine Tasting

The acidity in wine is an important component in the quality and taste of the wine. It adds a sharpness to the flavors and is detected most readily by a prickling sensation on the sides of the tongue and a mouth watering after taste. Of particular importance is the balance of acidity versus the sweetness of the wine and the more bitter components of the wine. A wine with too much acidity will taste excessive sour and sharp. A wine with too little acidity will taste flabby, flat and with less defined flavors.

Alcohols

Wine tasting is the sensory evaluation of wine, encompassing more than taste, but also mouth feel, aroma, and colour. The main aims of wine tasting are to: assess the wine's quality, determine the wine's maturity and suitability for aging or immediate drinking, detect the aromas and flavors of the wine, discover the many facets of wine, so as to better appreciate it. To assess a wine's quality, one must gauge its complexity of aroma and flavor, determine the, intensity of the aroma and flavor, check that the flavors and structural elements – such as acid,, tannin and alcoholic strength – are well balanced, and finally see how long the wine persists in, the mouth after tasting.Practiced wine tasters will gauge the wine's quality in other ways too.

Some techniques include malolactic fermentation or barrel fermentation. Wine professional look for wines that drinkers will like the most by studying their characteristics. Temperature of wine serving: To taste wine, we serve still wines at a temperature of 60 to 64 degrees Fahrenheit. This temperature is the best to easily detect the flavor and aroma of a wine. When serving wine cool, flaws of cheap wines can be hidden but when serving it warm you allow the complex smell to be expressed. This second option is the best one for expensive and aged wines. The exception to this convention is sparkling wine which is usually tasted chilled. The thinking behind this is that many sparkling wines can be unpleasant in the mouth when they are warm. A good rule of thumb is the Rule of 20: place red wines in the refrigerator 20 minutes before serving, and remove whites from the refrigerator 20 minutes before serving.

Aldehydes and Ketones

Nomenclature of Aldehydes and Ketones

Aldehydes and ketones are organic compounds which incorporate a carbonyl functional group, C=O. The carbon atom of this group has two remaining bonds that may be occupied by hydrogen or alkyl or aryl substituents. If at least one of these substituents is hydrogen, the compound is an aldehyde. If neither is hydrogen, the compound is a ketone.

The IUPAC system of nomenclature assigns a characteristic suffix to these classes, al to aldehydes and one to ketones. For example, $H_2C=O$ is methanal, more commonly called formaldehyde. Since an aldehyde carbonyl group must always lie at the end of a carbon chain, it is by default position #1, and therefore defines the numbering direction. A ketone carbonyl function may be located anywhere within a chain or ring, and its position is given by a locator number. Chain numbering normally starts from the end nearest the carbonyl group. In cyclic ketone's the carbonyl group is assigned position #1, and this number is not cited in the name, unless more than one carbonyl group is present.

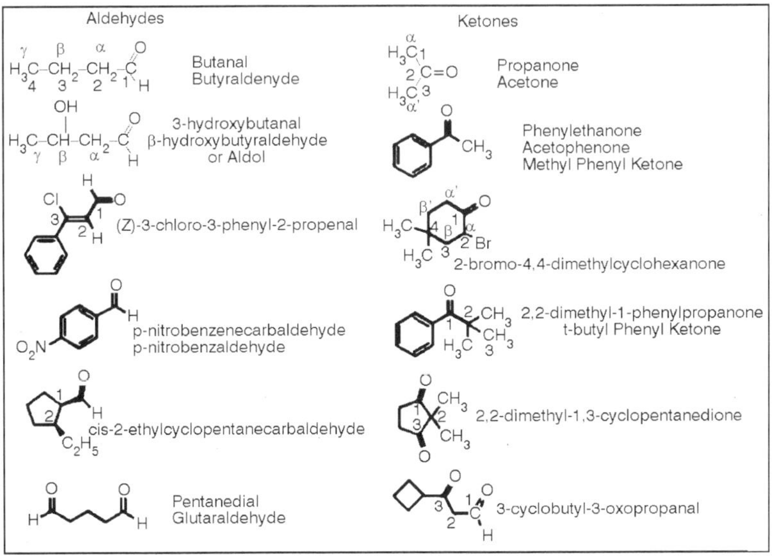

Aldehydes	Ketones
$H_3C{-}CH_2{-}CH_2{-}CHO$ (γ β α) Butanal, Butyraldenyde	$H_3C{-}CO{-}CH_3$ (α, α') Propanone, Acetone
$H_3C{-}CH(OH){-}CH_2{-}CHO$ (γ β α) 3-hydroxybutanal, β-hydroxybutyraldehyde or Aldol	Phenylethanone, Acetophenone, Methyl Phenyl Ketone
(Z)-3-chloro-3-phenyl-2-propenal	2-bromo-4,4-dimethylcyclohexanone
p-nitrobenzenecarbaldehyde, p-nitrobenzaldehyde	2,2-dimethyl-1-phenylpropanone, t-butyl Phenyl Ketone
cis-2-ethylcyclopentanecarbaldehyde	2,2-dimethyl-1,3-cyclopentanedione
Pentanedial, Glutaraldehyde	3-cyclobutyl-3-oxopropanal

Common names are in red, and derived names in black. In common names carbon atoms near the carbonyl group are often designated by Greek letters.

The atom adjacent to the function is alpha, the next removed is beta and so on. Since ketones have two sets of neighboring atoms, one set is labled á, â *etc.*, and the other á', â' *etc*. Very simple ketones, such as propanone and phenylethanone do not require a locator number, since there is only one possible site for a ketone carbonyl function. Likewise, locator numbers are omitted for the simple dialdehyde at the bottom left, since aldehyde functions must occupy the ends of carbon chains. The hydroxy butanal and propenal examples and the oxopropanal example depict the nomenclature priority of IUPAC suffixes. In all cases the aldehyde function has a higher status than either an alcohol, alkene or ketone and provides the nomenclature suffix.

The other functional groups are treated as substituents. Because ketones are just below aldehydes in nomenclature suffix priority, the "oxo" substituent terminology is seldom needed. Simple substituents incorporating a carbonyl group are often encountered. The generic name for such groups is acyl.

Three examples of acyl groups having specific names are.

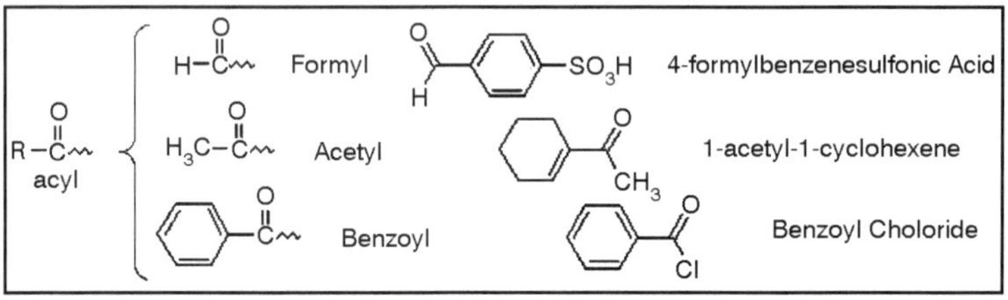

R–C(=O)– acyl

H–C(=O)– Formyl — 4-formylbenzenesulfonic Acid

H_3C–C(=O)– Acetyl — 1-acetyl-1-cyclohexene

C_6H_5–C(=O)– Benzoyl — Benzoyl Choloride

Occurrence of Aldehydes and Ketones

Natural Products

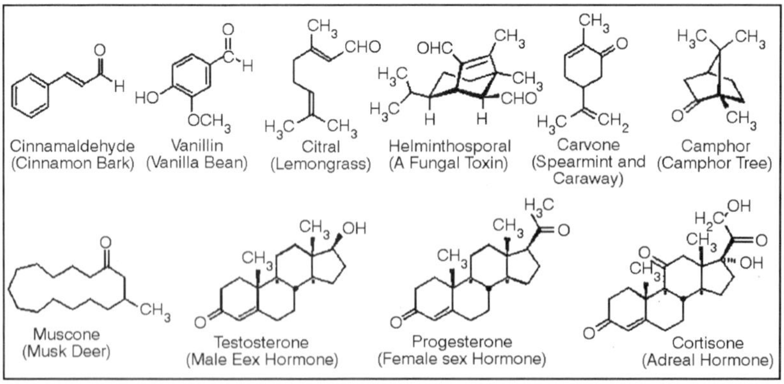

Cinnamaldehyde (Cinnamon Bark)
Vanillin (Vanilla Bean)
Citral (Lemongrass)
Helminthosporal (A Fungal Toxin)
Carvone (Spearmint and Caraway)
Camphor (Camphor Tree)
Muscone (Musk Deer)
Testosterone (Male Eex Hormone)
Progesterone (Female sex Hormone)
Cortisone (Adreal Hormone)

Aldehydes and ketones are widespread in nature, often combined with other functional groups. The compounds in the top row are found chiefly in plants or microorganisms; those in the bottom row have animal origins. With the exception of the first three compounds these molecular structures are all chiral. When chiral compounds are found in nature they are usually enantiomerically pure, although different sources may yield different enantiomers. For example, carvone is found as its levorotatory (*R*)-enantiomer in spearmint oil, whereas, caraway seeds contain the dextrorotatory (*S*)-enantiomer.

Note that the aldehyde function is often written as –CHO in condensed or complex formulas.

Synthetic Preparation of Aldehydes and Ketones

1. Oxidation of d1° and of 2° Alcohols

C_5H_{11}–C≡C–CH_2–OH → (PCC in CH_2Cl_2) → C_5H_{11}–C≡C–CHO

Cyclooctanol → (Jones' reag+acetone (CrO_3 in aq, H_2SO_4)) → cyclooctanone

2. Friedel-Crafts Acylation

Benzene + succinic anhydride → (AlCl$_3$ and Heat) → C_6H_5COCH$_2$CH$_2$CO$_2$H

2 Benzene + ClOC–CH=CH–COCl → (AlCl$_3$ and Heat) → C_6H_5CO–CH=CH–COC$_6H_5$

C_6H_5COCl + thiophene → (AlCl$_3$ in CS$_2$) → 2-benzoylthiophene

3. Hydration of Alkynes

1-ethynylcyclohexanol → (HgO in H_2SO_4 and H_2O) → [enol intermediate: C(OH)=CH$_2$] → 1-acetylcyclohexanol (OH, O, CH$_3$)

Bicyclic alkyne (CH$_2$, CH$_3$, C≡C–H) → (1. ($C_5H_{11})_2$BH Disiamylborane; 2. H_2O_2,NaOH) → [enol intermediate (CH$_2$, CH$_3$, OH)] → aldehyde (CH$_2$, CH$_3$, H, O)

4. Glycol Cleavage

1-methylcyclohexane-1,2-diol (OH, OH, CH$_3$) → (HIO$_4$ or pb (OAC)$_4$) → CHO / COCH$_3$ ≡ H–CO–(CH$_2$)$_4$–CO–CH$_3$

5. Ozonolysis of Alkenes

With the exception of Friedel-Crafts acylation, these methods do not increase the size or complexity of molecules. We shall find that one of the most useful characteristics of aldehydes and ketones is their reactivity towards carbon nucleophiles, and the resulting elaboration of molecular structure that results. In short, aldehydes and ketones are important intermediates for the assembly or synthesis of complex organic molecules.

Properties of Aldehydes and Ketones

A comparison of the properties and reactivity of aldehydes and ketones with those of the alkenes is warranted, since both have a double bond functional group. Because of the greater electronegativity of oxygen, the carbonyl group is polar, and aldehydes and ketones have larger molecular dipole moments than do alkenes.

The resonance structures on the right depict this polarity, and the relative dipole moments of formaldehyde, other aldehydes and ketones confirm the stabilizing influence that alkyl substituents have on carbocations.

We expect, therefore, that aldehydes and ketones will have higher boiling points than similar sized alkenes. Furthermore, the presence of oxygen with its non-bonding electron pairs makes aldehydes and ketones hydrogen-bond acceptors, and should increase their water solubility relative to hydrocarbons. Specific examples of these relationships are provided in the following table.

Compound	Mol. Wt.	Boiling Point	Water Solubility
$(CH_3)_2C{=}CH_2$	56	-7.0 ºC	0.04 g/100
$(CH_3)_2C{=}O$	58	56.5 ºC	infinite
$CH_3CH_2CH_2CH{=}CH_2$	70	30.0 ºC	0.03 g/100
$CH_3CH_2CH_2CH{=}O$	72	76.0 ºC	7 g/100
CH_2	96	103.0 ºC	insoluble
O	98	155.6 ºC	5 g/100

The polarity of the carbonyl group also has a profound effect on its chemical reactivity, compared with the non-polar double bonds of alkenes. Thus, reversible addition of water to the carbonyl function is fast, whereas water addition to alkenes is immeasureably slow in the absence of a strong acid catalyst. Curiously, relative bond energies influence the thermodynamics of such addition reactions in the opposite sense.

The C=C of alkenes has an average bond energy of 146 kcal/mole. Since a C–C σ-bond has a bond energy of 83 kcal/mole, the π-bond energy may be estimated at 63 kcal/mole (*i.e.* less than the energy of the sigma bond). The C=O bond energy of a carbonyl group, on the other hand, varies with its location, as follows:

$H_2C=O$ 170 kcal/mole
$RCH=O$ 175 kcal/mole
$R_2C=O$ 180 kcal/mole

The C–O σ-bond is found to have an average bond energy of 86 kcal/mole. Consequently, with the exception of formaldehyde, the carbonyl function of aldehydes and ketones has a π-bond energy greater than that of the sigma-bond, in contrast to the pi-sigma relationship in C=C. This suggests that addition reactions to carbonyl groups should be thermodynamically disfavored, as is the case for the addition of water.

$$>C=C< + H_2O \underset{\text{Very Slow}}{\overset{\text{Slow}}{\rightleftharpoons}} H{-}\overset{|}{\underset{|}{C}}{-}\overset{|}{\underset{|}{C}}{-}OH \qquad \Delta H^{o}_{add} \approx -10\,\text{kcal/mole, Requires Strong Acid Catalysis}$$

$$>C=O + H_2O \underset{\text{Very Fast}}{\overset{\text{Fast}}{\rightleftharpoons}} >C(OH)_2 \underset{\text{Fast}}{\overset{\text{Very Fast}}{\rightleftharpoons}} >C=O + H_2O \qquad \Delta H^{o} \approx +6\,\text{kcal/mole}$$

Although the addition of water to an alkene is exothermic and gives a stable product, the uncatalyzed reaction is extremely slow due to a high activation energy . The reverse reaction is even slower, and because of the kinetic barrier. The microscopically reversible mechanism for both reactions was described earlier. In contrast, both the endothermic addition of water to a carbonyl function, and the exothermic elimination of water from the resulting geminal-diol are fast. The inherent polarity of the carbonyl group, together with its increased basicity lowers the transition state energy for both reactions, with a resulting increase in rate. Acids and bases catalyze both the addition and elimination of water. Proof that rapid and reversible addition of water to carbonyl compounds occurs is provided by experiments using isotopically labeled water. If a carbonyl reactant composed of ^{16}O is treated with water incorporating the ^{18}O isotope a rapid exchange of the oxygen isotope occurs. This can only be explained by the addition-elimination mechanism shown here.

Acetal

An acetal is a molecule with two single bonded oxygens attached to the same carbon atom.

Traditional usages distinguish ketal from acetal. Current accepted terminology classifies ketals as a subset of acetals.

The plastic known as acetal is a polyacetal.

Formation of an acetal occurs when the hydroxyl group of a hemiacetal becomes protonated and is lost as water. The carbocation ion that is produced is then rapidly attacked by a molecule of alcohol. Loss of the proton from the attached alcohol gives the acetal.

Acetals are stable compared to hemiacetals but their formation is reversible as with esters. As a reaction to create an acetal proceeds, water must be removed from the reaction mixture or it will hydrolyse the product. The formation of acetals reduces the total number of molecules present and therefore is not favourable with regards to entropy. A way to improve this is to use an orthoester as a source of alcohol.

Aldehydes and ketones undergo a process called acetal exchange with orthoesters to give acetals. Water produced along with the acetal product is used up in hydrolysing the orthoester and producing more alcohol to be used in the reaction.

$R^1R^2C{=}O \underset{H^+}{\overset{R^3OH}{\rightleftharpoons}} [R^1R^2C(OH)(OR^3)] \underset{H^+}{\overset{R^3OH}{\rightleftharpoons}} R^1R^2C(OR^3)_2 + H_2O$

Ketone — Hemiacetal — Acetal

Acetals are important in nature, for example in solution the most stable form of glucose is its cyclic hemiacetal and maltose is an acetal made from two glucose units. Acetaldehyde diethyl acetal is an important flavouring compound in distilled beverages. Acetals are sometimes used as protecting groups for carbonyl groups in organic synthesis as they are stable with respect to hydrolysis by bases.

Hydrogen Sulfide

Hydrogen sulfide (H_2S) is generally thought to be a metabolic by-product of yeast fermentation in nitrogen limited environments. It is formed when yeast ferment via the sulfate reduction pathway. Fermenting wine is often supplemented with diammonium phosphate as a nitrogen source to prevent formation. The sensory threshold for hydrogen sulfide is 40-50 ìg/L. Hydrogen sulfide can further react with wine compounds to form mercaptans and disulfides.

Hydrocarbon Derivatives

- Organic compounds are divided into two main classes: hydrocarbons and hydrocarbon derivatives
- Hydrocarbon derivatives are molecular compounds of carbon and at least one other element that is not hydrogen
- Organic halides are organic compounds in which one or more hydrogen atoms have been replaced by halogen atoms.
- Common organic halides include freons and Teflon
- Naming halides uses the same format as branched-chain hydrocarbons.
- The branch is named by shortening the halogen name to fluoro-, chloro-, bromo-, or iodo-.
- In drawing organic halides using IUPAC names, draw the parent chain and add branches at locations specified in the name eg.

```
Cl Cl
||
H-C-C-H
 ||
 H H
```

1,2-dichloroethane

- Organic halides react fast which is explained from the idea that no strong covalent bond is broken – the electron rearrangement does not involve separation of the carbon atoms
- Addition of halogens could be added to alkynes which results in alkenes or alkanes
- By adding halogens to alkenes, the product could undergo another addition step, by adding halogens to the parent chain, the double bond has to become a single bond in order to accommodate the halogens eg.

```
 Br Br          Br Br
  ||             | |
H-C=C-H + Br-Br ⇒ H-C-C-H
                     | |
              Br Br
```

-By adding hydrogen halides to unsaturated compounds will produce isomers:

```
 H H H        H H H        H H H
  | | |         | | |         | | |
H-C=C-C-H + H-Cl ⇒ H-C-C-C-H OR H-C-C-C-H
  |           | | |         | | |
  H          Cl H H        HCl H
```

- Substitution reaction is a reaction that involves the breaking of a carbon-hydrogen bond in an alkane or aromatic ring and the replacement of the hydrogen atom with another atom or group of atoms.
- With light energy it enables the substitution reaction to move at a noticeable rate eg. C_3H_8 + BR_2 + light ⇒ C_3H_7Br + HBR.
- Through substitution reaction, in order to name the reaction product, just indicate the location number of the replacement, followed by the halogen prefix and then state the type of parent chain. Also indicate the second product created from substitution reaction *e.g.*, propane + bromine ⇒ 1–bromopropane + hydrogen bromide.
- Elimination is an organic reaction in which an alkyl halide reacts with hydroxide ion to produce an alkene by removing a hydrogen and halide ion from the molecule

```
 H H H       H H H
  | | |       | | |
H-C-C-C-H + OH ⇒ H-C=C-C-H + H-O + Br
  | | |          |      |
 H BrH           H      H
```

- Alcohols have properties that can be explained by the presence of a hydroxyl functional group attached to a hydrocarbon chain
- Short-chain alcohols are very soluble in water because they form hydrogen bonds with water molecules
- Alcohols are used as solvents in organic reactions because they are effective for both polar and non-polar compounds
- To name alcohols, the –e is dropped from the end of the alkane name and is replaced with –ol eg. Methane ⇒ methanol.
- Methanol is also called wood alcohol because it was once made by heating wood shavings in the absence of air.
- These days, methanol is prepared by combining carbon monoxide and hydrogen at high temperatures and pressure with the use of a catalyst
- Methanol, however, is poisonous to humans. Consuming a small amount could cause blindness or death
- When naming alcohols with more than two carbon atoms, the position of the hydroxyl group is indicated
- Alcohols that contain more than one hydroxyl group are called polyalcohols, their names indicate the positions of the hydroxyl groups eg. 1,2-ethanediol
- Alcohols undergo elimination reactions to produce alkenes through being catalyzed by concentrated sulfuric acid, which removes or eliminates a hydrogen atom and a hydroxyl group

```
  HH        HH
  ||        ||
H-C-C-H + acid  ⇒  H-C=C-H  +  H-O
  ||                 |
  H OH               H
```

ethanol + acid ⇒ ethene + water

- Ethers is a family of organic compounds that contain an oxygen atom bonded between two hydrocarbon groups, and have the general formula R_1–O–R_2.
- To name ethers add oxy to the prefix for the smaller hydrocarbon group and join it to the alkane name of the larger hydrocarbon group eg.

$$CH_3\text{–}O\text{–}C_2H_5$$

Ethoxyethane:

- Ethers have low solubility in water, low boiling points, and have no evidence of hydrogen bonding
- Ethers undergo chemical change only when treated with powerful reagents under vigorous conditions
- Ethers are formed by the condensation reaction of alcohols.
- Condensation reaction is the joining of two molecules and the elimination of a small molecule, usually water.

- The carbonyl functional group, -CO-, consists of a carbon atom with a double covalent bond to an oxygen atom.
- Aldehydes has the carbonyl group on the terminal carbon atom of a chain.
- To name aldehydes, replace the final –e of the name of the corresponding alkane with the suffix –al.
- Small aldehyde molecules have sharp, irritating odours whereas larger molecules have flowery odours and is used to make perfumes.
- A ketone has the carbonyl group present anywhere in a carbon chain except at the end of the chain.
- The difference in position of the carbonyl group affects the chemical reactivity, and enables us to distinguish aldehydes from ketones empirically.
- To name ketones, replace the –e ending of the name of the corresponding alkane with –one.
- The simplest ketone is acetone CH_3COCH_3 .
- The family of organic compounds, carboxylic acids contain the carboxyl functional group, -COOH, which includes both the carbonyl and hydroxyl groups.
- Carboxylic acids are found in citrus fruits, and other foods with properties of having a sour taste.
- Carboxylic acids also have distinctive odours.
- The molecules of carboxylic acids are polar and form hydrogen bonds both with each other and with water molecules.
- Carboxylic acids acid properties, so a litmus test can separate these compounds from other hydrocarbon derivatives
- To name carboxylic acids, replace the –e ending of the alkane name with –oic, followed by the word "acid".
- Methanoic acid, HCOOH, is the first member of the carboxylic acid family.
- Some acids contain two or three carbonyl groups such as oxalic acid, and citric acid.

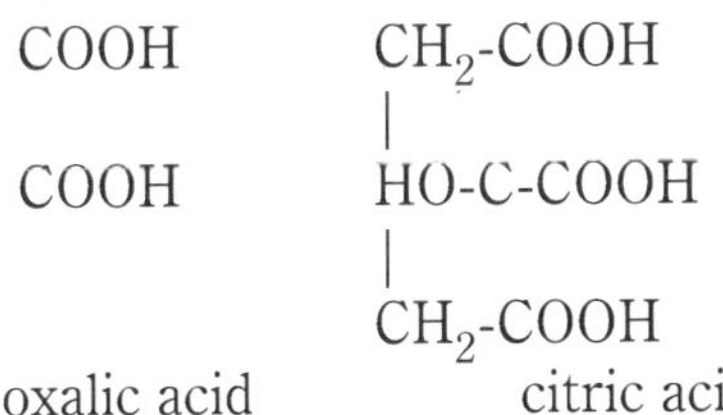

oxalic acid citric acid

- When carboxylic acids undergo a condensation reaction, in which a carboxylic acid combines with another reactant, it forms two products – an organic compound and water

- Esterification is the condensation reaction in which a carboxylic acid reacts with an alcohol to produce ester and water
  carboxylic acid + alcohol ⇒ ester + water
- The ester functional group is similar to that of an acid, except that the hydrogen atom of the carboxyl group is replaced by a hydrocarbon branch
- Esters are responsible for the odours of fruits and flowers and are also added to foods for aroma and taste
- To name an ester, determine name of the alkyl group from the alcohol used in the esterification reaction
- Next change the ending of the acid name from "–oic acid" to "–oate"
  ethanoic acid + methanol ⇒ methyl ethanoate + water
- Artificial flavorings are made by mixing synthetic esters to give similar odours of the natural substance
- An amide consists of a carboxyl group bonded to a nitrogen atom
- Amides could be formed in condensation reactions
- Amides occur in proteins, the large molecules found in all living organisms
- Peptide bonds is the joining of amino acids together in proteins
- To name amides, have the name of the alkane with the same number of carbon atoms, with the final –e replaced by the suffix –amide
- Change the suffix of the carboxylic acid from "–oic acid" to –amide to have the same name results eg. ethanamide
- Amines consist of one or more hydrocarbon groups bonded to a nitrogen atom
- Through X-Ray diffraction reveals that the amine functional group is a nitrogen atom bonded by single covalent bonds to one, two, or three carbon atoms
- Amines are polar substances that re extremely soluble in water as they form strong hydrogen bonds both to each other and to water
- Amines have peculiar, horrible odours
- The name of amines include the names of the alkyl groups attached to the nitrogen atom, followed by the suffix –amine eg. methylamine
- Amines with one, two, or three hydrocarbon groups attached to the central nitrogen atom are referred to as primary, secondary, and tertiary
- Primary amines is when a hydrogen atom attached to the nitrogen atom is replaced by a hydrocarbon group
- Secondary amines are when two hydrocarbon groups replaces the hydrogen atoms and tertiary amines replaces all of the hydrogen atoms with hydrocarbon groups
- Amines are used in the synthesis of medicines
- A group of amines found in many plants are called alkaloids

- Many alkaloids influence the function of the central nervous systems of animals
- *Substitution*: Alkane/aromatic + halogen + light ⇒ organic halide + hydrogen halide
- *Elimination*: Alkyl halide + OH ⇒ alkene + water | + water + halide ion
- *Elimination*: Alcohol + acid ⇒ alkene + water

Lactones

These are a kind of cyclic ester. They are formed when the acid and alcohol functions are part of the same molecule. In other words, they are cyclic esters and occur in a wide range of natural substances.

Wine Lactone

An ester with a sweet coconut odour was recently found to cause the smell and flavour of many white wines.

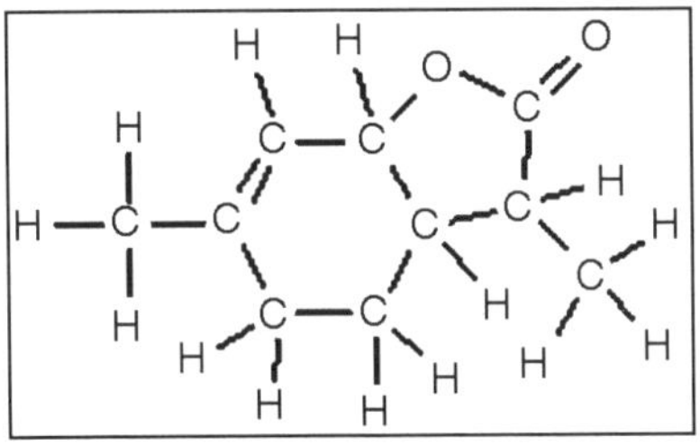

This molecule has been identified in a number of wines, as well as being synthesised. There are three chiral carbons, and the one of the eight isomers that has the highest activity has been identified; it is identical with the lactone found in the wines. It has also been found in orange juice and in black pepper.

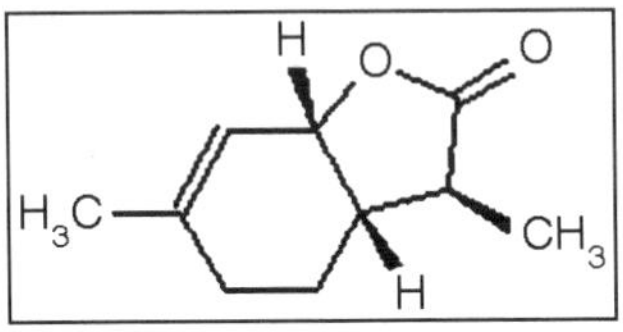

Aroma and Terpenes

Significant changes in wine aroma occur during maturation and aging. These include the loss of certain grape or yeasty aromas, retention of the varietal aroma, formation of new aromas integration of all flavors to produce a harmonious and pleasing fragrance. Many esters and higher alcohols formed by the yeast's metabolic activity contribute to the fermentation aroma. During wine storage, the esters are hydrolyzed and the fresh and fruity aroma is lost. Concurrent with the degradation of esters, a synthesis of new esters occurs. For example, the formation of isoamyl acetate and diethyl succinate.

In wines with strong varietal flavor, both qualitative and quantitative changes in aroma take place. For example, in muscat varieties, terpenes are the main odourous compounds. During maturation and aging, the concentration of monoterpene alcohol declines and monoterpene oxides are formed. This leads to the loss and alteration of floral aroma. In Riesling, linalool is found in significant amounts. This terpene compound gives a floral aroma to the wine. The oxide terpene derivatives, such as alphaterpineol, have a pine like odour; whereas, its precursor linalool, as indicated earlier, has a floral fragrance.

It should be noted that terpene compounds also occur in a bound form. In an acidic medium, such as wine, the bound terpenes are slowly converted to free volatile terpenes over time. When these reactions occur, the fruity aroma of a wine is enhanced during maturation.

Phenolic Compounds in Wine

The phenols compounds in wine include a large group of several hundred chemical compounds, known as polyphenols, that affect the taste, colour and mouthfeel of wine. This large group can be broadly separated into two categories-flavonoids and non-flavonoids. Flavonoids include anthocyanins and tannins which contribute to the colour and mouthfeel of the wine. Non-flavonoids include stilbenes such as resveratrol and compounds derived from acids in wine like benzoic, caffeic and cinnamic acid.

In wine grapes, phenolics are found widely in the skin, stems and seeds. During the growth cycle of the grapevine, sunlight will increase the concentration of phenolics in the grape berries with the development of phenolics being an important component of canopy management. Most phenols are classified as secondary metabolites and are not active in the primary metabolism and function of the grapevine. They are water soluble and will often secrete into the vacuole of grape berries as glycosides. In winemaking, the process of maceration or "skin contact" is used to increase the influence of phenols in wine. Phenolic acids are found in the pulp or juice of the wine and can be commonly found in white wines which usually doesn't go through a maceration period. The process of oak aging can also introduce phenolic compounds to wine, most notably in the form of vanillin which adds vanilla aroma to wines.

Flavonoids

In red wine, up to 90% of the wine's phenolic content fall under the classification of flavonoids. These phenols, mainly derived from the stems, seeds and skins are often leeched out of the grape during the maceration period of winemaking. The amount of phenols leeched is known as extraction. They contribute to the astringency, colour and mouthfeel of the wine.

In white wines the number of flavonoids is reduced due to less skin contact that they receive in winemaking. Within the flavonoid category is a subcategory known as flavonols, which includes the yellow pigment inducing phenol-quercetin. Like other flavonoids, the concentration of flavonols in the grape berries increases as they exposed to sunlight.

Some viticulturalists will use measurement of flavonols like quercetin as an indication of a vineyard's sun exposure and the effectiveness of canopy management techniques. There is on going study in the health benefits of wine derived from the antioxidant and chemopreventive properties of flavonoids.

Anthocyanins

Anthocyanins are phenolic compounds found throughout the plant kingdom, being responsible for the blue to red colours found in flowers, fruits and leaves. In wine grapes, they develop during the stage of *veraison* when the skin of red wine grapes change colour from green to shading from red to black. As the sugars in the grape increase during ripening, so does the concentration of anthocyanins. In most grapes anthocyanins are found only in the outer cell layers of the skin, leaving the grape juice inside to be virtually colorless.

Therefore to get colour pigmentation in the wine, the fermenting must needs to be in contact with the grape skins in order to extract the anthocyanins. For this reason, white wine can be from red wine grapes as in the case for many white sparkling wines which are often made from the red wine grapes of Pinot noir and Pinot meunier. The exception to this is the small class of grapes known as teinturiers, such as Alicante Bouschet, which has a small amount of anthocyanins in the pulp which produces pigmented juice.

There are several types of anthocyanins found in wine grapes which are responsible for the vast range of coloring found in wine grapes from ruby red to dark black. Ampelographers can use this observation to assist in the identification of different grape varieties. The European vine family *Vitis Vinifera* is characterized with anthocyanins that are composed of only one molecule of glucose while non-*Vinifera* vines such as hybrids and the American *Vitis labrusca* will have anthocyanins with two molecules. In the mid-20th century, French ampelographers used this knowledge to test the various vine varieties throughout France to identify which vineyards still contained non-*Vinifera* plantings.

The color variation in the finished red wine is partly derived from the ionization of anthocyanin pigments caused by the acidity of the wine. In this case, the three types of anthocyanin pigments are red, blue and colorless with the concentration of those various pigments dictating the color of the wine. A wine with low pH will have a higher occurrence of ionized anthocyanins which will increase the amount of bright red pigments. Wines with a higher pH will have a higher concentration of blue and colorless pigments.

As the wine ages, anthocyanins will react with other acids and compounds in wines such as tannins, pyruvic acid and acetaldehyde which will change the color of the wine, causing it to develop more "brick red" hues. These molecules will link up to create polymers that eventually exceed their solubility and become sediment at the bottom of wine bottles. Pyranoanthocyanins are chemical compounds formed in red wines by yeast during fermentation processes or during controled oxygenation processes during the aging of wine.

Tannins

Tannins refer to the diverse group of chemical compounds in wine that can affect the color, aging ability and texture of the wine. While tannins can not be smelt or tasted, they can be perceived during wine tasting by the tactile drying sensation and sense of bitterness that they can leave in the mouth. This is due to the tendency of tannins to react with proteins, such as the ones found in saliva. In food and wine pairing, foods that are high in proteins are often paired with tannic wines to minimize the astringency of tannins. However, many wine drinkers find the perception of tannins to be a positive trait-especially as it relates to mouthfeel. The management of tannins in the winemaking process is a key component in the resulting quality of the wine.

Tannins are found in the skin, stems and seeds of wine grapes but can also be introduced to the wine through the use of oak barrels and chips or with the addition of tannin powder. The natural tannins found in grapes are known as proanthocyanins due to their ability to release red anthocyanin pigments when they are heated in an acidic solution. The tannins are formed by enzymes during metabolic processes by the grapevine.

The amount of tannins found naturally in grapes varies depending variety with Cabernet Sauvignon, Nebbiolo, Syrah and Tannat being 4 of the most tannic grape varieties. The reaction of tannins and anthocyanins with the phenolic compound catechins creates another class of tannins known as pigmented tannins which influences the color of red wine.

Commercial preparations of tannins, known as *enological tannins*, made from oak wood, grape seed and skin, plant gall, chestnut, quebracho, gambier and myrobalan fruits, can be added at different stages of the wine production to improve color durability. The tannins derived from oak influence are known as "hydrolysable tannins" being created from the ellagic and gallic acid found in the wood.

In the vineyards, there is also a growing distinction being made between "ripe" and "unripe" tannins present in the grape. This "physiological ripeness", which is roughly determined by tasting the grapes off the vines, is being used along with sugar levels as a determination of when to the harvest. The idea is that "riper" tannins will taste softer but still impart some of the texture components found favorable in wine.

In winemaking, the amount of the time that the must spends in contact with the grape skins, stems and seeds will influence the amount of tannins that are present in the wine with wines subjected to longer maceration period having more tannin extract. Following harvest, stems are normally picked out and discarded prior to fermentation but some winemakers may intentionally leave in a few stems for varieties low in tannins in order to increase the tannic extract in the wine. If there is an excess in the amount of tannins in the wine, winemakers can use various fining agents like albumin, casein and gelatin that can bind to tannins molecule and precipitate them out as sediments.

As a wine ages, tannins will form long polymerized chains which come across to a taster as "softer" and less tannic. Oxygen can bind with tannin molecules to make them larger and seem also seem softer on the palate. The winemaking technique of micro-oxygenation and decanting wine use oxygen to partial mimic the effect of aging on tannins.

Other Flavonoids

Catechins are flavonoids that contribute to the construction of various tannins and contribute to the perception of bitterness in wine. They are found in highest concentrations in grape seeds but are also in the skin and stems. Catechins play a role in the microbial defence of the grape berry, being produced in higher concentrations by the grape vines when it is being attacked by grape diseases such as downy mildew.

Because of that grape vines in cool, damp climates produce catechins at high levels than vines in dry, hot climates. Together with anthocyanins and tannins they increase the stability of a wines color-meaning that a wine will be able to maintain its coloring for a longer period of time. The amount of catechins present varies amount grape varieties with varietals like Merlot and Pinot noir having high concentrations while Syrah has very low levels. As an antioxidant, there are some studies into the health benefits of moderate consumption of wines high in catechins. Myricetin, laricitrin and syringetin, flavonols which are present in red grape varieties only, can be found in red wine.

Non-flavonoids

Resveratrol is a phenolic compound found in highest concentration in the skins of wine grapes. Both red and white wine grape varieties have resveratrol but more frequent use of skin contact and maceration in red winemaking means that red wines will normally have 10 times more resveratrol than white wines. It generally produced by grape vines as a means of microbial defence, though production can be artificially stimulated by ultraviolet radiation. Grapevines in cool, damp regions with higher risk of grape diseases, such as Bordeaux and Burgundy, tend to produce grapes with higher levels of resveratrol than warmer, drier wine regions like California and Australia.

Additionally, different grape varieties are prone to differing levels with Muscadines and the Pinot family having high levels while the Cabernet family being noted for lower levels of resveratrol.

In the late 20th century, interest in the possible health benefits of resveratrol in wine was spurred by discussion of the French paradox involving the health of wine drinkers in France. Vanillin is a phenolic aldehyde most commonly associated with the vanilla notes in wines that have been aged in oak. Some trace amounts of vanillin are found naturally in the grapes themselves but they are most prominent in the lignin structure of oak barrels. Newer barrels will impart more vanillin, with the concentration present decreasing with each subsequent usage.

VOMERONASAL ORGAN

Biologists have long realized that the noses of most vertebrates actually contain two sensory channels. The first is the familiar olfactory system, which humans possess. The second channel is the vomeronasal complex, a system that has its own separate organs, nerves, and connecting structures in the brain. The function of the vomeronasal system is the detection of pheromones, chemical messengers that carry information between individuals of the same species. It was widely believed that humans had long ago discarded this sensory system somewhere along evolution's trail.

But convincing behavioral and anatomical evidence has since brought the notion of a human vomeronasal organ into the realm of scientific fact. Some thirty years ago, when anatomist David Berliner was studying human skin composition using scraped skin cells from the insides of discarded casts, he found that when he left vials containing skin extracts open, his lab assistants would become more friendly and warm than usual.

When, months later, he decided to cover the vials, the warm and relaxed behavior was noticeably reduced. These findings led him to investigate the possible existence of odourless human pheromones and a "sixth sense" organ to detect their presence, a VNO.

While this early evidence was not empirical, anatomists have since found that all humans display two tiny pits, with duct openings, on both sides of the septum just behind the opening of the nose. The duct leads into a tubular lumen lacking a thick, distinct sensory epithelium. However, there are cells in the lining of the lumen that may be VNO receptor neurons.

They appear to be bipolar neurons and respond to neuron specific stains. In a recent experiment, human VNO was reported to respond positively to puffs of air laden with substances claimed to be human pheromones. If the experiment is valid, it presents strong evidence supporting the hypothesis that the human VNO is functioning, not vestigial. In some respects, however, the proof is lacking. The human VNO lacks the characteristic capsule and large blood vessels of other mammals' VNOs. The sensory epithelium is not well developed. In addition, connections between the presumed VNO receptor neurons and the brain have not yet been confirmed in humans.

In other mammals, nerve impulses from the sensory cells of the vomeronasal organ enter brain structures known as the accessory olfactory bulbs and also project to brain structures that regulate sexual behavior and the secretion of gonadotropin, a pituitary hormone regulating the function of the testes. The accessory olfactory bulb, the normal termination of vomeronasal receptor-neuron axons cannot be distinguished clearly in the human brain.

But, the structural inconsistencies of the human VNO system do not prove that it is inactive. They merely indicate that it different, and perhaps less fundamental, than in our fellow vertebrates, a notion that is readily apparent from more cursory observations. Recent human behavioral studies, which will be discussed later, have tipped the conventional wisdom scales to the viewpoint supporting the presence of a functioning human VNO.

The VNOs of other vertebrates, thankfully, are somewhat less mysterious. This is, in part, because the anatomy and function of the VNO in snakes, some lizards, and nonprimate mammals are less disguised than in humans. It is also related to the ease with which researchers can remove or disable the VNOs of animals for experimentation. In humans, this highly invasive and damaging procedure is, for obvious reasons, not feasible.

Because the vomeronasal organ in non-human animals is typically situated in a pouch off the nasal cavity, airborne odourant molecules cannot efficiently enter the dead-end passage the same way that they reach the olfactory receptor cells. The VNO requires another delivery system. In snakes, environmental stimuli enter the vomeronasal organ through ducts that connect it with the oral cavity. During flicking, the tongue picks up molecules from the air and nearby objects.

As the tongue retracts into the mouth at the end of each flick, the molecules are drawn over the duct openings leading to the VNO. Mammals have evolved a different delivery system. When they lick and sniff, molecules from the environment are absorbed onto the nose and tongue, and are then transported into the vomeronasal organ in saliva. A pumping action that dilates and constricts the organ walls increases the motion of fluid in and out of the dead-end structure, moving stimuli rapidly into the chamber.

Vomeronasal sensory neurons are distinct from olfactory neurons in their morphology and in the signal transduction components that they express. The main olfactory system of mammals recognizes the universe of odourants using as many as a thousand related G protein-coupled receptors. Oddly enough, the sensory potential of this vast family is not exploited by the mammalian vomeronasal organ.

Vomeronasal neurons do not express the classical olfactory receptors. In a 1995 study by Dulac and Axel, VNO neuron receptors were identified using a single-cell PCR strategy to find genes expressed at high levels.

They found a family of 30-100 genes that encode proteins that are completely unrelated to the olfactory receptors. Only one or a few receptor proteins are expressed per cell, indicating possible cellular specificity to molecular stimulants. A majority of the research on vomeronasal function has been in rodents and snakes, and most has involved lesions of the vomeronasal or olfactory systems in order to reveal deficits in behavior or physiological function. In rodents, pheromone communication can produce dramatic effects on reproductive behavior and physiology and can be the basis for aggressive behavior. Many of these effects depend on chemosensory input from the VNO. For example, male mice and other rodents produce chemosignals that accelerate puberty in immature females of the same species. Female mice living in groups produce a urinary chemosignal that suppresses estrus in other females.

In both of these cases, removal of the VNO prevents the response. There is evidence that these effects are due to an influence of VNO input on hormone levels. In many species, both sexes show changes of luteinizing-hormone in response to chemical signals from opposite sex individuals. In mice and hamsters, removal of the VNO prevents the hormonal changes normally observed after exposure of males to female chemosignals.

When LH is injected into the brain, deficits in mating behavior caused by VNO removal are restored. Furthermore, in sexually naive mice and hamsters, the removal of the vomeronasal organs alone prevents mating behavior, while removal of the olfactory input alone does not. This is strong evidence that the VNO plays a critical role in facilitating certain preprogrammed behaviors in these mammals.

Knowing that the VNO system acts as an intermediary between chemical stimuli and the transmission of behavioral instructions, we should address how this is facilitated by neural wiring. The VNO receptor neurons have axons that leave the VNO capsule in bundles and carry electrical signals to the accessory olfactory bulb. The AOBs process VNO input and lie dorsal to the main olfactory bulbs, processors of smell input.

The VNO information from the AOB and the olfactory information from the MOB are carried via separate sets of "second-order" axons to the amygdala. From there the VNO system projects directly to the preoptic area and to the hypothalamus, areas known to be involved in reproductive behavior. Recent experiments indicate that the VNO-recipient area of the amygdala and the preoptic area are active during VNO-initiated male hamster mating behavior, and that the amygdala is activated when animals are stimulated by female pheromones. The main olfactory system did not show activation beyond control levels during pheromone stimulation.

So, what role, if any, does consciousness play our model of the VNO system? There is apparently no neo-cortical projection of the vomeronasal system. Based partly on this evidence that it bypasses the cerebral cortex, it has been suggested that vomeronasal sensory input may be unavailable to conscious processes. In other words, the recipient of pheromonal communication, despite exhibiting a behavioral response, may be unaware of the stimulus. This hypothesis is not yet provable. First, while the cerebral cortex is thought to be the location of conscious thought, it is likely that many brain structures integrate to create consciousness. As we know, the brain typically has several ways of fulfilling a given task, and consciousness is probably a particularly complex, demanding task, likely requiring the cooperation of various structures. We also don't know that rodents and other VNO possessing creatures have conscious awareness in the first place.

We cannot yet prove that they have an "I" function, a self that can think and feel. However, the concept that a higher organisms such as rodents or bears could have a highly developed, behavior-altering sense of which they are not "aware" is fascinating, and worthy of further exploration.

There is no question that humans are not aware of this sixth sense, if they do indeed have it. If we do receive chemical signals from people in our vicinity, these signals must compete with many other factors that influence our behavior. Yet our physiology may respond similarly to that of other mammals. Researchers at the Monell Chemical Senses Center in Philadelphia studying the effects of male odours on hormone levels in females have found that the length and timing of the menstrual cycle are markedly influenced by odours from the underarms of males.

These responses could be linked to the observation that the menstrual cycle of women living around men tends to be more regular. Another study has indicated that the long observed phenomenon of women living in close quarters developing synchronized menstrual cycles may be explained by the recognition of pheromones by the VNO. The researchers wiped pads under the noses of female subjects. They found that "compounds donated by women in the late follicular phase of their menstrual cycles accelerated the preovulatory surge of luteninizing hormone of recipient women, and shortened their menstrual cycles."

They also found that "compounds from the same donors, but collected later had an opposite effect, delaying the LH surge of recipients and lengthening their menstrual cycles." As compelling as the evidence is, neither case proves that the VNO is involved in the physiological responses. However, some sort of sensory processing at an unconscious level must be taking place to bring about these responses, and the VNO appears to be at the root of it.

If the human pheromonal system exists, it is logical to assume that it has an adaptive purpose. While every existing biological system does not necessarily have an adaptive purpose, evolutionary theory suggests that a species living in a unstable environment will, through thousands of generations, be trimmed of what is not beneficial to survival. It has been proposed that the purpose of the pheromonal system is not to attract the opposite sex, but to inform the individual reproductive system of the continued presence of a mate. There is no real need for humans to use odours to attract the opposite sex: we have excellent hearing and eyesight and can recognize each other at long distances.

Males and females are easy to differentiate because they have distinctive shapes. We live in groups, and can thus easily establish initial contact with potential mates. Many of the animals which rely on odours and pheromones to attract, find, and recognize mates live in environments in which meeting mates is much less convenient.

Let's consider the conditions under which humans are close enough to smell, the bodily emanation of another. This occurs through close contact, such as sleeping or cuddling with mates or potential mates.

Perhaps, then, the human VNO and pheromonal system serves to promote and maintain pair bonds, or increase the probability that such a relationship will lead to reproduction. So, how might this be selected for? If the effect of male pheromonal cues was to make the female more fertile, there would indeed be selection for male ability to emit the pheromones, and for female ability to receive them.

Males who lacked the mechanism for releasing the pheromones would produce fewer offspring from their matings. Females who lacked the apparatus for receiving the male pheromonal signals would be unable to adjust their fertility based on the presence or absence of a male, and would be out-reproduced by those females who did receive the signals. If males transmit pheromonal signals while cuddling with or sleeping with females, then it could help explain why humans are unusually sexual animals engaging in much non-reproductive sex, including copulation when the female is not in the fertile portion of her menstrual cycle.

If sexual contact serves to increase female fertility as the evidence suggests, it would help explain the selection for male and female desires for frequent sex.

There is anatomical, behavioral, physiological, and adaptive evidence for a human VNO. Research merely needs to take a final step, to witness the VNO in action. Human pheromones must also be structurally identified and better understood for the account to be complete.

OFF-ODORS

Volatile Acidity

Volatile acidity refers to the steam distillable acids present in wine, primarily acetic acid but also lactic, formic, butyric, and propionic acids. Commonly, these acids are measured by Cash Still, though now they can be measured by gas chromatography, HPLC or enzymatic methods. The average level of acetic acid in a new dry table wine is less than 400 mg/L, though levels may range from undetectable up to 3g/L.

The aroma threshold for acetic acid in red wine varies from 600 mg/L and 900 mg/L, depending on the variety and style. While acetic acid is generally considered a spoilage product, some winemakers seek a low or barely detectible level of acetic acid to add to the perceived complexity of a wine. In addition, the production of acetic acid will result in the concomitant formation of other, sometimes unpleasant, aroma compounds. These compounds have much lower sensory threshold than acetic acid—both acetaldehyde and ethyl acetate are detectable at less than 200 mg/L in wine. In addition to the undesirable aromas, both acetic acid and acetaldehyde are toxic to Saccharomyces cerevisiae and may lead to stuck fermentations.

Origins:

- The amount of volatile acidity found in sound grapes is negligible. It is a byproduct of microbial metabolism.
- Acetic acid bacteria is able to convert both glucose and ethanol to acetic acid.
- Yeast found in the vineyard—Kloeckera, Hansenula, and Metschnikowia—are able to produce large amounts of acetic acid and ethyl acetate early in a fermentation, but his generally occurs only with damaged grapes. This conversion can be prevented by the addition of sulfites at crush.
- Most lactic acid bacteria will produce acetic acid from glucose if they are present when there is still significant amounts of sugar.
- Of wine yeast, Saccharomyces strains will produce varying amounts, while Brettanomyces is a strong producer of acetic acid.
- Dessert wines produced from botrysized grapes often have higher levels of acetic acid. The Botrytis mold breaks open the grape skins, allowing the co-infection of the grapes with yeast or bacteria that produce acetic acid.

Prevention

Acetic acid bacteria require oxygen to grow, therefore, elimination of any air in wine containers and sulfur dioxide addition will limit their growth. Likewise, rejection of moldy grapes will prevent possible problems. Use of sulfur dioxide and inoculation with a low-V.A. producing strain of Saccharomyces may deter acetic acid producing yeast.

Treatment

A relatively new method for removal of volatile acidity from a wine is reverse osmosis. Blending may also help—a wine with high V.A. can be filtered and blended with a low V.A. wine, so that the acetic acid level is below the sensory threshold.

Ethyl Acetate

Ethyl acetate is formed in wine by the esterification of ethanol and acetic acid. Therefore wines with high acetic acid levels are more likely ethyl acetate formation, but the compound does not contribute to the volatile acidity. It is a common microbial fault produced by wine spoilage yeasts, particularly *Pichia anomala*, *Kloeckera apiculata*, and *Hanseniaspora uvarum*. High levels of ethyl acetate are also produced by lactic acid bacteria and acetic acid bacteria. The sensory threshold for ethyl acetate is 150-200 mg/L.

4-Ethylphenol

4-Ethylphenol, often abbreviated to 4-EP, is a phenolic compound with the molecular formula $C_8H_{10}O$. In wine and beer it is produced by the spoilage yeast *Brettanomyces*. When it reaches concentrations greater than the sensory threshold it can give the wine aromas described as *barnyard*, *medicinal*, *band-aids*, and *mousy*. In certain Belgian beer styles, a high 4-EP level may be desirable; however, very high levels of the compound in wine can render it undrinkable. The level of 4-ethylphenol is roughly proportional to *Brettanomyces* concentration and activity, and can therefore be used as an indicator of the yeast's presence. There are significant differences between strains of Brettanomyces in their ability to produce 4-Ethyl Phenol.

Fusel Alcohol

Fusel alcohols, also sometimes called fusel oils, or potato oil in Europe, are higher-order alcohols formed by fermentation and present in cider, mead, beer, wine, and spirits to varying degrees.

Composition and Taste

The compounds involved are chiefly:

- 1-propanol
- 2-propanol
- Butanol
- Amyl alcohol
- Furfural

Excessive concentrations of these fractions may cause off flavours, sometimes described as "spicy," "hot," or "solvent-like." Some beverages, such as whisky, Siwucha and traditional ales and ciders, are expected to have relatively high concentrations of fusel alcohols as part of the flavour profile. In other beverages, such as vodka and lagers, the presence of fusel alcohols is considered a fault.

Formation and Removal

Fusel alcohols are formed when fermentation occurs:

- At higher temperatures.
- At lower pH.
- When yeast activity is limited by low nitrogen content.

During distillation, fusel alcohols are concentrated in the "tails" at the end of the distillation run. They have an oily consistency, which is noticeable to the distiller, hence the other name "fusel oil". If desired, these heavier alcohols can be almost completely separated in a reflux still. Freeze distillation, on the other hand, does not remove fusel alcohols.

Health Effects

There is a popular belief that fusel alcohol contributes to hangover symptoms. One study indicated that fusel alcohol has no more significant undesirable health effects than ethanol, the primary active ingredient in all alcoholic beverages. However, it should be noted that this study involved an animal model of hangover, and its significance in humans is unclear.

Bibliography

A M Bagulia.: *Encyclopaedia of Travel Agency Management* (3 *Vols-Set*), Anmol Publications, Delhi, 2006.

A.P. Rastogi.: *Travel Agency Operations*, Aman Publications, Delhi, 2007.

Alan A. Lew, C. Michael Hall, and Allan M. Williams.: *A Companion to Tourism*, Rawat Publication, New Delhi, 2005.

Alexandru Nedelea and Babu P. George.: *Comparative TourismMarketing : Case Studies*, Abhijeet Publication, Delhi, 2010.

Amit Gaur.: *Adventure Tourism*, Sonali Publication, Delhi, 2011.

Amrita Bhagnani.: *Travel Agency and Tourism*, Abhijeet Publications,Delhi, 2012.

Anand Ballabh.: *Fundamentals of Travel and Tourism*, Akansha Publications, Delhi, 2005.

Anil Kathuria.: *Hotel Industry*, Sonali Publication, Delhi, 2008.

Anupama Srivastava and Keya Pandey.: *Anthropology and Tourism*, Serials Publications, Delhi, 2012.

Ashim Gupta.: *Travel Agency and Tour Operations: Concepts and Principles*, Centrum Press, Delhi, 2012.

B S Badan and Harish Bhatt.: *Transport for Travel and Tourism*, Commonwealth Publications, Delhi, 2007.

B. K. Goswami and G. Raveendran.: *A Textbook of Tourism*, Haranand Publications, Delhi, 2010.

Babu P. George and Sampad Kumar Swain.: *Advancements in Tourism Theory and Practice : Perspectives from India*, Abhijeet Publication, Delhi, 2005.

Banwari Lal Raheja.: *Food Management in Hotel, Travel and Tourism*, Arise Publications, Delhi, 2006.

Deepak Raj Gupta and Anil Gupta.: *Travel and Tourism Management: Contemporary Issues and Trends*, Abhishek Publications, Delhi, 2008.

Dinesh Kaushik.: *Financial Management of Travel and Tourism*, Vishvabharti Publications, Delhi, 2006.

Jack Randall.: *Agriculture Tourism*, Discovery Publishing House, Delhi, 2011.

Jagmohan Negi and Gaurav Manoher.: *Project Report Preparation : Hospitality Management and Tourism Development*, Aman Publications, Delhi, 2010.

Jagmohan Negi and Gaurav Manoher.: *Travel Agency Operations: Concepts and Principles (With Examination Questions)*, Kanishka Publications, Delhi, 2003.

Jagmohan Negi, Gaurav M.J., Suniti and Ritushka.: *Communication Skills for Hospitality Management*, Kanishka Publication, Delhi, 2012.

Jagpradeep.: *Hotel Management*, Murari Lal & Sons, Delhi, 2008.

Jitendra K. Sharma.: *Contemporary Tourism and Hospitality Management*, Kanishka Publication, Delhi, 2006.

Krishan K. Kamra and Mohinder Chand.: *Basics of Tourism: Theory, Operation and Practice*, Kanishka Publication, Delhi, 2002.

Lalita Sharma.: *An Introduction to Ecotourism*, Centrum Press, Delhi, 2003.

M C Metti.: *Advertising and Hotel Management*, Anmol Publication, Delhi, 2008.

M C Metti.: *Catering : Housekeeping and Hotel Management*, Anmol Publication, Delhi, 2008.

M C Metti.: *Customer Service and Hotel Management*, Anmol Publication, Delhi, 2008.

Rajesh Singh.: *HRM in Travel and Tourism Industry*, Sonali Publications, Delhi, 2011.

Rajiv Sabharwal.: *Role of ICTs in Travel and Tourism*, Pacific Publications, Delhi, 2011.

Ravee Chauhan.: *Advanced Book on Marketing of Tourism*, Vista International Publishing House, Delhi, 2011.

Romila Chawla.: *Accommodation Management and Tourism*, Sonali Publication, Delhi, 2006.

Romila Chawla.: *Agri-Tourism*, Sonali Publication, Delhi, 2006.

S W P Prabhakaran.: *Child Labour In Hotel Industry*, Discovery Publishing House, Delhi, 2011.

Saurab Kumar Dixit.: *Aspects of Tourism Development*, Mohit Publication, Delhi, 2005.

]Thomas Walsh.: *Adventure Tourism*, Discovery Publishing House, Delhi, 2011.

Thomas Walsh.: *Creative Tourism*, Discovery Publishing House, Delhi, 2011.

Index